P9-DMR-021

PRAISE FOR *Introduction to Middle School:*

"I am often asked to recommend an introductory text, but until this book, I had none to recommend, because they lacked a seriousness and depth that I sought. Your book satisfies those criteria. It ought to do well in the undergraduate market; it is a great balance."

● Paul S. George, *University of Florida*

Introduction to Middle School

second edition

Sara Davis Powell

Belmont Abbey College

Boston • Columbus • Indianapolis • New York • San Francisco • Upper Saddle River
Amsterdam • Cape Town • Dubai • London • Madrid • Milan • Munich • Paris • Montreal • Toronto
Delhi • Mexico City • Sao Paulo • Sydney • Hong Kong • Seoul • Singapore • Taipei • Tokyo

ALEXANDRIA LIBRARY
ALEXANDRIA, VA 22304

Senior Editor: Kelly Villella Canton
Editorial Assistant: Annalea Manalili
Senior Marketing Manager: Darcy Betts
Production Editor: Annette Joseph
Editorial Production Service: Ashley Schneider, S4Carlisle Publishing Services
Manufacturing Buyer: Megan Cochran
Electronic Composition: S4Carlisle Publishing Services
Interior Design: Denise Hoffman, Glenview Studios

Credits and acknowledgments borrowed from other sources and reproduced, with permission, in this textbook appear on appropriate page within text (or on page iv).

Copyright © 2011, 2005 Pearson Education, Inc., publishing as Allyn & Bacon, 501 Boylston St., Suite 901, Boston, MA, 02116. All rights reserved. Manufactured in the United States of America. This publication is protected by Copyright, and permission should be obtained from the publisher prior to any prohibited reproduction, storage in a retrieval system, or transmission in any form or by any means, electronic, mechanical, photocopying, recording, or likewise. To obtain permission(s) to use material from this work, please submit a written request to Pearson Education, Inc., Permissions Department, 501 Boylston St., Suite 901, Boston, MA 02116.

Photo Credits: Student school pictures courtesy of Carl Lackey of Carolina Photography. Photos on pages 66 and 321 courtesy of Rhonda VanPelt; photos on page 183 courtesy of KR MediaCenter; and photo on page 215 courtesy of Warren Cobb. All other photos taken by the author, Sara Davis Powell.

Library of Congress Cataloging-in-Publication Data
Powell, Sara Davis.
   Introduction to middle school / Sara Davis Powell.—2nd ed.
    p. cm.
   ISBN 978-0-13-704574-7
   1.   Middle school education—United States. I.   Title.
   LB1623.5.P69 2010
   373.236—dc22
                                            2010009110

10 9 8 7 6 5 4 3   RRD-VA 14 13 12 11

www.pearsonhighered.com

ISBN-10: 0-13-704574-3
ISBN-13: 978-0-13-704574-7

To my husband, Rus, who makes all aspects of our life together
a delightful partnership.

To Jesse, Cody, Travis, and Noah, my sons who continually
give me so much pleasure and reasons to be proud.

To middle school kids and teachers, who grow
and learn together every day.

About the Author

Sara Davis Powell is a teacher, from the middle school classroom to teacher preparation as professor and chair of education at Belmont Abbey College in North Carolina. She is a young adolescent advocate who writes about middle level teacher preparation, emphasizing a balance of theory with developmentally responsive and academically rigorous practice. She is actively involved in local classrooms and the middle school community through the facilitation of professional development, supervision of clinical interns, and research and writing about middle level issues. She is also a frequent speaker at regional and national conferences, where her enthusiasm for middle level education has proven contagious. Dr. Powell's most recent books include *An Introduction to Education: Choosing Your Teaching Path* (Pearson, 2009) and *Wayside Teaching: Connecting with Students to Support Learning* (Corwin, 2010).

Married, with four sons, three daughters-in-law, and two grandchildren, she enjoys watching the sun set over the lake outside her back door with her husband, Rus, and spending time with her sons and their families. When not on her dock, with her family, or writing at her desk at home, chances are she can be reached at Belmont Abbey College, 100 Belmont-Mt. Holly Road, Belmont, North Carolina 28012; (704)461-5059; sarapowell@bac.edu.

Brief Contents

Contents

CHAPTER **3**

Diversity among Middle Level Students   47

CHAPTER **4**   **Middle Level Teachers**   **81**

CHAPTER **5**

Societal Context of Middle Level Education   114

CHAPTER 6

Structures of Middle Level Education   141

CHAPTER **10**   **Planning for Teaching and Learning   258**

CHAPTER **11**

Maintaining a Positive, Productive Learning Environment   292

Preface

● New to This Edition

In this new edition of *Introduction to Middle School*, Sara Powell offers a contemporary and comprehensive body of knowledge while speaking directly to teacher candidates in a voice that invites them into today's middle level classrooms. The second edition is a compelling look at a variety of current issues and topics affecting young adolescents, their teachers, and their schools, including discussions of 21st century knowledge and skill requirements such as global awareness, information literacy, and ethical responsibility. Also addressed are new approaches to physical, emotional, and academic safety in the face of the current societal context, including two significant challenges—bullying and childhood obesity—both of which are increasing at alarming rates.

Despite all the changes both students and teachers face, the developmental needs of young adolescents remain predictable. Relevant and challenging curriculum, engaging instruction, ongoing assessment that is growth-promoting, developmental responsiveness, and strategies for creating and maintaining a positive and productive learning environment—represent some vital components of middle level education that must be firmly in place.

To help prepare middle level teachers who will be effective facilitators of learning, the following features are NEW TO THIS EDITION:

- *New Chapter:* **Societal Context of Middle Level Education**   Young adolescents don't leave their lives outside the schoolhouse door. This new chapter explores the differences among urban, suburban, and rural settings; bullying in its many forms; technology's impact on students; the effects of poverty; dilemmas surrounding English language learners; and wellness issues including substance abuse, sexuality-related issues, and childhood obesity. Each topic is followed by **Make a Difference**, ideas for addressing the issues presented.

- Increased Emphasis on **Diversity**   Coverage of diversity issues has increased by at least 25%, with issues identified using a new Diversity Icon. Suggestions for teacher attitudes and actions that positively impact all students are throughout the text.

**Young Adolescent
Diversity**

- *All New* **Focus Teachers**   In this edition we meet nine new focus teachers through scenarios and photos. They share their classroom experiences and appear as central characters in the end-of-chapter **Professional Practice** scenarios and Praxis II preparation items.

- *All New* **Focus Students**   In this edition we meet nine new focus students through scenarios and photos. We watch them grow from 6th to 7th to 8th grade in scenarios and as central characters in the end-of-chapter Professional Practice scenarios and Praxis II preparation items. Through both **Focus Students** and **Focus Teachers** the concepts of *Introduction to Middle School* come to life.

- *All New* **Professional Practice Features**   All Professional Practice features are 100% new and incorporate scenarios, multiple choice items, and constructed response opportunities based on experiences of the nine Focus Teachers and nine Focus Students.

- *New Feature . . .* **Teachers Speak**   The Focus Teachers speak directly to readers about their experiences with teaching young adolescents and working with teachers on their teams through photos, vignettes, insights, and advice.

- *New Feature . . .* **See How They Grow**   The Focus Students' experiences as they move from grade to grade are included in this new feature.

- **Virtual Field Experiences**   Throughout the second edition readers are directed to **MyEducationLab** to view videos of teacher interviews, student interviews, classroom lessons, a middle school tour, a principal discussing what she looks for in teachers, and a variety of stories about teachers making a difference. These Video Examples and Video Assignments and Activities afford opportunities for virtual observation experiences and reflection. References to the clips and assignment ideas will also be included in the Instructor's Manual.

- **Teacher Talk**   In each chapter readers will be directed to watch a brief video of a state Teacher of the Year explaining reasons for teaching. These inspirational "Why I Teach" segments of middle level teachers present a wide array of perspectives that showcase a variety of personalities and styles.

Overview

This content-rich, reader-friendly text presents a comprehensive introduction to the world of young adolescents and middle level education. *Introduction to Middle School, Second Edition,* models the ideals of middle level education in that it is both academically rigorous and developmentally responsive. It is academically rigorous because it is comprised of a comprehensive body of knowledge and developmentally responsive because it approaches these topics without intimidating or boring the reader. I am an experienced middle school teacher speaking to other teachers whether they are: teacher candidates completing bachelor or master degrees; career changers preparing to take their skills and backgrounds into the middle school classroom; elementary or high school teachers getting ready for the challenges and joys of spending their days with young adolescents; or teachers who desire to dig deeper into their profession, seeking insights and encouragement. Writing a book only allows me to speak, but not actually converse. My hope is that readers will talk to each other about middle grades education, prompted by my side of the "conversation."

Teachers are my heroes. They make the minute-by-minute decisions on which student success and well-being depend. If knowledge is power, and I believe it is, the more we understand about the nature of adolescence, with both its documented predictability and its absurd volatility, the more prepared we are to make the relatively insignificant, as well as life-changing, decisions.

Yes, experience is the best teacher. But opportunities to read, reflect, discuss, and speculate will sharpen our focus on, and widen our peripheral vision of, middle grades education and all that is involved in teaching young adolescents. This book provides such opportunities. The tenets of *Turning Points* (1989 and 2000), *This We Believe (2010)*, the underpinnings of the National Middle School Association, and the teacher preparation standards of NMSA/NCATE permeate every page. This strong conceptual foundation focuses us squarely on students and learning. As a unique phase of human development, early adolescence deserves continued, concentrated research and study that will further deepen our understanding of how best to meet the needs of the students in our charge.

The second edition of *Introduction to Middle School* presents the issues of teaching and learning with young adolescents including the development and diversity of young adolescent learners and the societal context of their lives; middle level curriculum, instruction, and assessment; practices for creating and maintaining a positive, productive learning environment; the impact of technology on young adolescents; challenges related to teaching English language learners; verbal, physical, and cyberbullying; health issues such as adolescent obesity and substance abuse; and the middle level teacher's responsibilities to differentiate to meet the needs of all learners. These issues are addressed in commonsense ways that infuse practicality with theory.

This book is a work of nontraditional scholarship—scholarly by way of knowledge base, and nontraditional by way of personalization. It is written in first person. I believe I best serve teachers, in whatever career stage, by speaking from both a research base and my own and others' experiences in the classroom. I welcome all readers to the adventure of exploring the landscape of middle school.

Features of This Book

In addition to the components that are New to This Edition, the second edition of *Introduction to Middle School* includes the following features:

NMSA/NCATE Standards   Throughout the book the Performance-Based Standards for Initial Middle Level Teacher Preparation are boxed for easy reference. The knowledge, dispositions, and performance standards are placed within the context of the topics they address. Elements of all seven standards are addressed.

Margin Notes   Concepts, that when approached together result in positive effects, are illustrated through the margin notes.

Activities   Following each chapter are a variety of activities. Group Activities require readers to work cooperatively to accomplish particular tasks. Individual Activities give readers opportunities to explore middle level concepts on their own. The Personal Journal section asks readers to reflect on their own experiences.

Internet Resources   Selected websites are annotated to provide additional sources of information on topics in each chapter. Most of the sites are quite large with links to other worthwhile websites.

Glossary   There exists an evolving common vocabulary that allows teachers to talk with mutual understanding. In addition, there are words and phrases that have specialized meanings and nuances when used within a middle level education context. Many of these terms are explained in the glossary.

Organization

This book is comprised of twelve chapters. Separating the body of knowledge of middle level education into discrete chapters seems arbitrary, but it is efficient to do so. Chapter 1 focuses on the history of middle school and the elements that have given it legitimacy and theoretical grounding. Chapter 2 is an overview of student physical, intellectual, emotional, social, and character development. Chapter 3 looks at the diversity among our students from cultural to socioeconomic, to learning styles, and more. Chapter 4 probes the characteristics of effective middle school teachers. Chapter 5 addresses the societal context of middle level education. Chapter 6 delves into the structures of people, time, and place, including teaming, flexible schedules, and classroom/school facilities. Chapters 7, 8, and 9 discuss curriculum, instruction, and assessment at the middle level, while Chapter 10 details all levels of planning for instruction. Chapter 11 deals with the important topic of the classroom environment and its management. Chapter 12 addresses 21st century knowledge and skills, family and community involvement, No Child Left Behind legislation, and the critical issues of transitioning into and out of middle grades.

Instructor Supplements

Because differentiation of instruction is valuable not only to young adolescent learners but also to preservice teacher learners, providing a variety of instructional approaches in our college classrooms is vital. While we all incorporate our own ideas and activities into teacher education courses, the instructor supplements for this text will help grow your repertoire and provide additional ways to address learning preferences of teacher candidates. In doing so we both model differentiation and add to the strategies in our future teachers' instructional tool boxes. The instructor supplements for *Introduction to Middle School* are located on the password-protected Instructor Resource Center at www.pearsonhighered.com. If you need assistance downloading these supplements, please contact your local Pearson representative.

Instructor's Manual and Test Bank

The Instructor's Manual provides a menu of instructional supplements for each chapter, including:

- Chapter Objectives
- More class activities in addition to individual, small group, and whole class assignments and activities included at the end of each chapter.
- Daystarter questions to post at the beginning of classes to activate prior knowledge of, and peak interest in, the content of each chapter.
- Suggestions for how to divide the content of each chapter to utilize the Jigsaw Model of cooperative learning that requires teacher candidates to teach content to their classmates.
- Possible responses to the *Professional Practice* features that accompany each chapter.

- Questions and activities to fully utilize each video segment specifically related to chapter content and available on MyEducationLab.
- Questions and activities to fully utilize each *Teacher Talk* segment available on MyEducationLab.
- Multiple Choice and True-False Test items for each chapter, along with answer keys.

PowerPoint™ Presentations

Ideal for presentations, discussion starters, and student handouts, the PowerPoint™ Presentation for each chapter includes key concept summaries and chapter figures.

PEARSON
myeducationlab
The Power of Classroom Practice
www.myeducationlab.com

"Teacher educators who are developing pedagogies for the analysis of teaching and learning contend that analyzing teaching artifacts has three advantages: it enables new teachers time for reflection while still using the real materials of practice; it provides new teachers with experience thinking about and approaching the complexity of the classroom; and in some cases, it can help new teachers and teacher educators develop a shared understanding and common language about teaching. . . ."[1] As Linda Darling-Hammond and her colleagues point out, grounding teacher education in real classrooms—among real teachers and students and among actual examples of students' and teachers' work—is an important, and perhaps even an essential, part of preparing teachers for the complexities of teaching in today's classrooms. For this reason, we have created a valuable, time-saving website–MyEducationLab–that provides the context of real classrooms and artifacts that research on teacher education tells us is so important. The authentic in-class video footage, interactive skill-building exercises and other resources available on MyEducationLab offers a uniquely valuable teacher education tool.

MyEducationLab is easy to use and integrate into assignments and courses. Whenever the MyEducationLab logo appears in the text, follow the simple instructions to access the interactive assignments, activities, and learning units on MyEducationLab. For each topic covered in the course you will find most or all of the following resources:

Connection to National Standards

Now it is easier than ever to see how coursework is connected to national standards. Each topic on MyEducationLab lists intended learning outcomes connected to the appropriate national standards. And all of the Assignments and Activities and all of the Building Teaching Skills and Dispositions in MyEducationLab are mapped to the appropriate national standards and learning outcomes as well.

---

[1]Darling-Hammond, I., & Bransford, J., Eds.(2005). *Preparing Teachers for a Changing World*. San Francisco: John Wiley & Sons.

Assignments and Activities

Designed to save instructors preparation time and enhance student understanding, these assignable exercises show concepts in action (through video, cases, and/or student and teacher artifacts). They help students synthesize and apply concepts and strategies they read about in the book.

Building Teaching Skills and Dispositions

These learning units help students practice and strengthen skills that are essential to quality teaching. They are presented with the core skill or concept and then given an opportunity to practice their understanding of this concept multiple times by watching video footage (or interacting with other media) and then critically analyzing the strategy or skill presented.

IRIS Center Resources

The IRIS Center at Vanderbilt University (http://iris.peabody.vanderbilt.edu)–funded by the U.S. Department of Education's Office of Special Education Programs (OSEP) develops training enhancement materials for pre-service and in-service teachers. The Center works with experts from across the country to create challenge-based interactive modules, case study units, and podcasts that provide research-validated information about working with students in inclusive settings. In your MyEducationLab course we have integrated this content where appropriate.

Teacher Talk

This feature links to videos of teachers of the year across the country discussing their personal stories of why they teach. This National Teacher of the Year Program is sponsored by the Council of Chief State School Officers (CCSSO) and focuses public attention on teaching excellence.

General Resources on Your MyEducationLab Course

The Resources section on MyEducationLab is designed to help students pass their licensure exams, put together effective portfolios and lesson plans, prepare for and navigate the first year of their teaching careers, and understand key educational standards, policies, and laws. This section includes:

- *Licensure Exams:* Contains guidelines for passing the Praxis exam. The *Practice Test Exam* includes practice multiple-choice questions, case study questions, and video case studies with sample questions.
- *Lesson Plan Builder:* Helps students create and share lesson plans.
- *Licensure and Standards:* Provides links to state licensure standards and national standards.
- *Beginning Your Career:* Offers tips, advice, and valuable information on:
  - Resume Writing and Interviewing: Expert advice on how to write impressive resumes and prepare for job interviews.

- Your First Year of Teaching: Practical tips on setting up a classroom, managing student behavior, and planning for instruction and assessment.
- Law and Public Policies: Includes specific directives and requirements educators need to understand under the No Child Left Behind Act and the Individuals with Disabilities Education Improvement Act of 2004.

Visit **www.myeducationlab.com** *for a demonstration of this exciting new online teaching resource.*

Acknowledgments

I want to thank the teachers, students, and principals who allowed me to wander the halls of their schools and take pictures of middle schools and young adolescents in action. My appreciation goes to Jesse White, Jermaine Joyner, Sadie Fox, Keith Richardson, Jennifer Kinnett, Joey Huber, Sarah Gardener, Traci Peters, Deirdre McGrew—all wonderful teachers. Also thanks to these wonderful young adolescents and their parents—Zach Hall, DeVante Mackins, KeMaurye McLean, Gabe Hernandez, Zaira Ortiz, Andrew Burgess, Sierria McGinnis, Taylor Szucs, and Nikolaus Gunawan. For their assistance, I thank Tonya Farbo and Audrey Devine at Belmont Middle School, and Becky Ford and Cristi Bostic at Cramerton Middle School.

Special thanks go to my editor, Kelly Villella Canton, and Annette Joseph for their guidance and prompt responses to my questions and requests. Special appreciation goes to those who reviewed *Introduction to Middle School* and offered thoughtful and useful suggestions. They include: Sue E. Anderson, Jamestown College; David W. Messer, Clayton State University; John A. Moore, Western Kentucky University; Paul T. Parkison, University of Southern Indiana; Jennifer Weber, South Dakota State University; and Lois J. Yocum, University of Arkansas–Fort Smith.

What Is Middle School?

Most schools designed for 6th through 8th graders now have the words *Middle School* in their names. What ever happened to Junior Highs? Does the name change imply a different philosophy, or is it just window dressing without meaningful alteration to what goes on inside? This chapter explores middle level education philosophy and how it can transform the way we educate *young adolescents*.

*t*he middle school movement is an educational success story unparalleled in our history. In little over three decades the face of American education has been remade; the intermediate level of education has been given a long overdue identity and has, in fact, been recognized as the level leading in instituting significant educational reform.

Lounsbury, 1997, p. xi

CHAPTER PREVIEW

Middle School and Middle Level Education
- A Brief History of the School in the Middle
- Middle Level Recognized

Legitimizing Factors
- Middle Level Teacher Preparation Standards
- Assessing Teacher Knowledge and Skills

Reflections on Middle Level Education

Rationale for Middle Schools
- National Middle School Association
- *Turning Points*
- *This We Believe*
- *Turning Points 2000*

INTRODUCTION

If a poll were taken today of all middle level teachers, the great majority would possess a fictitious MSBA degree. No, this doesn't refer to some esoteric mix of a master's degree and a Bachelor of Arts. Instead, it's a tongue-in-cheek degree symbolizing the "Middle School By Accident" reality. This reality is how most of us landed in the midst of the young adolescent odyssey, and the "degree" quantifies our years of on-the-job training and experience. Many started out intending to teach elementary students; others majored in a subject area and became certified to teach high school students. But, for a variety of reasons, including lack of our first teaching position choice, we found ourselves in a sort of "in between" school. In the 1960s and 1970s, these in-between schools were mostly junior highs, while in the 1980s and 1990s, and into the 21st century, most schools between elementary and high schools were, and still are, called *middle schools*. And most middle level teachers, whether in junior high or middle school, got there by accident.

As middle schools achieve the recognition they deserve on the educational landscape, the hope is that teachers will think of themselves as having a more relevant degree, an *MSBD—Middle School By Design*—rather than an *MSBA—Middle*

myeducationlab

To hear Traci Peters, 7th grade teacher at Cario Middle School, tell us that although she prepared to teach elementary students, she now loves spending her days with young adolescents, go to the Video Examples section of **Topic # 1: Schools and Teaching Today** in the MyEducationLab for your course and view the video entitled "Traci Peters' Interview."

School By Accident. With this purposeful choosing of the field of middle level education comes the cry for legitimacy. Teacher candidates now in programs to prepare them to enter the teaching profession more than likely attended middle school versus junior high. Granted, these schools may have been junior high in philosophy and practice, but chances are the sign out front reads "Middle School." So when the "teaching bug" hits, or the reasoned and thoughtful choice is made for a professional career in education, teachers most recently joining the ranks do so with an idea of what middle school is and who middle schoolers are. Most still enter with an MSBA, but they enter more prepared, having realized that there are three distinct levels of school, not just two.

Elementary schools conjure up images of eager children, full of curiosity and energy, adoring their teachers and revering them as wise and loving. High schools elicit images of maturing, sometimes smart-aleck, generally self-absorbed growing adolescents. They may often exhibit adult-like tendencies and behaviors and be capable of engaging in subject-specific discussions with teachers they consider experts. But what about middle schools? Is it possible to define the experience in such a way as to elicit testimonials of "Gee, I can't wait to become a middle school teacher"? Until we have a commonly held, legitimate identification of what a middle school is and what middle school students are like, entering the profession with an MSBD degree will be less common than entering with the nagging suspicion that the best use of our talents would be in an elementary or high school classroom.

In this chapter, we explore both the concept and the institution of middle school. In Chapters 2 and 3 we concentrate on middle school students, and in Chapter 4 we take a look at the profession of teaching middle school. In Chapter 5 we consider the societal context of teaching young adolescents. In Chapter 6, we examine the structures of people, time, and place in a middle level setting. In Chapters 7 through 9 we examine curriculum, instruction, and assessment. In Chapter 10 we discuss planning for instruction, and in Chapter 11 we explore the creation and maintenance of a positive and productive middle grades learning environment. In Chapter 12 we discuss the involvement of family and community members and the future prospects for middle level education.

Middle School and Middle Level Education

The National Middle School Association (NMSA) defines a *middle school* as one that is specifically structured to meet the developmental needs of young adolescents ages 10 to 15. NMSA uses characteristics such as goals, activities, and organizational attributes rather than merely the school's grade configuration to designate a school as a middle school. Alexander (1968) defined middle school as "A school having at least three grades and not more than five grades, and including at least grades six and seven" (p. 1). Alexander and McEwin (1989) refined and expanded this definition of a middle school 20 years later by stating that schools with grades 6–8 are likely to feature the following:

1. An interdisciplinary organization with a flexible day
2. An adequate guidance program, including a teacher advisory plan
3. A full-scale exploratory program
4. Curricular provision for such goals and curriculum domains as personal development, continued learning skills, and basic knowledge areas
5. Varied and effective instructional methodology for the age group
6. Continued orientation and articulation for students, parents, and teachers (pp. 84–85)

There are approximately 12,500 U.S. schools with the words *middle school* in their names. The most prevalent grade configuration is 6–8, but configurations of grades 5–8 and 7–8 also exist (McEwin, Dickinson, & Jenkins, 2003). National Middle School Association (NMSA) continues to set high expectations for what a true middle school should be like, one that is guided by developmental appropriateness and academic rigor.

Not all young adolescents are in middle schools. Some districts serve young adolescents in K–8 schools, while others utilize 7–12 grade bands, or even K–12. While NMSA strongly endorses the idea of a unique school in the middle (between elementary and high schools), staffed by adults who understand and appreciate young adolescents, the organization acknowledges that developmental appropriateness and academic rigor can be accomplished in a school regardless of the name out front or the grade level configuration within.

Middle level education is not without its critics. There are those who say that public education is failing to meet the needs of young adolescents, especially those who attend middle schools. When middle school national and international test results are weak, the critics' case is bolstered. Middle level philosophy as espoused by NMSA is blamed. But it's not the philosophy. Every aspect of middle level philosophy is developed distinctly for the unique stage of early adolescence. It's not the philosophy . . . it's the lack of conscientious implementation in so many schools that serve young adolescents. "There is nothing wrong with the middle school concept. The concept—a school for young adolescents based on their developmental needs—is as valid today as it was . . . at the turn of the 20th century or in the early 1960s. . . . It is a flexible, responsive, integrated concept with the aim of providing a safe, secure, and appropriate environment for a young adolescent to learn challenging content that will enable him or her to explore self, others, and the larger world" (Dickinson, 2001, p. 1).

Always keep in mind that this text is about the education and well-being of young adolescents, wherever and however that may occur. Specific grade configurations and practices may always be controversial. This fact keeps us fresh and on our toes. Controversy stretches us. But remember, it's all about the kids and our responsibility to do what's best for them.

● A Brief History of the School in the Middle

We won't spend a lot of time talking about the history of middle schools. The years involved are relatively few, with most accounts telling us the history is only about four decades old and that it began in the 1960s. There are some notable educators and writers who are responsible in great measure for catapulting the middle school concept/philosophy into our everyday lives. When we consider that most of the educators who invested their careers in the establishment and proliferation of middle schools are still with us, and are still inspiring our efforts, the history of the middle school movement comes alive as an ongoing progression of events. The pioneers of middle school have made, and continue to witness, significant progress.

Junior High Established   The first signs that a separate school organization was being established to bridge the gap between elementary and high schools began in 1909. These new schools were aptly named *junior highs* and were established to be preparatory schools for students going on to high school, where they would enter one of two defined tracks. The tracks had two broad purposes—to provide enriched curriculum for college bound students, or to provide vocational training for those preparing to enter the workforce (Manning, 2000). Even then, elementary schools were made up of self-contained grade level classes intended to provide consistency and security for young children, much as was experienced ideally in a family setting. As they are today, high schools at the beginning of the 20th century were basically departmentalized by subject area, with students changing classes four to eight times a day. The junior high resembled the high school in structure in 1909, but was generally smaller to allow for a greater sense of personalization, while functioning in a departmentalized fashion. Even though there was little written research about early adolescence, the junior high concept met a recognized need that made it a widespread and rapidly growing part of public education. By 1960, approximately four out of five high school graduates attended junior high as part of a 6–3–3 grade configuration—6 years of elementary, 3 years of junior high, and 3 years of high school. By the mid-1960s, variations began to emerge, resulting in middle level schools consisting of grades 5–8 or 6–8 (Alexander & McEwin, 1989).

Problems with Junior High   As early as 1945, some educators were troubled by what they observed in junior highs. An early advocate for the junior high wrote about what he perceived as persistent problems. His list included the following (Anfara & Waks, 2000):

- Curriculum that was too subject-centered
- Teachers who were inadequately prepared to teach young adolescents
- Classrooms that were teacher-centered and textbook-centered
- Students who were tracked (p. 47)

These problems are very similar to the ones addressed by what is considered middle level philosophy today.

● Middle Level Recognized

William Alexander broke ground for the establishment of what are now middle schools when he presented a "philosophy" of the characteristics needed in a transitional school at the Cornell University Junior High School Conference in the summer of 1963. Alexander urged the maintenance of the positive contributions of junior highs such as core curriculum, guidance programs, exploratory education, and vocational/home arts, and the elimination of high school practices such as competitive sports and subject matter orientation (Manning, 2000). He conducted a survey of middle level schools, then labeled junior highs, whose grade configurations had evolved into grades 5–8 or 6–8 from original 6–3–3, 6–2–4, and 6–6 grade structures. A total of 101 middle level schools were located by contacting state departments of education. The results of this study were published in *The Emergent Middle School* in 1968 by Alexander and Williams. This book described middle school as a new concept, not merely a rearrangement of junior high.

Twenty years later, in 1988, a second major research study was conducted with another in 1993. The results of a fourth study in 2001 are reported in *America's Middle Schools in The New Century* (2004) by McEwin, Dickinson, and Jenkins. Throughout this text, portions of this latest study will be referenced.

The overwhelming conclusion to be drawn from the 1968, 1988, 1993, and 2001 studies is that middle schools with varying grade configurations have grown at a rapid rate. Other studies have been conducted over the course of the last half of the 20th century that have informed middle school practice, including studies by McEwin and Clay in 1983; Calweti in 1988; Epstein and McIver in 1990; and Valentine, Clark, Irwin, Keefe, and Melton in 1993. These studies documented various aspects of middle schools, from numbers of students to philosophical bents and forms of practice. While it is important to have these aspects recorded and analyzed, it is perhaps more important to seek to understand the development and manifestation of the middle school qualities examined in separate sections of this book so that they may be considered in more depth and within the context of middle schools as we know them today.

A brief overview of some of the differences between junior high and middle school is in Figure 1.1. All of the components of middle school are discussed in subsequent chapters.

Rationale for Middle Schools

Middle school educators continue their quest for legitimacy that goes beyond mere numbers of schools. One sign of increasing legitimacy is the growing body of literature on the topic of middle level education. We find that the literature about middle school can be basically divided into two major categories—one justifies the rationale for, and existence of, the unique middle school organization; the second explores better ways of doing what we do within these schools.

You will notice that throughout this book, middle school is referred to in a variety of ways—middle level education, middle grades education, middle school, schools in the middle, and so on. By whatever name, we are referring to a philosophy of educating young adolescents that is different from elementary philosophy, high school

FIGURE 1.1 Differences between junior high and middle school

Junior High	Middle School
1. Subject-centered	Student-oriented
2. Emphasis is on cognitive development	Emphasis is on both cognitive and affective development
3. Organizes teachers in subject-based departments	Organizes teachers and students in interdisciplinary teams
4. Traditional instruction dominates	Experiential approaches to instruction
5. Six to eight class periods per day	Allows for block and flexible scheduling
6. Provides academic classes	Provides exploratory, academic, and nonacademic classes
7. Offers study hall and/or homeroom	Offers advisor/advisee, teacher/student opportunities
8. Classrooms arranged randomly or by subject or grade level	Team classrooms in close proximity

philosophy, or junior high philosophy. This philosophy of viewing both the needs and ways of meeting these needs will permeate the chapters to follow.

A unique philosophy is necessary because we recognize that middle school should be far more than a "holding tank" for children who are too old for the traditional elementary school and too young for high school. The junior high mindset viewed preparation for high school as sufficient justification for a transitional school. Middle level education can be, and should be, much more. Kienholz (2001) wrote, "the middle school movement attempted to close the gap between what we know about young adolescents and what we do with them in schools, to narrow the chasm between theory and practice in our public schools" (p. 21). As Jackson and Davis (2000) wrote in *Turning Points 2000: Educating Adolescents in the 21st Century:*

> Just as middle grades teachers need to know how, specifically, young adolescents are different from young children and older adolescents, they also need to understand that middle grades schools are different from elementary and high schools. This difference is much more than the sign on the front of the school; it lies in the philosophical foundations of middle grades education and the organizational structure that grows from and supports this philosophy (p. 100).

Four major occurrences grew out of, and at the same time helped shape, the middle school movement. We will look at them in chronological order.

● National Middle School Association

The first major contribution to the growing rationale for middle school was the establishment of the *National Middle School Association (NMSA)* in 1973. This organization is dedicated exclusively to the education, development, and growth of young

---

FIGURE 1.2   The National Middle School Association

The National Middle School Association is dedicated to improving the educational experiences of young adolescents by providing vision, knowledge, and resources to all who serve them in order to develop healthy, productive, and ethical citizens.

National Middle School Association
4151 Executive Parkway, Suite 300
Westerville, OH 43081
1-800-528-NMSA
www.nmsa.org

> Contributors to rationale for middle schools = National Middle School Association + *Turning Points* + *This We Believe* + *Turning Points 2000*

adolescents. The NMSA mission statement and contact information are in Figure 1.2. The organization provides a voice and a professional structure for middle level educators, and has grown to include members in all 50 states, Canada, and dozens of other countries. There are more than 50 affiliate organizations of NMSA that sponsor local, regional, and state activities focused on middle level education.

One very important affiliate of NMSA is the Collegiate Middle Level Association (CMLA). CMLA is a university student organization with student officers and activities. Each CMLA chapter promotes middle level teacher preparation through group meetings featuring professional development, involvement of CMLA members in local schools above and beyond field experiences, and fundraising to support attendance at state and national conferences. I have been privileged to be a faculty sponsor of a CMLA and can personally attest to what wonderful organizations they can be. For more information on beginning or enhancing a CMLA, look under the Professional Preparation tab on the NMSA website.

NMSA publishes a wealth of books and monographs, a variety of which are included in this book's reference section. In addition, NMSA publishes the *Middle School Journal,* a refreshing and informative compilation of articles that is highly regarded for both its topical and scholarly content. Alternating monthly with the *Middle School Journal* is *Middle Ground,* a very practical and entirely reader-friendly journal featuring regular columns written by practitioners. Membership in the National Middle School Association is accompanied by subscriptions to both *Middle School Journal* and *Middle Ground.* NMSA also publishes *Research in Middle Level Education Online,* several general newsletters, and videos. In addition to periodicals, NMSA publishes the largest selection of books written specifically for middle school practitioners. These are available through NMSA catalogs, at middle school conferences, and at www.nmsa.org.

The National Middle School Association website (www.nmsa.org) is an excellent resource featuring general information about NMSA, ways to advocate for young adolescents, professional development opportunities, professional teacher standards, the latest research on middle level education, and a publications shopping bonanza for all who are interested in early adolescence. In addition, the site contains

Source: National Middle School Association, 4151 Executive Parkway, Suite 300, Westerville, OH 43081, 1-800-528-NMSA, www.nmsa.org

NMSA position statements along with the latest in news items and legislation affecting middle level education. You will also find membership information. College students may join NMSA and enjoy all the benefits of membership, including monthly journals, for only $40 a year. I go to the NMSA site at least weekly to keep current in the world of middle level education.

One of the highlights provided by the National Middle School Association is the widely acclaimed NMSA annual fall conference. This conference draws more than 10,000 teachers, future teachers, principals, central office personnel, university faculty, state department officials, parents, and community members, all vitally interested in the promotion of developmentally appropriate practices. It's an exciting conference that all teachers should have the opportunity to attend. Lasting 3 days, the main events include keynote speakers, concurrent sessions on topics of interest to adults who work with young adolescents, and site visits to local schools to view exemplary practices. Perhaps the major inspiration provided by this annual conference comes from the realization that we are not alone, the knowledge that hundreds of thousands of adults concerned with young adolescent development and education are represented by those who attend.

● *Turning Points*

The second major factor shaping middle level education was the highly acclaimed document

Source: Illustration by Jill Ryerson.
© Carnegie Corporation of New York.
Reprinted with permission.

Turning Points: Preparing American Youth for the 21st Century, published in 1989 by the Carnegie Council on Adolescent Development. The Council's research showed that substantial numbers of American young adolescents were at risk of reaching adulthood inadequately prepared to function productively. As a result of this finding, the Carnegie Council developed a research-based document that has shaped middle school philosophy. This study continues to lead the way in both describing characteristics of young adolescents and prescribing ways to meet their needs within the school setting.

This groundbreaking work, which we will refer to simply as *Turning Points,* was undertaken because "A volatile mismatch exists between the organization and curriculum of middle grade schools and the intellectual and emotional needs of young adolescents" (*Turning Points,* 1989, p. 8). Authors of the study were spurred on by their belief that "for many youth 10 to 15 years old, early adolescence offers opportunities to choose a path toward a productive and fulfilling life. For others it represents their last best chance to avoid a diminished future" (*Turning Points,* 1989, p. 7). More than 100,000 copies of the full report and more than 200,000 copies of the abridged version have been disseminated. The eight tenets of *Turning Points* summarized in Table 1.1 provide a model of what a middle school can be. The tenets are interrelated elements that, when taken as a whole, provide a vision for teaching and learning appropriate for young adolescents.

myeducationlab

To hear Lee-Ann Stephens, the 2007 Minnesota Teacher of the Year, discuss her philosophy that teaching requires care, laughter, and relationship building, go to the Teacher Talk section of **Topic #1: Schools and Teaching Today** in the MyEducationLab for your course.

This We Believe

The third major contributor to our understanding of why middle schools are unique and necessary was the publication of the National Middle School Association's position paper, *This We Believe,* in 1995. The 2010 revision, *This We Believe: Keys to Educating Young Adolescents,* presents four essential attributes of effective education for young adolescents, including

Source: Reprinted with permission from National Middle School Association. National Middle School Association. (2010). *Keys to educating young adolescents.* Westerville, OH: Author.

1. Developmentally responsive: using the distinctive nature of young adolescents as the foundation upon which all decisions about school organization, policies, curriculum, instruction, and assessment are made.

2. Challenging: ensuring that every member of the learning community is held to high expectations.

TABLE 1.1   *Turning Points*

Turning Points: Preparing American Youth for the 21st Century **Carnegie Council on Adolescent Development, 1989**	
Creating a community for learning	Schools should be places where close, trusting relationships with adults and peers create a climate for students' personal growth and intellectual development.
Teaching a core of common knowledge	Every student in the middle grades should learn to think critically through mastery of an appropriate body of knowledge, lead a healthy life, behave ethically and lawfully, and assume the responsibilities of citizenship in a pluralistic society.
Ensuring success for all students	All young adolescents should have the opportunity to succeed in every aspect of the middle grade program, regardless of previous achievement or the pace at which they learn.
Empowering teachers and administrators	Decisions concerning the experiences of middle grade students should be made by the adults who know them best.
Preparing teachers for the middle grades	Teachers in middle grade schools should be selected and specially educated to teach young adolescents.
Improving academic performance through better health and fitness	Young adolescents must be healthy in order to learn.
Reengaging families in the education of young adolescents	Families and middle grade schools must be allied through trust and respect if young adolescents are to succeed in school.
Connecting schools with communities	Responsibility for each middle grade student's success should be shared by schools and community organizations.

Source: From *Turning Points: Preparing American Youth for the 21st Century* (pp. 37–70), by Carnegie Council on Adolescent Development, 1989, Washington, DC: Author. Reprinted with permission.

3. Empowering: providing all students with the knowledge and skills they need to take responsibility for their lives, to address life's challenges, to function successfully at all levels of society, and to be creators of knowledge.

4. Equitable: advocating for and ensuring every student's right to learn and providing appropriately challenging and relevant learning opportunities for every student (p. 13).

This We Believe seeks to isolate and quantify the unique aspects of young adolescents and identify the appropriate support, responses, and environment of a middle school. In doing so, it has provided both a mission statement and benchmarks for what the effective middle school should be and has contributed a framework

FIGURE 1.3   *This We Believe*

This We Believe

National Middle School Association believes successful schools for young adolescents include the following characteristics:

Curriculum, Instruction, and Assessment

- Educators value young adolescents and are prepared to teach them.
- Students and teachers are engaged in active, purposeful learning.
- Curriculum is challenging, exploratory, integrative, and relevant.
- Educators use multiple learning and teaching approaches.
- Varied and ongoing assessments advance learning as well as measure it.

Leadership and Organization

- A shared vision developed by all stakeholders guides every decision.
- Leaders are committed to and knowledgeable about this age group, educational research, and best practices.
- Leaders demonstrate courage and collaboration.
- Ongoing professional development reflects best educational practices.
- Organizational structures foster purposeful learning and meaningful relationships.

Culture and Community

- The school environment is inviting, safe, inclusive, and supportive of all.
- Every student's academic and personal development is guided by an adult advocate.
- Comprehensive guidance and support services meet the needs of young adolescents.
- Health and wellness are supported in curricula, school-wide programs, and related policies.
- The school actively involves families in the education of their children.
- The school includes community and business partners.

Source: Reprinted with permission from National Middle School Association. National Middle School Association. (2010). *Keys to Educating Young Adolescents.* Westerville, OH: Author.

within which decisions about programs can be made. This document also outlines sixteen general characteristics of successful schools for young adolescents. The characteristics of *This We Believe* are summarized in Figure 1.3.

Turning Points 2000

The fourth major contribution to basic middle level philosophy was the publication of *Turning Points 2000: Educating Adolescents in the 21st Century.* While the original *Turning Points* (1989) provided a framework for middle grades education, *Turning*

Points 2000 gives us in-depth insights into how to improve middle grades education. Strong emphasis is placed on curriculum, instruction, and assessment. The point is made that organizational changes (teaming, flexible scheduling, schools-within-schools, etc.) may be necessary, but not sufficient, for major improvement in academic achievement.

Turning Points 2000, written by Anthony Jackson and Gayle Davis, traces the progress of middle schools, and the levels of implementation of middle school philosophy, since the publication of the original *Turning Points* in 1989. *Turning Points 2000* reports that as schools implemented more of the tenets of *Turning Points,* and with greater fidelity, their students' standardized test scores in mathematics, language arts, and reading increased significantly. These results occurred at both the low and high ends of proficiency scales. The report also states that still to be reached are the schools that need improvement most—the ones in high-poverty urban and rural communities where lack of achievement is rampant and pockets of excellence are few and far between. Middle school philosophy has achieved its greatest level of acceptance and success primarily in suburban and upper-income areas (Jackson & Davis, 2000). *Turning Points 2000* provides practical applications for implementing what research tells us is best practice for young adolescents. In doing so, it has made some alterations in the original eight tenets. The newer document contains seven recommendations that have at their core the goal of ensuring success for every student, reflecting the centrality of teaching and learning.

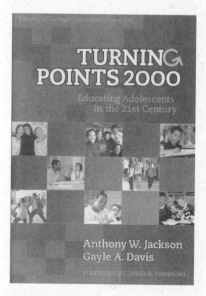

Source: Reprinted by permission of the publisher from Jackson, A. W. and Davis, G. A., *Turning Points 2000.* (New York: Teachers College Press, © 2000 by Jackson, A. W., and Davis, G. A. All rights reserved).

As you consider the recommendations of *Turning Points 2000* in Figure 1.4, keep in mind that there is no specific order in which a school must address improvements and make changes. As Jackson and Davis (2000) state:

> Schools are not blank slates on which this design or any other can be drawn without restriction or concern for the unique nature and status of the school itself. The *Turning Points 2000* design, like instruction for students, should meet schools where they are and help take them to where they need to go to ensure success (p. 25).

When one element in a school is changed, it inevitably affects other aspects of schooling. The recommendations are to be viewed as means to an end—improving classroom practice to lead to greater levels of student achievement. It is a continual process of change for the sake of improving, not just for the sake of change, as principals and teachers, and parents and communities embrace what is proving to be best for young adolescents.

FIGURE 1.4   *Turning Points 2000*

Turning Points 2000 calls for schools that

- Teach a curriculum grounded in rigorous, public academic standards for what students should know and be able to do, relevant to the concerns of adolescents and based on how students learn best.

- Use instructional methods designed to prepare all students to achieve higher standards and become lifelong learners.

- Staff middle grades schools with teachers who are expert at teaching young adolescents, and engage teachers in ongoing, targeted professional development opportunities.

- Organize relationships for learning to create a climate of intellectual development and a caring community of shared educational purpose.

- Govern democratically, through direct or representative participation by all school staff members, the adults who know the students best.

- Provide a safe and healthy school environment as part of improving academic performance and developing caring and ethical citizens.

- Involve parents and communities in supporting student learning and healthy development.

Source: Reprinted by permission of the publisher from Jackson, A. W., and Davis, G. A. *Turning Points 2000* (New York: Teachers College Press, © 2000 by Jackson, A. W., and Davis, G. A. All rights reserved.) pp. 23–24.

In addition to NMSA, the National Forum to Accelerate Middle-Grades Reform is working diligently to promote best practices for young adolescents. In 1999 the National Forum launched the *Schools to Watch* initiative. Through this initiative middle schools across the country are identified because they meet, or are making significant progress toward meeting, three specific criteria for high performance

- They are *academically excellent*—these schools challenge all students to use their minds well.

- They are *developmentally responsive*—these schools are sensitive to the unique developmental challenges of early adolescence.

- They are *socially equitable*—these schools are democratic and fair, providing every student with high-quality teachers, resources, and supports (www .schoolstowatch.org).

Each *School to Watch* faces its own unique challenges related to student population, levels of district support, location, and other variables. However, they all have some common threads, including the characteristics listed in Figure 1.5.

> **FIGURE 1.5   Common threads of Schools to Watch**
>
> - The schools know and articulate the academic outcomes they seek. In some cases, the outcomes are prescribed by the state or district; in others the faculty has adopted the outcomes recommended by their various disciplines.
> - The schools are taking deliberate steps to help students achieve those outcomes by making strategic changes in curriculum, teaching, and school services.
> - The schools have set benchmarks for implementing their strategies, and hold themselves accountable for specific results. We cannot stress too much the importance of data in the lives of these schools.
> - Each school strategically concentrates its energies on important focus areas. As a result, the changes in each school are burrowing deeply into its culture.
> - The schools have strong, visionary leaders who can articulate challenging goals, and motivate faculty and staff to reach those goals.

Source: From *What Are Schools to Watch?* By John Harrison, the National Forum to Accelerate Middle-Grades Reform, and the www.schoolstowatch.org website.

Legitimizing Factors

While educators convinced of the legitimacy of middle level education as a distinct and vital part of the K–12 sequence were building the philosophical foundation and supporting practices, validation of their efforts grew. We look at two major sources of legitimacy—the National Council for the Accreditation of Teacher Educators and the Educational Testing Service.

Legitimizing factors = NMSA Standards + Praxis Exams

● Middle Level Teacher Preparation Standards

A major step toward legitimacy occurred in 1995 when the *National Council for Accreditation of Teacher Education (NCATE)* recognized the need for the establishment of standards for the preparation of middle grades teachers. Most schools of education are either accredited, or are seeking accreditation, through NCATE. In 2000, NMSA and NCATE jointly established seven standards for middle level teacher preparation. Within each of the seven standards are objectives organized around teacher knowledge, dispositions, and performances. Figure 1.6 lists the standards that encompass adolescent development; philosophical underpinnings of developmentally responsive programs including curriculum, instruction, and assessment; the need for content-specific knowledge and training; the value of collaborative relationships; and the importance of professional development of teachers. Each standard is addressed within this book. Familiarize yourself with the standards and recognize that many of the recommended areas of knowledge, dispositions, and performances are addressed numerous times and in a variety of ways, chapter after chapter.

FIGURE 1.6   NMSA Performance-Based Standards for Initial Middle Level Teacher Preparation

Standard 1 Young Adolescent Development

Middle level teacher candidates understand the major concepts, principles, theories, and research related to young adolescent development, and they provide opportunities that support student development and learning.

Standard 2 Middle Level Philosophy and School Organization

Middle level teacher candidates understand the major concepts, principles, theories, and research underlying the philosophical foundations of developmentally responsive middle level programs and schools, and they work successfully within these organizational components.

Standard 3 Middle Level Curriculum and Assessment

Middle level teacher candidates understand the major concepts, principles, theories, standards, and research related to middle level curriculum and assessment, and they use this knowledge in their practice.

Standard 4 Middle Level Teaching Fields

Middle level teacher candidates understand and use the central concepts, tools of inquiry, standards, and structures of content in their chosen teaching fields, and they create meaningful learning experiences that develop all young adolescents' competence in subject matter and skills.

Standard 5 Middle Level Instruction and Assessment

Middle level teacher candidates understand and use the major concepts, principles, theories, and research related to effective instruction and assessment, and they employ a variety of strategies for a developmentally appropriate climate to meet the varying abilities and learning styles of all young adolescents.

Standard 6 Family and Community Involvement

Middle level teacher candidates understand the major concepts, principles, theories, and research related to working collaboratively with family and community members, and they use that knowledge to maximize the learning of all young adolescents.

Standard 7 Middle Level Professional Roles

Middle level teacher candidates understand the complexity of teaching young adolescents, and they engage in practices and behaviors that develop their competence as professionals.

Source: National Middle School Association, 4151 Executive Parkway, Suite 300, Westerville, OH 43081, 1-800-528-NMSA, www.nmsa.org.

● Assessing Teacher Knowledge and Skills

The *Educational Testing Service (ETS)* has developed a series of assessments designed to test teacher candidates according to the standards established by most states in the areas of basic academic skills, subject knowledge, knowledge of teaching methods, and classroom performance. These assessments form the *Praxis* Series. ETS tells us that there are three basic uses for the Praxis results: universities may use them to assess the knowledge of teacher candidates; states use them for granting initial licensure; and professional organizations require their successful completion as part of the criteria for certification.

You may have taken the Praxis I exam in conjunction with entry requirements for your teacher education program. The Praxis I exam assesses basic knowledge in reading, writing, and math. The Praxis II Series is designed to assess specific knowledge and skills aligning with your chosen level of teaching and/or subject area. Exactly which tests are required varies from state to state. One of the most widely used tests in the Praxis Series is the Principles of Learning and Teaching (PLT). This assessment is now divided into grade levels, with middle level defined as grades 5 through 9, encompassing the ways in which middle level education is configured. Success on the test requires knowledge of young adolescent development, curriculum, instruction, assessment, and maintenance of an appropriate learning environment. The Praxis II Series also includes subject-specific middle level tests in mathematics, science, literature and language studies, and history/social studies.

Reflections on Middle Level Education

Middle school philosophy is grounded in two areas—our understanding of the unique nature of young adolescents and how we choose to respond to their needs. Middle school philosophy is an attitude, a belief in possibilities. It's not necessarily quantifiable. It requires reflection and the renewal of resources, both physical and psychological. Middle school philosophy asks the adults who touch the lives of young adolescents to stretch and grow right along with their students.

With ongoing growth comes the ability to balance what we know and understand about young adolescents with how we respond to their needs. To maintain balance is to continually weigh what we know against what we do. Sound and reasoned judgment along with an eye for appropriateness will maintain this sensitive equilibrium.

For the remainder of the book, standards and accompanying knowledge, dispositions, and performances will be boxed and labeled in sections of the text where they are addressed. Please remember that even if you don't see a particular standard boxed, it may be addressed. There are some areas of standard knowledge, dispositions, and performances that are ongoing themes of the entire book. So far in Chapter 1 we have addressed a number of areas, specifically those listed in the box. By the time you work your way through this book, you will have a grasp of the enormity of our task and how our knowledge and dispositions are to be manifested through our performances as middle level educators.

STANDARD 1

Knowledge 4: Middle level teacher candidates understand the implications of young adolescent development for school organization and components of successful middle level programs and schools.

STANDARD 2

Knowledge 1: Middle level teacher candidates understand the philosophical foundations of developmentally responsive middle level programs and schools.

Knowledge 2: Middle level teacher candidates are knowledgeable about historical and contemporary models of schooling for young adolescents and the advantages and disadvantages of these models.

Knowledge 3: Middle level teacher candidates understand the rationale and characteristic components of developmentally responsive middle level schools.

Disposition 1: Middle level teacher candidates believe in the philosophical foundations that support developmentally responsive and socially equitable programs for all young adolescents.

Disposition 2: Middle level teacher candidates are committed to the application of middle level philosophical foundations in their practice.

GROUP ACTIVITIES

1. Obtain a wall map of your city and/or county. Locate and mark each middle school in your surrounding area. This will help put your future discussions of local middle schools in context.

2. As a class, begin a paper or electronic file to which you all have access. This file should have a section designated for each local (city or county) middle school. As data and observations are collected, add them to the file.

3. Assign each class member a middle school in your area to research. Go online to get the approximate number of students. Record the number of students and the published mission statement in your class file.

INDIVIDUAL ACTIVITIES

1. Establish a three-ring Middle Level Education binder for your work concerning middle grades. Use dividers for sections containing group activities, individual activities, your personal journal, observation and interview notes, helpful handouts, newspaper clippings, and other sections as the need arises.

2. Clip items from your local newspaper(s) (or print from newspaper websites) that deal with or impact middle grades education. Glue them

to notebook paper, include the date of the clipping, and summarize your reactions. You may be surprised at how many issues surface that are relevant to middle grades. Continue to collect clippings during your course.

3. Choose a mission statement from a local middle school. Write a brief assessment of the statement as you examine it for elements of *This We Believe.*

PERSONAL JOURNAL

At the end of each chapter, there are questions and/or prompts that require you to draw on your own experiences. Use the designated section of your Middle Level Education binder to respond to the personal journal items. Feel free to react to any portion of the chapter beyond the items asked for. This part of your binder should be for your eyes only and should be shared at your own discretion.

1. Describe the grade structure of your K–12 school experience. Was any part of it called *Middle School?*

2. What do you recall about the facility you attended during the middle level years? How was it different from your elementary and high schools?

Professional Practice

This is the first of the Professional Practice sections you will find at the end of each chapter. The scenarios, multiple choice questions, and constructed response items ask you to apply the knowledge in the text to classroom and school situations. The items are designed to provide practice for a variety of the Praxis II exams that may be required for certification. Most of the scenarios involve students you will meet in Chapter 2 and teachers you will meet in Chapter 4. When Lake Park Junior High changed the sign out front to Lake Park Middle School, it joined all the other middle level schools in the district. The community was growing and the decision was made to follow a national trend and move 6th graders from elementary schools to newly formed middle schools. Likewise, 9th grade was moved to the high schools where additions had been built to accommodate more students.

Lake Park principal, Mr. Hammond, was given the task by the district superintendent of exploring middle school philosophy and arranging for an August staff day where junior high

teachers would learn about how middle schools are different from junior highs and, more importantly, what to do with 6th graders in schools used to 7th, 8th, and 9th graders. He had read about the National Middle School Association in the National Association of Secondary School Principals (NASSP) journals and recognized NMSA as the best source for direction. He went online and found some information. He joined NMSA in order to receive the *Middle School Journal.* He ordered books on middle school philosophy and checked with the state to see if they could recommend middle schools for him to visit. It was June and he had little time to prepare for August.

1. In his efforts to explore middle level philosophy, which combination of sources of information might be most helpful?
   a. state education newsletters designed to share information on what's happening in local areas; *Middle School Journal;* NASSP Bulletin

    b. *Turning Points* from the Carnegie Corporation; NASSP Bulletin

    c. *Middle School Journal; Turning Points* from the Carnegie Corporation

    d. *This We Believe,* original 1995 version; *Middle School Journal; Turning Points* from the Carnegie Corporation

2. What will likely be the most significant barrier for Mr. Hammond as he moves forward and envisions the staff development day in August?

    a. principals who are resistant to change

    b. parental concerns about the district-wide change

    c. teachers who have not been specifically prepared for middle level education

    d. lack of viable role model schools in the area

3. Organizationally, perhaps the most difficult change for teachers will be that . . .

    a. emphasis shifts from cognitive growth to a mix of cognitive and affective growth.

    b. teachers will be grouped into interdisciplinary teams rather than subject-based departments.

    c. emphasis will be on the creation of small learning communities rather than viewing the school as a whole.

    d. they will share a group of students with a specific group of teachers.

Constructed Response

Will it be possible for the Lake Park Middle School (aka Junior High) staff to make significant changes in time for school to start in August? If you believe they will be able to change their philosophy and "look" different in late August, what changes do you think they will be able to make? If you believe they will not be significantly different, what emphases/initiatives do you think will take longer to put into place and why?

INTERNET RESOURCES

Association for Supervision and Curriculum Development (ASCD)

www.ascd.org

ASCD is the nation's largest organization of educators interested in curriculum and supervision of instruction. The website offers valuable resources for teachers on multiple topics and features a wide variety of outstanding publications, conferences, and professional development opportunities.

Middle Web

www.middleweb.com

This large site, sponsored by the Edna McConnell Clark Foundation, is dedicated to increasing achievement for all middle school students. It features numerous articles and dozens of links, along with a teacher chat room.

National Forum to Accelerate Middle-Grades Reform

www.mgforum.org

This group is dedicated to promoting academic performance and healthy development of young adolescents. They work across organizations to promote common goals and strengthen efforts to improve middle grades schools.

National Middle School Association (NMSA)

www.nmsa.org

NMSA maintains this valuable website to inform members and all others interested in middle grades education about the organization's philosophy and focus. Information is available for teachers, administrators, state level officials, and higher education faculty concerning events, resources, and position statements of NMSA. Online shopping for NMSA publications is available, as is information on professional development and conferences.

Schools to Watch

www.schoolstowatch.org

Schools to Watch, an initiative of the National Forum to Accelerate Middle-Grades Reform, is a program that identifies middle schools across the United States that exhibit characteristics of high performing middle level education according to National Forum standards (available at this website).

2 Development of Middle Level Learners

Physical development of young adolescents is accompanied by emotional and social development that shape relationships. Adults in their lives share responsibility for guiding middle level students through the maturing process.

Young adolescents are child-like and adult-like, mature and immature, sensitive and unaware, seekers of independence and clingers to dependence, concrete and idealogical, interested and detached. Sometimes all these characteristics are evident within a single individual and within a brief span of time. Adolescents are in a state of transition from a more predictable, prescribed, limited, and familiar place in the world to one less familiar, more unpredictable, more self-directed, and fuzzier in its boundaries.

Williamson & Johnston, 1998, p. 21

CHAPTER PREVIEW

Physical Development
- Mismatched Parts
- Puberty
- Sexual Maturity
- Timing
- Physical Development Issues

Intellectual Development
- Becoming
- Intellectual Development Issues

Emotional Development
- Variety of Emotions
- Interrelatedness
- Worry
- Emotional Development Issues

Social Development
- Adult Relationships
- Peer and Group Relationships
- Social Development Issues

Character Development
- Young Adolescent Character Traits
- School Programs
- Character Development Issues

Reflections on the Development of Middle Level Learners

INTRODUCTION

The middle school years represent a unique and significant period of human development. Young adolescents are in a world of their own and yet are keenly aware of their surroundings—the places, people, and things that make up their world. By middle school, students have begun to develop diversified views of themselves. Donna Marie San Antonio, a respected Harvard professor, provides some dichotomies that vividly describe wonderfully complex young adolescents (2006, p. 9). Think about these statements, altered slightly from the originals, as you continue preparing to be a middle grades teacher.

- Young adolescents may be fiercely independent, yet yearn for meaningful relationships with adults.
- Young adolescents may reveal emotional vulnerability, yet be deeply self-protective.
- Young adolescents may be capable of complex analytic thinking, yet be disorganized to the point of chronic forgetfulness.
- Young adolescents may be compassionate and altruistic in the desire to make the world a better place, yet capable of striking out cruelly at an unpopular classmate.
- Young adolescents may be able to understand and accommodate the needs of others, yet display a high level of self-centeredness.

San Antonio continues, "I believe that we cannot accomplish our academic goals without a purposeful and thoughtful focus on social development" (p. 13).

This chapter approaches young adolescent development from five broad perspectives—physical, intellectual, emotional, social, and character development. Each of these perspectives interact with, and influence, all of the others. In the ever-changing world of early adolescence, it is artificial to separate these areas of development. Exploring them separately must be considered only an organizing tool. Let the perspectives flow in and out of one another as you read and reflect.

Physical Development

Remember the days when self-consciousness took priority over everything else? Maybe you were one of the lucky ones with looks and self-esteem that gave you the confidence to be relatively free of trauma when it came to your physical appearance. But let's face it, even the cheerleaders and the coolest guy around had their moments of doubt. Perhaps the physical burden was never feeling quite good-looking enough. This desire to be physically attractive is part of the human condition and needs to be put in perspective. Easy to say as adults! However, we are concerned here with young adolescents who at times are completely devoid of perspective.

STANDARD 1

Knowledge 1: Middle level teacher candidates understand the major concepts, principles, and theories of young adolescent development—intellectual, physical, social, emotional, and moral.

Knowledge 2: Middle level teacher candidates understand the range of individual differences of all young adolescents and the implications of these differences for teaching and learning.

In the inconsistent world of early adolescence, there is one predictable factor. Physical development influences every other type of development that middle level students experience—emotional, social, intellectual, and character.

● Mismatched Parts

Young Adolescent Diversity

If we held up a bag of male body parts and asked a blindfolded 12-year-old boy to reach inside, grab parts randomly, and become the young adolescent that is the composite of those parts, the result would be a middle level student in sixth or seventh grade. There is no such thing as "typical" because these newly double-digit-aged kids so often appear to be "Mister Potato Heads" in this awkward stage of life! Ears too big, arms too long, voices too squeaky. Girls, too, often resemble creatures of mismatched parts. Their hips may widen before their breasts develop, their noses may be too big for their faces.

Growth spurts usually occur for boys between the ages of 12 and 14, but for some boys, rapid physical growth may be delayed well into high school. Growth is seldom even or gradual for young adolescents. Bones tend to grow more rapidly than muscles. So, while weight gain generally accompanies bone growth, without equivalent development of muscle, awkwardness and clumsiness are inevitable. Joint pain, leg aches, restlessness, and fatigue may accompany these uneven periods of growth. Outer extremities, such as hands and feet, grow before arms and legs. Have you ever heard someone say that you can predict the adult size of a puppy by looking at the size of its paws? Well, chances are that if a boy needs a size 13 sneaker by age 12, 30 × 28 jeans will be history by age 14! So in his new 32 × 34 jeans, he walks into middle school to greet his eighth grade year as a remarkably different-looking young adolescent than his sixth and seventh grade teachers experienced. As a middle school teacher, I never tired of gasping (to the delight of many a boy!), "This can't be the same Cody who sat by the window in my third period class last year!"

Each of these three boys is 11 years old. While we may think the boy in the center is the most mature, his teacher tells us he is actually less emotionally mature than his two much smaller classmates.

Girls generally experience rapid growth a year or two before boys. Remember middle school dances when the tall, gangly girls giggled in one corner while shorter, "cutie-pie" boys taunted each other to ask for a dance—only to find that their faces often matched up with developing breasts?

Puberty

Outward growth spurts indicate big changes on the inside. Between childhood and the beginning of young adulthood is the transition period known as *puberty*. The word *puberty* often causes parent and teacher alike to shudder. If we think it's scary as adults to spend time around kids in puberty, let's try to recall what it was like to have puberty actually taking place inside us. For many of us, it's a time best left in the past. But we are survivors! During puberty biological changes that make us taller, heavier, and more muscular are accompanied by hormonal changes that forever alter our bodies in equally significant ways. Although testosterone, the male hormone, and estrogen, the female hormone, are present in all of us, the balance of the hormones is broken during puberty so that one hormone takes over to influence sexual development. All of this is happening for some at the same time as those mismatched parts are appearing almost overnight. At this point, if you are thinking, "I'm supposed to teach these creatures subject-verb agreement and the Pythagorean theorem?" you are beginning to get the picture of some of the challenges involved in middle level education!

STANDARD 1

Knowledge 5: Middle level teacher candidates understand issues of young adolescent health and sexuality.

Many changes occur during puberty. Hair growth develops under arms, on legs, in pubic areas, and on the face. The voice changes as the larynx grows larger. Girls' voices may become more mellow, while boys' voices may go through those embarrassing falsetto-crack-bass-crack-falsetto moments. Oil and sweat glands may begin to function, resulting in all kinds of potentially embarrassing situations. Acne medication, shampoo, and deodorant appear on shopping lists, while longer, more frequent showers become part of a daily routine.

So you think you want to spend your career behind closed doors with as many as 30 of these creatures at a time? Read on!

Sexual Maturity

With puberty comes sexual maturation. Yes, these awkward, funny-sounding, often aromatic configurations we call young adolescents have all the parts necessary to reproduce themselves. Because the body often matures before mental and emotional decision-making skills, developing middle grades students are at high risk for either poor decisions or not thinking at all before acting. Ill-timed sexual experimentation can easily lead to multiple unfortunate consequences, only two of which are sexually transmitted diseases and pregnancy.

Timing

Perhaps at no other stage of life does timing play such an important role. Rapid physical changes, puberty, and sexual maturation generally take place, in starts and stops, between the ages of 10 and 14. Puberty, with all its miraculous changes, may qualify as a challenging period of life for many young adolescents. If we could say, "Okay, between March 20 and April 12 of the seventh grade year, you will all experience puberty. You will grow to full maturity and emerge April 13 as lovely, adjusted teenagers, all looking good in your 'Clearasiled' skin, wide-shouldered or B cup upper bodies, all deodorized and smelling of aftershave and perfume," what a wonderful world this would be!

However, we live in a less-than-perfect young adolescent world and the changes experienced by growing children happen sporadically, predictable only in the sense that there are growth patterns. These patterns happen rapidly and early for some, and slowly and haltingly for others. The "early bloomers" may be boastful, but are often embarrassed. The "late bloomers" are almost always self-conscious. There are emotional consequences associated with physical changes that can lead to long-lasting and very memorable scars on the psyche that haunt for a lifetime. Let's look at some issues that may accompany physical development and explore some ways we, as teachers, might make the "child-to-adolescent" passage a bit more tolerable.

Physical Development Issues

Physical development issues are many and are often uncomfortable for teacher and student alike. Here are some of the reasons for concern, along with suggestions for how we can make a difference, both as individual teachers and on school and district levels.

▶ ISSUE #1
Middle level students need information on physical development.

Not only do middle level students have a hard time finding answers, they can rarely define the question or problem when it comes to physical growth and changes. A comprehensive health education curriculum is invaluable. National and state standards are available that outline what 10- to 14-year-olds need to know about wellness, puberty, and sexual maturation. A health educator is needed in every school—someone who is honest, straightforward, trustworthy from a student perspective, and accessible. Boys and girls should be separated at times to allow for more honest and detailed questions and answers.

▶ ISSUE #2
Physical changes affect behavior.

Teachers serve students well when they recognize and accept a variety of behaviors that may result directly from the turmoil caused and/or aggravated by the biological aspects of puberty. When opportunities arise to address the unspoken questions and resulting behaviors, teachers should reassure students that their anxieties are normal, and even expected.

Middle level students are restless and uncomfortable much of the time. Because of varying growth rates and the excess energy that may accompany these periods of rapid growth, regulation desks arranged in rows do not always provide the physical setting students need. Providing a classroom with a variety of seating possibilities can prove very beneficial. Perhaps a couple of tables with chairs, desks of varying sizes, a few comfortable chairs, and a couch will provide ample choices. I realize that this gives students a lot of freedom, and many teachers are hesitant to build their classroom environments in this way. However, I have found that most middle level students respond positively when their needs are taken into consideration and when teachers do things that show respect for them.

The legitimate restlessness resulting from growing bodies may be exacerbated by long periods of sitting, regardless of the variety of chairs provided. It's no secret that active learning is more effective than passive learning. Movement stimulates the learning process. Find ways to get students up and moving as part of instruction.

▶ **ISSUE #3**
Rapid growth requires increased and balanced nutrition.

There are two problems when it comes to young adolescents increasing what they eat in a balanced way. Body image worries scream "thin" to many middle level students. And then, when they're hungry, their taste buds, along with peer pressure, often lead them to less nutritional food choices.

A comprehensive health program will include lessons on good nutrition. But the health educator can't do it alone. All of us need to emphasize healthy eating. When we have a snack, let's make it something nutritional like an apple or carrot. When we eat in the cafeteria, let's model healthy eating habits. Middle level kids are often hungry. If, as a faculty, a decision can be made to allow eating during the day other than at lunchtime, then find a way to let kids have snacks, perhaps mid-morning or mid-afternoon, provided the snacks follow healthy eating guidelines you and your team/administration have established. We discuss obesity and anorexia in Chapter 5.

▶ **ISSUE #4**
Young adolescents should not be stereotyped
according to physical characteristics.

Many growth issues factor into physical ability. Some middle level students experience athletic success as they mature. Others find themselves lacking the coordination and stamina they may have had in elementary school. Let's give middle level students the opportunity to explore athletics and find their talents and interests according to their own timing. Tall boys are not automatically talented at, or even interested in, basketball. Petite girls are not all destined to be gymnasts. While physical development may sometimes lead to a child's interest in a particular activity or sport, mental development also influences activity choices.

Plan ways to incorporate a variety of intramural opportunities that allow even less physically skilled students to participate in team and individual activities. Offer classes in exploratory time or after school that help students learn skills such as dancing, tennis, martial arts, and so on.

Chorus quality depends on vocal cord development. Some activities in home economics and home/shop arts require dexterity, and some art forms require coordination/spatial sense. While we would like all middle level students to experience success in all areas, we need to understand that while the brain may be willing, biological development may not have caught up. Let's make sure that exploratory courses and intramural activities are opportunities to experience and experiment in broad areas that allow for and accommodate differences in development.

▶ **ISSUE #5**
Many girls will experience the first signs of a menstrual period during the school day.

This development alone will cause most girls to be upset and anxious, depending on the amount of information they have or the level of openness they have experienced among friends and family. A common cause of absenteeism among young adolescent girls is menstrual pain. Teachers need to be very sensitive to girls' requests to leave the classroom suddenly, as well as to girls who are late to class or stay in the restroom longer than expected. Of course, the key to knowing the legitimacy of these events is knowing our students. Not every tardy girl is menstruating. Just be aware that questioning tardiness or restroom requests in front of other middle schoolers is not appropriate. Make sure your school clinic has feminine hygiene products available. Menstrual discomfort is real, not psychosomatic, and can't simply be willed away. As with other physical aspects of life, some will use cramping as an excuse to miss activities in class when perhaps it's not necessary. We should try to err on the side of belief, however, rather than punishing sincere girls who need our understanding.

▶ **ISSUE #6**
Some middle level students (and I'm not just talking about girls!) feel a compulsion to check themselves out visually on a regular basis.

I found that having a full-length mirror in an out-of-the-way place in the classroom served a positive purpose. I also placed a smaller mirror on the wall by the pencil sharpener, so it was never obvious who needed visual reassurance and who simply had pencils with bad lead! These mirrors were up in August and were a natural part of the classroom setting. As a result, I had very few problems related to them.

▶ **ISSUE #7**
Overactive glands may cause difficulties.

Because glands of all kinds may be newly activated or overactive in young adolescents, by mid-morning a student may realize that he forgot to use deodorant, or perhaps he feels the need for just a touch of something that smells good. Consider having a brown paper bag in a supply closet with spray deodorant and an inexpensive bottle of aftershave, along with a very light fragrance for girls. As with the mirrors, this may be an "extra" that some teachers may not be comfortable providing. Very few students will ever use these items, but you may save some 12-year-old a world of embarrassment. It's worth the effort!

If comfortable with both the issue and the students, we may have occasions to initiate a personal hygiene discussion with students who, for whatever reason, need our brown bags of smell-good items. A trusted guidance counselor may be a better choice than the classroom teacher for this kind of heart-to-heart. It all depends on the individuals involved.

The physical development of young adolescents may come in sudden spurts or with gradual subtlety. The changes accompanying physical development may be met with emotional turmoil or casual acceptance. In fact, all four of these descriptors may be manifested in one individual student. Regardless of student responses to physical changes, they are sure to affect the other areas of development. Let's look next at intellectual development.

Intellectual Development

Middle level students experience a transitional state between childlike thinking and adultlike thinking. Childlike thinking is characterized as concrete. This means that children organize information and experiences around things that are visible and familiar. They have difficulty visualizing concepts that they cannot see or touch. In the concrete stage, children have rigid patterns of thinking. Middle grades students who are concrete thinkers learn concepts much more readily when they are taught using manipulatives and hands-on activities that help bridge the transition from concrete to more adultlike abstract thinking and learning.

The intellectual transition that occurs in puberty opens whole new worlds for children progressing to the teen years. They begin to think in more general terms and to visualize events without having to see them. They can form mental connections, put things in perspective, and predict in more complex ways.

● Becoming

We must not lose sight of a very important word—**becoming**. As vital as it is to understand how the terms *concrete* and *abstract* apply to the thinking process, it is just as vital to understand the transition between the two distinct stages. Middle level students are generally concrete thinkers at age 10, and some may remain basically concrete through age 14. However, they may be concrete at age 10 and well on their way to abstract thinking capabilities by age 11. One thing is certain, they are becoming. Some researchers tell us that the complete transition into abstract thinking may not take place until the age of 17 or 18. In fact, research evidence now shows that some parts of the brain do not fully develop until the mid-20s.

Young Adolescent Diversity

While we may be able to identify and characterize stages of mental and intellectual growth, we must remember that the process of moving from concrete to abstract thinking is completely individual. In other words, becoming is idiosyncratic. It happens at different rates and at different ages for all of us. To complicate matters even further, the other areas of development impact this intellectual growth. By itself intellectual development is variable, but just think about how physical, emotional, social, and character development figure into the mix of progressing from childhood to adolescence and subsequently to adulthood. It's a complex and staggering period, to say the least!

Intellectual Development Issues

We should be aware of the varied manifestations of intellectual development in the classroom and of the issues they present to the teacher. This awareness leads us to seek ways we can assist in this important growth process.

▶ ISSUE #1

The attention span of young adolescents may not be as great as it was in late elementary school or will be in high school.

This issue has profound implications for instruction. Expecting a middle level student to sit through a 20-minute lecture, much less a 45-minute one, and gain a great deal of knowledge is ludicrous. Attention will wander and learning will be hit or miss at best. In Chapter 8 we explore instructional strategies intended to hold attention for appropriate lengths of time. Breaking up blocks of time into manageable segments is a technique that should be mastered by middle level teachers.

▶ ISSUE #2

Middle level students often have very vivid imaginations which can be linked to concepts as abstract thinking develops.

Purposefully channeling imagination into learning experiences, conjures up creativity that has not been possible before. Encouraging students to use their imaginations and creativity to discover nuances and possibilities, rather than simply feeding them information, helps them take advantage of this imagination-meets-abstract-thinking stage of life.

▶ ISSUE #3

Because intellectual development is so variable among young adolescents, a group of 25 seventh graders may represent a whole spectrum of developmental levels.

This is one of the biggest challenges of middle level education. The question is, "How do we facilitate the learning of a prescribed curriculum, that is, state and national standards, in a classroom filled with students who are at very different places in development?" As teachers, we must be observers, constantly monitoring what's working and what isn't, and for which students at which times. In Chapter 8, we discuss filling our "instructional toolboxes" to the brim with ways of teaching concepts and skills to students at variable levels of readiness. One size does not fit all!

As the shift from concrete to abstract thinking is ongoing, it is possible to lose opportunities to challenge middle level students. We must adjust and readjust our lesson components; we must watch closely and listen carefully to our students. We need to vary our instructional approaches to make the most of learning possibilities.

▶ ISSUE #4
Physical development and intellectual development happen concurrently.

Active learning should take precedence over passive learning. Let's get middle level students up and moving. They have a need to experience learning—to move, to touch, to manipulate, to search for meaning and understanding. The concept of inquiry, or discovery, learning should pervade what we do in the classroom.

▶ ISSUE #5
A major shift in the intellectual development of middle level students is their newly acquired ability to think about their own thinking, or to experience metacognition.

We "miss the boat" when it comes to helping students take charge of their own learning by failing to ask them to reflect on their learning processes. Knowles and Brown (2007) tell us that the emerging possibilities to think about thinking may be a source of frustration for students. They may become confused about their ability to be reflective. We can help them explore how their thinking takes place and what happens inside and outside the classroom that increases comprehension and makes learning specific skills easier and faster.

▶ ISSUE #6
Middle level students begin to understand what is meaningful and useful, with application to their lives.

This intellectual development issue has major implications for what we teach, or the curriculum. In Chapter 7 there are guidelines for a curriculum that weaves the knowledge and skills mandated by state standards with what interests and concerns middle level students. Framing our lessons in the context of real life makes learning a more natural process of satisfying intellectual curiosity that arises from this sense of purpose and usefulness. There are times when young adolescent intellectual development appears to be at the mercy of emotional development.

Emotional Development

Parents, teachers, and even young adolescents themselves often refer to the roller coaster of emotions that accompany the middle grade years as difficult to understand and impossible to predict. If you have ridden a roller coaster, you can no doubt close your eyes and recall the exhilaration of expectation, the sheer terror of the actual descents, and brief moments of calm during leveling off sections. But even in those "catch your breath" phases of the ride, there is an anticipation that keeps the adrenaline flowing and a sense of peace at bay. That's how early adolescence can be characterized.

Dan Goleman, author of *Emotional Intelligence* (1995), says that emotional intelligence determines about 80 percent of a person's success in life. His understanding of emotional intelligence is based in part on Howard Gardner's interpersonal and intrapersonal intelligences that we discuss in Chapter 3. Goleman tells us we need to include five dimensions of emotional intelligence into what we do in schools. These five dimensions are self-awareness, handling emotions, motivation, empathy, and social skills. He believes it is possible to raise the emotional intelligence of students by, among other things, being available to them with a sympathetic ear.

Variety of Emotions

Numerous descriptors are used when referring to the emotional states of early adolescence. Of course not every 10- to 15-year-old experiences all the characteristics, and, when compared to the student next to him at lunch, none to the identical extent. Young adolescents may have emotions that are unpredictable, extreme, and unstable. They may be moody, anxious, angry, and embarrassed by things that we don't see as important.

While these descriptors seem to be negative in nature, my experience leads me to add hopefulness, optimism, and excitement to the list. I see these positive emotions exhibited every day by young adolescents. The message here is that variability makes for a wide emotional spectrum of middle school students. All of the descriptors are tied into the concept of self. The development of a positive self-esteem is crucial but often elusive. The sense of losing control over the environment contributes to self-consciousness (Knowles & Brown, 2007) and this self-consciousness often results in loss of self-esteem. The transition from elementary to middle school carries with it a myriad of changes that to a 10- or 11-year-old may seem overwhelming. Add this transition to the physical changes continually experienced and it's entirely understandable that self-esteem would suffer. Developing a positive self-esteem, while universally challenging for young adolescents, may prove to be especially difficult for minority students. As teachers we must create learning environments that account for cultural, ethnic, and racial differences. In Chapter 3 we explore these, and other, differences.

Interrelatedness

Emotional development is interrelated with both physical and intellectual development. The physical changes described in this chapter are enough to cause emotions to occasionally go haywire. Imagine going from 4 feet 11 inches to 5 feet 8 inches in

Many factors contribute to the development of self-concept in young adolescents. The emotional roller coaster ride often includes dips that lead to periods of sadness.

the three short summer months between seventh and eighth grade. Or consider the creamy, smooth complexion that becomes embarrassingly blemished during first semester of the seventh grade. How about the unpredictable erections that occur while finding the surface area of a cylinder or discussing the merits of the Panama Canal? The list of physical changes that can provoke emotional responses could go on and on, with each of us adding our own personal traumas. Be keenly aware that each time you are in a classroom of 25 middle grades students in the process of *becoming*, there are potentially 25 cases of moodiness and insecurity and emotional distress in there with you. Dealing with the physical changes taking place in their bodies is a persistent emotional challenge for young adolescents.

Emotional development is also entangled with intellectual development in ways we are just now beginning to understand and document. Brain researchers tell us that emotions strongly influence our ability to pay attention and retain information (Wolfe, 2001). The implications of this for the way we approach teaching and learning are tremendous. Emotional concerns can impede academics unless middle school teachers know how to work with these factors and channel concerns into productive results by understanding the context of the student's world. "The affective side of learning is the critical interplay between how we feel, act, and think. There is no separation of mind and emotions; emotions, thinking, and learning are all linked" (Jensen, 1998, p. 71).

● Worry

Middle grades students worry about almost everything. Their fears have changed from those of childhood to concerns about social and appearance issues. "Do I fit in? Do my jeans look like everybody else's? Is my hair right? Will they want me to sit with them at lunch? Did he notice my braces? Will I be in the 'right' group on the field trip?" Worry, fear, and anxiety are common emotions of early adolescence. From an adult perspective, the sources of these negative emotions may seem trivial, but remember that our perceptions become our realities. To middle grades students, their worries are legitimate and quite real. To try to convince them otherwise is futile and potentially harmful. If we denigrate their concerns, we are, in students' minds, denigrating them and adding to their anxieties and uncertainties. Our responses should be tempered with understanding and the absence of judgmental attitudes. When a 12-year-old girl is crying because she found uncomplimentary notes written about her by kids she considered friends, the last thing she wants to hear is "It's no big deal, you'll find new friends." Instead, we should acknowledge that she is hurt. The gift of an understanding ear will allow her to express her feelings and know that someone cares. It won't take away the hurt, but it will legitimize her emotions and give her the opportunity to work through the grief of the moment.

Emotional Development Issues

As middle grades educators our goal regarding emotional development should be to help our students find their way toward emotional maturity. This task is compounded by the challenge of teaching socially acceptable ways of both controlling and expressing emotions. Along with displaying emotions in socially acceptable ways, emotional maturity must include dealing with personal emotions in mentally healthy ways. Middle schools must provide opportunities for students to see that a wide range of emotions is normal. Creating an environment that says "It's okay to feel the way you do" will enhance self-acceptance and allow emotional maturity to progress.

▶ **ISSUE #1**
Because emotions may occur suddenly and without warning, self-regulation is very difficult.

A sensitivity to the emotions of our students should make us acutely aware of the volatility they are experiencing. When an outburst of emotion or some sort of personal affront is aimed at us, we have the perfect opportunity to model self-regulation. The sage advice of "take a deep breath and count to ten" has a lot of validity in a middle grades setting. Show how it's done and encourage students to do likewise.

▶ **ISSUE #2**
Because of emotional variability, young adolescents may be at high risk of making poor decisions.

We can help students recognize that many emotions are fleeting, that what they feel at one moment may change quickly and unexpectedly. Through thinking out loud when a decision needs to be made, we can model the difference between reacting and responding. Reactions are emotionally triggered, while responses are the result of thinking through those emotions. We want our students to make decisions based more on rational thought than on emotions.

▶ **ISSUE #3**

Some incidences and events trigger emotions
to the point of disruption of the learning process.

As individual teachers, but preferably as a team of teachers, we have a very beneficial tool for dealing with emotions. That tool is providing a psychologically safe environment in which concerns may be aired. This environment may include appropriate readings and videos that present possible solutions to emotionally charged dilemmas and situations. Encouraging students to role-play and involve themselves in simulations may be a vehicle for venting worries, anxieties, and emotional distress and preventing the disruption of the learning process.

Not only can the learning process be affected by emotions, but social relationships and growth are often impacted by emotions.

Closely linked to emotional development is social development which, in turn, affects overall development of easily influenced and socially self-conscious young adolescents. Let's explore social development.

Social Development

As young adolescents become aware of the unique aspects of themselves, they also become acutely aware of others around them—most specifically, their peers. They develop an exaggerated view of themselves, often thinking that everyone's attention is on them. This perception may make them uneasy in social settings. The emotion-laden search for personal identity integrates experiences with developing bodies, biological drive, new thinking capacities, and expanding social roles (Knowles & Brown, 2007). While it may be uncomfortable, socialization plays a major role in the psychological growth process, as it is influenced by, and interrelated with, physical, intellectual, and emotional development. "Perhaps the most significant stress in a young adolescent's life is the sense of not fitting in. For most students, good adjustment and performance in school require some level of social comfort" (San Antonio, 2006, p.10).

PEARSON
myeducationlab)

As a six foot tall 12-year-old, David's physical development far exceeds his emotional, social, and cognitive development. To view an interview with David and his mother, go to the Video Examples section of **Topic #2: Today's Students** in the MyEducationLab for your course and view the video entitled "David McBeath's Interview."

The need for socialization is especially strong during early adolescence. As we explored in Chapter 1, middle level philosophy originated partially from the belief that the school can and should play a major role in both the cognitive and affective dimensions of the development of the whole child, including aspects of socialization.

STANDARD 1

Performance 9: Middle level teacher candidates deal effectively with societal changes that impact the healthy development of young adolescents.

NMSA

● Adult Relationships

Young adolescents often find themselves caught between their desire to be safe and secure (as in childhood) and their desire for freedom and independence. Because adults generally represent security, the struggle for change often revolves around relationships with them. While affirmation of parental love and teacher approval are secretly sought, young adolescents may act out in argumentative and rebellious ways against those closest to them, in many cases parents, guardians, and teachers. This rebellion, in its many forms, is normal and even necessary, as attempts are made toward demonstrating that they have minds of their own. Considering the options, perhaps rebellion during middle school years is preferable to rebellion at other times in life, when even more dangerous options become available.

Even as young adolescents tend to disassociate themselves from family, they may seek to emulate other adults (Knowles & Brown, 2007). They easily buy into fantasies about adults, often created in the media. This leads to hero formation, most likely of movie stars and sports figures. In fact, Mee (1997) found in a large-scale study that boys almost exclusively named sports figures as their role models. Both genders may fantasize that adult life can be (or is) glamorous; that money is easily made; that outward beauty equates to happiness; that TV sitcom life is realistic; that those successful, carefree people in the advertisements drinking beer and smoking do so with no consequences; that casual sex is desirable. . . . The list goes on.

● Peer and Group Relationships

As young adolescents begin to discover that it is unlikely that they can always please the adults with authority over them as well as the kids they hang around with, a loyalty shift usually takes place. Friends generally take on greater significance. Fear of being different, and therefore not accepted by peers, is a drive that for most is unavoidable. They adopt personalities and appearances that will win them placement in a group. I remember distinctly the groups that existed during my middle school (junior high) years, and I'm certain you remember yours too. "Natural selection" played a role in group formation. There were certain groups I knew I could not align with. The "cheerleader," for instance, was not a possibility for me because I didn't look the part, regardless of how I tried. I recognized the choices that were realistic and found my way into a group that was comfortable. Being part of a group provides security and is a source of feedback when experimentation and dilemmas occur. It seems that simply being part of a group is more important than which group. Since most of us don't choose our families or teachers, choosing friends and a peer group takes on importance as a factor in establishing identity and independence. It's a decision-making opportunity.

Group alignment creates peer pressure, the driving force created by the need/ desire to conform. Giving in to peer pressure is absolutely normal at any age. Peer pressure can have a positive or negative influence. If peer pressure dictates that good grades, church attendance, and politeness are the norm, then most adults cheer the influence. However, if peer pressure leads to smoking, drinking, drugs, vandalism, or early sex, then it is viewed as negative. Most peer pressure is somewhere in between

The alliances formed in early adolescence are often very strong.

and varies according to circumstances and timing. Like it or not, the influence of peers is a phenomenon that is inevitable. Adults can and should attempt to influence the choices of friends and peer groups, but the truth is that young adolescents will assert their need for independence and make choices that only locking them in their rooms until age 21 could prevent.

In the beginning of early adolescence, around ages 10 to 12, same-sex friendships are the most vital. The need for a "best friend" to whom there is uncompromising loyalty and from whom the same is expected is a driving force. Once the best friend status is achieved, the relegation to "second best friend" is a devastating prospect. This appears to be much more pronounced in girls than boys. Girls will bare their souls to best friends, while boys are often content to be in a group where they laugh at the same things and are physically active in the same interest areas. When and with whom opposite sex attractions occur occupies a place in young adolescent variability that exceeds most other aspects of the age. Some "puppy love" experiences heavily influence 11-year-olds, while in others opposite sex attractions do not wield a great deal of influence until age 16 or so.

The social development of early adolescence includes some notable paradoxes. In their quest for independence, adolescents will freely conform to fit in. They rebel against adult authority while doing what they can to become adultlike. Social development implies relationships with other people and yet this is an age of egocentricity and perhaps selfishness.

These paradoxes take place simultaneously with expanding possibilities for violence, bullying, aggression, and a variety of abusive scenarios that we discuss in Chapter 5 when we consider the societal contexts of middle level education.

● Social Development Issues

There are many issues involved in the social development of young adolescents. Our own memories of the pre- and early-teen years serve as acute reminders of just how significant social issues can be during this period of life.

▶ **ISSUE #1**

Young adolescents have a very strong need to be part of a social group.

Students who are part of advisory groups (more about these in Chapter 6) often feel a bond of trust, or at least a sense that they know the others in the group. Clubs give students chances to get to know others with similar interests. At a minimum, we should adhere to the *Turning Points* tenet that calls for us to create small learning communities. This translates into teams, the basic organizational foundation of middle school. We explore teams and teaming in Chapter 6. Giving students "free time" during the school day allows for informal socialization.

If we do not allow for socialization time, we are depriving our students of growth opportunities. Kids are going to talk, pass notes, send text messages, gather in groups, and so on. If we don't give them time for such activities, they will take the time from us. Showing that we understand socialization needs should be part of our visible attitude toward our students. Social validation is important.

▶ **ISSUE #2**

Some young adolescents are targets.

Kids often pick on others as a way of diverting attention away from themselves, their differences, or their insecurities. Regardless of the reasons, it happens. As educators, we need to do what we can to stifle this activity. Be sensitive to the kids who seem to be the outcasts and never say things like "stop picking on Sam" in front of Sam or other kids who aren't involved. This will just make things worse for unfortunate Sam as students tease him because the teacher has come to his rescue. Instead, we need to find interests and activities that Sam does well and capitalize on them. Identify kids with similar interests/skills and arrange for Sam to get together with them. We should also encourage Sam not to react to teasing. Then it will no longer be fun for the perpetrators and it will lessen the occurrences. As strange as it may seem, some kids who become "targets" actually thrive on it in a perverse way. Attention, even though it's negative, gives a sense of identity. These students would benefit from multiple visits with the school counselor.

▶ **ISSUE #3**

Early adolescence is a prime time for shyness, given the self-consciousness of the age.

Young adolescents may experience symptoms such as blushing, sweating, and increased heart rate. The need to conform to group norms may cause them to hide the symptoms and appear to be confident. Whether shyness is obvious, or not, it can be painful and viewed as a negative trait by peers and adults. As with Issue #1, providing a variety of outlets for socialization will help ease shyness. Offering activity opportunities that vary enough to appeal to a variety of students may help shy students find their talents and interests, and other students who share them.

▶ **ISSUE #4**

Teachers' social backgrounds may be different from their students' backgrounds.

This is a very common phenomenon. We may teach students with whom we have difficulty relating. Our realities may be very different from those of our students. Student learning will be more meaningful if teachers understand the young adolescent. Knowing student social realities will assist us in relating to them and connecting them more fully to school experiences. We look more closely at societal issues in Chapter 5.

In the next section we will see that social development and character development are closely linked.

Character Development

"The characters of young people are determined by what they do and what happens to them. But these take place in a concrete social medium, a complex web of human relationships. The content and quality of this social medium as a whole plays a significant, formative role in shaping the character of students" (Dobrin, 2001, p. 275). The discussion of character development has the potential to become value-laden as we deal with morals and ethics. Rather than steering clear of the topic because of possible controversy, or embedding it in discussions of emotional and social development, let's take a look at what appear to be the characteristics of early adolescence in terms of character development and explore how "what they do and what happens to them" may be dealt with in healthy ways within our middle schools. The "concrete social medium" referred to by Dobrin is the 24-hour-a-day, 7-day-a-week life of students. Time spent in school accounts for a major chunk of this time. So the school is an influential part of the social medium that shapes the character of students.

● Young Adolescent Character Traits

There are many generalizations that can be made about typical character traits of young adolescents. Here are some to consider. Young adolescents often

myeducationlab)

To hear Ruth Meisen, the 2008 Illinois Teacher of the Year, discuss her belief that teachers possess tremendous power to influence all areas of student development, go to the Teacher Talk section of **Topic #1: Schools and Teaching Today** in the MyEducationLab for your course.

● are concerned about fairness.

Telling a teacher "you're not fair" is a terrible rebuke. Middle grades students have definite ideas about what adults should be and should do in regard to treating students fairly. When adults disappoint them, students are not quick to forgive and forget.

- ask unanswerable questions.

  Middle grades students want to know answers to major questions, such as the meaning of life and what their roles should be in society. They usually realize that adults don't have all these answers, but they at least want adults to treat their questions seriously.

- need support, but seldom ask for it.

  To make wise decisions about moral issues, young adolescents need us to be positive role models to help them with issues of right and wrong.

- make poor decisions as a result of their strong need for peer acceptance.

  During the middle grades years, students often value social approval over moral convictions. This may lead to decisions that have harmful, often life-changing consequences.

School Programs

Understanding that young adolescents are continually struggling with character development, we naturally ask ourselves how we can help them. Over the years, schools have institutionalized many character-development programs delivered to students in a variety of ways. Classes and/or occasional meetings devoted to character development are often plagued with controversy over exactly what values and aspects of character should be promoted in public schools. Even with the controversy, there is a renewed call for schools to address character issues, perhaps due to the increase in violent incidents in our schools at the end of the 20th century.

Groups of citizens and educators often debate which character issues to emphasize. From Aristotle's universal values of wisdom, courage, temperance, and justice, to C. S. Lewis's list that includes respect, responsibility, honesty, compassion, and fairness, we struggle to impart a sense of right and wrong that will not conflict with religious values or be politically incorrect. Communities attempt to come up with what they consider universally (or at least locally) acceptable values.

In their article "Intrinsic Goodness: Facilitating Character Development," Richardson and Norman (2000) identified 10 attributes that are necessary for character growth. Five are intrapersonal and five are interpersonal. These attributes, contained in Figure 2.1, may be used as the basis of a character education program.

Most character-building curricula will specify qualities of good character. According to Gathercoal and Crowell (2000), the most commonly used terminology for the desired characteristics of many programs include

- Trustworthiness
- Respect for others
- Responsibility
- Fairness
- Caring
- Citizenship (p. 175)

> ### FIGURE 2.1   Necessary attributes for character growth
>
> **Intrapersonal Attributes**
> 1. Self-Discovery
> 2. Self-Management
> 3. Delayed gratification
> 4. Courage
> 5. Honesty
>
> **Interpersonal Attributes**
> 1. Empathy
> 2. Altruism
> 3. Problem solving
> 4. Tolerance
> 5. Social deftness

Source: From "Intrinsic Goodness: Facilitating Character Development," by R. C. Richardson and K. I. Norman, 2000, *Kappa Delta Pi Record, 36*(4), pp. 168–172.

As teachers we have the capacity to *be* the character-building program. Actually, we have no choice. Whether they acknowledge it or not, students watch us and count on us to model exemplary character. So, even if your district or school doesn't have an organized character-development program, your students are observing, and to some degree internalizing, the morals and values you exemplify.

● Character Development Issues

The issues involved in character development tend to be more dependent on the context of home and community than those in other developmental areas.

▶ ISSUE #1
Some students grow up in homes that emphasize a very strict moral code, while others live in homes where there are few moral guidelines or restrictions.

Young Adolescent Diversity

We need to understand that home life heavily influences the behaviors and attitudes of the kids in our classes. Through conscientiously being positive role models, understanding home influences, and finding ways to gently prod students toward what our communities consider good character, we will be teachers who make a difference. We cannot lose sight of the variability of influences outside the school. Individualizing our approach to character development is essential.

▶ ISSUE #2
Students are continually faced with contradictions concerning character.

We can't erase or deny contradictions. Creating a forum that allows students to candidly discuss their disappointments in adults, in their personal lives, or in the media will help them understand that they are not alone in their feelings. Through discussion comes opportunity for growth. We need to remember, however, that when kids come to us to talk about character, emotional, or social issues, sometimes they simply want to talk and need someone who will listen rather than give advice.

▶ **ISSUE #3**

Middle grades students are especially vulnerable to falling into the "wrong crowd."

Before values are established, being accepted by a group may take precedence. As we've discussed, socialization is a major force during the middle grades years. When socialization leads to the acceptance of values, morals, or ethics that result in undesirable behavior, we have a problem. As middle grades educators, we have the responsibility to expose kids to all kinds of relationships and groups. We can, in fact, act as engineers in our own classrooms as we build experiences that give our students social and value choices in a context that allows them to question and change their minds.

STANDARD 1

Knowledge 6: Middle level teacher candidates understand the interrelationships among the characteristics and needs of all young adolescents.

Knowledge 7: Middle level teacher candidates understand that the development of all young adolescents occurs in the context of classrooms, families, peer groups, communities, and society.

Disposition 1: Middle level teacher candidates are positive and enthusiastic about all young adolescents.

Disposition 2: Middle level teacher candidates respect and appreciate the range of individual developmental differences of all young adolescents.

Performance 1: Middle level teacher candidates establish close, mutually respectful relationships with all young adolescents that support their intellectual, ethical, and social growth.

Reflections on the Development of Middle Level Learners

There are as many possible combinations of developmental traits as there are middle grades students. All of our students are evolving and becoming—they are not finished products. Our challenge as teachers is to accept them as they are and do what we can to help them grow in healthy ways physically, intellectually, emotionally, and socially, and with positive and productive character traits. Williamson and Johnston (1998) tell us that, while not a homogeneous group, middle level students are "bound together by common threads." The common threads in the physical, intellectual, emotional, social, and character development of young adolescents weave patterns that form the students we nurture in our classrooms.

Now that we have briefly considered the development of young adolescents, you may be thinking, "What does all this have to do with teaching them how to factor binomials?" The answer is *everything*. Or perhaps you are thinking that your future students will be enamored with the American Revolution and will leave their prepubescent/pubescent selves behind when you grab their imaginations with your detailed lecture. *Think again*. The jolt of *becoming* is often so staggering, that learning is not a given, while mind-wandering is. Case in point . . . I read this years ago in a journal, the name of which I can't recall. The timing may not be scientifically derived, but the point is valid. An 8th grade boy likely thinks of sex every 20 seconds. Binomials and the American Revolution have some significant competition. Better have a plan for really engaging instruction!

As middle level teachers we contend with much more than content. Somehow we find ways to capture attention and keep it long enough to engage young adolescents in their own learning. The more we understand the developmental impact life itself has on our kids, the better we are at helping make early adolescence a period of growth in which they thrive.

GROUP ACTIVITIES

1. In small groups, make bulleted lists of possible characteristics or descriptors of middle level students for each of the five developmental areas discussed in this chapter. Feel free to add to what this text covers. It would take volumes to be comprehensive! Share your lists with other groups.

2. How do movies and television shows portray middle level students? As a class, brainstorm about all the 10- to 15-year-olds we see on TV and in movies. What characteristics from your lists do these fictitious kids exemplify?

INDIVIDUAL ACTIVITIES

1. Interview at least three of your friends and ask them to describe themselves as middle schoolers in the five developmental areas. Write brief sketches of them using your interview notes. Would you have predicted them to be as they are today given their self-described young adolescent personas?

2. Go to a place where you are likely to see groups of young adolescents. Try the mall, a fast food restaurant, a sporting event, or another after-school hangout. Describe what you observe during a 10- or 15-minute period. Include their physical size/shape, clothing, accessories,

hairstyles, socialization patterns, and so on. This exercise may bring back memories! Be prepared to share your observations with your class.

3. If you teach in a school that does not have a designated health/sex education teacher and/or class, are there ways you as an individual teacher might have a positive impact in this important dimension of young adolescent development? Write some notes on your own thoughts. Share them with fellow teacher candidates and your instructor to compile a list of possibilities that are both appropriate and within reasonable guidelines.

PERSONAL JOURNAL

1. Write an honest appraisal of yourself during early adolescence. Try to think about the span of sixth, seventh, and eighth grade rather than one particular time frame. Consider all five areas of development at each grade level.

2. Call at least two family members, if possible, to ask them to recall what you were like as a young adolescent. Assure them that you can remain objective about their comments because you are now a mature teacher candidate. Try the "if you'll be honest with me, I'll be honest with you" ploy. Of course, that tactic could backfire, as many of us would rather leave those years in the past! Compare your family members' observations to your own self-assessment.

Professional Practice

Jermaine Joyner

Jermaine Joyner has so much energy and is filled with ideas he wants to implement at Jefferson Middle School, a technology and communication magnet school in an urban area. Magnet status was given to Jefferson in 1998 in an effort to draw students from the suburbs to downtown to achieve both racial and socioeconomic desegregation. Magnet schools encourage students from across an entire school district to attend them based on a theme or special emphasis. The plan had worked. About half the Jefferson kids were from the immediate neighborhood and half from various areas in the district.

Mr. Joyner is the school's computer guru. He teaches all three grade levels and has been able to build a program that allows students to start at a basic computer literacy level and steadily progress to more advanced computer applications. One of his pet initiatives is the development of a television studio where 5-minute daily programs are taped and broadcast to the whole student body. The Broadcast Club meets before and after school.

DeVante • 6th grade

DeVante is one of the new 6th graders at Jefferson. The school is not in his immediate neighborhood, but he gave in to Granny's urging, reluctantly applied, and won a spot at the school through lottery selection. DeVante has a troubled past. He has failed twice and prefers to hang around with older kids, many of whom have gang ties. He's unhappy about having to leave his own neighborhood for school.

1. Which barrier is most significant for Mr. Joyner to overcome in his sponsorship of the Broadcast Club?
   a. getting kids interested in spending extra time the club requires
   b. finding ways to encourage kids from across a wide spectrum of lifestyles to work together
   c. convincing other teachers that the 5 minutes required for the broadcast is worth the time
   d. maintaining equipment and the expense required to do so

2. Which circumstance will likely have the most positive impact on DeVante?
   a. being in classes with a variety of students
   b. learning computer skills in Mr. Joyner's class
   c. being older and physically larger than other kids, which will help keep him from being a target
   d. joining the Broadcast Club at the insistence of Mr. Joyner

3. During his first few months at Jefferson, DeVante is hesitant to even crack a smile. He is attending the school begrudgingly. It wasn't his idea. About the first week in December Mr. Joyner sees a spark of interest as DeVante actually starts a conversation with him. What is the most likely reason DeVante shows signs of interest in the Broadcast Club?
   a. Having Mr. Joyner as a role model of a successful African American man is having an impact.
   b. He sees broadcasting as a possible career interest.
   c. He has made close friends with kids in the school.
   d. He has reconciled himself to the fact that Jefferson is his school and he might as well make the most of it.

Constructed Response

Explain the meaning of the San Antonio quote in Chapter 2 that says, "I believe that we cannot accomplish our academic goals without a purposeful and thoughtful focus on social development." How does this statement relate to middle level philosophy? Why is it a significant statement to consider when thinking about the challenges posed by DeVante's move to Jefferson Middle School?

INTERNET RESOURCES

Six Seconds
www.6seconds.org/

Six Seconds, a nonprofit service organization, provides information about emotional intelligence for schools, families, and communities.

Studies in Moral Development and Education
tigger.uic.edu/~lnucci/MoralEd

This site brings together educators and others who are interested in research and practices in the area of moral/character development.

Character Education Partnership
www.character.org

Character Education Partnership is an umbrella organization for character education, serving as a resource for people and organizations that are integrating character education into their schools and communities.

Diversity among Middle Level Students

3

Young adolescents display diversity in some obvious physical ways through attributes such as gender, skin color, height, and weight. Less obvious is their diversity in academic ability/achievement, learning style, and motivation. Diversity in family make-up, socioeconomic status, and the presence of disabilities challenges teachers as they work to provide opportunities for optimal growth during the middle school years.

*d*iversity is the hallmark of middle level learners. . . . The middle school population includes both sexes, members of many cultures, students representing a panoply of interests, students with a full range of learning profiles, as well as students who struggle greatly with academics, and those for whom academics mirror advanced scholastic talent.

Tomlinson, Moon, & Callahan, 1998, p. 3

CHAPTER PREVIEW

Gender Differences
- Boys
- Girls
- Our Approach
- Gay and Lesbian Students

Multiple Intelligences Theory
- More Than One Intelligence
- How Intelligences Look
- Applying MI Theory

Learning Styles
- Imaginative, Analytic, Common Sense, Dynamic Learners
- Learning Modalities

Cultural Differences
- Culture, Ethnicity, Race, Linguistics
- Desegregation
- Understanding Differences
- English Language Learners
- Multicultural Education

Socioeconomic Differences
- Socioeconomic Integration
- High Expectations

Family Differences
- Defining Family
- Involving the Family

Academic Differences
- Ability and Effort
- Self-Worth Theory and Underachievement

Students with Exceptionalities
- Students with Exceptional Abilities
- Students with Disabilities

Reflections on Celebrating Diversity

INTRODUCTION

Diversity exists in a myriad of forms. We explore the differences inherent in middle school students not to place labels on them, but to understand them. This chapter explores student differences in terms of gender, multiple intelligences, learning styles, family structures, academics, culture, socioeconomics, and special needs. These are by no means all the ways in which students differ, but, when viewed along with the five developmental areas discussed in Chapter 2, they provide an overview of some of the diversity you will likely encounter in your classroom. As you read, reflect on the characteristics of diverse populations as generalities rather than stereotypical images. "Generalizations are statements supported by data, whereas stereotypes are general statements based on incomplete or missing data. . . . Stereotypes are often based on misperceptions and usually involve a negative judgment" (Rasool & Curtis, 2000, p. 61).

STANDARD 1

Knowledge 2: Middle level teacher candidates understand the range of individual differences of all young adolescents and the implications of these differences for teaching and learning.

STANDARD 6

Disposition 5: Middle level teacher candidates value and appreciate all young adolescents regardless of family circumstances, community environment, health, and/or economic conditions.

Disposition 6: Middle level teacher candidates value the enrichment of learning that comes from the diverse backgrounds, values, skills, talents, and interests of all young adolescents and their families.

Gender Differences

Young Adolescent Diversity

Girls and boys are different. Ask parents who have both. Chances are they'll tell you that differences are apparent from birth.

According to King and Gurian (2006), researchers have actually identified over 100 structural differences between the male brain and the female brain. Some differences are genetic, while others appear to result from socialization. A partial list of these differences is in Table 3.1. So what can we do to better meet the needs of both girls and boys in our classrooms given the differences teachers have always perceived and science is now validating? Let's take a brief look at girls and boys separately and discuss some alternative approaches.

TABLE 3.1   Differences in brain functions of males and females

Category	Male	Female
Verbal/spatial	More mechanical aptitude; more spatial awareness	Use more words than males; think more verbally
Visual system	Rely on pictures and visual movement when writing	Excel at using words to represent color and other fine sensory information
Frontal lobe development	More impulsive; reading/writing production areas develop more slowly	Better able to sit still and read; read and write earlier and with more pleasure
Neural rest states	Rest states experienced often; drifting off likely; efforts to stay focused may become disruptive	Even when bored, brain stays active; retains ability to read, write, and listen for longer periods of time
Cross talk between hemispheres	Brain tends to compartmentalize; have a single-task focus; do better when following well-ordered steps	Multitasking is more natural; pay attention to more information at one time
Natural aggression	More naturally aggressive and competitive; more impulsivity	Less competitive; more relationship oriented; more compliant with others, including teachers

Source: From "Teaching to the Minds of Boys" by K. King and M. Gurian, 2006, *Educational Leadership, 64*(1), pp. 56–61.

● Boys

After years of believing that girls lagged behind academically, the tables are turning and girls are now outperforming boys in many areas. This has prompted the notion that boys may be in some sort of crisis. Researchers tell us that it's likely not a boy crisis, but overall they are not showing academic gains as rapidly as girls (Perkins-Gough, 2006). However, this change from boys always outscoring girls has prompted study of how boys and girls learn differently. And any new information is helpful to teachers, even if what prompts it turns out to be false.

A recent research study reveals that "Teachers tended to view the natural assets that boys bring to learning—impulsivity, single-track focus, spatial-kinesthetic learning, and physical aggression—as problems" (King & Gurian, 2006). Given that most schools are predominantly sit-and-listen environments, it's surprising that boys have held their own in the classroom.

Through the following suggestions for practice, you'll recognize some of the boy–girl differences, not as stereotypical, but as generalizations. Most of the suggestions are from the work of King and Gurian (2006).

- Hands-on learning appeals to the more kinesthetic-oriented boys. Anything that gets them moving, rather than sitting still with paper and pencil, will be beneficial.

- Let students choose topics that interest them for reading and writing assignments. Boys are more likely to complete assignments that interest them.

- Try to make learning relevant and purposeful. While girls appear to be more willing to complete assignments for the sake of completion, boys tend to need to see the purposefulness of the work they are asked to do.

- Male role models add much meaning to learning experiences. Providing people in their lives that they may want to be like, encourages boys to try harder and achieve.

Girls

Issues that lead to girls having difficulty with learning are generally more subtle than those of boys and are often not as blatantly obvious to teachers. Through research and experience, a group of teachers, counselors, and psychologists have pinpointed some stressors for young adolescent girls including

- Body image concerns and disordered eating
- Academic gender role stereotyping (for instance, boys are better at math)
- Sexual harassment
- Relational aggression

These same researchers tell us that teachers may be more effective in promoting girls' healthy development when they

- Understand gender-related challenges.
- Are open to listening to student opinions.
- Examine their own practices and beliefs regarding gender differences.
- Insist that girls and boys be treated fairly in their classrooms.
- Are available to serve as mentors who help process experiences that are important to students (Mendez, Young, Mihalas, Cusumano, & Hoffmann, 2006).

Our Approach

If we accept that gender differences exist, both physiologically and psychologically, we come to the conclusion that it's okay, a part of the human condition. Most of us are very happy that there are differences! Much of our social lives revolve around these differences. For middle grades students, acquiring social acceptance is rooted in gender.

Increasingly, middle level schools are experimenting with single-gender settings. Some schools are dividing boys and girls for particular classes. For instance, science may be taught as a single-gender subject while all the other classes are coeducational. In other schools, the whole core (language arts, math, science, social studies) may be taught in single-gender classes, while the non-core classes are coeducational. Still other schools are totally single-gender.

STANDARD 1

Knowledge 8: Middle level teacher candidates are knowledgeable about how the media portrays young adolescents and comprehend the implications of these portraits.

Kommer (2006) takes a commonsense approach and advises us to make our classrooms more gender-friendly by understanding that there are differences between girls and boys, and then using a broad array of instructional strategies. He tells us that "Gender-friendly classrooms are really models of effective instruction. . . . Being purposeful in the selection of methods and materials will send messages to boys and girls that they are indeed different from one another, but equally intelligent, equally important, and equally cared for in our schools" (p. 48).

Acknowledging gender differences is not the same as perpetuating stereotypes that may result in unfair treatment. Print and electronic media often portray gender differences in exaggerated ways. In selling products and/or services, the media will shamelessly capitalize on gender differences. A proactive way to approach gender differences while giving students a sense of perspective on the subject is to acquaint young adolescents with the impact magazines, television, movies, and advertisements have on our society. Frank discussions of how we are influenced in terms of gender stereotyping provide a valuable service to developing young adolescents.

When it comes to unequal treatment of girls and boys in educational settings, we need to find ways to avoid what many of us do naturally as a result of social conditioning. We are often unaware of how we interact with students. Unintentionally treating boys and girls differently often leads to allowing boys to interrupt girls, and then at times going so far as to praise girls for their patience. Avoiding such discrimination may be difficult even when we are aware of it. I don't think educators would intentionally create unequal opportunities for learning between girls and boys. But, many, myself included, have unintentionally treated them differently when it comes to expectations and classroom question/answer sessions. I became aware that I called on boys more frequently than girls when a practicum student kept a tally without my knowledge. She presented the results to me, and I have worked toward balance for two decades. Colleagues can help each other detect how we approach gender, or we can keep track of our own questioning using a seating chart on a clipboard. When we direct discussions, we can keep track of boy/girl talk time and try to achieve gender balance.

How well teachers cope with and compensate for gender differences, unequal opportunities, and stereotyping can have very real and lasting consequences by creating artificially different expectations in activities, social settings, or academic performance. Common sense tells us that equalizing expectations and opportunities will have an influence on perpetuating interest and, consequently, achievement in all subject areas by both girls and boys. We need to do all we can to encourage all students to participate fully in the education process.

Gay and Lesbian Students

Young Adolescent Diversity

A discussion of gender differences could not be complete without acknowledging gay and lesbian students, often referred to as the "invisible minority." These students often find that the two places where they spend the most time and encounter adults most frequently—home and school—are often the places where they are most misunderstood. Just as we have a responsibility to meet the needs of students who differ in other respects, we also have a professional mandate to address the needs of the sexual minorities. While many gay and lesbian students will deny their sexual preference in middle school, they will often acknowledge it in high school. It is important that gay and lesbian students and their parents experience a school environment that is supportive. Taylor (2000) tells us that a supportive environment is particularly important for these students because of the increased safety and health risks they often encounter. He reports that young adolescent gay and lesbian middle grades students are more likely to be verbally and physically attacked, to be threatened, to skip school, to drop out of school, and to attempt suicide. As educators committed to meeting the needs of all students in developmentally responsive ways, we should not ignore or sidestep the needs of gay and lesbian youth. In Chapter 5 we explore gay and lesbian issues and how we can support these students who are so often taunted by peers and underserved by adults.

Two excellent books on the subject of gender in adolescence are *Reviving Ophelia* by Mary Pipher (1994) and *Raising Cain* by Daniel Kindlon and Michael Thompson (1999). These authors delve deeply into the natural and societal forces that contribute to gender characteristics. The insightful material in both of these books provides food for thought and discussion with colleagues, and will help refocus your perspective regarding adolescent gender issues.

Multiple Intelligences Theory

Definitions of intelligence abound. Consideration of the cognitive process continues to intrigue us. Many educators have changed their view of the concept of intelligence, as illustrated in Figure 3.1.

More Than One Intelligence

Is it possible to move beyond the "old view" of intelligence to the "new view" in ways that are operational in a school setting? Howard Gardner's Theory of Multiple Intelligences, first presented in 1983 in *Frames of Mind*, does exactly that. Gardner added an "s" to intelligence. In other words, he espoused that intelligence is not unitary, but rather may be exhibited in many ways. In Multiple Intelligences (MI) theory he proposed a revolutionary revision of our thinking about intelligence by recognizing that through a unique relationship between nature and nurture, each person has a mix of intelligence strengths he labels "frames" (Willis & Johnson, 2001). Each of these "frames" is an intelligence.

FIGURE 3.1 How our definition of intelligence has changed

Old View

- Intelligence was fixed.
- Intelligence was measured by a number.
- Intelligence was unitary.
- Intelligence was measured in isolation.
- Intelligence was used to sort students and predict their success.

New View

- Intelligence can be developed.
- Intelligence is not numerically quantifiable and is exhibited during a performance or problem-solving process.
- Intelligence can be exhibited in many ways—multiple intelligences.
- Intelligence is measured in context/real life situations.
- Intelligence is used to understand human capacities and the many and varied ways students can achieve.

Source: So Each May Learn: Integrating Learning Styles and Multiple Intelligences by Silver, Strong, and Perini. Copyright 2000 by Silver Strong & Associates LLC/Thoughtful Ed Press. Reproduced with permission of Silver Strong & Associates LLC/Thoughtful Ed Press in the format Textbook via Copyright Clearance Center.

Gardner conceptualizes intelligence as "a biopsychological potential to process information that can be activated in a cultural setting to solve problems or create products that are of value in a culture" (Gardner, 1999, p. 33). In other words, he sees intelligences as potentials that can be mobilized and connected according to personal inclinations and cultural preferences. Since 1983 Gardner has added two intelligences for a total of nine.

- Verbal-Linguistic
- Logical-Mathematical
- Visual-Spatial
- Bodily-Kinesthetic
- Musical
- Interpersonal
- Intrapersonal
- Naturalist
- Existentialist

How Intelligences Look

We want to briefly discuss how these intelligences "look" in the classroom. A widely accepted method involves considering dispositional theory based on the work of Perkins, Jay, and Tishman (1993), who tell us that good thinkers have dispositions that influence their ability to process and make sense of information. In *So Each May Learn*, multiple intelligences are linked to dispositional theory like this:

> Dispositional theory provides a productive means of looking at multiple intelligences. A sensitivity may lead to an inclination for using that intelligence and, in the right environment and under the right circumstances, an inclination can be translated into an ability to use the intelligence in a variety of contexts. (Silver, Strong, & Perini, 2000, p.10)

Table 3.2 gives us ways of thinking about the intelligences in terms of dispositional theory. Note that existentialist was added after 2000.

It is widely accepted that all children demonstrate abilities in at least one area, while none have exceptional abilities in all. Individual differences arise when unique combinations of intelligences, and degrees of those intelligences, are manifested. Knowledge of the nine intelligences helps teachers recognize and appreciate student differences. To make the most of teaching/learning opportunities, teachers should help students discover and nurture their primary intelligences and foster the development of intelligences that may not be as "natural" to them.

Applying MI Theory

Young Adolescent Diversity

Program after program has evolved based on MI theory. Howard Gardner himself cautions us in terms of application and tells us "MI theory is in no way an educational prescription" (Gardner, 1999, p. 89). He views MI theory as an "endorsement of three key propositions: we are not all the same; we do not all have the same kinds of minds; and education works most effectively if these differences are taken into account rather than denied or ignored" (p. 91). In Chapter 8 we will explore instructional strategies that align with Gardner's view of differences. We must keep in mind, however, that superficial application of MI theory may not only be ineffective, it may actually harm students if labeling is all that occurs and measures to increase each student's capacity to perceive and understand are not implemented.

Learning Styles

myeducationlab

To hear Linda Reid, the 2007 Oklahoma Teacher of the Year, talk about the impact even little gestures have on student relationships and motivation, go to the Teacher Talk section of **Topic #4: Motivation** in the MyEducationLab for your course.

Individuals have unique styles of learning. We adapt these styles, usually unconsciously, to varying circumstances according to the learning demand. Many psychologists and educators have observed, and attempted to label, the ways we learn.

Multiple intelligences and *learning styles* are linked in practical ways. Intelligences are "biological and psychological potentials and capacities" (Gardner, 1999, p. 82). Decisions about how to use these capacities may depend on style

TABLE 3.2 Intelligences as dispositions

Disposition/Intelligence	Sensitivity to	Inclination for	Ability to
Verbal-Linguistic Intelligence	Sounds, meanings, structures, and styles of language	Speaking, writing, listening, reading	Speak effectively (teacher, religious leader, politician) or write effectively (poet, journalist, novelist, copywriter, editor)
Logical-Mathematical Intelligence	Patterns, numbers, and numerical data; causes and effects; objective and quantitative reasoning	Finding patterns, making calculations, formulating hypotheses, using the scientific method, deductive and inductive reasoning	Work effectively with numbers (accountant, statistician, economist) and reason effectively (engineer, scientist, computer programmer)
Spatial Intelligence	Colors, shapes, visual puzzles, symmetry, lines, images	Representing ideas visually, creating mental images, noticing visual details, drawing and sketching	Create visually (artist, photographer, engineer, decorator) and visualize accurately (tour guide, scout, ranger)
Bodily-Kinesthetic Intelligence	Touch, movement, physical self, athleticism	Activities requiring strength, speed, flexibility, hand-eye coordination, and balance	Use the hands to fix or create (mechanic, surgeon, carpenter, sculptor, mason) and use the body expressively (dancer, athlete, actor)
Musical Intelligence	Tone, beat, tempo, melody, pitch, sound	Listening, singing, playing an instrument	Create music (songwriter, composer, musician, conductor) and analyze music (music critic)
Interpersonal Intelligence	Body language, moods, voice, feelings	Noticing and responding to other people's feelings and personalities	Work with people (administrators, managers, consultants, teachers) and help people identify and overcome problems (therapists, psychologists)
Intrapersonal Intelligence	One's own strengths, weaknesses, goals, desires	Setting goals, assessing personal abilities and liabilities, monitoring one's own thinking	Meditate, reflect, exhibit self-discipline, maintain composure, and get the most out of oneself

TABLE 3.2   Intelligences as dispositions (Continued)

Disposition/Intelligence	Sensitivity to	Inclination for	Ability to
Naturalist Intelligence	Natural objects, plants, animals, naturally occurring issues	Identifying and classifying living things and natural objects	Analyze ecological and natural situations (ecologists, rangers), learn from living things (zoologist, botanist, veterinarian), and work in natural settings (hunter, scout)

Source: So Each May Learn: Integrating Learning Styles and Multiple Intelligences by Silver, Strong, and Perini. Copyright 2000 by Silver Strong & Associates LLC/Thoughtful Ed Press. Reproduced with permission of Silver Strong & Associates LLC/Thoughtful Ed Press in the format Textbook via Copyright Clearance Center.

preference. Style determines our approach to intelligences. To clarify this concept, consider a person with strong musical intelligence. This intelligence may manifest itself in the careers of conductors, performers, composers, and music critics, or it may be manifested in a talent that is enjoyed as an avocation. Learner preferences and styles contribute to how intelligences are used and developed.

To use our understanding of learning differences to the benefit of students, we need to analyze our own inclinations as well as those of our students. Then we must help our students see how they can learn best so they can both use their dominant characteristics and enhance their less dominant characteristics. All this involves understanding of self. Carl Jung's (1923) work has contributed greatly to our ability to do just that. He divides all human behavior into two categories—perception and judgment. To perceive is to find out or discover. To judge (or process) is to decide, evaluate, and take action. Each of us spends time perceiving and judging, individually tending toward one over the other.

● Imaginative, Analytic, Common Sense, Dynamic Learners

Bernice McCarthy (1997) describes four major learning styles: imaginative, analytic, common sense, and dynamic. She explains these styles, using Jung's conception of perceiving and judging. *Imaginative learners* perceive information in concrete ways and then process it reflectively. Imaginative learners prefer interaction and integration and sharing rather than the "sit and git" traditional classroom style. *Analytic learners* perceive information abstractly and then process it reflectively. They value established knowledge and detail. Because they prefer sequential, step-by-step learning, the traditional classroom approach works well for them. *Common sense learners* perceive information abstractly and then process it actively. They desire real-life applications of learning and thrive with hands-on instruction. Traditional classroom instruction will frustrate them unless they can see immediate uses for the skills/knowledge presented. *Dynamic learners* perceive information concretely and process it actively. They do not care about order and sequential learning, but prefer to take risks and tackle new challenges. They are often frustrated by traditional classroom methods.

McCarthy's learning styles = Imaginative + Analytic + Common sense + Dynamic

Given this theory of learning styles, it appears that traditional classrooms, generally recognized for material presentation, guided practice, and assessments, and characterized by lecture, notetaking, occasional demonstration, and testing, are places where analytic learners thrive most. In our chapter on instructional methods, we explore ways to better motivate all learners, regardless of their learning styles.

Learning Modalities

Learning styles and learning modalities are often spoken of interchangeably. Modalities refer to how students use their senses in the learning process. We commonly consider four modalities: *visual* (seeing), *auditory* (hearing), *kinesthetic* (moving), and *tactile* (touching). As you might guess, the more senses or modalities we activate, the more learning will take place.

Four basic learning modalities = Visual + Auditory + Kinesthetic + Tactile

The great majority of students can learn using all four modalities, but we all have preferences that can be enhanced and weaker leanings that can be strengthened. In our classrooms, we must provide an environment that is conducive to all four modalities. Traditional classrooms rely heavily on auditory stimulation with lecture and discussions. Now that we have considered the developmental characteristics of young adolescence, we realize that visual, kinesthetic, and tactile modalities also play strong roles in adolescent lives. Figure 3.2 will help us understand characteristics we may observe in students who learn best through hearing, seeing, moving, and touching.

It is important to discover as much as we can about how we, as teachers, learn. Because it is natural to teach in the same ways we learn, knowing our own styles, modalities, and preferences will help us recognize when we are doing that rather than teaching in a variety of ways to meet the needs of more of our students. We should first know ourselves as learners, and then discover the ways in which our students learn in order to help them understand their own ways of learning. It is our responsibility to use a variety of instructional strategies to address as many learning styles and modalities as possible.

Cultural Differences

In Washington, D.C., 96% of the students in public schools belong to a minority race. In Maine and Vermont, the percentage is 4. Other states fall somewhere in between these two extremes. Of the approximately 50,000,000 students in K–12 public schools in the U.S., about 20,000,000, or 40%, are considered minorities (National Center for Education Statistics, 2006).

FIGURE 3.2 Traits of auditory, visual, kinesthetic, and tactile learners

Auditory Learners Tend to . . .

enjoy reading and being read to.
be able to verbally explain concepts and scenarios.
like music and hum to themselves.
enjoy both talking and listening.

Visual Learners Tend to . . .

have good spelling, notetaking, and organizational skills.
notice details and prefer neatness.
learn more if illustrations and charts accompany reading.
prefer quiet, serene surroundings.

Kinesthetic Learners Tend to . . .

be demonstrative, animated, and outgoing.
enjoy physical movement and manipulatives.
be willing to try new things.
be messy in habits and surroundings.

Tactile Learners Tend to . . .

prefer manipulatives when being introduced to a topic.
literally translate events and phenomena.
tolerate clutter.
be artistic in nature.

Young Adolescent Diversity

We are told that by the year 2050, the percentage of Latinos in the United States population will almost triple; Asian students will more than triple; and African Americans will increase about 3%. The American teaching force is heading in the opposite direction, with about 9% non-White in 2001, and predictions that even fewer teachers in the future will reflect diversity (Jorgenson, 2001).

Culture, Ethnicity, Race, Linguistics

In most discussions concerning cultural similarities and differences, certain phraseology is used. As commonly used as the words *culture, ethnicity,* and *race* are, various scholars define them in different ways. We'll settle on what appear to be widely accepted definitions. *Culture* refers to specific shared values, beliefs, and attitudes (Rasool & Curtis, 2000). *Ethnicity* simply refers to an individual's country of origin (Gollnick & Chinn, 2006). *Race* categorizes individuals into groups (such as White, Black, Asian) based on certain outward physical characteristics (Rasool & Curtis, 2000).

Along with differences in culture, ethnicity, and race often come linguistic differences. In 2000, as many as 42% of public school students were language minority students. "There is a wide gap between what they understand in English and what they can say in English . . . , between how they conceptualize in English and how they conceptualize in their native languages" (Teemant, Bernhardt, Rodriquez-Munoz, & Aiello, 2000, p. 30).

So what once was thought of as the majority is rapidly becoming the minority in American schools. Numerous books and articles address the topic of differences in culture, ethnicity, race, and language. This same topic permeates most teacher education and staff development programs. I encourage you to take advantage of growth opportunities dealing with this vital topic. What is offered here is only an overview.

Desegregation

The 20th century was a time of extremes in how public education was delivered to a diverse population. Segregation of Whites and Blacks (then the single largest minority population) was the norm until the 1954 Supreme Court decision of *Brown v. Board of Education* after which the United States began efforts "to dismantle entrenched racial segregation in public schools" (Kahlenberg, 2000, p. 17). Where desegregation occurred, Black achievement rose sharply and White scores did not decline. Unfortunately, in the 1990s a series of court cases stated that previous desegregation rulings were temporary and school districts were freed from federally mandated desegregation remedies (Kahlenberg, 2000). Now in the second decade of the 21st century, there appears to be a resurgence of segregation. Whether in racially segregated schools, or in schools where segregation is subtly accomplished, racism is ugly and detrimental.

Understanding Differences

Young Adolescent Diversity

As educators, we should avoid racism in any form. In order to do this, we need to examine our own deeply held beliefs and prejudices. For many, this is a lifelong endeavor. The sooner we begin, the more effectively we will meet the diverse needs of our students. It is easy to misinterpret the behaviors of those from whom we differ. Because statistically most teachers in the United States are Caucasian and were raised in predominantly Caucasian communities, knowledge of other races is often limited. Figure 3.3 contains information from *Multicultural Education in Middle and Secondary Classrooms* (Rasool and Curtis, 2000, p. 61). The authors urge us to use caution as we consider generalizations in order to avoid racial/ethnic stereotyping. Recall the differences between generalizing and stereotyping discussed in this chapter's Introduction. The generalizations in Figure 3.3 represent compilations of learning characteristics that are often cited as typical. Please view them as such. It is important to note that while generalizations pertaining to learners can be made, many educators and researchers tell us that learning styles are not culturally, ethnically, or racially dependent. While these factors may affect student learning, no single learning style applies to a particular group of people.

FIGURE 3.3   Generalizations of learning characteristics

African American learners . . .

- are more global, focusing on the whole picture rather than on parts.
- often approximate space, numbers, and time rather than being tied to precise accuracy.
- prefer inferential reasoning.
- rely on nonverbal as well as verbal communication patterns.
- sometimes distrust mainstream people and institutions.
- prefer visual and aural cues.

Hispanic/Latino learners . . .

- are more group-oriented and inductive thinkers.
- are peer-oriented and more likely to perform well in small groups.
- have a more external locus of control.
- prefer more personal and informal relationships with authority figures.

Native American learners . . .

- prefer sharing and cooperative learning versus competitive learning environments.
- have a different concept of time from the mainstream perspective.
- frequently exhibit behaviors that seem to indicate a lack of interest in learning.
- are more reflective than impulsive.
- are more visually and imagery oriented than verbally oriented.
- more often have an internal locus of control and are self-directed.
- view teachers as facilitators of learning.

Asian American learners . . .

- prefer formal relationships with teachers and other authority figures.
- are autonomous and conforming.
- are obedient to authority.
- are usually conservative and reserved.
- are more introverted.

Source: From *Multicultural Education in Middle and Secondary Classrooms: Meeting the Challenge of Diversity and Change,* 1st edition, by Rasool/Curtis, © 2000. Reprinted with permission of Wadsworth, a division of Thomson Learning: *www.thomsonrights.com,* Fax 800-730-2215.

Teachers need to be particularly aware of the unique concerns presented when adolescents of mixed race or mixed ethnic backgrounds are present in the classroom or school. The number of biracial, multiracial/biethnic, or multiethnic children has increased dramatically, and these children populate our schools in statistically significant numbers. Since much of a child's self-identity and self-esteem are tied to a

In her bilingual history class, Ynez benefits from writing notes in both Spanish and English, as well as illustrating events and concepts.

sense of pride in cultural or racial background, children of mixed heritage can experience significant pressure to identify with only one of their ethnic or racial backgrounds (usually the one of color). At the same time, society often makes them feel alienated, belittled, and often insignificant as they experience insensitivity from both mainstream and minority groups. Identity issues may intensify during the middle school years as a facet of the young adolescent's search for self-awareness. Schools can and should be sensitive to these issues by including specific staff training in their agenda, reviewing curriculum for undue emphasis on any one cultural or racial group to the exclusion of others, and supporting an atmosphere of positive cross-cultural attitudes, perceptions, and behaviors (Wardle, 2000).

English Language Learners

Young Adolescent Diversity

A controversial issue in education revolves around children whose first language is not English. As our nation becomes more and more diverse, the number of languages spoken in the homes of students increases. *English language learners* are often placed in low-ability groups where they are labeled as poor readers. They may be segregated in bilingual programs or mainstreamed into English-speaking content classes with only limited assistance in sporadic *English as a Second Language (ESL)* pull-out programs. At the other end of the spectrum are the total immersion programs that place non-English speakers in all-day programs where they concentrate only on the development of English language skills before they are assimilated into regular classes. The selection of a plan by a community depends on political and demographic profiles in the local population, as well as on what the district or state embraces philosophically. As "regular" classroom teachers, we may find ourselves in a variety of situations with regard to English language learners. Take advantage of whatever assistance is offered.

Multicultural Education

"A safe, secure learning environment is a place where teachers are aware of their students' race, ethnicity, gender, religion, socioeconomic status, first language, ability challenges, and other unique characteristics" (Dyck, 2006). This awareness, together with promotion of equal education opportunities and celebration of differences, amounts to multicultural education. To be culturally responsive teachers, we should respect diversity, create safe and encouraging learning environments, and motivate all learners to grow and excel. James Banks (2004) tells us that three of the goals of multicultural education are:

- creation of opportunities for students of all cultures to succeed
- development of the knowledge, skills, and dispositions to function successfully in a diverse world
- promotion of communication and interaction among diverse groups

In order to accomplish what Dr. Banks envisions, we must have high expectations for all students, make sure materials in classrooms reflect a wide array of contributions and perspectives, and use different teaching strategies as needed by the children we serve. In Chapter 8 we look closely at instructional strategies that help tailor our instruction for the young adolescents in our classrooms.

Too often what passes for multicultural education is a poster or two depicting Martin Luther King or César Chávez. Teachers may give lip service to Black History Month, Kwanzaa, or the Chinese New Year. That's not multicultural education. The sense that differences are not only accepted, but are also celebrated, is needed. Respect and appreciation for differences should permeate our classrooms and interactions.

In *Educating Everybody's Children* (1995), Carbo tells the story of Joe Sweeny, a middle school teacher in New York City. In his school, 58% of the students are Hispanic, 12% are Asian, and the other 30% represent 25 different countries. Sweeny organizes neighborhood workshops using volunteer interpreters. He assigns math problems that call for collection and analysis of data relevant to problems such as homelessness and graffiti, with some projects actually leading to social change for neighborhood residents. According to Sweeny, "School cannot be an isolated site that exists only from 9:00 to 3:00. The whole community must get involved with the school. If everyone works together, our schools will succeed" (p. 7). While Joe Sweeny has obviously found ways to communicate with the students and families he serves, we are all in danger of the miscommunication that can occur in culturally diverse settings. Multiculturalism requires teachers to understand the norms and preferences, along with the verbal and nonverbal patterns of alternative cultures (Chesebro, Berko, Hopson, Cooper, & Hodges, 1995). Louanne Johnson (1998), author of the book that served as the basis for the film *Dangerous Minds*, tells us that, "Cultural differences create many opportunities to put your foot in your mouth" (p. 157). She goes on to tell us that students will readily forgive us if they are assured that we genuinely care about and respect them.

In Chapter 5 we examine aspects of cultural diversity and positive ways we can impact the lives of all students.

Socioeconomic Differences

Young Adolescent Diversity

Ten percent of America's children live in poverty. A family of four—two adults and two children—are considered to be living in poverty if the family income is less than $20,000 per year (U.S. Census Bureau, 2006). A child may qualify for free or reduced-price meals and live in a low-income home that's above the poverty level.

The socioeconomic gap in the United States is often referred to as the *privilege gap*. Students in U.S. middle schools reflect the fact that there are haves and have-nots in our country. This is recognized by the U.S. government as well. Title I funding is the U.S. government's method of assisting schools with over 50% of its students qualifying for free or reduced-price meals. Our government is correct in the notion that it takes more money to educate a child who lives near or below the poverty line. As a matter of fact, there are statistics that tell us it takes about 40% more money to educate a child from a poor home than a child from a middle income home (Azzam, 2005).

● Socioeconomic Integration

Kahlenberg (2000) proposes that if using race to promote integration is problematic, then perhaps we should promote integration through students' economic status. Given the strong correlation between race and socioeconomic class in the United States, *socioeconomic integration* would likely produce racial diversity. Many educators believe that access to education among a core of children of middle class families may be the best predictor of school quality. Therefore, socioeconomic integration would give all students access to quality schools.

Students who qualify for free or reduced-price lunch provide a measure that our government uses to appropriate funds; hence, this statistic is kept by all schools, districts, and states. In some schools, as many as 98% of the students fall within free or reduced-price lunch guidelines. However, simply giving extra money in the form of Title I funds to high poverty schools doesn't always have the desired effect of enhancing the quality of education offered.

Given the statistics concerning students who are poor and the below-average performance of most high poverty schools, even with additional funding, Kahlenberg's suggestion of socioeconomic integration may hold the key to giving every student the opportunities offered in basically middle class settings. It would mean redistricting and busing, and would require major legislation and bold moves by policy makers.

● High Expectations

While a mandated attempt at a solution may be years away, individual teachers can make a difference in the lives of students who are poor. Given all we have explored in terms of young adolescent development, even middle school students with unlimited financial resources struggle with the passage from childhood to adolescence. Think about how much more difficult it may be for those young adolescents who live in low income settings. To add to their problems, many studies show that teachers expect less of students from lower socioeconomic strata than they do of middle class students. We must examine what part we play in the ongoing failure of poor students by communicating to them that they lack potential (Rasool & Curtis, 2000). Teachers must believe their students can achieve before they put forth their best effort to teach them. Likewise, students must believe that they can achieve before they are willing to try.

We discuss socioeconomic differences in more detail in Chapter 5.

Family Differences

Some of the family structures experienced by middle school students today are far different from what was considered "normal" during much of the last century. Regardless of the family/home structure, it strongly influences a child's development. Likewise, as young adolescents try to figure out who they are within the family unit, their struggle affects the way family members interact with each other.

STANDARD 6

Knowledge 1: Middle level teacher candidates understand the variety of family structures.

Knowledge 2: Middle level teacher candidates understand how prior learning, differing experiences, and family and cultural backgrounds influence young adolescent learning.

Disposition 1: Middle level teacher candidates respect all young adolescents and their families.

● Defining Family

Young Adolescent Diversity

With only about one-fourth of school-age children living in traditional, two-biological parent homes, we need to examine the structures in which our students live. The U.S. Census Report for 2000 reveals that the U.S. divorce rate exceeds 50% and is the highest in the world. The number of single-parent homes rose by 300% from 1980 to 2000, reaching an incredible 12 million homes. This translates into almost half of our students spending at least part of their childhood in homes with only one parent. Some studies reveal that as many as one-fourth of the babies born at the turn of the 21st century were born to unwed mothers. Add the staggering number of 45 million people (almost 20% of the U.S. population) who moved in 1999–2000, and it becomes obvious that there is a general lack of stability pervading families today. Young adolescents in middle schools may live with

- two biological parents
- one biological parent
- one biological parent and a stepparent

- one stepparent
- grandparents
- aunts and uncles
- adult siblings
- foster families
- other students in a group home

It is not uncommon for students to "time share" in two houses because their parents have joint custody following a divorce. These houses may have any number of others living there as well (stepparent, stepsiblings, halfsiblings, etc.). Our migrant family population is also significant. These families often move repeatedly according to the season and the available work, so that children are in several different schools during the year. A relatively new family structure for which there are no statistics as yet are same-sex partners who choose to be parents. And we must never forget the children, who by themselves or in a variety of family units, find themselves homeless.

● Involving the Family

All of these different family structures carry with them inherent strengths and weaknesses in terms of the amount of support offered to our students. When we hear teachers complain that more and more is expected of the school when it comes to "raising" children, it's easy to understand why the roles we play have been altered. We may be the central stability and only consistent factor in a student's life. Only by

Some students are fortunate enough to have family support and encouragement, while others rarely see sparks of interest in what they do in or out of school.

knowing the home situations and understanding the challenges of students whose lives we touch, will we know best how to help our students grow.

Getting to know the adults with whom our students live is more difficult in middle school when parental involvement often plummets. The parents of middle grades students are only half as likely to attend parent conferences as the parents of elementary students. Overall, parent involvement drops around the sixth grade (Downs, 2001). Developmental changes occurring during early adolescence not only affect the children themselves, but everyone else in the household, too. Parents/guardians are often caught off guard by the rapid and unexpected changes they see in their young adolescents. Adults in the home are confused and often look for faults on which to blame behavior changes, not recognizing that many of the changes have very little to do with them. As students strive for greater independence, the adults in their homes may interpret the struggle, rightly or wrongly, as a signal to disengage (Downs, 2001). When students enter middle school, they leave what many experience as the comfort zone of the self-contained elementary classroom. School becomes more complex with class changes, course options, and larger numbers of students with which to contend. Middle school parents or guardians often feel as if they are lost in the maze. Their attitudes may turn to merely hoping to survive the middle grades experiences of their children.

Parents and other adults in the home play significant roles in the academic achievement of middle school students. Teachers often tell us that lack of home support is a major obstacle to raising student achievement (L'Esperance & Gabbard, 2001). So far, the picture I've painted of family and home structures of our middle grades students has been generally negative. We need to acknowledge, however, that there may be many adults in the lives of our students who are very supportive. There are whole schools that experience overwhelming support from the majority of parents and guardians, resulting in an environment conducive to increased student achievement. This valuable partnership should be nurtured so that we are not guilty of Fege's (2000) lament of, "Twenty-first century families attempting to partner with twentieth-century school organizations" (p. 40). He encourages us to accommodate parents/adults in our students' education by offering unique settings such as weekend and weeknight volunteer opportunities, child care, and transportation. In Chapter 12 we explore ways to make the most of family and home structures that benefit our students.

Academic Differences

PEARSON
myeducationlab

To hear Deirdre McGrew, reading and remediation teacher at Cario Middle School, explain working with students with learning disabilities and those with records of low achievement, go to the Video Examples section of **Topic # 13: Inclusion and Special Needs** in the MyEducationLab for your course and view the video entitled "Deirdre McGrew's Interview."

As discussed in Chapter 2, middle grades students experience intellectual development at varying rates and to varying degrees. This variance, along with other developmental changes taking place within the context of a student's world, contributes to academic success, or the lack of it. We should not expect all students to learn the same things in the same ways at the same rate.

Young Adolescent Diversity

Ability and Effort

Academic success is dependent on both ability and effort. In any heterogeneous middle school classroom, we may find IQ scores ranging from about 70 to 140 and beyond. In terms of effort, the variability may be just as wide. As shown in Figure 3.4, the wide variances in, and interplay between, both IQ and level of effort can lead to failure by very capable students as well as success by only marginally capable ones. Most students exhibit moderate levels of both IQ and effort. It is our responsibility as educators to attend to both ability and effort.

Self-Worth Theory and Underachievement

We have explored the role that developing self-esteem plays in the lives of young adolescents. Strahan (1997) tells us that how students perceive ability and effort is a critical factor in a student's academic self-esteem. He says that if students experience academic success, they will assign more importance to academic self-esteem. On the other hand, if students do poorly in school, they face a difficult psychological dilemma. In an attempt to preserve some measure of self-esteem, these students will discount academics. They may adopt a "school doesn't matter" attitude. When children are young, they see ability and effort as one and the same. If they try hard, they are successful. By middle grades, students tend to see the "smart" kids appearing not to try as hard for good grades. Assuming that, if you have ability, effort isn't important, their logic leads them to believe that if you have to try hard, you must not be very "smart." In an attempt to avoid failure, students may appear not to try so they can get away from feeling unable. They may display lack of effort, procrastination, putting blame on others, and purposefully turning in wrong assignments. Strahan (1997) cautions us that if these behaviors are ". . . unchecked, these failure-avoiding tactics can become self-fulfilling prophecies and make it increasingly difficult for students to succeed" (p. 37).

Psychologist Sylvia Rimm (1997) tells us that when academically unsuccessful students complain that the work is boring, they may be masking feelings of inadequacy.

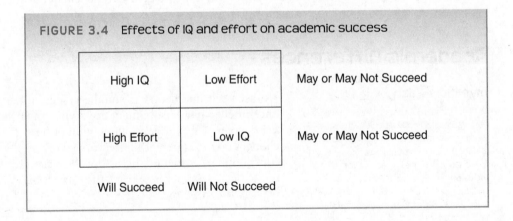

FIGURE 3.4   Effects of IQ and effort on academic success

High IQ	Low Effort	May or May Not Succeed
High Effort	Low IQ	May or May Not Succeed
Will Succeed	Will Not Succeed	

Here's how she defines *underachievement:* "Underachievement is a discrepancy between a child's school performance and some index of the child's ability. If children are not working to their ability in school, they are underachieving" (p. 18). Our role as educators should include recognizing when our students are not working up to their potential, and then taking appropriate action.

Academic differences exist, whether stemming from levels of ability or levels of effort. Williamson and Johnston (1998) give us an appropriate challenge when they write, "High achieving schools, where all students succeed, embrace the conversations about achievement, about rigor and challenge, about raising standards, and about serving students more appropriately. They understand the importance of achievement and unabashedly promote it as their school's primary goal" (p. 8). Our mission is to meet students where they are in terms of ability and effort and then find ways to design/choose curriculum, instructional strategies, and assessments to move them forward.

Students with Exceptionalities

Millions of students are receiving special services in American public schools. The delivery of these special services is the source of continual controversy regarding which students to serve, and how and where to serve them. This section is a broad overview rather than a comprehensive look at special services for students with exceptionalities.

Students with *exceptionalities* are those who have abilities and disabilities that set them apart from other students. Students with enhanced abilities are often referred to as gifted and talented. Students with disabilities fall into a wide gamut of descriptors. In both cases, identification and intervention are very important. We need to know who fits what category, and then how best to help develop each student's potential. Let's first consider students designated as gifted and talented.

Students with Exceptional Abilities

Young Adolescent Diversity

Students who are considered gifted and/or talented are identified in a variety of ways, from IQ scores of 125 or more, to teacher and/or parent recommendation, to observation of a particular gift that may be nonacademic such as music and art. Students designated as gifted and talented may excel in intellectual, creative, artistic, and/or leadership abilities.

Susan Rakow (2007) specializes in the study of gifted and talented middle level students. She emphasizes that gifted and talented young adolescents face the same challenges of others their age, but with some twists that may make their lives even more complicated. For many, going from elementary school where having an "A" paper posted by the teacher meant a good day, to middle school where achievement may be ridiculed by insecure peers, may be reason to shrink from the spotlight and stop achieving. Rakow says that being labeled "nerd" or "weirdo" is enough to cause some to underachieve. African American students who achieve at high levels are sometimes accused of "acting White."

Services for gifted and talented students vary significantly and include pull-out programs, one period a day with other gifted students, grade skipping, learning the curriculum at a faster pace (compacting), and tracking with other gifted and talented students for part or all of the school day. As classroom teachers we need to be flexible and accepting of novel ideas and approaches to problem solving. We must not be intimidated by students who may have higher IQ scores than our own and encourage them to use their gifts and talents in positive ways. In Chapter 8 we discuss differentiated instruction that helps us meet the learning needs of those with exceptional abilities, as well as those with disabilities.

Students with Disabilities

About 12% of public school students receive special education services (Goldstein, 2003). Disabilities that impair daily functioning like orthopedic impediments and vision impairment are generally diagnosed at a very young age.

The largest category of disabilities, learning disabled (LD), is often not diagnosed until late elementary school or middle school. Almost half of the students receiving services are LD. A student with a learning disability has a significant discrepancy between learning potential and achievement, and most often displays problems understanding and using language (Turnbull, Turnbull, & Wehmeyer, 2007). Because LD has so many forms, it is often misdiagnosed or not diagnosed at all. Many kids find ways of coping and compensating, while others do not.

Students with speech and language impairments comprise about 20% of those receiving services, with about 10% of those receiving services exhibiting mental retardation.

History of Services   The "official" history of special services delivery is very recent. Until 1975, a student with disabilities was accorded no federal rights to an education. Children with disabilities were often denied access to public education and placed in separate schools to be educated, often minimally, with other children with disabilities. The legislative act known as the 1975 Education for All Handicapped Children Act (PL 94–142) mandated, among other things, that all children with handicaps be given the right to a free and appropriate public education in the *Least Restrictive Environment (LRE)* guided by an *Individualized Education Plan (IEP)*. All handicapped children are entitled to a nondiscriminatory evaluation and parental participation in the development of the IEP (Rasool & Curtis, 2000).

In 1990, PL 94–142 was reauthorized as the *Individuals with Disabilities Education Act (IDEA)*. The disabilities listed in the 1990 law include autism, deafness, deaf-blindness, hearing impairment, mental retardation, multiple disabilities, orthopedic impairments, other health impairments, serious emotional disturbance, specific learning disabilities, speech or language impairments, traumatic brain injuries, and visual impairments. The 1990 legislation reiterated the principles of the 1975 law and added guidelines for transitioning of students. Grade-to-grade transitions for regular

Trista is a cheerleader. Trista has Down syndrome. Surprised? With support, young adolescents with disabilities can thrive.

education students are generally uneventful, requiring minimal support. However, for students with developmental disabilities, transitions may be quite traumatic.

In 1997, the law was reauthorized with an emphasis on accountability, requiring districts and states to include students with disabilities in their assessment plans and to provide appropriate alternative assessments when needed. Other highlights included the mandate for schools to support professional development for all staff to better involve them in the IEP process and to raise academic expectations and performances of students with disabilities. The law also called for more involvement of students with disabilities in extracurricular activities (Rasool & Curtis, 2000).

myeducationlab

As a young adolescent with Down syndrome, Trista Kutcher finds success in many areas of her life because of tremendous support at home and in school. To view interviews with Trista, her sister, and her mother, go to the Video Examples section of **Topic # 13: Inclusion and Special Needs** in the MyEducationLab for your course and view the video entitled "Trista Kutcher's Interview."

Inclusion   Rather than focusing on who is served and how, the most hotly debated question may be where to serve students with disabilities. The Least Restrictive Environment in a school is the regular classroom. The assignment of students to the regular classroom for some or all of the day is known as *inclusion* (*mainstreaming* is a term often used interchangeably with inclusion). Because middle school philosophy espouses heterogeneity in learning settings, inclusion is a natural fit. Inclusion supports social development and awareness as it gives all students the opportunity to interact.

Because writing an IEP involves both special education and regular classroom teachers, placement of students in inclusive settings is a collaborative effort. While most general education teachers agree that inclusion can be a positive practice, they don't necessarily feel adequately prepared to serve the wide range of needs often accompanying inclusion. In fact, not all parents of children with disabilities believe that inclusion provides the most effective learning environment for their children. Ruder (2000) tells us that for teachers the two biggest enemies of successful inclusion are time and fear: time to plan, to search for resources, to assess needs, and so on, and fear of moving beyond their comfort zone and failing to meet the needs of all students. To be successful, inclusion requires close collaboration among staff members and, ideally, a special educator actually present in the regular education classroom.

Schools are required by IDEA to have a continuum of alternative placements available that vary in terms of restrictiveness since a particular level of inclusion is not mandated by law. The "where" of the delivery of services is based on the individual student's IEP and must be revisited annually. Placement decisions often pose scheduling difficulties, as well as staffing, planning, and resource dilemmas. No single model of services can be prescribed.

Attention Deficit Disorder   Encountered more and more in the classroom, and only coincidentally assigned to any kind of special education setting, are those with *Attention Deficit Disorder* (*ADD*) and *Attention Deficit Hyperactivity Disorder* (*ADHD*). Students are not considered disabled because of a diagnosis of ADD or ADHD. Students with ADD try to pay attention to everything rather than focusing attention on the task at hand. ADHD adds two dimensions to ADD—hyperactivity and impulsivity. Hyperactivity is defined as "age-inappropriate increased activity in multiple settings" while impulsivity refers to the "tendency to act rashly and without judgment or consideration" (Schlozman & Schlozman, 2000, p. 28). Most researchers say that ADD and ADHD have biological causes and behavioral symptoms. To be diagnosed with either, symptoms must be excessive and long-term. More than 7% of all children ages 4 to 17 are diagnosed with ADD or ADHD. Many take medication such as Ritalin in attempts to manage the condition. In some schools, as many as 10% of the students are on medication for ADD and ADHD (Brown, 2007). They must, however, have some other disabling characteristic to receive special education services.

Many educators and researchers think that ADHD is overdiagnosed and/or misdiagnosed. They say the causes of disruptive behavior often associated with ADHD may actually be from overcrowded classrooms, lack of self-discipline skills, or teachers who demand inappropriate amounts of attention. Still others bemoan the fact that many students whom they suspect have the disorder go undiagnosed and experience what Jensen (1998, p. 50) calls "a horror movie they can't escape."

The symptoms of ADD and ADHD may be mild to extreme within a class that includes a number of diagnosed students, or within a single day, with a single child. Schlozman and Schlozman (2000) tell us that "Tight budgets, large classrooms, and often multiple students with the same diagnosis who require different teaching strategies substantially challenge the educator's primary objective: to teach and inspire every student dynamically and efficiently" (p. 28). In addition to medication, behavioral interventions may be used in the classroom—social skills groups, daily report cards, positive reinforcement, preferred seating, "time out" arrangements, and so on.

Reflections on Celebrating Diversity

We have explored a variety of diversity issues and should consider both the richness these differences represent, and the opportunities they lend, as we plan all aspects of our classrooms. Our responsibility is to affirm each individual and help all students appreciate each other both for what they have in common and for the diversity that is inevitable. As the demographics of the population of the United States shift and change, our classrooms will become more diverse places. Creating environments that go beyond tolerance of diversity in its many forms to a real celebration of diversity both in the classroom and in the school, should be a major goal of middle level education. "In a world in which we are trying to recognize, accept, appreciate, and champion differences, we must teach our children how their differences can be used to make a positive impact" (Caram, 2001, p. 73).

▶ Meet the Students

Reading about student development and diversity serves as foundational knowledge. When we see the concepts through real kids, we internalize them. That's why including focus students is a vital part of this textbook. Here you meet our nine focus students in 6th grade. They represent only a portion of the elements of diversity among young adolescents. These kids are included in the Professional Practice exercises at the end of the chapters, as well as in a feature called **See How They Grow** as we watch them grow from 6th to 7th to 8th grade. Get to know these students and think about how you might use what you read in subsequent chapters to be a more effective teacher for them.

Zach ● 6th grade, Lincoln Middle School

Zach is basically a good kid. He experienced his own bouts of trouble in elementary school, but is doing fine so far in 6th grade. Zach's mom, Melinda, teaches at Lincoln Middle School where Zach is now a student. She lives near the Title I school because, as a single mom with responsibility for her aging parents and her son, the house they all share is less expensive. Her concern is that Zach is one of the few Caucasian kids at Lincoln. She knows as a teacher that skin color shouldn't be an issue, that it's really socioeconomic, but she still worries. There are discipline and motivational issues at Lincoln that other schools, primarily in the suburbs, don't face as frequently. She hopes that Zach is growing up to be well-rounded and culturally sensitive and that those qualities will serve him well.

Zach was diagnosed with ADHD in 3rd grade. Mom and his teachers watched him carefully for two years before going to his pediatrician with their concerns. Melinda didn't want Zach "labeled" unless there was a significant problem and a promise of help through either behavior modifications or medication or both. Zach began taking Ritalin in the beginning of 4th grade and the medicine appears to be helping him concentrate and learn, while assisting with behavioral issues he faced earlier.

(*Continued*)

DeVante ● 6th grade, Jefferson Middle School

DeVante is surviving as a beginning 6th grader at Jefferson Middle School, but life wasn't always so good for him. After failing both kindergarten and 3rd grade, DeVante is considerably taller and more socially streetwise than others about to enter middle school. His granny and sole guardian was at her wits' end. She didn't like the neighborhood school, but didn't know what else to do. She needed help and managed to get DeVante into the Boys and Girls Club near their downtown apartment the summer after 5th grade. It was difficult to convince him to try it because he only wanted to hang out with the kids his age (13) rather then the 11-year-olds who just completed 5th grade with him. One of the volunteers at the Boys and Girls Club told DeVante's grandmother about Jefferson, a magnet school not far away. DeVante reluctantly applied and was accepted.

DeVante's granny gets by on food stamps and other government assistance. This means, as a 6th grader, he rarely has spending money. When he hangs out with the older kids, they buy him things—food, shoes, an occasional beer. They like DeVante. And that's a problem. The 13- to 15-year-olds in the neighborhood are being groomed by a local gang. Most will do whatever gang members say and actually idolize the older boys who have dropped out of high school. No wonder Granny is concerned.

Emily ● 6th grade, Madison Middle School

Emily is shy and immature. Her mom worries that she is too young for middle school. She was allowed to start kindergarten at age 4 and it's quite obvious that another year in elementary would have been good from a social standpoint. Mom divorced when Emily and her older brother were quite young. Emily spends one weekend a month with Dad and his second wife. Her mom remarried two years ago and, in the bargain, Emily got three young stepsiblings.

Emily has a speech impediment that accounts for some of her shyness. If she just says a few words, it's not obvious. More than that, and it's easy to pick up on. In elementary school she spent time each day with a speech therapist and dreads doing the same thing in middle school. Now that she's in 6th grade, she's just waiting for the first day when someone comes to the door and asks for her. She's quite nervous about being singled out.

Kim ● 6th grade, Jefferson Middle School

Kim could have been a character on *The Cosby Show*. Dad is a doctor and Mom is a bank executive. She has an older brother and a younger sister. Life for three generations on both sides of the family has been good, with lots of successful careers and lifestyles to match. Kim is a good student, but not particularly interested in math, science, or social studies. She likes to write and begged her parents to let her attend Jefferson Middle School, an inner-city magnet school focusing on technology and communications. They were reluctant, but decided to give the school a chance. Kim has wanted to be a television news anchor ever since her aunt became a successful broadcaster in Atlanta.

Kim is very visual. She learns best when she sees what's supposed to be learned, and graphic representations appeal to her. Just hearing something often goes right past her. Kim's elementary teachers understood this. Mom and Dad are a little concerned about her transition to Jefferson. Kim's visual learning style is accompanied by a seemingly nonstop need to talk.

Gabe • 6th grade, Valley View Middle School

Gabe is a quiet, small-for-his-age Hispanic boy who was born in the U.S. His mom, dad, and two younger sisters speak Spanish at home. Dad works as a farmhand 10–12 hours a day to provide a meager living for the family. For three months a year the family moves across the Kansas border so Dad can work in a restaurant when he's not needed on the farm. This poses a problem for Gabe now that he is a 6th grader at Valley View Middle School. He seems pretty happy at school, but doesn't stand out, either in a positive way or as a behavioral problem.

The fact that Gabe is a U.S. citizen makes his parents happy. They know their three children will have more opportunities than they had. They adore Gabe and his sisters, but have found that helping Gabe with homework is a thing of the past. In the middle of 4th grade they were at a loss to help, and Gabe's teacher assumed it was because of language difficulties. But that's not the whole reason. Gabe's parents completed only the equivalent of 6th grade in Mexico.

Janie • 6th grade, Cario Middle School

Janie has always liked school and done well. Her circle of girl-friends has been together since kindergarten. They go to the mall and the movies and talk on the phone incessantly. She has lived in the same neighborhood since she was two. Her dad is a successful realtor; her mom cares for Janie and her 7-year-old brother full time in their home. As she happily enters 6th grade, Mom and Dad are confident that Janie will be fine at Cario Middle School. Their only concern about her actually has a possible positive side. The summer after 5th grade Janie became conscious of her weight and started cutting back on sweets and spent more time riding her bike. She wanted to lose weight for middle school.

Janie loves to read. She was a Judy Blume fan in elementary school and read some of the books three times. She anxiously awaited each Harry Potter book before she could read them with comprehension. She knew her parents would read them to her. Now she has discovered Jodi Picoult. Mom thinks the books are a little old for her, but she's just glad Janie's love of reading continues.

(Continued)

Andy • 6th grade, Hamilton Middle School

Andy lives in a trailer on the outskirts of a small southern town. He's an only child whose mom died of cancer two years ago. Andy and his dad hunt and fish every weekend during the school year. He's not at all out of place in his rural community where there are definite social strata. The two quite distinct groups of people get along as groups, but a look at the children in the school gym shows that some of their lifestyle priorities and resources are quite different.

Andy has been heavy all his life. When he was a baby, everyone thought he was adorable. Now that he's in 6th grade, he has become more conscious of his size but still doesn't care very much. Unfortunately, he has started using chewing tobacco. He is often distracted in class and sometimes makes inappropriate remarks to other students. He's always been an average student who does much better when he experiences a concept rather than reading about it or doing paper and pencil work.

Darma • 6th grade, Lake Park Middle School

Darma, his parents, and younger brother emigrated from Indonesia when he was 6. He is a very interesting boy who enjoys playing chess and collecting comic books. He has a close group of friends and doesn't really care to socialize with other kids outside this circle. He's fine with going to middle school and knows he will continue to be in an academically gifted class where he is very comfortable. Darma's last name is Suparman, a common surname in his native country. His friends, of course, call him "Superman," a nickname he actually likes.

In Indonesia many people speak both Indonesian and English. Darma has grown up speaking English outside his home, so language is not a problem for him. While he does well in all his classes, Darma is fascinated with patterns and sequences making math a favorite subject. He is meticulously organized and has trouble relating to kids who don't share his passion for order. Teachers, of course, look forward to having Darma in class because he consistently meets or exceeds their expectations.

Maria • 6th grade, MLK Middle School

Maria was born in Mexico and came to the U.S. when she was seven years old. Her dad took her brothers back to Mexico to help care for his parents, and she hasn't seen them in three years. Her mom is a housekeeper at a downtown hotel and works evenings and weekends. Since she was in 4th grade, Maria has been staying by herself after school until Mom returns after midnight. On weekends she watches TV and mostly sits around, locked in her apartment. Her mom wants her to have all the advantages she didn't have, but Maria is sad most of the time. Her mom hasn't learned much English, and neither has Maria.

Each year Maria barely passes to the next grade. Teachers have suspected a learning disability, but, because she's an English language learner, it's been hard to pinpoint. In middle school she may fall even further behind. Emotionally and socially Maria is growing more and more restless. She doesn't want to stay inside anymore now that she's in middle school. This worries Mom, but she doesn't know what to do about it. She wants Maria to be successful in school and to have nice friends.

GROUP ACTIVITIES

1. Refer to your class file of local middle schools. Divide them among class members to find the total number of students, the percentage of free and reduced lunch students, and a breakdown of racial identification in each school. All schools should have this data. They may refer you to the district office. If so, only one call may be necessary to acquire the information. Add the data to your class file.

2. Together, brainstorm ways that you as middle school teachers might help create an appreciation of diversity among your students.

INDIVIDUAL ACTIVITIES

1. Why is it important for your students to understand their particular strengths in terms of multiple intelligences? Is there value in students understanding the areas where they have less strength?

2. Choose a subject area and a topic you can imagine teaching. Think of ways you might approach the topic that could address each of the four learning modalities. Write a brief description of each approach and be ready to share your ideas with your class.

PERSONAL JOURNAL

1. Describe yourself in terms of the diversity categories in Chapter 3.

2. Did you experience any kind of prejudice because of ways you may have been different from other kids in middle school? This may be painful to remember, but "reliving" it and writing about it may lead you toward a better understanding of your students.

3. Are there certain areas of diversity that make you more uncomfortable than others? Do you have personal experiences that contribute to your comfort levels?

Professional Practice

Cario Middle School has a diverse population, even though the majority of the kids are middle to upper income Caucasian. In a growing and mostly prosperous town, Cario has recently seen an influx of students from various parts of Asia, mostly to fill professional positions, as well as immigrants from Mexico who have come to work in service industries. At Cario the socioeconomic gap seems to be increasing, as is the academic gap, and teachers are scrambling to cope with their changing student population.

● **Traci Peters**   ● **Deirdre McGrew**

Traci Peters teaches 7th grade math and Deirdre McGrew teaches kids who are at risk for academic failure in a program called *Cario Academic Recovery and Enrichment* (CARE). Both teachers are concerned that Cario is not keeping up with the rapid student population changes, and, therefore, not meeting the needs of the kids who walk through the doors now. Most of the teachers are well aware of the middle school philosophy that recommends that kids from a wide array of achievement backgrounds be placed in classes together whenever possible. They have had staff development sessions about how to successfully manage this heterogeneous grouping. But nothing prepared them for the realities of this new demographic situation.

1. Ms. Peters looks around her classroom during an algebra class and is struck by how white it appears. There are two students from Japan and the rest are Caucasian. This group looks so very different from the mix of kids she supervised in the gym this morning before school. How might Ms. Peters work with 6th grade teachers to attempt to have a more diverse 7th grade algebra class next year?

   a. explore the backgrounds of some of the students who show academic promise in 6th grade to see what their achievement levels had been in their previous schools, even if outside the U.S., with the intent of putting them in an algebra class in 7th grade

   b. ask the principal to assign an ethnic balance of students next year to an algebra class without pretesting or teacher recommendation to see if having high expectations of all of the kids will bring about success in algebra

   c. Both a and b

   d. Neither a nor b

2. Ms. McGrew is used to working with the kids who have been placed in CARE in the past. She knew that most would be African American from the lower SES areas of the community. What she was not prepared for were the new students in her group from Mexico and Southeast Asian countries who speak little English. Even with only 15 students in her class, when four speak two different languages, she is at a loss to know how to meet their needs. Which course of action is likely to have the most immediate benefit for all the kids in CARE?

   a. meet with all the parents of her students to ask about their learning styles

   b. ask her principal to explore the idea of an assistant who will work with CARE kids on English language development

   c. increase the variety of the instructional strategies to increase student understanding

   d. check with the publisher of her materials to see if tapes are available so students can listen and follow along in order to increase their reading skills in English

Constructed Response

What could Cario teachers do to establish stronger relationships among themselves and their students, even as the school becomes more diverse? How might they build a sense of community among all the adults and students? What steps could they use to validate that all learners are capable of contributing positively in class and to the school in general?

INTERNET RESOURCES

Council for Exceptional Children (CEC)
www.cec.sped.org

The CEC is an international professional organization dedicated to improving education outcomes for individuals with exceptionalities, students with disabilities, and gifted students. This site gives information about professional development, publications, and conferences along with links to articles and other organizations.

Inclusive Education
www.uni.edu/coe/inclusion/index.html

This site gives practical information to teachers, administrators, and parents about how to implement inclusive practices. Resources are provided along with links to other sites about inclusive education.

Multiple Intelligences Development Assessment Scales (MIDAS)
www.miresearch.org

This site concentrates on characteristics of students as exhibited through Howard Gardner's theory of multiple intelligences.

National Institute on the Education of At-Risk Students
www.miresearch.org

This organization is supported by the U.S. Department of Education and sponsors a wide range of research and development activities designed to improve the education of students who are at risk for failure due to poverty, race, geographic location, socioeconomic status, and/or limited proficiency in English.

Texas Education Network
www.tenet.edu/halls/multiculturalism.html

This site provides an extensive list of other websites, many addressing issues related to multicultural education.

Citizen Schools
www.citizenschools.org

Citizen Schools partners with middle schools to expand the learning day for low-income children across the country. Since 1995, students at Citizen Schools have developed the academic and leadership skills they need to succeed in high school, college, the workplace, and civic life. Citizen Schools serve over 40 campuses in 7 states utilizing volunteers as afternoon educators who provide academic support and leadership development.

Girl Talk
www.desiretoinspire.org

Founded in 2002, Girl Talk is a student-to-student mentoring program that pairs middle school girls with high school girls who serve as mentors. Weekly meetings are held before or after school, during which the high school leader conducts valuable lessons that address issues middle school girls face every day.

Multicultural Pavilion
www.edchange.org/multicultural

This site offers 20 *(Self-) Critical Things I Will Do to Be a Better Multicultural Educator*, a tool for identifying teacher biases, prejudices, and cultural oversights.

National Association for Gifted Children

www.nagc.org

The National Association for Gifted Children (NAGC) is an organization of parents, teachers, educators, other professionals, and community leaders who unite to address the unique needs of children and youth with demonstrated gifts and talents as well as those children who may be able to develop their talent potential with appropriate educational experiences.

National Center for Culturally Responsive Educational Systems

www.nccrest.org

The National Center for Culturally Responsive Educational Systems (NCCRESt), a project funded by the U.S. Department of Education's Office of Special Education Programs, provides technical assistance and professional development to close the achievement gap between students from culturally and linguistically diverse backgrounds and their peers, and reduce inappropriate referrals to special education. The project targets improvements in culturally responsive practices, early intervention, literacy, and positive behavioral supports.

About Gender

www.gender.org.uk/about/

This site addresses gender roles, gender variance, and gender identity.

The Consortium on Race, Gender and Ethnicity

www.crge.umd.edu/

The Consortium on Race, Gender and Ethnicity (CRGE) works to explore the intersections of race, gender, ethnicity and other dimensions of difference. The group's goal is to influence behaviors within complex social relations. The site is sponsored by the University of Maryland.

Learning Disabilities Association of America

www.ldanatl.org/

The Learning Disabilities Association of America provides support to people with learning disabilities, their parents, teachers, and other professionals.

Middle Level Teachers

Teachers may not support the whole world on their shoulders as focus teacher Joey Huber is pretending, but in many ways they hold the futures of the students in their classes in their hands. Both inside and outside the classroom we have opportunities and responsibilities that are challenging and satisfying.

𝑀iddle level teachers are special. Those who observe them day after day presiding over their volatile, active charges know they have a distinctive quality that sets them apart from elementary and high school teachers. Their example, their caring, along with the effectiveness of their instruction have enduring influence. Perhaps more than any other group of teachers, middle level teachers shape the future.

Arth, Lounsbury, McEwin, & Swaim, 1995, p. 1

CHAPTER PREVIEW

Preparing to Teach
- Traditional Path
- Alternative Paths

Teachers as Learners
- Learning Individually
- School as a Community of Learners
- Formal Staff Development

Characteristics of Effective Middle Level Teachers

Reflections on Being a Middle Level Teacher

Teachers Inside the Classroom
- Classroom Community of Learners Defined
- Creating a Classroom Community of Learners

Teachers Outside the Classroom
- Within the School
- Within the System of Education
- Within Our Personal Circles
- Within the Broader Community

INTRODUCTION

As a young girl I vividly remember "playing school." Of course, I was always in the role of teacher. In my bedroom, I lined up my stuffed animals and dolls and held class on a regular basis. I loved school supplies (and I still do!). I was delighted by a new box of 64 crayons—who would not be thrilled by the sight of a periwinkle blue that had never touched a drawing pad! How about a new Big Chief tablet with freshly sharpened pencils? I liked school. The thought of being a teacher directed my behavior as a student. I wanted to please my teachers, to have them know they could rely on me to make their jobs easier. OK, so I was a geek. But I know there are others just like me who have come to realize—but perhaps won't admit it publicly—that the desire to teach may have its roots in utero!

While most middle grades teachers prepare for the profession as traditional students, more and more people are choosing to teach as a second or third career. They have been successful engineers, full-time homemakers, business executives, factory workers, or military men and women—you name it, and we probably have teachers who have done it. Whether the "calling" to be a teacher comes early or later in life makes absolutely no difference. The enthusiasm of youth or the wisdom gained through life's experiences are both invaluable in the classroom. So from "always knowing it" to "I'm ready for a change," and every degree in between, we have teachers dedicating their professional lives to the welfare of students. Many elementary teachers report choosing the career of teaching because they love children. Many high school teachers report choosing the career because they love their particular subject area. Here we are between the two. We draw from the richness of both. A commitment to students in the middle grades entails caring for them as special individuals as well as both caring about, and knowing deeply, our chosen subject(s).

We come to the profession for a variety of reasons and with an even greater variety of perspectives. This diversity is strength. Fortunate are the middle school students who travel from class to class during the course of the day, greeted by men and women who present positive role models of adulthood garbed in personalities and life experiences. While we each have our own unique teacher fingerprints, we immerse ourselves in the lives of our students. Michael Fullan (1993), noted expert on the subject of educational change, tells us that "teaching at its core is a moral profession. Scratch a teacher and you will find a moral purpose" (p. 12). Public Agenda conducted an in-depth survey of more than 900 teachers who had been in the classroom for 5 years or less. The results, shown in Figure 4.1, are reported in *Educational Leadership*, May 2001. They reveal teaching to be a satisfying profession.

Eighty-six percent of the teachers in the Public Agenda survey believe that only those with "a true sense of calling" should pursue the profession of

---

FIGURE 4.1   Why we teach

Percentage of teachers who have taught five years or less who say:
  Teaching is work they love to do   96%
  They would choose teaching again if starting over   80%
  Teaching is a lifelong choice   75%
  They get a lot of satisfaction out of teaching   68%
  They fell into teaching by chance   12%

Source: A Sense of Calling: Who Teaches and Why (Public Agenda, 2000) as published in "Why New Teachers Choose to Teach ('Why Teachers Teachm' p. 25)," by Deborah Wadsworth, 2001, *Educational Leadership* 58(8). © 2001 by ASCD. Reprinted with permission. Learn more about ASCD at www.ascd.org.

teaching. Overwhelmingly they pointed out that our profession requires a sense of mission; so although we express our individuality in the classroom, we seem to share a common notion of calling. In his insightful book *Meet Me in the Middle*, Rick Wormeli (2001) says, "It is a privilege to be in education. Not everyone is called to such a noble cause" (p. 1).

Teaching is a profession that just about everyone in the United States feels qualified to critique. We were all students, weren't we? We had good teachers and bad teachers, and those of every descriptor in between. Because we all went to school, sizing up the teachers in classrooms across the country is something that many feel obliged to do—and rightly so. Most of us have spent 12 years, many of us 16 years, and a considerable number 20 plus years in the classroom as students. We have been on the receiving end and can justifiably offer criticisms and suggestions. Public school teachers are paid with public funds collected from "we the people." Public engagement is to be expected, the more positively directed the better. We would be hard pressed to find a politician anywhere who has not placed education near the top of his or her agenda. Scrutiny, criticism, quickly formulated and loudly expressed opinions, and occasional greatly appreciated support all come our way.

Consider how teachers are portrayed in movies. This is a particularly good thing to do after a tough week in the classroom. On the flattering side, we have *Stand and Deliver* in which Edward James Olmos stars as Jaime Escalante who shows his dedication and skill in teaching kids at Garfield High School in East Los Angeles. And how about Michelle Pfeiffer portraying the real life of LouAnne Johnson in *Dangerous Minds?* Pfeiffer and Johnson, both knockouts in real life, show us how to tame some incorrigibles with the "you're not going to get the best of me" attitude that leads to student learning. Fictional teachers inspire us in *Mr. Holland's Opus, The Prime of Miss Jean Brodie, Up the Down Staircase, To Sir, with Love,* and *Goodbye, Mr. Chips.* These movies resonate positively with most viewers. For laughs, there are a couple of movies I occasionally watch that portray teachers in less than glowing light. *Fast Times at Ridgemont High* stars Sean Penn as a surfer dude who challenges his teachers at every turn. A movie that makes me smile at the very thought of it—and laugh out loud from the opening scene to the closing credits—is *Ferris Bueller's Day Off.* Ferris, portrayed with sheer genius by Matthew Broderick, and his friends use every ploy imaginable to fool the system. After years of therapy (not really!) I have concluded that I am so enamored of Ferris because he is the opposite of my geekish self that I described earlier. What many people remember about teaching and teachers from *Ferris Bueller's Day Off* is the character played by Ben Stein, who attempts to illicit student responses concerning the Hawley Smoot Tariff Act with his monotone drone "Anyone? . . . Anyone?" While these last two movies should never be considered staff development tools, they do give us occasion to laugh and be good sports.

Any profession that calls for dedication, selfless giving, patience, and creativity will also necessitate renewal. In Chapters 2 and 3 we took an in-depth look at the students who fill our middle grades classrooms. If ever there was a challenging profession, teaching young adolescents is it! Later in this chapter, we'll discuss ways to bolster our resolve and renew our spirits through reflection and continual learning. While pep talks and chants, as seen occasionally in news magazine shows, seem to do the trick, at least temporarily, for Walmart employees, auto manufacturing workers, and Mary Kay sales associates, they have little to do with the way we respond to students, parents, and administrators on a daily basis. Renewing our resolve as teachers must resonate in very personal ways. In *The Courage to Teach*, Parker Palmer (1998) tells us that the "self-hood of the teacher is key" (p. 7). He encourages us to recover continually "the inner resources that good teaching always requires" (p. 7). Maintaining inner balance is vital, but at times difficult, in this profession filled with ups and downs. Knowles and Brown (2007) exhort us, "Hold onto your hat. We believe working with young adolescents will be the most exhilarating ride you will ever take" (p. 9).

Preparing to Teach

We come to the middle school classroom equipped with different knowledge, skills, and dispositions obtained in a variety of ways: some through a school of education four-year degree program, some through graduate programs in education, some through alternative programs. Teacher certification requirements vary by state.

STANDARD 7

Knowledge 1: Middle level teacher candidates understand their evolving role as middle level education professionals.

The NMSA Middle Level Teacher Preparation Standards discussed in Chapter 1 are based on an earlier set of standards outlined in 1995. These standards for middle level teacher preparation programs were validated in a 1999 study conducted by McEwin, Dickinson, and Hamilton (2000). Of the first 81 teachers to successfully obtain National Board Certified Young Adolescence/Generalist certification, 73 responded to open-ended questions concerning preparation. (National Board Certification will be discussed later in this chapter.) All of them responded "yes" when asked, "Are there important ideas, principles, understandings that an effective middle level teacher needs to know?" When asked to give examples, their responses included statements about the uniqueness of early adolescence, the importance of the learning environment, the value of active interdisciplinary instruction, the need to work cooperatively in teams, and the need to know content well. The authors note that "Clearly, the pattern of responses from these highly accomplished teachers offer further confirmation of the importance of specialized middle level teacher preparation programs" (p. 213).

Traditional Path

The fact that you are reading this book indicates that you are likely to be part of a college class studying middle level education. Terrific! This may be the only course you take focusing exclusively on the education of young adolescents, or it may be part of a comprehensive middle level program. Keep in mind that while textbooks, class discussions, and lectures by middle grades experts provide background knowledge, most of the skills you will need to be successful teachers at the middle level will be learned on the job. David Berliner, a noted researcher in the area of teacher expertise, says that we cannot completely pre-train teachers and that a college degree prepares us to be beginners in the complex world of the classroom (Scherer, 2001). We hope to emerge from teacher preparation programs with understanding and skills, but knowing when and how to apply our learning takes real-life situations to see how to pull strategies apart and determine how best to use them to meet the needs of particular students (Tolan, 2001). The National Board Certified teachers referred to earlier recommend that middle level teacher preparation include more real-life experiences with students and teachers in the classroom (McEwin et al., 2000). These experiences may be part of your preparation program. If not, I highly recommend that you pursue them on your own.

● Alternative Paths

Alternative paths to teacher certification are rapidly increasing due, in part, to the need for more teachers (particularly in middle and high school), but also as a result of mid-career changers who decide to enter the profession after working in other fields. Almost all states recognize some form of alternative certification. About 35,000 people enter the profession through alternative routes each year (Feistritzer, 2005). These programs vary widely and are sometimes controversial.

Perhaps the best known of all the alternative programs is Teach for America (TFA). College seniors, recent graduates, and professionals are recruited to teach in high-needs areas for a minimum of two years and are given, in return, forgiveness for part or all of their college loans, with other financial and professional growth incentives. TFA teachers receive professional development to equip them to teach America's most challenging student populations. TFA has more than 6,000 teachers in classrooms across the U.S. and plans to increase this number (Teach for America, 2009).

Now let's look at some characteristics of effective middle level teachers.

Characteristics of Effective Middle Level Teachers

I've come to the frightening conclusion that I am the decisive element in the classroom. It's my personal approach that creates climate. It's my daily mood that makes the weather. As a teacher, I possess a tremendous power to make a child's life miserable or joyous. I can be a tool of torture or an instrument of inspiration. I can humiliate or humor, hurt or heal. In all situations, it is my response that decides whether a crisis will be escalated or de-escalated, a child humanized or de-humanized (Ginott, 1993, p. 15).

myeducationlab

As a 7th grader, Patrick tells us his hopes for his future and what he likes and doesn't like about teachers. To view an interview with Patrick and his mother, go to the Video Examples section of **Topic # 2: Today's Students** in the MyEducationLab for your course and view the video entitled "Patrick Sutton's Interview."

Being a teacher is an awesome responsibility. I purposefully focus on the Haim Ginott quote on a regular basis. It is posted in my office and next to my desk at home. I give it to each of my students at the beginning of every semester. So how do we use this "tremendous power," accorded to us simply because we are teachers, in wise and positive ways? I firmly believe that teachers who understand that they have the power to make or break the experiences of young adolescents will seek out ways to be more effective. Once we understand that "we make the weather," the sobering reality of it should drive us to be the best teachers we can be.

From what we know about young adolescents, we recognize that effectively teaching them requires us to do more than merely survive. We need to find ways to thrive. There are basic differences between surviving and thriving in the classroom—the main difference being the ability to balance conflicting demands of the profession. On one hand, we should teach "the whole child," nurturing development in every way. On the other hand, we are held accountable for "covering" the curriculum and increasing test scores. Teachers who thrive, not merely survive, find ways to do both. They integrate their care for students as people with their efforts to enrich instruction and curriculum. John Lounsbury (1991) tells us, "There is no conflict between academic effectiveness and developmental responsiveness at the age of early adolescence" (p. 97). Supporting student development and structuring educational experiences in ways that promote success is what Strahan (1997) refers to as "caring in action."

In their book, *Middle Level Teachers: Portraits of Excellence* (1995), four major contributors to our knowledge of middle level education provide us with 16 research-based traits of effective middle level teachers. Al Arth, John Lounsbury, Ken McEwin, and John Swaim tell us that effective middle level teachers should strive to possess the characteristics listed in Figure 4.2. While this material may seem dated, the wisdom is sound, aligning with NMSA teacher preparation standards.

As you continue reading this book, refer back often to this list of characteristics. You will be able to link them to structures within middle schools (Chapter 6), curriculum development (Chapter 7), instructional and assessment strategies (Chapters 8 and 9), lesson/unit planning (Chapter 10), learning environment creation and maintenance (Chapter 11), and relationships with parents and community (Chapter 12).

It is appropriate to listen to middle level students concerning their views of effective teachers. Ed Lawton, a respected expert in the field of middle level education, as well as my own personal mentor, wrote a monograph for the National Association of Secondary School Principals in 1993 titled *The Effective Middle Level Teacher*. In it he reports on comments of students at Prospect Heights Middle School in Orange, Virginia. Very simply, the students give us a clear picture of their views on good teachers and not-so-good teachers in Figure 4.3. Again, while 1993 may seem like ages ago, young adolescent expectations of us are basically the same today.

FIGURE 4.2 The effective middle level teacher

1. Is sensitive to the individual differences, cultural backgrounds, and exceptionalities of young adolescents, treats them with respect, and celebrates their special nature.
2. Understands and welcomes the role of advocate, adult role model, and advisor.
3. Is self-confident and personally secure—can take student challenges while teaching.
4. Makes decisions about teaching based on a thorough understanding of the physical, social, intellectual, and emotional development of young adolescents.
5. Is dedicated to improving the welfare and education of young adolescents.
6. Works collaboratively and professionally to initiate needed changes.
7. Establishes and maintains a disciplined learning environment that is safe and respects the dignity of young adolescents.
8. Ensures that all young adolescents will succeed in learning.
9. Has a broad, interdisciplinary knowledge of the subjects in the middle level curriculum and depth of content knowledge in one or more areas.
10. Is committed to integrating curriculum.
11. Uses varied evaluation techniques that both teach and assess the broad goals of middle level education and provide for student self-evaluation.
12. Recognizes that major goals of middle level education include the development of humane values, respect for self, and positive attitudes toward learning.
13. Seeks out positive and constructive relationships and communicates with young adolescents in a variety of environments.
14. Works closely with families to form partnerships to help young adolescents be successful at school.
15. Utilizes a wide variety of developmentally appropriate instructional strategies.
16. Acquires, creates, and utilizes a wide variety of resources to improve the learning experiences of young adolescents.

Source: National Middle School Association, 4151 Executive Parkway, Suite 300, Westerville, OH 43081, 1-800-528-NMSA, www.nmsa.org

Teachers Inside the Classroom

Teaching is a profession that permeates who we are. At 4:00 P.M., we don't become frogs after being princes all day—and we certainly hope the opposite isn't true. Just like the poem says, a rose is a rose is a rose. And a teacher is a teacher is a teacher. This doesn't mean we have no lives outside the classroom. I do—and you will, too! However, your students, your lessons, your colleagues, your curriculum, and so on are never far from consciousness. The good things we do professionally, and the deep satisfaction that follows, give life a sweeter flavor. For organization's sake, I want us to think separately about life inside the classroom and life outside the classroom.

FIGURE 4.3   Student perceptions of teacher effectiveness

Good Teachers . . .	Not-So-Good Teachers . . .
• make learning more fun	• are not prepared
• give clear instructions	• are always cranky
• give you ways to remember things	• make a lot of threats
• review before the test	• lecture students in front of the class
• let students know how they feel	• don't review tests
• change their tone of voice	• single kids out and make them feel bad
• don't take anger out on kids	• take it out on kids when they are in a bad mood
• demand students' attention	• don't say anything when you give a wrong answer
• care about students' feelings	• teach only one way
• are strict but not mean	• won't call on you
• treat kids with respect	• act like a kid
• get students involved doing projects and experiments	• spend too much time ragging on kids who don't do their work
• move around	• sit at desks and read magazines or books
• are organized, know what they are going to do	• tell students to read the chapter and don't give notes
• start classes right away	

Source: From *The Effective Middle Level Teacher* (p. 13), by E. Lawton, 1993, Reston, VA: National Association of Secondary School Principals. Copyright 1993 National Association of Secondary School Principals. www.principals.org. Reprinted with permission.

When I say inside, I literally mean within the four walls or wherever we take our students to experience learning. Outside the classroom will include other places—from the school hallways to the grocery store, from school board meetings to dozing in the overstuffed living room chair with a book in your lap and the TV blaring.

Most middle school teachers conduct three to six classes a day, each made up of 15 to 30 students. In Chapter 6 we explore a variety of scheduling options that are frequently seen in middle school settings. Most elementary teachers teach the same 15 to 30 students all day in what we refer to as a self-contained setting. They have what some would consider the luxury of seeing the whole child as the day progresses, as moods ebb and flow, as subject areas intertwine, as progress is made or not made. The middle school teacher generally sees his or her students for 45 to 90 minutes a day, experiences a variety of moods and subject matter interests, and sees progress or lack of it—all limited to the time frame of class. Five minutes later there's another group of 15 to 30 students finding their places in the classroom. I can assure you of one thing—teaching in the middle grades is never boring!

So here's the challenge. We are to mold our students in ways that facilitate cognitive growth and meet the developmental needs of young adolescents. And we must do this four to six times every day. This requires more than classrooms with doors to contain our charges and bells to signal the beginning and end of each class period. Our responsibility is to create a community of learners.

● Classroom Community of Learners Defined

"Educational researchers and policy makers have agreed that one of the most power-ful factors in promoting accomplishment is the extent to which the classroom is a learning community" (Strahan, Smith, McElrath, & Toole, 2001, p. 46). The more we explore and articulate beliefs about teaching and learning, the deeper our definition of *community of learners* becomes. You have probably heard the phrase and/or discussed it in education courses. Sergiovanni (1996) tells us, "Communities are collections of individuals who are bonded together by natural will and who are together bound to a set of shared ideas and ideals. This bonding and binding is tight enough to transform them from a collection of 'I's to a collective 'we'" (p. 48). This is an inspiring definition, especially the last part about the results—the sense of "we" is a noble goal for the classroom.

Creation of community = Changing collection of "I's" to "we"

But let's face it, few middle school classrooms are made up of kids who come together 5 days a week out of what Sergiovanni refers to as "natural will." This fact makes our quest to create communities of learners more dif-ficult. We are attempting to transform a captive audience of individual young ado-lescents into a "we," bound together by shared ideas and ideals. As difficult as this may sound, it is possible. I have seen it, I have experienced it, and I assure you it is happening all across our country.

The two operative words in "community of learners" are both vitally important. There are benefits in creating a sense of community; there are benefits in making sure learning takes place. When the two are combined, the whole is definitely greater than the sum of its parts. This is called *synergism.* Bringing together a group of students with some, or all, of the diverse characteristics discussed in Chapters 2 and 3 for the purpose of studying a distinct body of content knowledge is what we do in middle school. Students may be in four or five, or up to seven, groups a day. How do we manage to create communities of learners so our young adolescents can experience this special synergism?

● Creating a Classroom Community of Learners

All the characteristics of effective teachers apply. The discussion of balancing the affective side of teaching with the curricular material of our subject areas is applica-ble, as is the reference to thriving versus surviving. Creating a community of learn-ers is when the "big picture" of classroom teaching comes into focus. All the components are snapshots and, when the snapshots are in their places, they form an album that showcases a community of learners.

A community of learners is characterized in *Turning Points* (Carnegie Council on Adolescent Development, 1989) as "a place where close, trusting relationships with adults and peers create a climate for personal growth and intellectual development" (p. 37). The authors of *Turning Points 2000* tell us that since the original document "an enormous amount has been learned from schools across the nation about how these kinds of middle grades learning communities can be created" (Jackson & Davis, 2000, p. 123). A recent study reports on two basic components that contribute to the creation of a community of learners: the teacher's personal commitment to the students, which often results in students and teachers learning side by side, and the translation of this commitment into "procedures that fuse academic and social accomplishment" (Strahan et al., 2001, p. 46).

STANDARD 1

Performance 1: Middle level teacher candidates establish close, mutually respectful relationships with all young adolescents that support their intellectual, ethical, and social growth.

Commitment to the creation of a community of learners requires us to both recognize and increase the progress of our students. John Lounsbury (1991) tells us that our commitment should be manifested in ways that have the effect of multiplying, as well as adding, so we help students multiply their knowledge while adding to their capacity to learn. We are helping to "grow" them and their abilities; that is, increase their capacities and expand their knowledge and skills. Think about water balloons—sometimes only about 2 inches by ½ inch empty. They look innocuous enough, but put them under the faucet and watch them fill their original size and then continue to expand as the water flows in. Then watch out—they can pack quite a wallop. Commitment to students calls for us to see them as they are, help them fill up, and then be catalysts that stretch them.

Rick Wormeli (2001), a middle school educator who regularly contributes to our profession with his insights, advises us on ways to invite students to be part of our community of learners (Figure 4.4).

FIGURE 4.4   Inviting students to participate in the classroom community

- Be pleasant to students.
- Call them by their first names.
- Greet them at the door.
- Smile often.
- Catch them doing something well.
- Crack a few jokes.
- Ask questions that show your interest.
- Applaud risk-taking.
- Share excellent homework or test responses with the rest of the class.
- Allow occasional democratic voting in the class.
- Refer one child who is an expert on something to another child who needs help, and make sure you rotate the expert's role.
- Ask students to tutor their peers after school.
- Give them responsible jobs in the classroom or school.
- Point out moments of caring among peers that occur in class.

Source: From *Meet Me in the Middle: Becoming an Accomplished Middle-Level Teacher,* by Rick Wormeli, 2001, Portland, ME: Stenhouse Publishers.

myeducationlab

To hear Carol Bartlett, principal of Cario Middle School, tell us that the first trait she looks for in a new teacher is an obvious enjoyment of young adolescents, go to the Video Examples section of **Topic #1: Schools and Teaching Today** in the MyEducationLab for your course and view the video entitled "Carol Bartlett's Interview."

Maintaining a classroom that is more than four walls with students and a teacher, a classroom that houses a community of learners, requires a teacher who has "a strong sense of self-awareness, a positive self-concept, and a controlled ego" (Lawton, 1993, p. 6). This kind of teacher passes the test of authenticity and is prepared to be a vital part of a community of learners.

Now let's take our assertion that "a teacher is a teacher is a teacher" outside the classroom walls.

Teachers Outside the Classroom

We are teachers within the school, within the sphere of education, in our homes and personal lives, and in the community at large. David Berliner, in an interview with Marge Scherer (2001), tells us,

> Teachers need to provide more leadership, to be more politically active, and to show that they are concerned about the community. No one else can change the perception of the teachers except teachers themselves, but there are three million of them. And they ought to be out there—and much more active than they are now (p.10).

Let's explore our roles within the school, the broader system of education, our personal circles, and the surrounding community.

Within the School

Wayside Teaching   Between classes, at lunch, at the bus departure/arrival areas, on the field—we are with our students at important times during the day outside our classrooms. While our encounters may not be planned, and certainly are not scripted, they are nonetheless very important. In the world of middle school, we teach as much by who we are as we do with our planned curriculum. So although we don't have lesson plans for passing periods or the lunchroom or the chance meeting on the way back to class from an errand, our attitudes toward our students dictate the interaction. John Lounsbury (1991) calls this *"wayside teaching"* (p. 29). It's not math or science or social studies or language arts, but it's teaching. Students are learning about life, about adulthood, about relationships. We can't fool them. Yes, they're wrapped up in themselves and their friends. So much is going on inside of them developmentally that it's only natural to be self-absorbed. That doesn't keep them from noticing us and paying attention to how we respond to them outside the classroom. Saying "How are you, Travis?" or "How's it going, Maresha?"—using names, showing concern, and demonstrating the simple fact that we actually like them—makes a difference to young adolescents.

STANDARD 7

Knowledge 2: Middle level teacher candidates understand the importance of their influence on all young adolescents.

Sometimes your classroom responsibilities will stretch outside your lesson plans and your classroom. You will have before school, after school, and lunch duties. Yes, these responsibilities may interfere with planning time and may require you to walk the halls or the field when you might rather have a second cup of coffee. Like everything else in life, attitude makes a difference. Try to view duty responsibilities as opportunities to interact with a student who needs an extra nudge toward cooperation, or maybe a "lost soul" who needs your caring touch.

Wayside teaching is more than a series of casual encounters; it's an attitude that fosters growth and learning. A wayside teaching attitude leads us to view young adolescents as whole children, build on strengths, not hold grudges or harbor low expectations, take the high road and forgive with a fresh start always available, care deeply, listen with respect, and respond with good judgment and compassion (Powell, 2010).

STANDARD 1

Disposition 5: Middle level teacher candidates are enthusiastic about being positive role models, coaches, and mentors for all young adolescents.

STANDARD 7

Disposition 4: Middle level teacher candidates believe in maintaining high standards of ethical behavior and professional competence.

Positive relationships among teachers and administrators are essential to creating and maintaining a community of learners.

Adult Relationships   Our relationships with fellow teachers weigh very heavily in terms of job satisfaction. Age and interests may determine the teachers we gravitate toward as "buddies," but paying attention to all the teachers in your building, noticing their composure and their attitude toward students, creates learning experiences for us. We all have our own styles and individual characteristics, but there is a bond among teachers that people outside the teaching profession don't understand. We teach young adolescents; we teach middle school. We're in this profession together. Take advantage of opportunities to observe and listen and learn. Be a team player when at all possible. Contribute and compromise—always for the sake of the kids.

The administrators in your building are important to you as a teacher. The role of principal is a difficult one; the buck often stops with them. They have the responsibility of coordinating and directing every aspect of their school. They answer to students, teachers, parents, district office personnel, school board members, the community, and their own conscience. Ideally, you will have a principal you respect and value, someone who makes the tough choices and puts the pieces together with the ultimate goal of serving students. As teachers, we may question decisions that principals make. That's healthy. Ask questions and make suggestions, but don't undermine. Because principals often see issues from different and wider perspectives, their decisions often reflect variables to which teachers are not privy.

Your school will have at least one guidance counselor and perhaps an assistant principal or two. These are valuable people with varying responsibilities. One thing's for sure—they're always busy with phone calls to return and students to see on top of the wide range of other duties assigned to them. Use their expertise and keep them informed of student issues from your perspective.

Two other important positions in the school are those of secretary and custodian. These are vital positions, and the people who fill them deserve our respect and our gratitude. Without them the school would not function.

STANDARD 7

Knowledge 4: Middle level teacher candidates understand the interrelationships and interdependencies among various professionals that serve young adolescents.

Disposition 2: Middle level teacher candidates perceive themselves as members of the larger learning community.

Disposition 7: Middle level teacher candidates value collegiality as an integral part of their professional practice.

Within the System of Education

The District   The school district is an important organizational entity. Many areas of policy-making, administration, services, coordination, programmatic issues, budget, and more are the functions of the district organization. I taught one year in Gilpin County, Colorado, where the district consisted of one school—a K–12 building with about 350 students. My duties, by the way, went from elementary music to senior Algebra II. The following year, I taught eighth grade math at Hill Middle School in Denver, a school district of 122 schools with more than 70,000 students. As you can imagine, the district offices looked very different. But each performed responsibilities and was governed by a school board. School boards are often very political groups made up of elected citizens who may or may not have any understanding of education or schools or teaching and learning beyond their own memories of "back in my day." Good or bad, like it or not, school boards have a great deal of power over the forces that shape what we do in our schools and in our classrooms. They can be supportive, positive influences that clearly understand their charge to keep the welfare of children uppermost in their decision-making, or they may become mired in special interests and be far removed from the realities of the classroom. As teachers, we need to be attentive to both thoroughly researched policy decisions and those made on what appear to be hunches or whims. We should be aware and active, with the faces of our students always in focus in the lenses we use to view decisions and directions.

Districts have superintendents, or Chief Executive Officers of schools, along with a wide variety of personnel who oversee curriculum, instruction, staff development, subject areas, personnel, testing, payroll, facilities, and so on. Get to know your district and the people who hold these administrative positions. If they are doing their jobs right, they will welcome your interest, questions, and opinions.

The district level provides common ground for middle level educators to talk and share with peers. No doubt there will be opportunities for you to get to know teachers at other middle schools near you. Take these opportunities to ask how things are done in other schools and to be an instigator of sharing. We all have so much to learn from one another.

Not only is it important for middle school teachers to talk to each other, it is also important for us to have ongoing conversations with teachers in the elementary feeder schools from which our students come, as well as the high schools our students will attend within our school districts. The transition into middle grades and then the transition into high school from middle school are big events in the lives of our students. We can gain insights from our students' former teachers and serve as resources for their future teachers. We consider transitions into and out of middle school in Chapter 12.

State and National Your state will have a State Department of Education with departments very similar to large school districts, plus departments that deal with certification and state political forces. Most states have established special committees charged with writing, updating, and overseeing curriculum standards. State oversight also includes departments that handle accountability issues addressed in Chapter 9 where we delve into assessment. Most states also have their own affiliate of the National Middle School Association. Some of these affiliates are flourishing organizations with staff development opportunities, summer curriculum and instruction institutes, conferences, newsletters, and journals, all with the purpose of helping us to serve our students better. State middle school organizations provide camaraderie and growth opportunities that shouldn't be missed.

Although education is deemed a state right and responsibility, the federal government has influence. The Department of Education in Washington, D.C., is headed by a national Secretary of Education whose staff influences federal policy-making, program-funding, and goal-setting. However, federal funding for schools amounts to only about 5% of district budgets, while state and local funding often share the remaining 95% relatively equally. By the time federal policies trickle down to the classroom level, a new administration may be at the helm, with priority shifts on the way. Throughout this book we have considered the broadest reform effort so far in the 21st century, the No Child Left Behind legislation, a product of President George W. Bush's administration.

STANDARD 7

Disposition 3: Middle level teacher candidates believe that their professional responsibilities extend beyond the classroom and school (e.g., advisory committees, parent-teacher organizations).

Performance 4: Middle level teacher candidates engage in and support ongoing professional practices for self and colleagues (e.g., attend professional development activities and conferences, participate in professional organizations).

Universities Many universities now offer courses leading to bachelor's and master's degrees in middle grades education. It would be to your benefit to explore what's available in your area. If you will soon student teach or be a clinical intern, or have already completed the experience, you realize how important this on-the-job training is. Someday you will be in a position to be a cooperating teacher for aspiring middle grades teachers. When you are ready, don't hesitate to do your part in assisting others. You don't need to have all the answers—none of us do. What's required is a genuine love of the profession and the young adolescents in your classroom.

Within Our Personal Circles

The personal lives of teachers span all the possibilities within the general public. We may be young, middle-aged, or beyond; single or married; parents or not. We are individuals. After all my years in the teaching profession, there is one thing I can say with certainty—only those who have been classroom teachers truly understand what it's like. We can, and do, talk about our days with friends and family. While others listen to us with interest, and support us to varying degrees, they can't identify with the responsibility, the care, the exhilaration, and sometimes the depth of despair we experience. Don't expect complete understanding, but keep talking and confiding in those you love.

Be good to yourself. You will find yourself thinking about your students, your lessons, your colleagues, and your school at times when you might rather concentrate on other areas of your life. In spite of this, treat yourself to personal interests. If you enjoy baseball, join a league; if you enjoy the water, swim or boat; if you enjoy travel, get away as often as you can. Go to movies, read what teachers often call "summer novels," take martial arts classes, begin guitar lessons, sing in civic or church groups, or learn to cook exotic foods. Do whatever makes you smile.

Our profession is important, and we are major players in the lives of our students. The old saying "we can't take care of others if we don't take care of ourselves" applies here. Taking care of ourselves keeps our profession and our personal lives in balance and better equips us to be our best in both areas. Our friends, our spouses, our extended families, our own children—all the people we love—deserve our attention and want to care for us. Enjoy yourself!

Within the Broader Community

Schools exist in communities. Here I am using the word *community* as the local area and the people who live there. Almost everyone has opinions about education, and many voice those opinions freely and attempt to influence us. That's how it should be. Schools and teachers are vital components of communities and can contribute in monumental ways to the lifestyles of everyone in them. Some teachers choose to live in the communities in which they teach. They may be involved in civic organizations or choose not to be. Other teachers prefer to live in areas outside the immediate communities of their schools. They choose to drive longer distances to achieve some sense of anonymity, where they can separate their personal and professional lives to a greater degree, where running into students and their parents in the mall or a restaurant is less likely. It's a matter of personal choice.

Teacher in school = Public relations agent in community

Here is something we must take very seriously concerning our communities. We are our own best, or worst, public relations agents. To a large extent, we influence public opinion regarding education. What we say matters. The media, both print and electronic, will follow test score improvement or lack of it, violent acts as well as humanitarian ones within the schools, programs that succeed or fail. We have some control, but not much, over media coverage. What we do have total control over is how we portray our students and our profession. If things aren't going like you think they should on your team or in your school, keep your opinions within the system. Outsiders are not going to understand the variables we complain about, but you can be sure they will both sense our negative attitude and zero in on any issue that signals trouble within "their" schools.

Bottom line—be professional and be positive! Even if things aren't going the way you might like, remember whom we serve. Our young adolescents are our focus. Spread the news about what great kids they are, or can be. And spread the news that there are thousands of middle grades teachers who do the best they can for kids every day and in every community! Like any professional, we should strive to be a part of the solution, not the problem.

STANDARD 6

Knowledge 4: Middle level teacher candidates know how to communicate effectively with family and community members.

Knowledge 5: Middle level teacher candidates understand that middle level schools are organizations within a larger community context.

Disposition 2: Middle level teacher candidates realize the importance of privacy and confidentiality of information when working with family members.

Teachers as Learners

We have explored preparation for entering the teaching profession, as well as characteristics of effective teachers. We know that graduation from a teacher education program or certification through an alternative route signals the beginning of a lifetime of learning that takes place through a dynamic combination of individual effort, teacher-to-teacher collaboration, and formal development opportunities. "We expect teachers to give their all to the growth and development of students. But a teacher cannot sustain such giving unless the conditions exist for the continued growth and development of the teacher" (Sarason, 1993, p. 62). In this section, we look at some possibilities for professional growth.

Lifetime of learning = Individual effort + Teacher-to-teacher collaboration + Formal staff development

STANDARD 7

Disposition 1: Middle level teacher candidates value learning as a life-long process.

Learning Individually

We want students to take responsibility for their own learning; we want them to want to learn. As teachers, taking responsibility for our own learning is vital as well. We can model for students the value of questioning, examining, seeking answers and reasons, and allowing each learning experience to prompt new questions that send us off in other learning directions. It's an attitude, a state of readiness, an openness to new ideas. Not only will our students benefit from our modeling, they will also be the recipients of the insights and practices we learn about teaching—and life.

Reflection   Learning occurs when we actively analyze our actions. Individual *reflection* about teaching is not daydreaming or passive recollection of the day. It is purposeful and thoughtful. Keeping a journal of classroom events—some significant, some seemingly trivial—and our responses to them, will help frame reflections. This is likely to lead to insights that will be learning experiences for us. The style of your journal writing is your personal choice. Some teachers keep a notebook and vow to write reflectively about their day before leaving school each afternoon. Some days call for pages and pages, while others may boil down to a few sentences. The key is consistency. It's a habit that makes us better because, as we write, situations will generally become clearer in our minds, and that clarity often leads to actions or changes in our practice. It may be helpful to establish a two-column journal with events and actions on the left, and our responses and thoughts about the occurrences on the right. This allows us the opportunity to go back later and respond as things "sink in."

STANDARD 7

Knowledge 8: Middle level teacher candidates understand the need for continual reflection on young adolescent development, the instructional process, and professional relationships.

I often recommend to student teachers, as well as practicing teachers, that they turn off their radios or CDs in the car after school and try to use the drive time to reflect on the day. Sometimes all we want to do is jump in the car, turn up the volume of our favorite music, and let our minds change channels from middle school to Mozart or Mariah Carey or Marvin Gay. Before going there, take some time to go back over your day, recalling what went right, what could use improvement, and what appeared at the time to be disastrous. Learn from your own experiences and resolve to grow.

myeducationlab

Go to the Assignments and Activities section of **Topic #16: Professional Responsibilities** in the MyEducationLab for your course and complete the activity entitled "Learning from Each Other."

Learn From Others In our determination to create a community of learners in our classrooms we shouldn't leave ourselves out. We are an essential part of the classroom learning cycle. Sure, we wear the name of teacher, but it's a two-way street—although some days it may feel more like a 20-lane superhighway. We facilitate learning and, in turn, we learn from our students. Remember to include yourself in your community of learners.

A trusting mentoring relationship with an experienced teacher provides many advantages for new teachers.

There is a world of expertise in your building. None of us are perfect in the classroom, but we all have areas where we excel. Some of us are better than others at classroom management techniques, some are masters of class discussion, some use a sense of humor in marvelous ways, some are organized in ways we never dreamed possible. Many of us learn best by observing. We may read about strategies and techniques, but to see a teaching tool and its benefits in action makes it come alive. Teachers have reputations for certain attributes, which are usually apparent if you're observant. If your students come to you excited about a project they are doing in social studies, ask the teacher who assigned the project to explain it to you and reveal his "secrets" for motivating the kids. You may hear students simply say, "Ms. Newton is awesome!" Have a conversation with Ms. Newton. Look for her spirit. If your planning period allows, observe her classroom.

Many school districts have mentor-mentee programs. If you are fortunate enough to have an official mentor, take advantage of opportunities to ask questions, talk through dilemmas, express emotions, and rely on an experienced teacher to provide guidance in trivial, and not so trivial, matters. If you are not assigned a mentor formally, choose a teacher or two who seem to enjoy their jobs and like their students. Tell them you know you have a lot to learn and ask for advice. Most teachers are flattered and are willing to help in any way they can.

STANDARD 7

NMSA

Disposition 6: Middle level teacher candidates are committed to refining classroom and school practices that address the needs of all young adolescents based on research, successful practice, and experience.

Read, Watch, Listen   A wealth of information is available on teaching. Reading "musts" for middle grades teachers are the two journals published by NMSA and discussed in Chapter 1, *Middle School Journal* and *Middle Ground*. The articles are current and practical, and I look forward to the journals arriving monthly in my mailbox. Most schools have institutional memberships in NMSA and should have the journals on hand. Access www.nmsa.org often. You are guaranteed to be a better teacher for it!

Videos are available on the subject of teaching. Pop some popcorn, invite a teacher friend over, and watch a video about teaching practices in the middle school. No, I don't do this on Friday or Saturday nights, or at least not very often. But I do make it a habit every month, or more often. There's so much to learn!

School as a Community of Learners

The section on "Teachers Inside the Classroom" earlier in this chapter was framed around the concept of a community of learners. In "Teachers Outside the Classroom" that followed we explored the adults who inhabit schools. These adults, plus the students, form the potential for a community of learners that encompasses everyone in a middle school.

You will likely encounter efforts to create *Professional Learning Communities,* a phrase popularized by Richard DuFour and others in books such as *Learning by Doing* (2006) and *Whatever It Takes: How Professional Learning Communities Respond When Kids Don't Learn* (2004). A Professional Learning Community (PLC) is composed of teams of educators working collaboratively toward common goals. It's a systemic process in which teachers work interdependently to improve classroom practice.

DuFour and others take us through the need for such a community, the changes necessary to create it, ways to identify the signs of learners coming together as a community, and methods to keep such a community vibrant. Whether part of an organized program or not, it is imperative that we understand the role of an individual teacher in supporting collaborative, collegial learning. Simple things like joining a discussion of curriculum and instruction, talking about solutions to dilemmas rather than just bemoaning their existence, sharing articles that spark your interest with other teachers—these build community and lead to learning.

A phrase I use often is "We are our own best teachers." It's true. When you have middle school teachers sitting around a table, you have collective knowledge and expertise that consultants and special seminars are hard pressed to match. Sometimes it takes a question or prompt to get the conversation going, but once middle level teachers become engaged in a topic, solutions and new ideas are not far behind. Listen, learn, and contribute.

One of the most effective vehicles of learning is the team organization. In middle school we have the privilege of working very closely with teachers with whom we share students. Some of my most valuable learning experiences have resulted from interactions with my teammates. In Chapter 6, we look in-depth at the practice of teaming.

● Formal Staff Development

Schools, school districts, and state departments of education provide staff development opportunities. Some of them are mandated, while others are voluntary. Some of them are very valuable, while others may seem like a waste of time. Even those that are less than thrilling will no doubt put you in situations in which you can interact with other teachers. When that happens, there's potential for learning.

Conferences and special institutes are available to teachers. The intense focus on teaching and learning has great potential, and the sense of camaraderie is inspiring.

Universities in almost every state offer graduate degrees in your content area and/or middle grades education. If you have access to an appropriate graduate program, continuing your formal education may be a viable option.

STANDARD 7

NMSA.

Performance 5: Middle level teacher candidates read professional literature, consult with colleagues, maintain currency with a range of technologies, and seek resources to enhance their professional competence.

> **FIGURE 4.5   Five propositions of accomplished teachers**
>
> 1. Teachers are committed to students and their learning.
> 2. Teachers know the subjects they teach and how to teach those subjects to students.
> 3. Teachers are responsible for managing and monitoring student learning.
> 4. Teachers think systematically about their practice and learn from experience.
> 5. Teachers are members of learning communities.

Source: Reprinted with permission from the National Board for Professional Teaching Standards, *http://www.nbpts.org.* All rights reserved.

National Board Certification was mentioned earlier in this chapter. The *National Board for Professional Teaching Standards (NBPTS)* was formed in 1987. Its purpose is to establish high standards for teachers that cut across state lines where certification requirements vary. The National Board process was always intended to be, and remains, voluntary. It is a nonprofit, nonpartisan organization governed primarily by classroom teachers. The five core propositions of the National Board are listed in Figure 4.5.

Teachers may apply in various categories, which are classified by developmental level and subject area. Early adolescence Certification is available for Generalist plus four subject areas: Mathematics, Science, Social Studies-History, and English Language Arts. To qualify, candidates spend months creating portfolios that include lesson plans, student work samples, assessment measures, and videotapes of their teaching, as well as evidence of their work with colleagues, parents, and communities. Candidates also write extensive commentaries evaluating their goals for instruction, rationales for practice, and effectiveness in the classroom. When this work is complete, they must pass a 6-hour written examination designed to measure knowledge and skills in their certification category.

Rick Wormeli (2001) was in the first group to receive certification. He says that the benefits he appreciates most are those that helped him increase his professionalism and led him to be a better teacher. He learned how to more effectively view and improve his own teaching and how to discuss instruction and assessment in more productive ways. He also experienced greater influence on educational policy as his opinions were sought out by political leaders. Wormeli calls the certification process a "journey to excellence" (p. 186).

Reflections on Being a Middle Level Teacher

We come to the profession of teaching for a variety of reasons and through a variety of paths. We prepare to teach in different ways. There is an abundance of literature on what it means to be a teacher, along with advice on how to be the best teachers we can be. Because there is diversity in our ranks and among our students, reading

myeducationlab

To hear David Wooten, the 2008 Pennsylvania Teacher of the Year, tell us that he is a teacher because of the influence of his own teachers who inspired him, go to the Teacher Talk section of **Topic #1: Schools and Teaching Today** in the MyEducationLab for your course.

about and meeting teachers who appear to excel in diverse ways is valuable. If we desire to grow professionally, we must continually assess our own strengths and weaknesses, and seek professional development.

In the May 2001 issue of *Educational Leadership*, Jamie Sawatzky (Tell, 2001, p. 18) reflects on his entrance into the teaching profession. His sincere words as a new seventh grade U.S. History teacher speak volumes. Listen with both your head and your heart.

I noticed the change in myself the first time I walked into my classroom. I was no longer Jamie. That was the name of the young man who had delivered pizzas or worked at the office. My new found teaching life had metamorphosed me into "Mr. Sawatzky." My previous work experiences had taught me a variety of skills, but accepting the title of teacher brings with it responsibilities that do not appear on most job descriptions. Walking through the classroom door has cast me into a world where I am charged with the awesome responsibility of sculpting young minds and preparing students for positive participation in their community.

When asked why they entered the profession, many teachers respond, "I wanted a chance to make a positive change in the world." In my case, perhaps selfishly, I wanted to be in a profession that would make a positive change in me. With my first year of teaching about to conclude, I can say that I am happy to be a teacher and happy to be "Mr. Sawatzky."

► Meet the Teachers

Let's get to know nine teachers. They are real teachers, but some of their circumstances have been altered in these profiles. Their backgrounds, personal attributes, education, teaching styles, and attitudes mirror teachers I have known. We will meet the teachers now and learn from their experiences in the Professional Practice sections to come. They will interact with one another, with other teachers, and with the students you met in Chapters 2 and 3 and other students, as well as administrators, community members, and parents. As with the students we have met, pictures of the teachers are provided so you will feel even better acquainted with them. Beginning in Chapter 5 they talk directly to you in a feature called "Teachers Speak." Here's who we meet:

- Jermaine Joyner, 6th/7th/8th grade technology, African American, age 31
- Sadie Fox, 8th grade science, Caucasian American, age 26
- Keith Richardson, 6th grade language arts, Caucasian American, age 40
- Carmen Esparza, 6th/7th/8th grade bilingual language arts and social studies, Hispanic American, age 34

(Continued)

- Jesse White, 8th grade social studies, Caucasian American, age 29
- Traci Peters, 7th grade math, Caucasian American, age 36
- Deirdre McGrew, 6th/7th/8th grade remedial language arts and social studies, African American, age 48
- Joey Huber, 7th grade student teacher, Caucasian American, age 22
- Sarah Gardner, 6th grade student teacher, Caucasian American, age 21

● Jermaine Joyner

This is my fourth year working in a public school. Right after I got my degree in computer science I went to work for a large chain store and made house calls with *Geek* on my name badge. After a year or so I was unhappy with my job and decided to teach computer classes at a private school. After qualifying for state certification, I took a position at Jefferson Middle School, an inner-city school that was converted to a magnet school in the mid-1990s. I am almost finished with my master's degree in administration and I would really like to be an assistant principal here in a few years.

Jefferson's magnet status is based on technology. We have laptop carts, handheld computers, 30 iPods, and 30 video cameras. This year we made our goal of a SmartBoard in each classroom. Students apply to Jefferson and are chosen by lottery. Those who apply must have at least a C average and a good attendance record. We have been able to attract quite a few kids from the suburbs. Those from the neighborhood around the school qualify for free lunch. The kids from the suburbs are wealthy enough to have private transportation to get here from outside the city. Actually, I think the mix works.

I am the computer teacher and I teach six 45-minute periods a day, two for each grade level. Computer science is a related arts course, and all the kids take it for one semester a year. I'm able to build on what they know and can do from 6th to 7th to 8th grade. My job at Jefferson gives me lots of room to be creative. Two years ago I took a back room in the library and turned it into a TV station. It fits right in with our technology focus. I wrote grants and checked with the district and other schools trying to obtain all the equipment we would need to do daily student broadcasts. Now I have a small group of kids who come to me before and after school as the Broadcast Club. We tape a daily broadcast shown each morning. Makes my day!

● Sadie Fox

You know, I had a lot of careers from which to choose. In college I thought about law school and pre-med. I know I could have been an attorney or a medical doctor, but I'm not. I chose, instead, to spend my days with kids and I love it! They are quirky and unpredictable. Watching them grow is a delight.

I translated my love of science into teaching the subject to kids who often don't seem to care very much. My challenge is to catch them enjoying some aspect of a lesson and then get them hooked by doing something just a little off the wall. Some of them get so interested that they begin to ask questions. My standard answer is, "Hey when you find out, share it with us." That sends them to the Internet or to the library. It's great.

I guess I've always been pretty competitive. I began a science club at Valley View four years ago when I first started teaching. It grew quickly as we entered a Science Olympiad competition, and we won! We continued to win and made it to the national level. Each year since, we have excelled. For a rural area with people scattered over almost 1500 square miles with only a few places to shop and eat, having a team of 8th graders win national science competitions . . . well, let's just say that the kids enjoy near rock star status.

Since I started teaching at Valley View I have finished a master's degree in science education and achieved National Board Certification. It's been a lot of work, but totally worth it. One of these days I plan to go back to graduate school and get a Ph.D. I think I would enjoy teaching at the university level.

● Keith Richardson

Right out of high school I went to a community college and, as I worked in a local restaurant, completed an associate's degree. That qualified me for a job in a textile mill where my dad and his dad worked for years. I got the job I wanted and got married at age 20. I received several promotions and had two kids. The problem was that I wasn't very satisfied with how I was spending my days. I left the house at 7 A.M. and often didn't get home until 6:00 in the evening. I was often asked to work swing shifts when someone called in sick. With two weeks of vacation a year and my sons growing quickly, I started reconsidering my choices.

I decided to go back to college and get a 4-year degree so I could teach middle or high school language arts. This decision wasn't really based on the time constraints of my job at the mill. I was always an avid reader and often wrote short stories for fun. I have taught Sunday School since I was a teenager and was often told I was a natural for getting people to understand things. As a teacher, the dilemma of not enough time with my family was solved. This was a decision I could live with!

I think I fit middle school. I'm patient, I can laugh at myself, and kids seem to like my easy-going style. I get restless with traditional instruction, and I know the students do, too. I try to keep them hopping by doing active things. They read anything they want during DEAR (Drop Everything And Read). The catch is that they have to tell the class about what they are reading twice every nine weeks, and they can't do regular book reports. They come up with some pretty crazy stuff, but the bottom line is, *they read!*

(Continued)

• Carmen Esparza

I'm a second generation American. My parents came to the U.S. when they were teenagers. They made a lot of sacrifices so my three brothers and I could have all the opportunities we enjoy today. We were born in Colorado and, therefore, are U.S. citizens. My oldest brother and I went to Colorado State. He is an engineer, and I majored in Spanish and minored in secondary education. After teaching high school Spanish for a few years near Denver, I went back to school and got a master's degree in English. I read a lot about bilingual education and made the decision to pursue a position in a middle school. I guess there aren't many of us around with degrees in both Spanish and English and I got a job right away. About that time I became pregnant. When my baby girl was born, I decided to be a stay-at-home mom for a while. Three babies later, I am back!

Teaching whole classes of English language learners is exhausting. I teach both language arts and social studies, about half in Spanish and half in English. I teach all the kids who need bilingual education grades 6–8, each grade level in a separate class. The trick is to engage the students in their own learning and use lots of visuals.

The longer I teach the more the reality sinks in that I can't "save" kids by myself. I can influence them and maybe help a few stay in school, but it's an uphill battle when I consider the strikes against them. Many aren't citizens and live in fear of being sent back to Mexico or Central America. I try to stay positive and help my kids get to the place where they have choices in life.

• Jesse White

I've been teaching for six years, all of them at Lincoln Middle School. I taught 7th grade science the first two years, and then a social studies position opened on the 8th grade Wildcats team. I jumped at the chance to be on a team with a couple of teachers I not only admired, but who stepped in and served as informal mentors to me. I've been here ever since, and I'm quite happy with what I do.

Lincoln is a Title I school. We have mostly Black and Hispanic students, and most get free breakfast and lunch. They almost all live within walking distance of the school. Funny thing . . . they're never really anxious to leave campus. During the day they often act like school is the last place they want to be, but then they stick around after school. I made a commitment my first year to be a teacher who's always accessible, so I stick around, too. If I'm going to be here anyway, I figure I might as well help with the football and soccer teams. So I help coach and find that I get to talk with kids on the field who rarely participate in class. It's a good outreach for me. I rarely get home before 6:00, but, if I worked in business or industry, I would have about the same length of workday. The difference is that once I get home, sometimes I'm not really finished with my work.

One thing I really appreciate about teaching on a team is team planning time. We teach three 90-minute blocks, with one block for planning, 45 minutes for individual planning and 45 minutes with my team. As the social studies teacher, I find that I can integrate all kinds of things into American history. When we talk about our teaching plans for the week, I can often support what's happening in language arts by emphasizing what's being taught. For instance, if they are learning about poetry, I find poems written in the period of history we're studying. If I can find something about an invention that goes along with the science curriculum, I throw it in. I like making connections. We still haven't done a true interdisciplinary unit. That's one of my goals for next year.

• Traci Peters

I'm a 7th grade math teacher, and I can't imagine doing anything else. I loved math as a student, but planned to teach elementary school. Well, I ended up in a middle school math classroom, and I'm so glad because it suits me. I enjoy organization and being prepared. These two qualities serve me well with my two algebra classes and two pre-algebra classes. I have a super team to work with. We all like each other and that makes going to work fun! And, of course, the kids make it fun, too, and also sometimes very frustrating. But that's OK. Overall, it's the best job anywhere. I have National Board certification and that has added to my income and my sense of professionalism.

I am married to a wonderful man who supports me in my career. I have a beautiful son who isn't in school yet. That's the one negative thing about teaching, but my mom takes care of Robbie for me and probably would throw a fit if I hinted at staying at home. I'm very fortunate.

Most of my students do really well on standardized tests. It's hard to show a lot of progress in three of my classes because their scores are already good. The students I have in 7th grader algebra and pre-algebra are the ones who achieve at math. My fourth class is a mix of students who have never excelled in math and those who have recently come to the U.S.

Our school is in a fairly well-to-do suburb, and most of the parents of my algebra and pre-algebra students are college educated. All the technology gadgets out there are likely in the hands of my students. They take to graphing calculators naturally. But when it comes to basic math concepts, I still rely on a whiteboard and an overhead projector. I use as many manipulatives as possible, like pattern blocks and paper folding. My philosophy is that experiencing math is the way to go.

• Deirdre McGrew

Teaching is my fourth career. I started out as a journalist. Then I went to work for a publishing house, and then I became an associate minister at my church. Along the way I got two master's degrees, a husband, and five children! Quite a life, don't you think?

I've taught elementary school and both language arts and social studies in middle school. When my principal heard about what some schools were doing to meet the needs of kids at risk

(*Continued*)

for failing, she started thinking about how we could adapt the plan at Cario. We don't have a real large population of kids at risk, but we are always looking for new ways to reach them. Because my principal knows what a soft spot I have for kids who struggle, she suggested that we think about starting CARE, Cario Academic Recovery and Enrichment. I have a group of 12–15 students in grades 6–8 for half a day for language arts and social studies, and a colleague has 12–15 students in grades 6–8 for half a day for math and science. We switch kids at lunch.

Through CARE we can make instruction very personalized. I have eight computers to use with the Scholastic Read 180 program. I do whole group instruction on basic skills for just a little while each day. Then the kids read and work on projects that combine the language arts and social studies standards. I am able to spend individual time with each student each day. I can see regular progress. Makes it worth the planning and effort!

Will I teach for the rest of my career? I honestly don't know. Life is full of surprises, and I'm always open to them.

● Joey Huber

I'm a student teacher. I have to keep saying it to believe it! I'm a student teacher. Most of my friends are business majors and have no idea what they'll do when we graduate. They're thinking maybe they'll need to go to graduate school to get a job in their fields. They've done internships, and most dreaded getting up in the morning to go. But not me! I love being a teacher! To be in my school all day every day for 16 weeks, I had to give up playing college baseball. I had a partial scholarship for the first seven semesters of college, but gave it up for one semester to be in the classroom. No regrets!

When I did some field work at my school, I figured I needed to befriend my students. I wanted to be their buddy and I accomplished it. But that wasn't smart, as I soon found out. There's a line teachers can't cross and still be the *teacher*. I'll tell you more about this later.

At my school the 6th graders are divided into teams with just two teachers. The 7th and 8th grade teams have 3 teachers on them. We have a math teacher, a language arts teacher, and a teacher who teaches science and social studies on a rotating basis. There are 86 kids on the starfish team. Our classes are heterogeneous, with some really high achievers, some with IEPs, and lots in between. My cooperating teachers are different from each other, but they each seem to reach the kids in unique ways.

After school I am an assistant coach of the baseball team. This is one of the best experiences I have ever had that more than makes up for not playing the game myself. I can teach them all I know and demonstrate how to play. I know that when I teach I want to coach as well.

● Sarah Gardner

I always knew I wanted to be a teacher. I was in Teacher Cadets in high school and went to college knowing that teaching was in my future. I loved the classes and now I am crazy about student teaching! I am assigned to a 6th grade team with two wonderful cooperating teachers. They are very responsive to the students, and I know I will learn so much from them. Half the students on our team are in the AIG program for academically and intellectually gifted students. The other half are considered regular learners, most of whom make adequate progress, but aren't designated AIG.

I will teach math and social studies for eight weeks, and then language arts and science for eight weeks. Math is really my favorite subject, but, because my certification will be in all the subjects for K–6, I need to experience all the areas. My plan is to teach middle school next year, though. I understand that I can take the Praxis II exams in math and maybe language arts and then be able to teach 7th and 8th grade in these subjects.

Something that bothers me a lot is that when we have the AIG classes we have mostly White students. When we have the other students, we have diversity. Everything I learned in my classes in college tells me that this is a problem. I remember learning about what's called the *soft bigotry of low expectations*. My question is "How has this happened?" When I ask my cooperating teachers they say it seems to have been this way for their whole careers. By the time students get to middle school, they have been labeled as AIG or not. I don't mean to say that average achievers are not succeeding. If they are working hard and making progress, then they are succeeding. But did these students' elementary teachers not expect them to be really bright? Would I have done any better? I'm starting to think about going to graduate school to learn more about gifted education. I'm interested in figuring out some answers to my questions.

GROUP ACTIVITIES

1. To your school files, add the number of teachers for each school. School offices can give you this information. If possible, find out how many teach in each broad area—core subjects (math, language arts, science, social studies), related arts (P.E., art, music, etc.), and special education. These numbers can be estimates. Compare the ratios of teachers to the information on total number of students collected in Chapter 3.

2. Designate someone in your class to find information on your state NMSA affiliate. As a class, write a letter or send an e-mail to the organization asking for information concerning membership and activities if the affiliate doesn't have a website.

3. In Chapter 2 you considered how middle level students are portrayed in the electronic media. Now consider how movies and television shows portray teachers. As a class, brainstorm all the instances you can think of in current or past productions. Are the majority of portrayals positive or negative? Do any appear to be realistic and, if so, in what ways?

INDIVIDUAL ACTIVITIES

1. At what point in your life did you decide to be a teacher? Was it an "Ah-ha!" moment or a gradual realization? Be prepared to share your answers with other teacher candidates.

2. Briefly explain in your own words what the phrase "thriving versus surviving" means for middle grades teachers.

3. Pretend that the school at which you teach has recently received some very bad publicity involving unethical behavior of a teacher. What is your responsibility in terms of school image when you meet and are questioned by community members at the mall, in church, at a soccer game, etc.?

4. Why is an attitude of "I can't wait until graduation. No more learning for me!" inappropriate for teacher candidates?

PERSONAL JOURNAL

1. Reread the Haim Ginott quote at the beginning of the "Characteristics of Effective Middle Level Teachers" section. How do Ginott's words affect you? Reflect on the implications for teacher responsibility.

2. Refer to Figure 4.3. Think about a "good" teacher from your days in middle school. Which of the characteristics listed apply to this teacher? Now think of a "not-so-good" teacher you had in middle school. Which of the characteristics apply to this teacher?

3. Do you recall a teacher who did an exceptional job of what Lounsbury calls "wayside teaching"? Write about how the teacher accomplished this.

Professional Practice

(It would be helpful to reread the description of Emily in Chapter 3.)

Joey Huber is in his sixth week of student teaching at Madison Middle School with teachers Ms. Lawson, Mr. Jenkins, and Ms. Moore. He's fascinated with the different styles of teaching and unique personalities of his cooperating teachers. Even with their differences, their personalities mesh and they get the job done, from what Joey can observe. Ms. Lawson brings over 20 years of middle school teaching experience to the mix and is a real math whiz. She obviously loves the subject, and kids recognize this.

Mr. Jenkins brings a good-natured "granddad" sense to the team. He teaches both science and social studies and works hard at making connections among the topics in both subjects. Kids rotate between the two subjects each nine weeks. Because the blocks of teaching time are 90 minutes, and they take science and social studies for a total of a semester each, kids get only half as much science and social studies as math and language arts which are taught daily all year. Ms. Moore brings extensive knowledge of American literature to the team and teaches language arts. This is her fourth year in middle school after

12 years of teaching high school literature. What Joey brings to the team, along with his enthusiasm, is explicit preparation for teaching young adolescents from a middle grades college teacher preparation program.

● Joey Huber

Joey is already teaching math and will begin teaching social studies in a week. Then he will pick up language arts. At the 9-week change he'll trade social studies with science.

Joey is very impressed with the way Ms. Moore plans lessons around literature. She carefully outlines her lectures, questions, and student prompts. Her expectations are high for her students. She puts thought and effort into what happens in the classroom.

Joey hates to criticize Ms. Moore, but, for all her careful planning, she doesn't seem to enjoy students outside the classroom. In a grade-level meeting last semester when Joey was just observing as part of a field experience, he heard the three 7th grade teams talking about how all teachers need to be in the halls between classes. Ms. Moore still doesn't see this as part of her responsibilities.

The students notice the difference between Ms. Moore and the other team teachers. They enjoy their language arts/reading class with her, but are aware that she doesn't participate in their world outside the class. She will smile at them in the hall, but her enthusiasm for young adolescents just doesn't carry over.

Emily ● seventh grade

Emily, a younger-than-most, shy 7th grade girl, has noticed that Ms. Moore's enthusiasm ends at the classroom door. After a year in middle school speech therapy, her confidence has grown some, but Emily still hesitates to speak in class. She has

responded very well, however, to Joey. His genuine love of kids and what he's doing makes him very approachable. Emily confided one afternoon that she thinks Ms. Moore is unfriendly because of her speech impediment. He assured her that her notion was absolutely not correct. A friend overheard the conversation and jumped in to say that Ms. Moore had taken a personal interest and helped her through a rough time.

1. Joey is concerned by Ms. Moore's apparent unwillingness to participate in her students' lives outside the classroom. Which of the following represents the least important reason for his concern?
   a. Students are sensitive to interactions with teachers, and Ms. Moore is offending some of them who notice her lack of interest outside the classroom.
   b. The other teacher team members are not pleased with Ms. Moore's reticence to pull her weight outside the classroom. It is a source of team discontent.
   c. Joey is not getting the full benefit of Ms. Moore as a role model and may be at risk for adopting a similar attitude toward students outside the classroom.
   d. Ms. Moore is missing out on teachable moments that happen between classes and in the lunchroom, and the students are missing out on lessons in life she might be teaching them.

2. In his middle grades program at the university, Joey learned about what John Lounsbury calls "wayside teaching." Which of the following is the most important reason for extending our lessons beyond the classroom door?
   a. We all need to adhere to the duty roster as designated by the administration.
   b. Middle grades students are learning about life inside and outside our classrooms.
   c. Part of the fulfillment of teaching is embodied in our relationships with students.

    d. The presence of teachers in the hallways helps the flow of student traffic and reduces between class disturbances.

3. Emily is obviously disturbed by Ms. Moore's lack of involvement with students outside the classroom. Using what we know about young adolescent development, how could Joey best address the situation?

    a. Remind Emily that according to her friend, Ms. Moore involved herself in positive ways in her life.

    b. Talk with both Ms. Lawson and Mr. Jenkins and convey what he observes, as well as Emily's comments.

    c. Because he has a good relationship with Ms. Moore, he could ask her about her view of responsibilities inside and outside the classroom in an effort to understand her behavior.

    d. Encourage Emily to talk to other students and organize a group to confront Ms. Moore.

Constructed Response

Joey Huber is very satisfied with his student teaching experience, but is still bothered by Ms. Moore's demeanor outside the classroom. Keeping NCATE Standard 8, Disposition 7 in mind (Middle level teacher candidates value collegiality as an integral part of their professional practices), briefly describe an approach Joey might take if he chooses to speak with Ms. Moore concerning wayside teaching.

INTERNET RESOURCES

Education World

http://educationworld.com

This large site has a section called First-Year Teachers. The section contains more than 100 subsections addressing the needs and apprehensions of new teachers. In addition, there are helpful strategies for planning the first days of school, organizing a classroom, communicating with parents, and much more.

National Board for Professional Teaching Standards (NBPTS)

www.nbpts.org

The NBPTS is a nonprofit organization responsible for the first nationally recognized standards for teachers. This site details the levels and subject areas in which board certification is possible, and provides specific information for teachers interested in applying for national board certification.

National Education Association (NEA) Resources for Teachers

www.nea.org

NEA is the largest national teacher union, with affiliate organizations in each state. Their mission is to advance the cause of public education. This site provides information on resources available to teachers, as well as information on current education issues and legislative efforts.

Public Education Network (PEN)

www.publiceducation.org

PEN is a nonprofit organization with the mission of promoting quality education for all children. Teachers can sign up to receive weekly updates on current issues in education with links to numerous articles on a wide variety of topics.

Teach for America

www.teachforamerica.org

Teach for America is a national corps of recent college graduates and professionals of all academic majors and career interests who commit two years to teach in urban and rural public schools and become leaders in the effort to expand educational opportunity.

5 Societal Context of Middle Level Education

The societal context of middle level education is both positive and negative at the same time. Some events and circumstances result in growth and happiness, while others present challenges that must either be confronted and overcome, or managed through coping skills. The more we understand about the societal context of our students, the better equipped we will be to celebrate the positive, and help correct or compensate for the negative.

there's a saying that goes "We cannot control the wind, but we can adjust our sails." Teachers recognize the social issues that negatively affect our students are complex and multidimensional. They don't begin with us, and most won't be completely resolved through us. However, with that reality in view, we can begin to focus on positive steps to prevent and/or halt risky behaviors and their impact on children and adolescents. Controlling the wind may not be within our reach, but adjusting our own, and our students', sails, is indeed possible.

Powell, 2009, p. 317

CHAPTER PREVIEW

Suburban, Urban, and Rural Settings
- Suburban Setting
- Urban Setting
- Rural Setting

Bullying
- The Harm of Bullying
- Gender Differences in Bullying
- Lesbian/Gay/Bisexual/Transgender Bullying
- Target Kids
- The Bystander

Technology and Young Adolescents
- Cyberbullying

Poverty and Schooling
- Need for Qualified Teachers

English Language Learners
- Variability among Students
- Programs Designed for ELL Students

Wellness Issues
- Substance Abuse
- Sexuality-Related Issues
- Childhood Obesity

Reflections on the Societal Context of Middle Level Education

INTRODUCTION

Each generation considers itself unique. And every generation is. To say that the current societal context of middle level education is unlike any other is true. The 21st century is well underway, ushered in by the Columbine tragedy of 1999, followed closely by September 11, 2001, a date that defines much of the political and social climate in which we live today. Protracted wars, economic upheaval, the fast-paced lives of both adults and children, our rapidly changing American population . . . all contribute to the societal context of education. We are told that students need a new 21st century skill set to function productively, contribute positively, and succeed. In Chapter 12 we look more closely at these new skills. Keep in mind that the 21st century skill set does not replace traditional skills but, instead, builds on them.

The societal context of our students' lives includes lots of positive aspects—a supportive family for many, community opportunities, higher education possibilities, and the rapidly expanding information highway, to name a few. Other societal aspects are, obviously, not so positive and include significant challenges. The topics in this chapter are not treated equally in terms of length and detail. Each can be explored as your interests lead. We begin by considering the impact of where students live, including suburban, urban, and rural settings. As a follow-up to Chapter 3 in which we talked about diversity among young adolescents, we explore bullying, a pervasive and ever-present part of many young adolescents' lives. Then we briefly look at how technology impacts young adolescents, along with the newest kind of bullying, cyberbullying. We then consider how poverty affects learners and learning. Next we discuss English language learners and the challenges associated with meeting their needs. We conclude the chapter with a discussion of wellness issues. This is not a "happy" chapter, but one that's necessary. Let's stick together through these less-than-positive topics and think about how we can make a difference concerning each issue.

STANDARD 1

Knowledge 7: Middle level teacher candidates understand that the development of all young adolescents occurs in the context of classrooms, families, peer groups, communities and society.

STANDARD 5

Performance 6: Middle level teacher candidates establish equitable, caring, and productive learning environments for all young adolescents.

STANDARD 6

Performance 2: Middle level teacher candidates act as advocates for all young adolescents in the school and in the larger community.

Suburban, Urban, and Rural Settings

**Young Adolescent
Diversity**

Where kids live and go to school shapes their experiences in many ways. There's nothing we can do about where kids grow up, but if inequities exist because of location we can try to correct them and/or compensate. The three principal settings of schools are suburban, urban, and rural. Suburban settings are generally on the outskirts of cities or small-to-medium sized towns. They typically have distinct neighborhoods or subdivisions. Urban areas are large cities with downtowns in the center. Rural areas are communities with lots of open spaces and limited retail (U.S. Census Bureau, 2002).

Suburban schools account for 46% of all public schools. Urban schools make up 25% of the schools, with rural schools accounting for 31% (National Center for Education Statistics, 2003). Let's look first at suburban schools.

STANDARD 6

NMSA

Knowledge 3: Middle level teacher candidates understand the challenges that families may encounter in contemporary society and are knowledgeable about support services and other resources that are available to assist them.

● Suburban Setting

Most kids who attend suburban schools live in single-family homes or in apartment complexes. There are generally lawns, schools, churches, recreational options, shopping malls, and well-lighted streets and sidewalks.

The school experiences of students in suburban settings include attendance at neighborhood schools with the friends on their block. Even with the increasing mobility of our society, many students in suburbs attend K–12 with the same kids. They may move to a different house, but the chances are pretty good that their schools will be stable. Most suburban schools offer afterschool options, some for fun and others for extra help with school work. There is a sense of safety and continuity that perhaps isn't prominent in urban settings.

Even in tough financial times, suburban schools provide the necessities for learning. Facilities are maintained. Parents and communities pull together and provide those things not considered necessities like band uniforms, afterschool sports, field trips, and so on . . . the stuff that so often hooks kids and keeps them in school.

In education we are fond of saying "Kids are kids are kids." By this we mean that they are alike in so many ways. And that's true. But for many students, life in urban schools presents challenges suburban kids may never face.

● Urban Setting

What I write about urban schools are generalizations, just as they are about suburban schools. The difference is that the picture painted of suburban schools tends to not offend. By generalizing about urban settings and schools, I run the risk of offending those who live and learn in them. This is not my intent.

Urban schools are usually older facilities with common problems concerning heating/cooling, restroom sanitation, limited parking, vandalism, and so on. Almost half of the students who attend urban schools do so with the majority of their classmates living in homes plagued with poverty (Urban Schools, 2000). As we've discussed, schools with the majority of students living in poverty receive extra government funding. This is research-supported because it takes more resources to provide education for students in disadvantaged settings. Is it enough? Obviously not, since achievement levels among students in urban settings generally fall well below those of students in suburban and rural settings (U.S. General Accounting Office, 2002).

The kids who attend urban schools may live in crowded apartment buildings and/or government project housing. They may have unstable home lives that often accompany poverty. They may find themselves in dangerous situations simply by walking on the streets that lead to their schools. We discuss poverty more in the next section as part of the societal context of middle level education.

Some urban schools have been converted into magnet schools, as discussed in Chapter 6. With intriguing themes, the promise of specialization, and the draw of expert teachers and perhaps small, specialized classes, some urban magnet schools have successfully recruited kids from suburban and rural areas, creating a healthy diversity among students. Two of our focus students, DeVante and Kim, attend Jefferson Middle School, an urban magnet. Read more about them in **See How They Grow**.

Going to school in a large city is quite different from going to school in a rural setting. Let's explore rural settings next.

▶ See How They Grow

DeVante and Kim • eighth grade

If you look back in Chapter 3 at DeVante and Kim as sixth graders, you'll see how much they have grown by 8th grade. While attending Jefferson Middle School, an urban magnet school for technology and communication, DeVante and Kim became good friends. She first approached DeVante as a "bad boy" she needed to "fix." By 7th grade she was viewing him as an intelligent, charismatic buddy. Through Kim, and several other students and teachers, DeVante began to see life as full of possibilities, and that he wasn't destined to join a gang and live in the conditions in which he had grown up. Kim and her "Cosby-like" family introduced him to the possibilities of college and careers. By 8th grade DeVante and Kim were almost inseparable.

● Rural Setting

In communities where kids live in very small towns, or are perhaps scattered across large areas of land, there may be K–12 schools out of necessity with fewer than 100 students. In Alaska, 20% of schools have three or fewer teachers. In Montana,

70% of the schools are rural. While most rural schools are small, some are actually as large as suburban and urban schools. Students may be bused to very large K–2, 3–4, 5–6, 7–8, and 9–12 schools, some as large as 1000 students per grade span.

Rural areas tend to be fairly stable, with the possibility of increasingly large populations of migrant farm families who may move with the season. This is a particularly challenging situation for some rural educators. When we talk about English language learners later in the chapter, you'll see why this is a dilemma.

Some of the other challenges of rural schools include the relative isolation of students and the resulting lack of the various forms of diversity (cultural, social, etc.). It may also be difficult to hire new teachers, many of whom want more social and graduate educational opportunities than many rural areas offer. It may also be harder to provide extracurricular opportunities for kids in widespread locations. Bus transportation may be difficult to arrange and pay for. Small schools may find it challenging to offer a wide range of courses because of lack of teacher expertise and few students having the same interests.

Rural settings have a number of advantages. With stable populations there may be a real sense of community and continuity. In smaller schools teachers and students may know each other better. The school may be the center of community life, with families involved in athletics, spelling bees, school carnivals, and so on. In many rural settings, the teachers sense that they are really extended family to students. They know parents and grandparents and often watch children grow through elementary, middle, and high school. They cheer them on through college. Yes, it sounds idyllic, but it's the reality of many living in rural areas. Remember that again we are dealing in generalities. Not all rural settings mirror Mayberry. (If this reference eludes you, try watching reruns of *The Andy Griffith Show*. Ron Howard wasn't always a famous director!)

STANDARD 2

Disposition 4: Middle level teacher candidates are committed to developmentally responsive and socially equitable teaching, learning, and schooling in a variety of organizational settings.

STANDARD 3

Performance 3: Middle level teacher candidates incorporate the ideas, interests, and experiences of all young adolescents in curriculum.

MAKE A DIFFERENCE

You may spend your entire career in one setting. Or you may have a chance to teach in two or three. Even though what you have just read is an overview, you will likely find parts that hold true for each setting. We know they are not alike. Our responsibility as teachers is to provide the most effective learning opportunities possible for our students, regardless of where we are.

Advocate for kids, wherever you may teach. That advocacy may look different based on circumstances. Be sensitive to needs and be vocal about what you, the school, the district, and the state need to do to make opportunities for learning and growing available for your students.

We now turn our attention to a societal issue that transcends home and educational settings. Bullying happens in the suburbs, the inner city, and in rural areas all across our country.

Bullying

Let's begin with what bullying is . . . and what it is not. Bullying is aggression with intent to harm; it is about exerting power over another person. Bullying is using this power in a relationship where one person (the bully) hurts and humiliates another (the bullied), often to the indifference or amusement of those who watch (the bystander). Bullying is not a rite of passage, nor an expectation of growing up. Bullying

PEARSON
myeducationlab

Go to the Assignments and Activities section of **Topic #1: Schools and Teaching Today** in the MyEducationLab for your course and complete the activity entitled "Eliminating Bullying in School."

does not include spontaneous acts that arise in particular circumstances; it is willful and intentional. "Bullying is a life-and-death issue that we ignore at our children's peril" (Coloroso, 2003). "Bullying is a weapon of people driven by the need for power. Bullying can be a single interaction—verbal, physical, or emotional—but it is always crafted to cause fear and to exert power" (White-Hood, 2006, p. 30).

Middle school kids know about bullying. They see it in the halls, in the cafeteria, on the playground, and, unfortunately, right under our noses in the classroom. Many experience bullying through the Internet in the form of cyberbullying. In fact, almost twice as many middle school kids experience bullying as do their elementary and high school counterparts (U.S. Department of Justice, 2005).

Bullying may be physical aggression in the form of slapping, kicking, bumping, or shoving. It may relate to possessions and involve vandalizing or stealing. Or bullying may be verbal in the form of taunting, gossip, or talking about students behind their backs or online. Young adolescents are daily faced with the possibility of being a target of bullying, and/or being a bystander. And obviously some choose to be the bully. No one is immune from involvement. This inevitability doesn't mean that it's OK to just let it happen. Because school, and middle school in particular, is where social interactions continually occur and self-concepts are formed and reformed, it is the place where students must learn civility and what it means to be humane.

The Harm of Bullying

We can imagine why bullying is harmful. But statistics take what we intuitively know and bring the very real consequences of bullying to our consciousness. Let's consider a few.

- Both bullies and their victims are more likely to engage in substance abuse.
- Victims of bullies have fewer friends and are prone to depression.

- Bullies are 4 times more likely to engage in criminal behavior by age 24.
- About 20% of those who are bullied experience severe negative psychological reactions with long-term effects.
- 60% of boys classified as bullies are convicted of at least one crime by age 24.
- Absenteeism may often be related to the avoidance of bullies.
- Kids who are bullied will not learn as much as they otherwise would. (Lemonick, 2005; *Stop Bullying Now*, 2004; Kass, Evans, & Shah, 2003)

In "The Under-Appreciated Role of Humiliation in the Middle School," authors Frey and Fisher (2008) report that when a large sample of teachers and students were asked about the causes of humiliation, the most common topic raised was bullying. When asked about the effects of being bullied, many talked about the deep level of shame it caused, as well as behaviors that were either violent or avoidant. In extreme cases, reactions to bullying have included suicide.

Gender Differences in Bullying

Young Adolescent Diversity

Both boys and girls are bullies and/or victims, and there are generalizations we can make about each. But when it comes to verbal bullying, they do it about equally (Coloroso 2003). Verbal bullying amounts to name-calling. It may be done quietly in a whisper or yelled on the field. It is a quick way for a bully to powerfully use words to hurt a victim. Racial slurs, sexual innuendo, cruel jokes aimed at hurting feelings, taunts such as "retard," "fag," and "geek" will continue if not dealt with by adults, and could possibly lead to even more severe forms of bullying.

Boys tend to use physical bullying more than girls. It's more visible than other forms. Choking, punching, pinching, tearing clothes, breaking or stealing possessions—these forms of bullying are used by boys who are older or bigger or who have more social capital than their victims. Girls who engage in physical bullying are most often the larger girls who tend to be louder and dependent on fear to hold onto others as companions.

Relational bullying, most often practiced by girls, is the "systematic diminishment of a bullied child's sense of self through ignoring, isolating, excluding, or shunning" behaviors (Coloroso, 2003, p. 17). What a list! I feel bad just writing the words. Imagine having these things done to you. Maybe they have been.

Socially aggressive behavior involved in relational bullying may be just as harmful, or more so, than physical bullying (Pollock, 2006). Facial expressions alone can be a devastatingly effective bullying tactic. Girls are often very sensitive to a particular look that tells them in no uncertain terms that they are not welcome at a table in the cafeteria. Emotional games that girls play that result in hurt feelings and make themselves appear powerful leave lasting scars on the girls who fall victim.

Relational bullying is a kind of psychological warfare and, therefore, is often hard to detect. Victims are often hesitant to tell anyone, much less accuse a classmate. Ratting on a peer is often forbidden in the social order of early adolescence.

Lesbian/Gay/Bisexual/Transgender Bullying

A recent survey found that almost 80% of teenagers questioned say they hear on a regular basis verbal bullying of kids thought to be homosexual (Brown University Child and Adolescent Behavior Letter, 2003). As reported in Pollock (2006), words such as *fag* and *homo* are used to taunt the approximately 3,000,000 people between the ages of 10 and 20 who are either bisexual or homosexual.

Lesbian/Gay/Bisexual/Transgender (LGBT) youth are at high risk of being victims of bullying. They often have nowhere to turn if they are not accepted in their own homes, and then are bullied in school. Renold (2002) tells us that, when kids don't mirror what's accepted in society as normal, they become more prone to being bullied, often suffering isolation, verbal abuse, and humiliation. Pollock (2006) advises us to explore our own biases as teachers and be sensitive to sexual orientation issues.

Target Kids

Everyone has a right to be treated with dignity, no matter how he or she fits in, or doesn't fit in, with others. Kids who are targets of bullies may be passive, physically weak/unattractive, have low self-concepts, be socially unskilled, cognitively/academically gifted, lesbian, gay . . . or maybe just new to the area. Targets come in all shapes and sizes, all races and ethnicities. Young adolescents often are convinced that there's nothing that can be done about bullying. We need to show them that they're wrong. Boynton and Boynton (2005, p. 164) recommend that we teach those who are bullied to

- relax and consider the options
- say "stop" and walk away
- stand by an adult
- bore the bully

Some student behaviors and mannerisms make them more likely to be targets of bullying. While we don't want to harm a student's self-concept by telling him to stop acting in ways that may seem very natural to him, we also don't want the target status to continue. Teacher-student relationships that include respect and trust help us talk with students in ways that can help, not harm, their sense of self.

- use humor
- act like you don't notice the bullying
- agree with everything the bully says and walk away
- tell a teacher

The Bystander

We are all bystanders. We have all seen bullying in progress and done nothing . . . if not as adults, then certainly as kids. It's understandable that 12-year-olds would perhaps watch and then turn away out of fear of being called names and ostracized, or out of a sense of helplessness. But for adults, it's unforgivable.

Again we turn to Boynton and Boynton for tips to teach bystanders of bullying.

- Don't join in.
- Don't watch.
- Tell the bully to stop.
- Be nice to the victim.
- Encourage the victim to leave with you.
- Get an adult.

For the bullied and the bystander both, these are tall orders. Let's consider what teachers, as bystanders with an acute responsibility to make a difference, might do to prevent and/or intervene when bullying occurs.

STANDARD 3

NMSA

Knowledge 12: Middle level teacher candidates understand how to develop, implement, and assess advisory and other student advocacy programs that attend to the social and emotional needs of young adolescents (e.g., mentoring, conflict resolution).

MAKE A DIFFERENCE

While making a difference in terms of perpetrator and victim in a bullying scenario may seem like a natural fit for teachers, in reality too many teachers either ignore bullying as part of kids growing and learning to make their way in life, or they are not tuned in to what's happening around them. It may be easy to spot overt bullying and send a student to the principal or the counselor. But just stopping the behavior isn't enough. We have to get at the cause in order to eradicate it. That's the tough part. When bullying occurs, it creates ready-made teachable moments not to be missed by effective middle grades teachers. Helping our students understand that we all deserve to be respected in spite of how we differ is part of being developmentally responsive. In addition, here are some ways we can make a difference with regard to bullying.

- Create a climate where "telling" is not only OK, but expected. Reporting bullying should be viewed as a classroom community responsibility where an open atmosphere consistently says that all are welcome and valued.

- Be totally present in mind, body, and spirit. This means our personal problems wait for us in the car for the trip home and do not interfere with giving our students our full attention.

- Practice "withitness." This is a term coined decades ago that means we act as though we have eyes in the back of our heads. We see all, hear all, and protect all.

- Use discussion groups, advisory periods (discussed in Chapter 6), literature focusing on tolerance and civility, and other means of continuing conversations about why bullying is wrong.

- Know what bullying looks like. Learn to recognize both the bully and the bullied. Act on what you see; act on what you hear.

- Never underestimate the fears of a student. Take reports seriously and don't stop interventions until the bully is put out of the bullying business and the victim is able to function in the school setting.

- Step in when there is an unhealthy imbalance of power. The better we know our students, the easier it will be to spot these situations.

- Consistently intervene, protect, and teach civility.

Some communities are taking bullying very seriously. Districts are establishing anti-bullying policies with uniform consequences. States are passing legislation requiring school personnel to report all suspicions of bullying to school administration. In the legislation, characteristics that motivate harassment are often listed. A compilation of these characteristics include race, color, religion, ancestry, national origin, gender, socioeconomic status, academic status, gender identity, physical appearance, sexual orientation, and mental/physical/developmental/sensory disability. So, concern about bullying goes well beyond the schoolhouse door. In fact, it's quite difficult to isolate anything inside the school, given the proliferation of technology.

Technology and Young Adolescents

Young adolescents are digital natives. We are urged by Prensky to "Listen to the natives" (2006, p. 9). Not only do the ways children now relate to technology have implications for how we teach and how they learn, we are in classrooms with kids who take to technological innovations in natural ways. Instead of the tired references to the "me" generation, some refer to today's kids as the "media generation" (McHugh, 2005, p. 33). For young adolescents, technology is definitely an attraction, often a distraction, and may become an obsession.

Cell phones, camera phones, iPods, iPhones, BlackBerrys, blogs, instant messaging, twittering, social networking sites, and whatever is new on a given day allow kids to be in touch with friends, family, and the whole world through the Internet. Possibilities are simply mind-boggling. Mark Springer tells us ". . . today's young adolescents seem fiber-optically wired to accept data streams faster and from multiple sources simultaneously" (2009, p. 23). Does all this change their lives? You bet! Many of the changes are positive, with one particularly negative phenomenon, cyberbullying.

Cyberbullying

Cyberbullying is bullying accomplished through technology. It's insidious, pervasive, and almost always accomplished under the proverbial radar screen of most adults. In 2006, Tom Erb, then editor of *Middle School Journal*, and always a voice of reason when it comes to the education of young adolescents, wrote this insightful statement:

> Dealing with bullying in school used to be about breaking up fights in the hallways, counseling students who spread rumors or passed vicious notes, or responding to racist or homophobic language in the classroom. Those "good old days" are fast slipping into history. Although the traditional forms of bullying continue to be used, young adolescents have at their disposal a growing number of new tools for the purpose: email, blogs, Internet chat rooms, instant messaging, and cell phone text messaging. (p. 2)

Erb tells us that cyberbullying shares the same basic elements as traditional bullying because it's about relationships, power, and control. There are, however, some different characteristics that we haven't dealt with before, including

- Anonymity is commonplace and perpetrators can very easily remain unknown.
- The bullying message can be spread widely by one click of the mouse.
- Cyberbullies are rarely held responsible for a variety of reasons, anonymity included.
- Cyberbullying may not take place on a school campus, so there are questions as to the legality of the school being involved with the solutions.
- Most adults are not privy to the cyber world of young adolescents and did not experience anything quite so sinister.
- Kids are hesitant to tell an adult about cyberbullying, partially because they don't want their technology tools/toys taken away.

One of the most frightening and potentially harmful types of cyberbullying is known as *sexting*. Yes, it's texting about sex. Many kids think that sending, or passing along to others, nude or suggestive photos and text, is fun and/or semi-innocent flirting. However, it's much more, with social and legal consequences they never imagine. For the sender who thinks only a select person or group will see or read the message, the surprise is that with a single click, it can all be on the Internet where millions may view what was assumed would remain private. For the receiver who decides to broadcast the images of a minor, child pornography charges are possible, with his or her inclusion on pedophile lists. Parents and school personnel are justified in their concern that unthinking actions of kids may haunt them for the rest of their lives.

Cyberbullying is a recent phenomenon that will require our best thinking and concentrated effort to figure out how to help our students avoid being damaged by those who may use technology to harm them, whether intentionally or unintentionally.

STANDARD 1

Performance 9: Middle level teacher candidates deal effectively with societal changes, including the portrait of young adolescents in the media, which impact the healthy development of young adolescents.

MAKE A DIFFERENCE

It is important for middle level teachers to know what's going on around them. We can't simply say "I have no use for all this technology so I'm not going to be smart about it." For one thing, most technological advances have tremendous potential as teaching tools. But even if that's not the intent, we need to be aware of what our kids have access to in terms of technology. We need to see it all both as positive new means of communication and as potentially harmful innovations when used improperly.

There are safeguards we can teach kids, accompanied by serious discussions about the harm that may come to them if they do not follow the guidelines that include

- Never give identifying personal information such as home address, social security number, telephone number, etc.
- Never send pictures that are in any way incriminating.
- Never give out online passwords to anyone other than parents.
- Never "meet" anyone online.
- Never pass along anything hurtful about anyone.
- Never download software without parental permission.

Of course, the list could go on and on. As middle level teachers we must remember that the decision-making capabilities of our students are not fully developed. What we consider common sense may not even cross their still developing minds.

Some students have very serious concerns on their developing minds, like surviving from day to day and justifiably worrying about their futures. Let's next consider students who may need us the most—those living in low socioeconomic status (SES) homes and neighborhoods.

Poverty and Schooling

**Young Adolescent
Diversity**

In Chapter 3 we discussed kids and socioeconomic status as a diversity issue. It deserves a second look, a third, and a fourth . . . until we find better ways of providing learning opportunities for the kids who begin life at risk and enter school the same way.

Not all kids in homes with low SES lack encouragement or grow up without parents/guardians who do what they can to ensure success. Many are living in very loving homes with parents who sacrifice every day to provide shelter, food, and other life necessities. Their lives may be difficult, but they are supported by family. Then there are other kids in situations that are not only difficult financially, but also in terms of support. Still others live in neighborhoods where gunfire is common and safety is illusive.

There are foundations and philanthropic groups that study poverty and ways to alleviate its negative effects on children in schools. The Sodexo Foundation found that hunger threatens 35 million in the United States and 10 million of those are children who struggle to learn and succeed in school while dealing with the impact of poor nutrition on their ability to learn. Children who live in poverty miss more days of school and are far less likely to be able to learn when they do attend classes. Behaviorally, children who are poor and sometimes hungry have difficulty paying attention and concentrating. They may be more disruptive and are more likely to need special educational services. Many organizations strongly urge that public school children who live in poverty be given breakfast, lunch, and dinner (Sodexo Foundation, 2008). This is even more vital for students who are homeless. They have a whole different set of problems that we can only begin to imagine.

● Need for Qualified Teachers

Kay Taylor, an educational researcher at Kansas State University, tells us that educators need to understand the multiple dimensions of poverty. "Teachers are placed in the forefront of this dilemma, and many have no personal experience or educational background to address issues of poverty in their classrooms" (*Science Daily*, 2009). The more we know about our students' life circumstances, the better able we are to meet their needs. Taylor says that, when a child acts out, we need to consider that the actions could be from the effects of poverty. She says we should be respectful, caring, and empathetic as we provide a solid foundation upon which learning can be built.

A problem cited over and over in the literature is the lack of qualified teachers in schools with high percentages of kids in poverty. Yes, they have special challenges and, no, it's not easy. But think about the progress that's possible. One of our focus teachers, Jesse White, is a teacher who has chosen to focus his efforts on kids who live in low SES settings. As you read in the last chapter, he has options each year to teach in suburban schools and makes the choice to stay in an urban setting with kids who need him most. Read what he has to say about his decision in **Teachers Speak**.

▶ Teachers Speak

● **Jesse White**

My university teacher preparation program was for K–8 certification. When it came time to student teach, I asked for 4th or 5th grade. I was placed in an upscale elementary school where all but two of my 4th graders were Caucasian. Dream assignment, right? Well, that's what I thought. I was the envy of other student teachers. But I discovered early on that my heart wasn't in it. The kids were great, and my cooperating teacher was supportive. But something was missing. When I walked through the front door of Lincoln Middle School, I knew what it was. It took a while for me to put it in words, and sometimes it's still difficult to express my "calling" to other people, even to teachers. The kids at Lincoln both won my heart, and broke it at the same time. You see, they all live in public housing projects, qualify for free breakfast and lunch, are almost all Black or Hispanic, and many have already failed a grade or two by the time they get to our 8th grade team. There are a few stars, but not many. And it seems like when one student begins to do well and stand out as an academic star, he or she will often slip back very quickly because standing out isn't cool.

I try to celebrate progress, no matter how small, in ways that are special and not embarrassing to the kids. It's a fine line. There are days when there's absolutely nothing to celebrate . . . days when there's a cloud over our team of kids. Parent arrested, cousin shot, or rumblings among gangs are frightening, and they know something's up. Unfortunately, some of my kids are already junior gang members; some have no choice but to join. Then there are other days when what we're discussing or experiencing in social studies strikes a positive chord or catches their interest. One of my goals is to relate what's in the curriculum standards to something the kids can understand.

This is my 6th year in the classroom. It's time for me to begin a master's program, and I'm sure I will soon. Some of my teacher friends are in administrator-prep programs, but I don't see myself leaving the classroom. It may sound hokey, but I love my students. When I see a light bulb come on in their heads as they get a concept, or when they just can't help but grin when I return a paper on which I've written a compliment, or they walk down the hall saying, "What's up, Mr. White?" I know I am where I need to be, and where I want to be.

STANDARD 6

Knowledge 7: Middle level teacher candidates know about the resources available within communities that can support students, teachers, and schools.

MAKE A DIFFERENCE

A number of teachers and researchers have provided ideas and actions teachers can try to help students in low SES settings succeed in school. What follows is a compilation of some of their suggestions.

myeducationlab

To hear James Bell, the 2008 North Carolina Teacher of the Year, express that education is the key to giving students hope and bright futures, go to the Teacher Talk section of **Topic #2: Today's Students** in the MyEducationLab for your course.

- Know students well, acknowledge their challenges, and do what's necessary to understand how poverty affects them.
- Look for student strengths, and find ways to build on them.
- Reject deficit theories that concentrate on what kids in poverty lack.
- Reach out to families, and involve them in ways that suit their availability.
- Fight to ensure school meal programs are accessible.
- Teach a curriculum that includes people from all arenas of life.
- Increase reading instruction and reading activities to build basic skills.
- Teach the whole student, not just what relates to the curriculum.
- Build relationships with students.
- Monitor progress, and celebrate even small successes.

Many young adolescents living in poverty have an additional challenge. English is not their first language.

STANDARD 6

NMSA

Knowledge 2: Middle level teacher candidates understand how prior learning, differing experiences, and family and cultural backgrounds influence young adolescent learning.

Disposition 5: Middle level teacher candidates value and appreciate all young adolescents regardless of family circumstances, community environment, health, and/or economic conditions.

Performance 1: Middle level teacher candidates establish respectful and productive relationships with family and community members that maximize student learning and well-being.

English Language Learners

More than 5 million students in U.S. schools are English language learners (ELL). That's 10% of our total school population (National Clearinghouse for English Language Acquisition, 2006). These students are either non-English speakers or have limited proficiency in English. Another recognized category of students are those

Young Adolescent Diversity

who are limited English proficient students (LEP). It is interesting to note that 57% of LEP students were born in the United States, making them second and third generation residents (Batalova, Fix, & Murray, 2007).

While the largest and fastest growing group of ELL students are part of immigrant families primarily from Mexico, they are joined in this category by students from countries around the world (Scherer, 2009). Over 14 million students in K–12 schools are language-minority students, with some in the ELL category and others who speak English adequately to learn at expected rates in English, but for whom English is not their first language (Garcia, Jensen, & Scribner, 2009). These kids are all around us, in suburban, urban, and rural settings. Not long ago ELL students were mostly living in California, Texas, and New York. Now rural areas in the Midwest, medium-sized towns in the Northwest, and cities along the Southeast coast have large populations of these students, many of whom are at risk for academic failure for multiple reasons, not just language differences.

Variability among Students

Rance-Roney (2009) uses an analogy of a quilt to describe the variability of ELL students when she says, "There is a quilt of English language learner profiles—a quilt rich with diverse life experiences, but loosely woven with common learning needs" (p. 34). The life circumstances among ELL students are as varied as within any other student population group. Most live with what Agirdag (2009) calls "cultural discontinuity" (p. 21) between what ELL students experience at home and what they experience at school. The following variables illustrate some reasons why we haven't made the discontinuity go away:

- How long they have lived in the U.S.
- English proficiency of parents and other family members
- Educational attainment of parents and family members
- Ethnic/racial minority status
- Economic and social resources
- Permanency of lifestyle
- Literacy level in native language
- Academic success in native country

While some ELL students come to us from families where parents are professionals with good jobs and have a record of academic success, others arrive in our classrooms for short periods of time from families who struggle to support their children through intermittent work they must follow in order to survive. Some are legally in the United States, while others must continually look over their shoulders to watch for a U.S. immigration official who may send them back to their native country. Hear this loud and clear . . . these students are young adolescents who deserve our very best efforts in providing teaching and learning environments that help them succeed not only in efforts to speak and comprehend English, but to learn all of the content in our standards. Tall order.

Bilingual teacher Carmen Esparza teaches 90 minutes a day in each of three classes, one with 6th graders, one with 7th graders, and one with 8th graders. She teaches language arts and social studies, about half in English and half in Spanish. Students concentrate on becoming fluent in English, while strengthening their skills in Spanish as well.

Programs Designed for ELL Students

Most agree that proficiency in the English language is necessary for academic success in U.S. public schools. The optimal path for getting there is controversial. Our quest to find solutions has become politicized, adding to the already difficult task of figuring out what to do. Here are some options that some states and districts are trying.

- *Structured English Immersion (SEI)*—This program is based on the premise that simply teaching in English is not teaching kids English. Kids are grouped according to their English proficiency levels, and they spend significant time each school day in classes emphasizing pronunciation, listening skills, vocabulary, verb tense, sentence structure, grammar applications, and English reading and writing.

- *Bilingual Education*—In order for a bilingual education to work, a school must have enough kids who are ELLs to make up a class. In most schools, the only language minority that qualifies for bilingual instruction are those who speak Spanish. And because most of our U.S. teachers who speak another language speak Spanish, bilingual classes are usually Spanish. If, for instance, there is a large population of Hmong students in a school, finding a bilingual teacher of English and Hmong is almost impossible. The premises of a bilingual program are: (1) continued development of both languages contributes to both educational and cognitive development, and (2) literacy-based abilities in one language enhance those abilities in another (Estrada, Gomez, & Ruiz-Escalante, 2009).

- *English as a Second Language (ESL)*—In ESL programs, students receive one-on-one or small group instruction two to three times a week. Chances are that ESL teachers will have limited proficiency in any language other than English. Instruction is in English only with little effort to preserve the native language. In schools where there is not a large population of ELLs, ESL programs are less expensive and may be the only alternative for providing attention to our English language learners.

MAKE A DIFFERENCE

The literature about language diversity contains many suggestions concerning English language learners in the classroom. Some are doable for teachers with little or no formal training in instructing ELLs, while others require more expertise and professional development than is currently available. Here are some things that may be within your reach in your middle level classroom.

- Know your students and their English proficiency levels. (Remember that no learning can be student-centered until we know our students.)
- Do what you can to activate the prior knowledge of ELL students.
- Use as many relevant graphics and visuals relating to your curriculum as possible.
- View a variety of languages as an asset. Demonstrate and verbalize this with your attitudes and actions.
- Make real objects part of your instruction to illustrate concepts.
- Use clear scoring rubrics that enable you to be culturally sensitive in feedback.
- Monitor learning problems as best you can, given language barriers.
- Try peer-assisted learning if you have bilingual students in your classes.
- Encourage family involvement in your classroom/school.
- Utilize translating services for home communication.
- Make all languages visible through welcome signs, directions for routines, etc.
- Validate other cultures in your classroom with artifacts, posters, anecdotes, inclusion of cultural customs, and persons of diversity in the curriculum.

Our efforts to meet the needs of English language learners will no doubt change as more research and teacher experiences are incorporated into the body of knowledge. You will likely have ELLs in your classroom, whether in the small towns of Maine or in the metropolises of California. Be innovative, be sensitive, and be respectful.

Now we focus on issues that cross cultural, language, and socioeconomic lines—wellness issues.

Wellness Issues

This section of the chapter could comprise many whole books and still only scratch the surface of health issues affecting young adolescents. We will focus on just a few, including substance abuse, sexuality-related concerns, and childhood obesity. In

Turning Points 2000, we read, "Healthy lifestyles and academic success are tightly interwoven—improvement in one leads to improvement in the other, both directly and indirectly" (p. 24). Day-to-day choices matter. Following each of the three main topics—substance abuse, sexuality-related concerns, childhood obesity—there's a **Make a Difference** section.

● Substance Abuse

Alcohol, tobacco, and drugs (including illegal, prescription, and over-the-counter) are readily available to middle level students. While many studies indicate that substance abuse among teens has not increased overall since the 1980s, three categories of substance abuse appear to be rising—sedatives, OxyContin, and inhalants. By some reports these are the very substances with which young adolescents experiment (Powell, 2009).

The consumption of alcohol by teenagers is still problematic for many reasons, including alcohol poisoning and impaired judgment, to name just two. The images of car accidents involving teen driving are seared into our minds even as Mothers Against Drunk Driving (MADD) and Students Against Drunk Driving (SADD) spread the word about the dangers of drinking and driving. The negative consequences of tobacco use are equally as publicized, but kids keep on experimenting with cigarettes and smokeless tobacco. Marijuana can be easily obtained from older "friends," and information about abusing over-the-counter substances is a click away on the Internet. We can't take the substances away. So what can we do?

STANDARD 1

Knowledge 5: Middle level teacher candidates understand issues of young adolescent health and sexuality.

Disposition 5: Middle level teacher candidates are enthusiastic about being positive role models, coaches, and mentors for all young adolescents.

Performance 8: Middle level teacher candidates create and maintain supportive learning environments that promote the healthy development of all young adolescents.

MAKE A DIFFERENCE

Amid all the planning for instruction and creating a positive environment and the seemingly endless tasks of teaching middle level, we must also do what we can to steer kids away from substances that will harm them. Here are some things to consider:

- Know the warning signs of substance abuse.
- Model good judgment in use of legal substances and abstinence of illegal substances.
- Develop strong, trusting relationships with students so that they will confide in you and respect your opinions.
- Make information available not only about the harm of substances, but also about community resources kids can contact for support and help.

Next let's explore sexuality-related issues.

● Sexuality-Related Issues

It's hard to imagine that Jenny, as we see her in her 7th grade school photo, would know about sexual intercourse, much less actually experience it. But she did. She's 12 and pregnant. Jenny lives with her grandparents and plans to keep her baby. She tells me the father of her baby, age 16, will be involved in her life and the life of the precious child she will soon have. Four out of five teen mothers are unmarried, a fact that puts them and their babies at high risk of living in poverty (Infoplease, 2004).

Teen pregnancy rates have actually declined steadily since the 1960s. That fact doesn't matter now to Jenny. Too many young adolescents are engaging in sexual activity, and many are suffering physical, as well as psychological, consequences. Sexual experimentation can result in sexually transmitted diseases (STDs) and transmission of the HIV virus that can lead to AIDS (Education Vital Signs, 2006). While their bodies may accommodate sexual activities, young adolescents aren't ready for the emotional and social dilemmas that accompany early sexual activity.

MAKE A DIFFERENCE

This is a sensitive area of development that some schools address in well-conceived health education programs, while others don't address the issues in any kind of

In her school picture, Jenny is a pretty, emerging young adolescent. Months after this picture was taken what sets her apart among her 12- and 13-year-old friends is that she'll soon be a mom.

organized, effective way. Young adolescents need information delivered in under-standable, matter-of-fact ways. As with any form of self-destruction, students' ability to use refusal skills increases with their own sense of self-worth and self-confidence. Teachers can be very instrumental in helping kids become better decision makers, armed with knowledge of what's wise and healthy.

Childhood Obesity

The number of children who are obese has tripled since the 1970s (Haskins, Paxson, & Donahue, 2006). Tripled . . . it's an epidemic with no legal remedy. Food is legal, and abundant for most children; exercise isn't mandated. Obese children are well above the normal weight for their age and height. The causes of this obesity epidemic are numerous and well documented.

Causes of Childhood Obesity   The causes are many and varied. One group of re-searchers list the following among them:

- Increases in media options leading to young "couch potatoes"
- Proliferation of fast food restaurants
- Working parents who rely on the first cause for babysitting and the second for dinner
- Increases in sugary snacks in stores
- Suburban sprawl and urban crime, both of which keep children from outdoor activities (Paxson, Donahue, Orleans, & Grisso, 2006).

I'll add two more. It has been my experience in public schools that even though states and districts mandate physical education time frames and amounts of activity measured in minutes per week, these policies are often not adhered to in reality. As pressure to perform on standardized tests increases, fewer minutes per week actu-ally find students participating in physical activities.

Childhood obesity may set today's youth apart from all others in the history of our country. Because of health problems related to obesity, this generation of kids may live shorter, less-healthy lives on average than their parents.

Another contributing factor to childhood obesity is adult obesity. It seems that with each passing year, the parents of my students have gotten fatter and fatter. I understand that I'm not being politically correct to say this, but it's true. When I meet some parents I think, "This poor child doesn't stand a chance of being a healthy weight." Home role models of healthy living are becoming harder and harder to find.

Consequences of Childhood Obesity   For the first time in generations, today's adolescents may live, on average, shorter and less-healthy life spans than their parents. And it's not drugs, alcohol, tobacco, or early sexual activity that will prove to be the culprit. It's unhealthy food, accompanied by a sedentary lifestyle. Serious health problems once thought to strike only adults are becoming commonplace among overweight adolescents—type 2 diabetes, heart disease, high cholesterol, joint dysfunctions, to name a few (Paxson et al., 2006). Childhood obesity may also contribute to serious social and psychological disorders resulting from low self-esteem, loneliness, and teasing that often accompany obesity (DeAngelis, 2004).

MAKE A DIFFERENCE

The Child Nutrition Reauthorization Act of 2004 mandated that school districts develop wellness policies that address what students eat in school, the kinds and amounts of physical activity they experience, and the provisions for health education. Most schools have removed machines that offer sugary drinks and unhealthy snacks.

Schools can help young adolescents live healthier lives by providing snack choices that promote better nutrition.

However, some cafeteria food contributes to both lack of nutrition and obesity. When choices routinely include pizza, hamburgers, and fries, kids will likely gravitate to them. When students may or may not participate in exercise, many will opt out.

We can be role models for our students. We can make wise choices in terms of nutrition and be physically active. We can be vocal advocates for young adolescents' health. To not do so contributes to this growing, serious problem of childhood obesity.

Reflections on the Societal Context of Middle Level Education

For many young adolescents, it's not easy growing up. This isn't a new phenomenon, but as a future middle level teacher you should be aware of the societal context in which your students live. There are some issues we are helpless to affect, but there are others where we can make a difference. Be that difference for your students. They're depending on you.

Sometimes as teachers we feel like so much of what happens in the lives of our students is out of our control. And it's true. As part of a school, we have about seven hours a day, 180 days a year, to have a positive impact. That's a big chunk of time, but time alone with young adolescents won't change many developmental aspects of their lives, their homes, neighborhoods, socioeconomic status, health-related choices, and so on. What we can control is ourselves—our attitudes, our levels of effort, our careful consideration when making decisions, our passion for our profession and its inherent responsibilities and opportunities. This chapter began with a quote that we should consider again as we close the chapter.

> There's a saying that goes "We cannot control the wind, but we can adjust our sails." Teachers recognize the social issues that negatively affect our students are complex and multidimensional. They don't begin with us, and most won't be completely resolved through us. However, with that reality in view, we can begin to focus on positive steps to prevent and/or halt risky behaviors and their impact on children and adolescents. Controlling the wind may not be within our reach, but adjusting our own, and our students', sails is indeed possible.
>
> Powell, 2009, p. 317

GROUP ACTIVITIES

1. As a group, think about the negative societal context issues the young adolescents in your area may be most likely to encounter. Other issues to consider include violence, theft, neglectful parents, and child abuse. Decide on several and, in small groups, do Web searches for more information about them. Share what you discover.

2. Brainstorm ways teachers might positively affect the decision-making skills of students on issues such as substance abuse, sexuality-related issues, and obesity.

3. Have a discussion about where and when you have experienced or witnessed bullying. What harm occurred because of the incidences?

INDIVIDUAL ACTIVITIES

1. Why is it important for teachers and schools to be involved in student wellness issues? Why do you think some educators hesitate to do so? What role do you think parents and the community play with regards to any limits that should be set for school involvement in sensitive issues?

2. Think about the subject(s) you want to teach. At what point in your curriculum do you think you might address one of the societal issues discussed in this chapter?

3. Have you encountered English language learners either as a middle school student or as an adult? If so, what do you remember about the experience(s)?

PERSONAL JOURNAL

1. Think about the societal context in which you grew up. What influenced you most?

2. What societal elements have the most influence on you today? Are there influences that you have now that are also applicable to young adolescents?

3. Have you ever been bullied? If so, what were the circumstances? Have you ever been a bully? If so, what were the circumstances? Have you ever been a bystander of bullying? If so, what were the circumstances?

Professional Practice

(It will be helpful to reread the descriptions of Keith Miller in Chapter 4 and Andy in Chapter 3.)

● **Keith Richardson**

Because Keith is only in his second year of teaching, after an 18 year career in business, he is still looking at students through new eyes. A number of things bother him. One problem he sees not only in his classroom, but also in his community, is obesity. In fact, there are times when he goes to Walmart or to a restaurant and has a hard time spotting people around him who are not overweight. He and his wife have talked about this growing problem for years. They are both fit, as are their children. Now that Keith is a teacher, he is continually reminded of the problem when he looks at the 6th graders on his team and the rest of the young adolescents at Hamilton Middle School.

Kids at Hamilton take P.E. one semester each year. That's not enough to meet the state guidelines, but no one appears concerned. There are still unhealthy snack machines in the hallway and frequent lunch choices include fries, hot dogs, hamburgers, and pizza. Because Keith is a relatively new teacher, he hesitates to speak up for fear of offending his grossly overweight principal, as well as one of his team teachers.

Andy • sixth grade

One of Keith's students who is well on his way to being obese is Andy. Recall from Chapter 3 that Andy is the only child whose mom died a couple of years ago. Andy's dad is overweight. Besides being overweight, Andy shows signs of being a bully. He doesn't display overt bullying behaviors that get him into trouble, at least not yet. Keith is observing subtle signs of bullying. He watches Andy and the looks he gives a couple of the smaller boys on the team. The looks are "evil," with squinting eyes and a frown. The other boys look away, and walk away. As he becomes more watchful, he notices that the two other boys often end up without their supplies and lunch money. He suspects this may have something to do with Andy. He wonders if Andy's expanding size has anything to do with what appears to be bullying behavior.

1. Keith wants to start an initiative that might have an impact on the activity level of the kids at Hamilton. He wants to develop a walking trail on the school property that consists of five fenced-in acres. Here's the problem he wants to address with his initiative. When kids finish lunch, they are allowed to either go outside or stay in the cafeteria. Those who stay inside just sit and talk. Those who go outside generally do the same. The few kids who are active are those who are normal weight. Keith wants to propose that all kids go outside, weather permitting, when they finish lunch and walk the trail until it's time to go back to class. Which of the following obstacles will be the most critical for Keith to overcome?
   a. His principal may not see the need for the project.
   b. It will take time and energy, along with volunteers, to make the trail a reality.
   c. The teachers at Hamilton will have to be "on board" and support the initiative for it to work.

d. There will be some expenses involved in the project.

2. If Keith's initiative is put in place, the students at Hamilton can simply be told that this is how they will spend their lunch breaks. However, for the walking trail to succeed in not only increasing activity for 15 minutes a day, but also in affecting how students view fitness, which of the following actions will likely have the most impact?
   a. Teachers enthusiastically walk the trail and show obvious enjoyment of the experience.
   b. The kids are encouraged to both run and walk to see who can make the most laps.
   c. Each student is given a pedometer so data can be kept and math problems developed around this authentic experience.
   d. The walk includes a weekly scavenger hunt for items on the trail.

3. While Keith is working on his plan, he is trying to figure out how to approach the fact that Hamilton P.E. classes don't provide either enough minutes or the activity levels that are addressed in state guidelines. What should he do?
   a. make a suggestion at a faculty meeting that the issue be addressed by the principal
   b. talk with the P.E. teacher to become smarter about the history of P.E. at Hamilton to better understand why classes are not full-year and why many days are spent indoors in a classroom rather than outside or in the gym
   c. call the district office and speak with the director of Health and Physical Education
   d. continue working on the walking trail and wait until he has accomplished the initiative before tackling another

Constructed Response

While Keith may never know for sure if Andy's weight contributes to what he is now certain is bullying, he knows something needs to happen. What are three things Keith might do to address this issue?

INTERNET RESOURCES

Sodexo Foundation

www.SodexoFoundation.org

The mission of the Sodexo Foundation is to be a driving and creative force that contributes to a hunger-free nation. They commission studies to find ways to impact undernutrition on children. They strive to find a solution that maximizes the potential for U.S. schoolchildren.

Stop Cyberbullying

www.stopcyberbullying.org

This site discusses what cyberbullying is and how it works. There is information on why it happens and how to prevent it.

National Coalition for the Homeless

www.nationalhomeless.org/

The National Coalition for the Homeless, founded in 1982, is a national network of people who are currently experiencing or who have experienced homelessness, activists and advocates, community-based and faith-based service providers, and others committed to a single mission of ending homelessness.

Mayo Clinic

www.mayoclinic.com/health/childhood-obesity/DS00698

This site is a comprehensive look at childhood obesity from the experts at the Mayo Clinic, including risk factors, causes, complications, prevention, and treatment.

TeensHealth

http://kidshealth.org/teen

Teens can access information on all kinds of health issues. Site users select a topic and then may read straightforward, useful information.

Structures of Middle Level Education

6

Close relationships are fostered through middle level structures such as teaming and advisory. These 8th graders know each other well because they spend the majority of the school day together. Group identity is so important to young adolescents.

*f*lexible structuring helps to create a responsive environment—in which needs can be recognized and adjustments made in form and function when necessary in order to maximize results. The best middle level schools are ever-changing, learning organizations.

Jackson & Davis, 2000, p. 90

CHAPTER PREVIEW

Structures of People
- To Track or Not to Track
- Teaming
- Creative Grouping Alternatives
- Advisory Programs

Structures of Place
- The Inviting Classroom
- Classroom Inventory
- Planning the Basic Set-up
- Home Away from Home

Structures of Time
- Traditional Schedule
- Block Schedule

Reflections on Structures of People, Time, and Place

INTRODUCTION

Structure gives shape and support to middle level education. Developmentally responsive structures provide both framework and opportunity for the middle level educator to build on best practices with as few impediments as possible. However, assuming that putting certain structures in place will automatically lead to developmentally responsive middle grades education is a fallacy. For instance, organizing teachers and students into interdisciplinary teams is an organizational change and not a guarantee that the potential benefits of teaming will be realized.

This chapter looks at possible structures of people, time, and place that are believed to be appropriate for middle grades students. These are elements to look for when determining a school's degree of adherence to middle level philosophy as articulated in *Turning Points* and *This We Believe*.

Structures of middle school = People + Time + Place

STANDARD 2

Disposition 3: Middle level teacher candidates are supportive of organizational components that maximize student learning.

Structures of People

As dynamic, living organizations, middle schools revolve around relationships that set the tone and determine the climate. Our challenge as teachers is to create structures of people that best promote learning and growth. In this section, we'll examine homogeneous and heterogeneous grouping, interdisciplinary teaming, multiage grouping, looping, schools-within-a-school, and advisory programs.

To Track or Not to Track

Perhaps the most controversial of all philosophical dilemmas concerning the structuring of people within middle level settings is the homogeneous versus heterogeneous grouping debate. *Homogeneous ability grouping,* or *tracking* as it is commonly called, has been the norm in most levels of schooling for many years. It seems to make sense to test students and put them into classes based on their abilities and achievement levels so curriculum and instruction can be tailored to meet their specific needs. It appears reasonable to expect teachers to teach at their best when presented with groups of students who fall within narrow bands of intelligence and aptitude. What "makes sense" and "appears reasonable" dictates what often prevails in practice, in direct opposition to middle level philosophy.

Turning Points 2000 clearly calls for *heterogeneous grouping* of students, meaning that students in any given class represent the spectrum of ability levels in the school student population. Still, homogeneous grouping is prevalent in schools that otherwise follow the tenets of middle grades education. The arguments for and against ability grouping/tracking have been the same for decades. It seems clear that ongoing research is needed on the topic of homogeneous versus heterogeneous grouping.

The Case for Tracking   The literature available on the topic of tracking indicates that the case for *ability grouping* is based on the following propositions: tracking helps schools meet the varying needs of students; tracking provides low-achieving students with the attention and slower pace they require; high-achieving students are provided challenges when tracked; tracking is necessary for individualizing instruction; and tracking will prevent low-achievers from hindering the progress of high-achievers.

It is easier to plan for instruction of a homogeneous class. Materials and teaching methods can be chosen specifically for the ability level of the students. High-achieving groups can sometimes "teach themselves." They often seem to thrive regardless of the curriculum and instruction. At the other end of the spectrum, teaching a class of low-achievers has been, and often still is, a matter of drill and practice in a worksheet-rich environment if the teacher is not committed to a type of instruction that is more interesting and challenging to students, and more difficult to plan. Perhaps it's not the grouping but the quality of instruction that makes a difference. We explore this later.

The Case against Tracking   The literature available on tracking indicates that the case against it relies on the following propositions: tracking is detrimental to young adolescent peer relationships; it is harmful to the self-esteem of low-achievers; it perpetuates class and racial inequities; the grouping process is often biased; it reinforces inaccurate assumptions about intelligence; and the least experienced teachers are typically assigned to low-achieving classes.

Young Adolescent Diversity

Finding Balance   Research can be found that both supports and refutes the value of tracking. However, organizations such as the National Middle School Association and the National Forum to Accelerate Middle-Grades Reform strongly recommend that heterogeneous grouping be used in most middle grades settings. San Antonio (2006) tells us that in her 30-year long experiences of studying the world of young adolescents, "No area of my study surprised me more than the connections among ability grouping, social class, and the development of social perceptions. Students in accelerated classes were more than three times more likely to be from wealthier communities than from poorer ones" (p.10). Her findings extend to the reality that most gifted classes consist primarily of Caucasian students from middle income or above homes.

Middle level philosophy in *Turning Points 2000* states that "Classes should include students of diverse needs, achievement levels, interests, and learning styles, and instruction should be differentiated to take advantage of the diversity, not ignore it" (Jackson & Davis, 2000, p. 23). The reality of what actually occurs in our schools often does not follow this philosophy. A major benefit of the team structure, which we will discuss later in the chapter, is that it supports heterogeneous grouping of students while allowing for grouping and regrouping as determined by individual student needs and the curriculum.

To make heterogeneous grouping successful, instructional practices should respond to student needs. Chapter 8 explores strategies that will enable us to differentiate instruction. There are numerous teaching practices that give students opportunities to learn in diverse ways. This variety of teaching practices is essential in creating a developmentally responsive classroom, one that embraces heterogeneous groups.

Some middle schools restrict grouping to subjects that are overtly hierarchical in nature. A common configuration of courses involves tracking in math and language arts with heterogeneous grouping in science and social studies. In *America's Middle Schools in the New Century* (2003), we learn that almost 75% of middle schools in this large study track students in math, with about 25% tracking in language arts and reading. In social studies and science, only about 10% of middle schools track students. For those adamantly opposed to any kind of tracking, it may be difficult to accept this compromise. However, tracking is deeply embedded in our schools and is unlikely to be eliminated. Chances are you will encounter some form of tracking in your school and may have no choice as to whether or not to practice it.

To track or not to track is a serious issue with potentially far-reaching consequences. It's, therefore, an issue that merits our best thinking and our most thoughtful actions. We've only scratched the surface; please take time to explore the homogeneous and heterogeneous grouping issue in greater depth. Keep in mind that a homogeneous middle school class is really an oxymoron. There are not 2, much less 20, middle school students who respond in the same way and at the same time to any given scenario.

Magnet Schools   A *magnet school* is a public school that offers something different from traditional public schools. This difference may involve specialized curriculum, instruction, or both. Magnet schools may bring together academically gifted students, students with an expressed interest in a specific curricular area, or perhaps students with distinct career aspirations. Because students in a magnet school share aptitude and/or interests, they tend to be more homogeneous. In some cases, magnet schools represent overt tracking. During the 1970s, districts devised magnet plans to draw students from the suburbs into urban areas to create racially mixed populations. Magnet schools are viewed by some as forces for integration.

Magnet schools are considered by many to be vehicles for improving scholastic standards, providing a broad range of curricular choices, and allowing students to concentrate on distinct interests and talents. Some magnet schools require proof of academic achievement and aptitude through high scores on standardized tests. Once admitted, students must maintain high achievement levels to remain in the school. Some magnet schools require auditions in areas such as music, theater, and dance. Their programs then provide talented students in these areas with opportunities to enhance their skills and to use them in performance. Some middle schools declare a curricular focus such as math and science. They increase their resources and teacher expertise and invite students with interest in, and/or aptitude for, the chosen focus to apply. Still other magnet schools declare a focus on, for instance, military or career preparation. Interested students are asked to apply, and attendance is determined by lottery.

Magnet schools are more likely to have greater monetary and staff resources. They cost more to operate. So, although magnet schools are part of public education, they are inherently unequal to nonmagnet schools in what they can offer students. They often compete with private and charter schools to draw students and parents who are looking for alternatives.

● Teaming

"No single educational idea has come to characterize the middle school concept as certainly as has interdisciplinary *teaming*" (Lounsbury, 1991, p. 58). Creating teams of teachers and students is vitally important to the development of a middle grades learning community. This partnership of shared time, space, instructional and curricular emphases, and philosophy can make a large school feel smaller and reduce anonymity for young adolescents and adults alike. Within a team, a small group of

A Middle School Team = A distinct group of teachers and students learning together

teachers takes primary responsibility for facilitating academic and social growth of a specific group of students. I am convinced that the adage "An individual can make a difference: a team can make a miracle" is true!

As with any organizational structure, teaming is as powerful as the people involved choose to make it. The structure provides the opportunity, but teacher determination and creativity are necessary for successful implementation.

STANDARD 2

Knowledge 5: Middle level teacher candidates understand the team process as a structure for school improvement and student learning.

Team Organization   Teams in middle school are most often interdisciplinary. Each teacher on a team is responsible for one or more subject areas and, when a team is formed, they represent at least the subjects considered core areas—language arts, social studies, science, and math. Research indicates that positive results are achieved from a wide variety of team sizes. Teams commonly consist of as few as two teachers and 40 students to as many as four core teachers plus related arts, special education, and resource teachers and more than 125 students. Because "one size fits all" does not make sense when it comes to team configurations, many decisions are required about the composition of teacher expertise, space, time, student demographics, and other relevant variables. The goal is to create an effective organizational scheme that produces a learning environment that meets the needs of middle level students. Smaller teams of two or three teachers are often created for fifth and sixth grade to more closely resemble self-contained classrooms, while larger teams are dominant in seventh and eighth grade. Regardless of the size of the team, teachers planning together is vital to ensure success.

STANDARD 7

Knowledge 6: Middle level teacher candidates understand teaming/collaborative theories and processes.

Performance 3: Middle level teacher candidates work successfully as members of interdisciplinary teams and as part of the total school environment.

Common Planning Time   To function effectively, team teachers need adequate time to meet and plan. *Common planning time* is time set aside during the instructional day when teams of teachers meet to plan their days with young adolescents. Teachers report that this time together allows them to use their collective knowledge to be on the same page in terms of recognizing student needs, planning for instruction, and providing stability for young adolescents (Picucci, Brownson, Kahlert, & Sobel, 2004). Almost 95% of middle schools have common planning time according to a 2001 study by McEwin, Dickinson, & Jenkins (2003). Jackson & Davis (2000) refer to common planning time as the "daily professional development 'huddle' as teachers reflect critically on their purpose and approach to teaching" during common planning time (p. 141). The frequency and length of common planning time have major impact on the effective functioning of teachers on a team. Team planning time typically occurs during students' related arts classes when all the core teachers are available to meet. A recent study indicates that teams of teachers that meet for 45 minutes four to five times a week function more effectively than teams that meet less frequently. This same study shows that there is a positive correlation between the frequency of team planning time and contact with other building resource staff. Teams that meet frequently have more interaction with counselors, resource teachers, and administrators. This is good news for students because of the active involvement of greater numbers of professionals in their education (Erb & Stevenson, 1999).

As team members, we should respect team planning time by being on time and focused. So much can be accomplished by teachers working together. Having an agenda for topics to be discussed and decisions to be made over the course of a week helps teachers stay on task. Team planning time should be separate from, and in addition to, individual planning time. A school and administration that values effective team functioning will arrange the schedule to accommodate both. Having to choose between using a planning period for individual planning or team planning is no choice at all. Both are vital to instructional effectiveness with young adolescents. Figure 6.1 gives you an idea of the variety of decisions and projects that teams of teachers confront. This list is by no means exhaustive. So many issues, so little time!

FIGURE 6.1   Possible agenda Items for team planning

- Upcoming thematic unit
- Student progress reports
- Scheduling of parent conference(s)
- Student disciplinary issues
- Overlapping curricular topics
- Special education referrals
- Field trip to museum
- Problem with graffiti in boys' bathroom
- Book fair approaching
- Bulletin board display rotation
- Choosing liaison to district committee
- Encouraging parent participation
- Rotating responsibility for student teacher
- Participation in writing competitions
- New rules during construction on field
- Use of computer lab time
- Discussing article given to team by principal
- Jointly grading unit projects
- Discussion of individual students as need arises
- Preparing for long-term substitute for teacher requiring maternity leave

Recommendations for Teaming   Middle grades educators appreciate the concept of teams and have given lots of consideration to what elements contribute to team success. While effective teaming cannot be reduced to a checklist of components, there are guidelines that help promote successful functioning.

The choice of teachers and students who will comprise a team should not be random. Teams need to bring together teachers who have varying subject area expertise, different backgrounds to add diversity, and personalities that will combine to give the team collective power. Best friends do not necessarily make the best teammates.

The composition of students on a team is as important as the mix of teachers. A team should be a microcosm of the whole school, reflecting heterogeneity in terms of ethnicity, socioeconomic background, gender, special education status, and academic achievement. We should be careful not to weight a team heavily with either high-achievers or low-achievers (Jackson & Davis, 2000).

The quality of teaming is enhanced by staff development, both before implementing teaming and on a regular basis after teams are established to promote increased effectiveness. Learning how to set goals, provide consistent support, communicate openly, and collaborate willingly requires concerted effort and training.

A recommendation that enhances the well-made choice of team members, staff development to help members grow, and efficient use of team planning time is the stabilization of team continuity for at least 3 years. Newly formed teams function differently than teams that have been together for a number of years. If norms have been established that foster effectiveness, then keeping teams together makes sense (Jackson & Davis, 2000).

Members of an effective team grow together and enhance one another. Effective teams

- Establish a team name and motto
- Build ownership and enthusiasm
- Spend time together in productive ways as they show care and concern for one another and for students
- Come to consensus on a philosophy, and then publicize and teach according to that philosophy
- Take advantage of opportunities to alter their schedule within flexible blocks of time
- Group and regroup students for instruction
- Work together to accomplish all the items on their ever-growing, ever-changing agenda
- Meet with students and confer with parents as a unit
- Plan curriculum together and make connections among concepts and topics as they use varied instructional strategies

Student welfare guides all decisions and actions. Effective teams of teachers put students first.

Team Leadership and Membership   Every team needs a designated facilitator, usually called the team leader. This task is sometimes rotated among members for varying lengths of time. Being a team leader takes more time than being a team member. Agendas must be made, extra meetings are often required with school-wide leadership teams, communication among team members and school administrators generally falls to the team leader, and the day-to-day functioning of the team relies in great measure on the team leader's efficiency.

Being a good team member is a task to be taken seriously and that cannot be defined by one set of standards. However, there are some traits that are common among those who are valued team members including

- Participatory, carrying through with all team decisions
- Collaborative, even when things aren't going their way
- Pleasant, even when circumstances make it difficult
- Responsible, completing tasks and showing up on time
- Energetic, finding ways to do what's needed when it's needed
- Honest and trustworthy, avoiding talking behind teammates' backs
- Open-minded, willing to learn and try new strategies
- Caring, always putting student needs first

Benefits of Teaming   As you can imagine after reading the preceding discussion, effective teaming has far-reaching benefits. The benefits listed in Figure 6.2 are referred to throughout the rest of this text.

FIGURE 6.2   Benefits of teaming for teachers and students

Benefits for Teachers	Benefits for Students
Teachers get to know students well.	Teachers get to know students well.
Procedures and routines are consistent.	Learning environment is more personalized.
Decisions are made collaboratively.	Sense of belonging is created.
Collegiality and professionalism are enhanced.	Connections among curricular areas are more obvious.
Synergy is created by combining strengths.	Support from teachers is comprehensive.
Intellectual stimulation is the result of collaboration.	More opportunities for grouping and regrouping exist.
Instructional strategies may be shared.	
Curriculum integration is easier to implement.	
Assessment is enhanced by joint evaluation.	
Classroom management is more consistent.	

myeducationlab

To hear Beth Oswald, the 2008 Wisconsin Teacher of the Year, express her love of middle level education and the value of being a lifelong learner, go to the Teacher Talk section of **Topic #1: Schools and Teaching Today** in the MyEducationLab for your course.

In *Meet Me in the Middle,* Wormeli (2001) views curriculum integration as one of the major benefits of teaming. He tells us that curriculum integration works well when it helps students understand who and why and how. It's not about making forced connections, but rather looking for and being conscious of natural links. Teams of teachers can coordinate assignments, focus on larger skills and concepts, and progress logically through subject matter. Subject integration shows students that "real jobs are seldom separated into pure disciplines" (p. 137). In Chapters 7 and 8 we explore curriculum integration and interdisciplinary instruction.

Involving Other School Professionals   Most middle school teams are limited to core curriculum teachers. Our students spend the majority of their school time with this group of two to five teachers. However, involving other school professionals makes the teaching/learning connection more viable.

STANDARD 7

NMSA

Knowledge 4: Middle level teacher candidates understand the interrelationships and interdependencies among various professionals that serve young adolescents (e.g., school counselors, social service workers, home-school coordinators).

Courses taught outside the core are sometimes called related arts, exploratory curriculum, wheel courses (referring to the fact that they are rotated), or encore courses. Perhaps the most generic term is *related arts,* so we'll stick with that. Related arts courses are vital to middle level philosophy. They provide skills training, use talents, and motivate students to pursue real-life activities. As you will see in the next section of this chapter, *related arts teachers* and their courses are the main reason teams are able to benefit from common planning time. While appreciating related arts teachers for the valuable learning resources they provide to our students, we also realize that without them core teams could not function effectively.

The *principal* plays a pivotal role in the success of teaming. When first implemented, teaming requires fundamental changes in any school's organization. To make the logistics work, principals have to rethink staffing, time allocations, and use of facilities. To begin and then continue the structure of teaming requires the principal to understand and support the concept of interdisciplinary teams.

As discussed in Chapter 3, the structure of special education in middle school is increasingly inclusive. This means that students who qualify for special services are part of both core and related arts courses. If the schedule can be arranged, everyone involved benefits from having *special educators* in the classroom alongside core and related arts teachers, all working in concert with students with special needs and other students in need of assistance. Some schools have even arranged schedules that support co-planning and co-teaching. As teams of students reflect the school population, they also share equally the students who have physical and learning differences. Many schools designate special education teachers to be part of specific teams and serve the students of those teams. In smaller schools, the special educators may serve the entire population of students with special needs.

Guidance counselors can have a tremendous influence in middle school. As discussed in Chapter 2, middle grades students sometimes appear to be on social, emotional, and/or physical roller coasters. Counselors who are compassionate, committed, and specially trained to work with young adolescents have the potential to make significant differences in the life of a school. Teams of teachers should communicate regularly with guidance counselors about the students they serve.

Creating Team Identity   The teachers' vision for their team leads the team to a unique persona, an identity that is recognizable. An element of "this is who we are" does much to unify and motivate both teachers and students.

A team name is essential. Don't announce to students in August that they should be proud to be members of team 7B. Screams excitement, doesn't it? How about "Welcome to the Stargazers! Stargazers dream big and aspire to reach the stars," as the lights go out and stars are projected around the room. Some teams of teachers choose a name and a theme and stick with it year after year. They accumulate "stuff" that speaks to their theme. It grows with time. Other teams allow students to choose a name and theme each year. They let the students experience the democratic process and take ownership of team identity. There are pros and cons with each method. No matter how it's chosen, the team's name and theme should be proudly displayed in each team classroom and used in fun ways all year.

Choosing team colors and a team chant helps students feel that they belong. If fabric painting is part of art, then banners and T-shirts can be made. The music teacher may help students write a chant or song. Most 6th graders will participate willingly, while many 7th graders will consider it all pretty silly, although they may secretly take a good deal of pride in their team identity. Eighth graders will often take a renewed interest in team identity and relish being the "big guys" of the middle school. Students of each grade level will generally reflect the enthusiasm of the team teachers. Team identity will be as meaningful as teachers choose to make it.

While the vast majority of middle schools are organized in teams by grade level, there are other possible organizational structures. In some schools, more than one structure is operating and variations of basic organizational schemes can be found. It would be impossible to describe all the possibilities, so as we briefly discuss three of these structures, keep the basics of teaming in mind.

▶ Teachers Speak

● **Sadie Fox**

For me, teaching is all about the kids. Yes, I love science and teaching it to my students, but I decided to teach so I could make a difference in the lives of kids. I chose middle school for a number of reasons. One reason is that I enjoy their sense of humor—biazarre and unpredictable! I also am drawn to the concept of teaming. When I was in college, I was president of our chapter of the Collegiate Middle Level Association and attended two National Middle School Association conferences. There I participated in sessions on teaming and found the concept to be the best thing going!

I think the enthusiasm of the younger teachers at Valley View convinced other teachers to make the most of the concept. When I started teaching here, teams were in place, but if you walked down the halls you couldn't tell one team from another. Several of us got together and decided the 8th grade teachers and students would change that. We decided to develop team identities and come up with names, colors, chants, logos, and anything else the kids could think of. We had several team meetings and brainstormed with the kids. Our team decided they wanted to be the Valley View Vampires. I wasn't crazy about it, but decided to let them run with it. They chose red, of course, for blood and resurrected the old Monster Mash song as the theme. I went to the dollar store that evening and surprised them with plastic vampire teeth. Well, we all put them on and posed for a team photo. I had the photo enlarged to poster size and we hung it in our team hall. The kids wanted to get a vampire movie and read books about vampires. We agreed to study the legend of Dracula, but the only movie we could show in school about vampires was "Scooby-Doo and the Legend of the Vampire." This wasn't exactly what they had in mind, but we used it as a behavior incentive for the end of the term, and the kids had a great time at the event, complete with red soda and popcorn.

Can we do splashy team events all the time? No, of course not. But has a team identity with lots of student input brought us closer together, involved reluctant kids, and motivated participation in not only activities but also in learning? You bet! Teaming is at the heart of middle school. It makes sense and makes teaching more effective and enjoyable.

● Creative Grouping Alternatives

The possibility of creating alternative structures is very real. "The knowledge and experience required for such organizational transformation to take place is available; only the will needed for more widespread implementation is lacking. For the sake of the education of young adolescents, it must be done" (George & Lounsbury, 2000, p. 113). Let's explore three possibilities.

Multiage Grouping   Do you remember reading about the one-room school in an introduction to education class? Maybe you've seen the reruns of "Little House on the Prairie." Some communities, like the village of Romulus, New York, have renewed interest in their local education history. The folks of Romulus actually restored their historic one-room schoolhouse and moved it to the campus of the current high school to celebrate their education heritage. Today we perceive the concept of the one-room school as a form of *multiage grouping.*

In middle schools, multiage grouping refers to students of two or more grade levels being placed on the same team and even in the same classroom as ability levels and interests dictate. If a school serves grades 6, 7, and 8, students spend 3 years with others who are their same age and students who are younger and/or older than they are. At the end of each year, one-third of the students in the multiage group go on to high school to be replaced by the incoming sixth graders the following fall. One-room schools were formed out of necessity due to the size of the communities and the economics dictated by limited population, resources, and qualified teachers. Today multiage grouping is driven by the benefits derived from long-term relationships. Discipline becomes less of a problem as relationships are maintained over three years. Beginnings and endings of the year are much smoother. Parent relationships are more positive and productive. Interethnic relationships improve. When there are signs of difficulty of any kind, multiage problem solving and growth are possible. Teachers, students, parents, and administrators who practice multiage grouping have discovered that many school processes work better when more permanence is part of school relationships (George & Lounsbury, 2000).

More research is definitely called for concerning multiage grouping. This research needs to follow students and teachers for 3 or more years to capture the complexities of this creative alternative. Affective outcomes appear to be positive, while the effects of multiage grouping on academic achievement are mostly unknown.

Looping   The rationale for this grouping alternative is that if teams of students and teachers have many benefits, why not extend those relationships, and consequently the benefits, over longer periods of time? A continuous year-to-year instructional plan involving the same team of students and teachers has been called teacher rotation, student-teacher progression, and, most recently, *looping.* "Looping . . . promotes real communication, mediation, resolution, and deeper understanding of other perspectives that foster a sense of community and teach our students lessons about maintaining the relationships in their lives" (Fenter, 2009, p. 29).

While research is sparse concerning achievement benefits, anecdotal accounts tell us that looping is a very positive experience. Some have reported that this gift of time is experienced in the second and third years when moving ahead instructionally is not hampered by the necessity of getting acquainted, becoming familiar with achievement status, and working out procedures. In *Making Big Schools Feel Small* (2000), a medical analogy is given. George and Lounsbury relate that the idea of finding a new dentist or doctor for a child every year makes no sense. If it's important for physicians to know their patients as they develop, how can we not see that it's equally important for teachers to know their students as they grow? This is a powerful argument.

Schools-within-a-School This third alternative method of grouping also takes advantage of long-term relationships. In large middle schools, separate community systems may be established composed of a sixth grade team, a seventh grade team, and an eighth grade team (or teams). *Schools-within-a-school* is also known as a house plan. The original *Turning Points* (Carnegie Council on Adolescent Development, 1989) document recommended that "The student should, upon entering middle grade school, join a small community in which people—students and adults—get to know each other well to create a climate for intellectual development. . . . One successful solution to unacceptably large middle schools is the schools-within-a-school or house arrangement" (pp. 37–38).

In this grouping, each *house* is a microcosm of the total school population. If facilities permit, each house has its own distinct area of the building(s), where at least the core classes are held. Ideally each house has its own administrative area, along with related arts classrooms. If this isn't possible, houses stay together for core classes and then join others on individual grade levels for related arts and intramural activities.

Schools-within-a-school have been around for years. The organization requires fewer alterations and less effort than multiage grouping and looping. Teachers remain with a team of students for one grade level. The benefits are derived from grade to grade by teams continuing to work together closely as a unit. They can plan for ongoing themes as they build a curriculum for a specific group of students. Sixth graders know who their teachers will be in subsequent years. They also know that the students on their team will remain constant. So the benefits of a small learning community can be realized without the complexities inherent in other arrangements (George & Lounsbury, 2000).

Regardless of the organizational structure of a middle school, or any school that serves young adolescents, advisory programs are developmentally appropriate.

● Advisory Programs

A special time regularly set aside for small groups of students to meet with specific adults is known as *advisory* period. Some schools call it advisor/advisee or home-based guidance or teacher-based guidance. Typically advisory groups meet for 20 to 30 minutes, at least three days a week.

Turning Points (1989) directs middle schools to provide opportunities such as advisory periods for each student to have a close relationship with an adult within the school.

> Every student should be well known by at least one adult. Students should be able to rely on that adult to help them learn from their experiences, comprehend physical changes and changing relations with family and peers, act on their behalf to marshall every school and community resource needed for the student to succeed, and help to fashion a promising vision of the future. (p. 40)

Turning Points 2000 (Jackson & Davis, 2000) supports the intention of the original document and contends that the advisory period is important to the development of strong interpersonal bonds.

STANDARD 7

Knowledge 5: Middle level teacher candidates know advisory/advocate theories, skills, and curriculum.

Performance 2: Middle level teacher candidates serve as advisors, advocates, and mentors for all young adolescents.

Organizing Advisory   Schools vary in their approaches to advisory. Some are quite structured with all advisory periods following basically the same plan—possibly a prescribed program using purchased materials to guide discussions and activities. Other schools leave advisory up to individual teams that decide how to best use the time. Some advisories are organized by day. For instance, Monday may be used for housekeeping activities, Tuesday for planned discussion, Wednesday for intramurals, Thursday for silent reading, and Friday for test preparation and homework completion. This kind of arrangement closely resembles the traditional homeroom and doesn't meet the developmental and affective needs of the middle school student in optimal ways. It does, however, afford the advisor a daily forum within which developmentally appropriate topics may be addressed if desired. Another approach might be for the team to decide on weekly or monthly themes that guide discussion and activities. Possible themes include self-awareness, respect, the dangers of substance abuse, healthy lifestyles, and celebrating differences.

The primary purpose for advisory is to meet the developmental and affective needs of students. Whatever schedule may be in place and regardless of the "plan," advisors should respond to crisis situations by giving advisees opportunities to ask questions, express fear or frustration, and, in general, draw comfort and guidance within the advisory setting. Incidents of school violence, crises of the 9/11 proportion, local happenings, or whatever is of concern to our students is appropriate advisory content.

Benefits of Advisory   Here's a list of some of the benefits of establishing and maintaining viable advisory periods in the middle grades.

- Because all young adolescents want to be heard, advisory periods provide opportunities for peers and a trusted adult to listen.
- All kids have occasional struggles as they make their way through early adolescence. Advisory periods provide a forum for discussions of their struggles and a safe place to explore options and solutions.

- Advisory groups serve to fortify identity. They bring together kids who normally may not have a lot of contact and who don't naturally gravitate to each other in social settings. This diverse group of kids has a unique identity as they spend time together.

- In stressful times, whether personal, school-based, regionally-generated, or as a result of national or international crisis, young adolescents gather in advisory and can vent their fears and anxiety under the watchful guidance of a trusted adult.

- Advisory period provides administrative functions much like traditional homerooms when needed.

Roadblocks to Advisory   While advisory by definition and in practice is a major tenet of middle grades philosophy, its widespread implementation remains elusive. Only about half of America's middle schools implement advisory periods (McEwin, Dickinson, & Jenkins, 2003). Most middle schools have a nonacademic and nonrelated arts period during the day that serves as an administrative time, like a homeroom, but may have the label "advisory." Close examination is required to determine if the period is being used for purposes similar to those described in this section. As with so many concepts, having a designated period provides opportunity. What is done with the period makes the difference. Many teachers view advisory as another preparation and are often unwilling to commit the time to make it valuable for students. Comprehensive staff development is vital to the successful implementation of advisory that realizes the benefits in the previous section.

Please consider carefully how advisory can make a difference in the lives of middle grades students. You may find yourself in a school where advisory exists in name only. If you have the designated period, use it with your kids and for their direct benefit. The effort will be worth it. And remember that advisory is an attitude more than a program. It's an attitude that leads us to commit to know our students well, to advocate for them when possible, and to wear our advisor hats all day, every day.

Now that we have considered structures of people in middle level settings, let's explore structures of time.

Structures of Time

"Time is perhaps the most important but least available resource in American education" (Jackson & Davis, 2000, p. 131). We typically have 180 days with our students. That's a constant. How we choose to use these days is a critically important variable. As with other variables in life, there isn't just one right way. Fortunately, there are many options and variations. As educators, we have an awesome responsibility for organizing the time our students spend with us so optimal benefit is achieved. While some configurations appear to be more developmentally conducive than others, ultimately schools have to choose a schedule that facilitates their priorities

(George & Alexander, 2003). In this section we will delve into how days can be scheduled for student growth through their middle level experience.

This We Believe (2010) calls for flexible grouping, scheduling, and staffing, with teams designing and operating much of the program. *Turning Points* (1989) calls for teams to have the power to ". . . create blocks of instructional time to best meet the needs of students, rather than tailoring learning to fit a rigid schedule. Teacher control of scheduling can . . . make learning come alive for students" (p. 16). *Turning Points 2000* echoes this point by recommending that team teachers lengthen and shorten classes, as well as determine the frequency and order of classes to reflect instructional and student needs.

Sounds great, doesn't it? With flexible scheduling we can have team autonomy to use time in ways that respond to the needs of students. Reality? Rarely.

● Traditional Schedule

Although opportunity exists for flexibility and creativity in scheduling, the majority of middle school class periods remain 45 to 55 minutes long. Many schools schedule six or seven fixed periods a day, every day, all year long. I'll be the first to say that a well-planned instructional period of 50 minutes is far preferable to a 90-minute period, half wasted. Limiting instructional time in each subject to an arbitrary 50 minutes is traditional, but perhaps not as effective as alternatives. If we view time as a resource rather than an element of schooling to be managed, we see that perceived obstacles to using time in more constructive ways are worth overcoming.

Dissatisfaction with both the limits of shorter classes and the inflexibility of traditional schedules has led increasing numbers of schools to reconfigure the way students and staff spend their days. No schedule is perfect, nor should any schedule be considered permanent. There are advantages and disadvantages to each that grow or recede in importance based on numerous variables. It's not necessary—and indeed prohibitive or downright impossible—to wait until all the anticipated kinks are ironed out of any given plan. While schedules need to stay fixed for given periods of time, they should be evolving and moldable from semester to semester, year to year.

● Block Schedule

The word *block* is used in many ways when discussing schedules. A block of time is a chunk of time—a longer period than the traditional 50-minute period. A *block schedule* is any schedule that allows for more time in class. It is important to understand that whatever the configuration of a block schedule, there are three major distinctions to be considered.

- Some forms of block scheduling increase the time spent in a given class period, but because the class may not meet every day the total minutes allotted to the class over the course of the year don't change.

- Some forms of block scheduling not only increase the time in a particular class, but also the total minutes for the year because the number of times the class meets is not altered.

- Flexible block scheduling provides time that is divided by teachers as appropriate for the day's academic plan. Let's look at a variety of block scheduling models.

4 × 4 Semester Block Model   The 4 × 4 is used in many high schools, and some middle schools are adapting the basics of the plan. In this model, four courses are completed during each semester. Figure 6.3 illustrates a variation for middle schools. In this sample, the student would have 90 minutes of math and 90 minutes of language arts every day of the year, but 90 minutes of science or social studies every day for only a semester. This plan would work well for a three-teacher team—one math, one language arts, and one science/social studies.

FIGURE 6.3   4 × 4 semester block model: sample of a schedule for one student on a team

	Semester I	Semester II
8:00–9:30	Math	Math
9:30–11:00	Language Arts	Language Arts
11:00–12:00	Lunch and Advisory	Lunch and Advisory
12:00–1:30	Science	Social Studies
1:30–3:00	Related Arts	Related Arts

The unique personalities and learning styles of middle level learners call for flexibility in scheduling. These same personalities add so much joy to our profession!

Alternating Day Model   This model is also popular in high schools where it's often referred to as the A/B schedule. In middle school this model allows for three related arts periods or a course repeated daily. Figure 6.4 illustrates the basics of this model using eight periods on a 2-week cycle. Like the 4 × 4, a benefit of this model is that students change classes only four times a day and thus spend more minutes in each period.

A variation of the previous model is the alternating day model that follows a weekly cycle as illustrated in Figure 6.5, allowing for each class to meet three times a week rather than some two times and some three.

FIGURE 6.4   Alternating day model (2-week cycle)

Time	Monday	Tuesday	Wednesday	Thursday	Friday
8:00–9:25	1	5	1	5	1
9:25–10:50	2	6	2	6	2
10:50–12:10	Lunch/Advisory/Recess				
12:10–1:35	3	7	3	7	3
1:35–3:00	4	8	4	8	4

Time	Monday	Tuesday	Wednesday	Thursday	Friday
8:00–9:25	5	1	5	1	5
9:25–10:50	6	2	6	2	6
10:50–12:10	Lunch/Advisory/Recess				
12:10–1:35	7	3	7	3	7
1:35–3:00	8	4	8	4	8

Time	Sixth Grade	Seventh Grade	Eighth Grade
10:50–11:15	Advisory	Recess	Lunch
11:15–11:40	Lunch	Advisory	Recess
11:40–12:10	Recess	Lunch	Advisory

FIGURE 6.5   Alternating day model (weekly cycle)

Time	Monday	Tuesday	Wednesday	Thursday	Friday
8:00–8:45	1	1	5	1	5
8:45–9:30	2				
9:30–10:15	3	2	6	2	6
10:15–11:00	4				
11:00–12:00	Lunch/Advisory/Recess				
12:00–12:45	5	3	7	3	7
12:45–1:30	6				
1:30–2:15	7	4	8	4	8
2:15–3:00	8				

FIGURE 6.6   Daily plus alternating day model

Time	Monday	Tuesday	Wednesday	Thursday	Friday
8:00–9:30	1	1	1	1	1
9:30–11:00	2	2	2	2	2
11:00–12:00	Lunch/Advisory/Recess				
12:00–1:30	3	5	3	5	3
1:30–3:00	4	6	4	6	4

Daily Plus Alternating Day Model   Some schools declare curricular emphasis in certain subjects such as science and math. Others have a "back to basics" approach that invests more time in math and language arts. The daily plus alternating day model in Figure 6.6 shows how a schedule can create time frames to accommodate some classes having twice as much time as others. This model still provides the benefit of longer class periods for all subjects.

Flexible Block Model   The schedules presented so far provide longer class periods and, for some courses, considerably more total time. What the schedules don't provide for is flexibility. The model that best approximates the vision for scheduling in *This We Believe* and *Turning Points* is the *flexible block* schedule. This model provides large blocks of time allotted to teams to be used for instruction. "All middle schools should adopt some form of flexible block scheduling that provides teachers with multiple opportunities to make sound decisions regarding curriculum and instruction for the young adolescents they teach" (McEwin, Dickinson, & Jenkins, 2003, p. 50).

A sample flexible block schedule is shown in Figure 6.7. Grade levels, and, therefore, interdisciplinary teams, have two large blocks to use as they deem appropriate. Early in the section, I wrote that even when given the opportunity to use

FIGURE 6.7   Flexible block model

Time	Sixth Grade	Seventh Grade	Eighth Grade
7:35–8:00	Homeroom/Advisory	Homeroom/Advisory	Homeroom/Advisory
8:00–8:25	Related Arts/ Exploratory	Instructional Block	Instructional Block
8:25–8:50	Related Arts/ Exploratory	Instructional Block	Instructional Block
8:50–9:15		Instructional Block	Instructional Block
9:15–9:40		Instructional Block	Instructional Block
9:40–10:05	Instructional Block	Instructional Block	Instructional Block
10:05–10:30	Instructional Block	Instructional Block	Instructional Block
10:30–10:55	Instructional Block	Related Arts/ Exploratory	Lunch
10:55–11:20	Instructional Block	Related Arts/ Exploratory	Recess
11:20–11:45	Lunch	Related Arts/ Exploratory	Instructional Block
11:45–12:10	Recess	Related Arts/ Exploratory	Instructional Block
12:10–12:35	Instructional Block	Lunch	Instructional Block
12:35–1:00	Instructional Block	Recess	Instructional Block
1:00–1:25	Instructional Block	Instructional Block	Related Arts/ Exploratory
1:25–1:50	Instructional Block	Instructional Block	Related Arts/ Exploratory
1:50–2:15	Instructional Block	Instructional Block	Related Arts/ Exploratory
2:15–2:40	Instructional Block	Instructional Block	Related Arts/ Exploratory

flexibility in scheduling, most middle school periods remain fixed. Examining Figure 6.7 will reveal how easily a team could take their 250 minutes and divide them into five neat periods—math, language arts, science, social studies, and reading. Or they might divide them into four periods of 60+ minutes with one split around lunch or related arts. That is OK to do as a base schedule. It is not OK to do every day for 180 days.

STANDARD 2

Knowledge 6: Middle level teacher candidates understand that flexible scheduling provides the context for teachers to meet the needs of all young adolescents.

NMSA

To make optimal use of the flexible block, teams of teachers should spend time devising about five different ways the schedule might be altered and brainstorm reasons for making the alterations. For instance, the science teacher plans to have students conduct a lab experiment that requires more than 50 minutes. The schedule is altered so that one science class meets for 150 minutes each day. The other teachers divide the remaining students (in the case of a four-person team, that would be 75% of the students) and rotate them through their subjects. Perhaps the team wants to see a special exhibit at the local museum. They would have 150 minutes for the trip without interrupting related arts schedules.

When teams have the autonomy to use their time, it is possible to rotate classes from day to day. We discussed the changeability of middle level students, how they may behave very differently from one day to the next. In fact, a student may approach school at 9:00 A.M. very differently than at 1:30 P.M. Teachers who rotate student schedules on a regular basis report that students respond differently to their teaching depending on the time of day. Not surprisingly, they find that their teaching styles and attitudes also vary—some are "morning people" and others function more enthusiastically as the day goes on. Thus, there are benefits in rotating classes of students to spread out the advantages, and to share the low moments equitably. On Monday, you may see groups A, B, C, and D in that order (ABCD). On Tuesday, you would see them in BCDA order and then on Wednesday in CDAB. Given uninterrupted team time, rotation is possible without interrupting schedules outside the team.

Perhaps the greatest benefit of the flexible block is that it accommodates *interdisciplinary instruction*. We explore this concept in detail in Chapters 7 and 10. With the flexible block, time is available for large group experiences, uninterrupted video viewing, co-teaching, grouping/regrouping, guest speakers, joint projects—the list can go on and on.

Utilizing Longer Blocks of Time   Two elements are absolutely necessary to make longer blocks of time the effective instructional tools they can be. One element is

Making longer blocks work =
Continuing staff development +
Planning

continuing staff development. A 90-minute lesson is not two 45-minute lessons back to back. Teachers need strategies appropriate for longer class periods. George & Alexander (2003) tell us that the most frequently reported outcome of longer blocks is better teaching—teaching that is more creative and innovative. More hands-on learning is possible with time for projects and opportunities for active student participation.

The second necessary element is planning. With adequate staff development, teachers are equipped to open their instructional toolboxes and apply varying strategies to longer blocks of time. To do so in effective ways, both individual and common team planning time are necessary.

Both traditional and alternative scheduling can provide opportunities for curricular and instructional improvement. Maximizing the potential of any structure requires commitment, energy, and ever-developing expertise.

Now let's explore guidelines for effectively structuring the places where we teach and learn.

Structures of Place

An important feature in the life of a middle school team is shared space. The core classes should be as close together as possible—either next door to one another, or at least on the same hallway. Proximity means fewer minutes lost in changing classes, fewer discipline problems in the hallways, and more opportunities for informal teacher-to-teacher contact (Jackson & Davis, 2000). Having an identifiable part of the building to call our own is a vital aspect of teaming. This is generally a built-in feature if a facility is constructed to accommodate middle level philosophy. Ideally there is a pod of classrooms including a science lab and a teacher workroom. With flexible scheduling, teams need to be free to move from classroom to classroom without disturbing other teams.

While we may have little control over the existence or location of shared team space, we have a great deal of control over our individual classrooms and the environments we create. What do we do inside our classrooms to make them livable, pleasant, and efficient? To answer this question requires thought and planning. There's not a lot we can do about the amount of money the school district has, or chooses to spend, for physical amenities, and the size of the classroom is rarely a matter of choice. Sometimes the only variable within our sphere of influence is our own creativity.

The Inviting Classroom

We want our rooms to serve as an initial and continuing invitation to students. The environment should say to students "Welcome. This is a place where you are wanted." The amount of effort we put into the classroom environment is evident to our students.

First impressions are crucial. Having your classroom ready to go on the first day of school with a big WELCOME banner to greet your students will set the tone. Try standing by the doorway and shaking each student's hand as he or she enters and saying a personal "Welcome! I'm _____." Most 10- to 14-year-olds are not used to being greeted in such an adult way. It will make a lasting impression! Most of them will look away and giggle and give you what my daddy used to call a "dead-fish" handshake. After a week or so, you can talk about the greeting. Ask students how it felt to be welcomed with a handshake. Talk to them about exuding self-confidence, a firm handshake, and eye contact. Repeat the greeting every few weeks.

Students need to feel safe and secure and comfortable. For some, these three factors don't exist outside the classroom. Their home and/or neighborhood environments may be less than desirable. You may bear the responsibility of providing one of the only inviting atmospheres they are currently experiencing. What a burden—and what an opportunity!

If you have the luxury of being hired in early summer for a position that begins in late August, you will have plenty of time to prepare your classroom. Some of you may be hired after school has already started because the enrollment allows the principal to add a position, or perhaps an emergency has led to the need to replace a teacher. Preparation may mean nights and weekends—whatever it takes to create a desirable environment.

STANDARD 5

Performance 6: Middle level teacher candidates establish equitable, caring, and productive learning environments for all young adolescents.

● Classroom Inventory

It is vital to begin the creation of your classroom environment with a thorough inventory. Find and list the items available. Figure 6.8 will give you an idea of things to look for. Once you know what you have, list any standard or basic items that are missing. They may be available somewhere in your building. Share your list of needs with your team, the custodial staff, and the main office staff. Don't be afraid to ask.

● Planning the Basic Set-up

The kind of environment we create may depend on the subject(s) we teach and on our personal preferences. There are two imperatives for basic room arrangement. When setting up desks or student tables, we must provide for teacher **access** to all

---

FIGURE 6.8   Classroom inventory

- Chalk/dry erase boards—don't cover them
- Assignment board (don't use valuable chalkboard space)
- Two trash cans
- Class work/homework baskets
- Podium on table or music stand
- Materials—appropriate for subject(s)
- Bulletin boards
- Place for posting rules
- Pets, plants
- Audiovisual equipment
- Computer(s)
- Windows/blinds/curtains
- Lighting accessories
- Desk
- Filing cabinet
- Shelves
- Bookcases
- "Cubbies," lockers, coat racks

---

students and ways for students to **transition** from individual to small group to whole class instruction.

myeducationlab

To watch Deirdre McGrew's room tour at Cario Middle School, showing distinct areas, each with a purpose, go to the Video Examples section of **Topic #3: Classroom Management** in the MyEducationLab for your course and view the video entitled "Deirdre McGrew's Room Tour."

Access   You need room to walk. You need to be able to reach each student in your classroom quickly. Proximity to students has both instructional and management advantages. Having a walking loop is an important way to accomplish proximity.

The configuration of desks in rows was typical in the recent past, and this configuration still persists in many classrooms. If lecture is the most frequently used form of instruction, then rows will work. Rows are easy to keep orderly. However, desks in rows also confine the teacher to the front of the room in the traditional power position. For standardized testing days or days dedicated to strictly individualized work, desks in rows may be advantageous. But on typical days in a middle school classroom filled with active involvement, there are other configurations that allow for greater teacher access to all students. Students always need to feel the teacher's presence.

Transitions   Whether you have 45 or 90 classes, your students will have *transitions* to make while following your lesson plans. If you are fortunate enough to have a large classroom that allows for easy movement, there are many room configurations that will work. If you are cramped for space by either a small classroom or a large number of students, your options may be limited.

Arranging desks or tables in small groups is the most usable and flexible configuration. If space permits the seating arrangement to be changed for transitions to individual and whole class work, that's terrific. If not, students can work individually or as a whole class from small group configurations.

Efficient room arrangement =
Access + Transitions

When tables or desks are in small group configurations, make sure students understand your expectations for individual work. They may simply pull their desks apart or may turn them so they are not directly facing one another. For transition to whole class instruction, be sure all students can see and hear what's going on.

Furniture, Equipment, and Materials   Once you have a basic set-up of desks or tables, it's time to plan the rest of the room. Your desk is an important feature of the classroom for you, but not for the students. It is an organizational tool for you where you may want to lay out materials you plan to use and keep information to which you need to refer. But the teacher's desk is not the focal point of a middle grades classroom. I suggest you choose a corner for a file cabinet, your desk, and a chair. It is your space and students need to respect that. Don't sit behind it and allow it to be a barrier between you and your students.

Learning centers are locations in your classroom where topics can be explored by individuals or small groups. Designate a table and shelves for a learning center. We talk more about setting up and maintaining these centers in Chapter 8.

A classroom library is appropriate regardless of the subject(s) you teach. Having interesting books, both fiction and nonfiction, on shelves for students to peruse and check out encourages reading.

If you have a computer(s) in your classroom, provide easy access and a method students follow for using technology. Frequency of use will depend on the subject you teach, the software available, and your encouragement. Do not allow your computer area to become a dumping ground for books and newspapers and jackets. If you are fortunate enough to have computers, by all means use them with your students.

As you plan for instruction, there will inevitably be materials involved. Maybe you'll use graph paper, newspapers, markers, maps, and so forth. Having materials organized and readily accessible will save valuable instructional time. Plastic crates and boxes that stack neatly work well. Teaching students good organizational habits will pay off. They need to know how to access and how to put away instructional materials. There's a knack to making all this organization work. The key is habit. Instill efficiency and respect for materials in your students from day one. These routines will pay off for each of the other 179! In Chapter 11 we discuss additional valuable routines.

Classroom wall space can be a dynamic teaching tool. Bulletin boards can be teaching tools in themselves. Many teachers merely purchase an assortment of posters, put them on the walls and bulletin boards, and then leave them all year. This is boring, and the posters rapidly become wasted instructional space once students have lost interest. You may have a few favorites that seem appropriate for the entire year, but choose carefully. Class/team/school rules may be left up and some inspirational posters are acceptable to use as permanent displays, but changing bulletin board displays is a creative and efficient way of bringing new information into the classroom. Bulletin board displays need to correspond to what's being learned. Make them interesting and interactive. Have groups of students design and make displays. Use student art or class work and display projects.

There should be a designated area where assignments and necessary books/materials are posted. This should be in a consistent location. Each afternoon before leaving for the day get into the habit of posting information for the following day. You do not necessarily need to write out the exact assignment, but have the space ready so you only have to fill in the details when it's appropriate.

You may want to add personal touches like plants to your classroom (let students rotate the responsibility for their care), couches, comfortable chairs, lamps, and so on. These items are a matter of space and availability and your own style. If time for individual reading is part of your day, seating options are enjoyed by students. Again, if they are in the habit of moving about the room in respectful ways, they will not abuse the privilege of sitting on a rug or in an overstuffed chair occasionally to enjoy silent reading.

Home Away from Home

Think about it—at least 7 of every 24 hours of every school day are spent mostly within the walls of our classrooms. Let your classroom reflect you, your care for students, and your interest in learning. Chances are you will experiment with configurations and move things around as the year goes by. You will learn what works best for your students in terms of your access and their transitioning. Learning centers will change and bulletin boards will develop in direct proportion to your creativity and the time you spend to make it happen. Remember that students are

Comfortable spaces welcome students and encourage reading.

watching. Their curiosity and subsequent motivation depend on your keeping an organized and comfortable environment as part of your instructional planning. Use your classroom as a haven of security, a motivator of interest, and a workshop for organizational habits.

Reflections on Structures of People, Time, and Place

How we choose to structure people, time, and place in the middle grades affects school climate and academic success. Some of the effects have been verified through research, while others are reported anecdotally. While many structures fall within an acceptable range, some follow more closely the tenets of *Turning Points* and *This We Believe*.

Creating smaller learning communities is a hallmark attribute of middle level philosophy. The middle grades teacher/student team is most widely accepted as the optimum people structure. As we've seen in this chapter, there are many possible team configurations, some incorporating tracking, and some that group entirely heterogeneously. Some are quite small, and some are large. Some teams of teachers and students stay together for 1 year, others for 2 years, and, in extreme cases of looping, some stay together for 3 years.

Time, as a tremendous resource, is ours to use every school day. As educators, we are obligated to make the most of the 180 or so days we spend with our students. Longer blocks of time in classes provide opportunities for complete cycles of introductory experiences, inquiry, understanding, practice, reflection, and assessment. Putting blocks of time together for optimal learning and then incorporating flexibility both serve vital functions in the middle grades.

Manipulating our physical environments may be an ongoing process of working toward efficiency and comfort. Choices of desk/table arrangements, use of wall space, walking and storage areas, and the atmosphere we create are all ours to make. The total effect of place relies in great measure on our efforts.

While the structures described in this chapter suit middle grades philosophy, there are schools all across America that are successfully educating young adolescents through responsive dispositions without many of the structures we have discussed. Understanding and appreciating the development of young adolescents and framing curriculum, instruction, and assessment around their needs and unique qualities will produce an atmosphere that fosters healthy physical, intellectual, emotional, social, and moral growth. It is possible for a school for middle grades students to be subject-area based with six classes a day and without clustering of classrooms, and still meet the needs of the students. It's possible, but certainly more difficult than if structures are in place that accommodate middle level philosophy. Keep in mind that structures aligning with middle level philosophy provide opportunities. They don't guarantee success. It's up to us to take full advantage of the opportunities provided by developmentally responsive structures of people, time, and place.

GROUP ACTIVITIES

1. In groups of two or three arrange to visit with teachers from a school in your file. Your instructor will give you guidelines for arranging the visit. Your group will want to spend about 30 minutes with the teacher you visit to find out about their structures of people, time, and place. Using this chapter as a reference, work with your class to formulate questions/prompts that will lead to an understanding of the degree to which the teachers and students team, if and how tracking is used, the format of advisory, the schedule, and the physical layout of the building as it is used by teams and/or grade levels. The results of the school visits will be added to your school file.

2. Divide your class into four groups. Each group will be assigned one of the following structures of people: grade level teams, looping, multiage grouping, and schools-within-a-school configurations. Each group will formulate their best reasoning in support of their structure. They will present their reasoning to the class as "panels of experts." If possible, invite other students (education majors and others) to listen to the panels and then allow the audience, even if it's only your classmates, to critique the panel discussions.

INDIVIDUAL ACTIVITIES

1. Knowing what we do about the development of middle grades students, write a description of what you would consider to be the most appropriate use of a week of daily 30-minute advisory periods.

2. Given the classroom inventory in Figure 6.8, draw an overview diagram of a classroom arrangement you might want for the subject area you plan to teach. Be prepared to explain (and possibly defend) your arrangement choices.

3. How do you feel about the "to track or not to track" debate? Specifically, what kind of grouping (and regrouping) do you feel might be most appropriate for your chosen subject area?

4. Explain in your own words the statement, "An individual can make a difference: a team can make a miracle."

PERSONAL JOURNAL

1. Think back to your days in middle grades. Was tracking used at your school? Was it formally orchestrated so that it was obvious to everyone, or was it more covertly arranged and just understood by students? Were you in a particular track in certain subjects? How did you feel personally, and how do you think you were perceived?

2. Do you remember classrooms that seemed to "invite" students? If so, what qualities did the classroom have? Was it a function of the physical amenities or of the teacher's personality? Was it a combination? If you don't remember any of your classrooms as obvious "invitations," what elements might have created this kind of atmosphere?

3. Do you think you have the personal skills to function as a cooperative and effective member of a teaching team? If so, what personal qualities give you this ability? If not, and if you want to be part of teaming, what personal qualities do you want to cultivate to allow you to participate productively on a team?

Professional Practice

(It would be helpful to reread the descriptions of Sarah Gardner in Chapter 4 and Darma in Chapter 3.)

● Sarah Gardner

Sarah Gardner is student teaching with two teachers who each have over 20 years in the classroom. They are comfortable with young adolescents and the subjects they teach. The only thing Sarah finds to question is their use of time set aside for advisory. Ms. Morris and Ms. Cunningham each have a group of about 25 kids for the 30-minute period. So far she hasn't seen the daily 30-minute period utilized the way she has read about in the *Middle School Journal*. It's a homeroom where lunch money is collected, announcements are made, and homework is finished. On Fridays they go outside or to the gym for games. It's not a bad use of time, just not what it could be.

Darma ● sixth grade

Kids like Darma thrive during the daily session. His homework already done, he uses the time to trade comic books or play chess or cards. His advisory group is the same as his first period class—all AIG (academically and intellectually gifted) students who meet with Ms. Morris. The other 25 kids meet with Ms. Cunningham.

1. Sarah is disappointed in the use of advisory time. What is the most likely cause of her disappointment?

a. She wants the time to be structured around academic assistance.
b. She thinks the time would be better spent for an additional related arts class.
c. She would rather divide the 30 minutes among the core courses so there would be more time in them.
d. She would like to address nonacademic topics that will help kids grow.

2. Which of the following would not be appropriate for Sarah's team teachers to do to change the way they have always approached advisory period?
a. call the district office and ask if anyone knows of a middle school that uses advisory in ways they don't at Lake Park Middle School
b. ask kids to come up with topics and then write reports and present topics to the whole advisory group
c. look into programs that address the affective side of young adolescent development and consider following a daily plan based on themes of the program
d. make a plan for each day of the week like current events on Monday, character traits on Tuesday, intramurals on Wednesday, and so on

3. Darma enjoys the 30-minute period each day. Given what we know about him, which of the following would likely not be Darma's reaction to changes in format?
a. Darma would go along with changes.
b. Darma would ask to change teams if Sarah got her way and mixed the two groups.

c. Darma would still complete his homework early and take a wait-and-see attitude toward changes.

d. Darma would actively work with his friends on whatever projects were planned.

4. Knowing Sarah as we do, what one thing would she want most to change about advisory that links to her interests in graduate school?

a. She would like to mix the AIG and "regular" kids in advisory period.

b. She would like to design a research study on student perceptions of advisory.

c. She would like to visit each team's advisory periods to observe differences.

d. She would like to plan focused reading and discussion.

Constructed Response

Advisory is one of the most underutilized facets of middle level philosophy. One reason for this cited in research studies is that teachers view advisory as another course preparation. What ideas do you have for taking advisory from the realm of drudgery or ambivalence to a pleasure for teachers and students?

INTERNET RESOURCES

Ability Grouping

www.reading.indiana.edu/ieo/bibs/ability.html

The current research on, and practices of, ability grouping are the focus of this website. The information is derived from websites, libraries, bookstores, and other sources.

Block Scheduling

www.education.umn.edu/carei/blockscheduling

The University of Minnesota College of Education maintains this site featuring research and information on block scheduling.

Design Share

www.designshare.com

The characteristics of an ideal middle school facility are featured on this site. Floor plans that support middle level philosophy of structures of people, time, and place are displayed.

7 Middle Level Curriculum

We are all teachers of reading. For many young adolescents, the key to enjoying reading is often found in stories filled with humor and adventure. Sparking the interest of young adolescents in reading will lead to greater proficiency and comprehension. Without reading skills, success in school is impossible.

Curriculum is the primary vehicle for achieving the goals and objectives of a school. In developmentally responsive middle grades schools, curriculum encompasses every planned aspect of the educational program. It includes not only the basic classes designed to advance skills and knowledge but also school-wide services and programs such as guidance, clubs and interest groups, music and drama productions, student government, service activities, and sports.

National Middle School Association, 2010, p. 17

CHAPTER PREVIEW

This We Believe about Curriculum

- Relevant
- Challenging
- Integrative
- Exploratory

Connecting Curriculum

- Complementary Content and Skills
- Multidisciplinary Approach
- Interdisciplinary Approach
- Integrative Curriculum

Curriculum Standards

- State and National Standards
- Standards in the Classroom

Service Learning

Subject-Centered Curriculum

- English Language Arts
- Mathematics
- Science
- Social Studies
- Related Arts

We Are All Teachers of Reading

- Strategies for Encouraging Reading
- Writing

Reflections on Curriculum for Middle Level Education

INTRODUCTION

Writing a chapter on middle level curriculum is complex. At first, it seems straight-forward, even simple. After all, curriculum is the "what" of teaching. It's the meat, the content. We should simply discuss language arts, math, science, social studies, and related arts. Yes, indeed, that's the curriculum . . . according to one all too common level of thought. However, so simplistic a discussion is inadequate and unfair to you. Books, articles, and conversations about curriculum run the gamut from shallow coverage to deeply insightful. What you will read in this chapter is an overview. It will, however, give you a glimpse of just how complex and challenging the issue of curriculum, and in particular, middle level curriculum, is.

Chapter 1 helped us build a rationalization and a foundation for middle level education. In Chapters 2 and 3, we examined the development of, and diversity among, our students. In Chapter 5, we discussed the societal context of middle level education. We looked at ourselves in Chapter 4. In Chapter 6, we considered how middle level education is organized.

Understanding who we are and how, where, and when we come together (Chapters 1 through 6) is essential before going on to examine what we do when we are together (Chapters 7—curriculum, 8—instruction, and 9—assessment). While in many ways separating curriculum, instruction, and assessment is artificial, it serves our purposes to explore the various aspects of each before attempting to understand their interdependence. Let's begin our discussion of curriculum with the guidelines provided by the National Middle School Association, the organization that is both the result and the voice of our dedication to middle level students.

STANDARD 3

Middle level teacher candidates understand the major concepts, principles, theories, standards, and research related to middle level curriculum and assessment, and they use this knowledge in their practice.

This We Believe about Curriculum

Our guiding document tells us that "curriculum embraces every planned aspect of a school's educational program" (2010, p. 19). So *curriculum* consists of specific classes, core and otherwise, as well as guidance, advisory, activities of all kinds, and provided services. Whatever is intentionally designed to support and accomplish the mission of the school is curriculum along with what's accomplished through wayside teaching. A developmentally responsive middle level school will embrace a curriculum that is relevant, challenging, integrative, and exploratory, finely tuned to the characteristics and needs of young adolescents.

> Middle level curriculum = Relevant + Challenging + Integrative + Exploratory

To begin our discussion, let's summarize *This We Believe* as it pertains to curriculum. Following this summary, the remainder of the chapter will "flesh out" the concepts of *This We Believe* (2010) and add others. In this section, all page numbers after quotes refer to the *This We Believe* document.

STANDARD 3

Knowledge 1: Middle level teacher candidates understand that middle level curriculum should be relevant, challenging, integrative, and exploratory.

● Relevant

"Curriculum is relevant when it allows students to pursue answers to questions they have about themselves, content, and the world" (p. 20). A relevant curriculum will result in student understanding of the connected, "holistic nature of all knowledge" (p. 20). A relevant curriculum will be "rich in all personal meaning" (p. 21). By creating new interests, a relevant curriculum will stretch "students to higher levels of learning" (p. 21).

> Relevant curriculum = Holistic + Personal meaning = New levels of learning

● Challenging

To be challenging, a curriculum must address three issues. Let's look at them separately.

A challenging curriculum must include "substantive issues and skills . . ." (p. 18). Substantive issues are those that are worthwhile in the eyes of both adults and students. They are issues that are important enough to study in depth. This in-depth study uses basic principles along with alternative points of view involving skills that are contextually based. A challenging curriculum addresses both why and how things happen.

> Challenging curriculum = Substantive + Multileveled + Responsibility building

Given the diversity exhibited by middle level students, implementing a curriculum that is appropriate for their varying levels of understanding is a daunting task. Finding ways to meet our students where they are, build on prior knowledge and experiences, and continue to challenge them should become our daily ritual requiring multilevels of curriculum.

The third issue requires that the curriculum enable students to take responsibility for their learning. Exercising decision-making must be a component of a developmentally responsive curriculum that is challenging.

● Integrative

"Curriculum is integrative when it helps students make sense of their lives and the world around them . . ." (p. 21). To be integrative, *This We Believe* tells us curriculum must be coherent, must connect school to students' daily lives, and must encourage students to grasp the totality of their experiences. Applications, connections, construction of knowledge—making sense of content and experiences is what *integrative curriculum* is all about.

> Integrative curriculum = Connections + Sense-making

● Exploratory

This We Believe tells us that "the general approach for the entire curriculum at this level should be exploratory" (p. 20). Exploratory, then, does not refer to a set of courses, but rather an attitude and an approach. Discovery and choice are embedded in the disposition that encourages exploration.

> Exploratory curriculum = Discovery + Choice

This We Believe states that "Exploration, in fact, is the aspect of a successful middle school's curriculum that most directly and fully reflects the nature and needs of the majority of young adolescents" (p. 20).

What we teach in the middle grades is influenced by a number of factors. For decades, school districts and states used curriculum guides for each subject and grade level that were only occasionally altered. Changes in accountability have precipitated changes in how we view and use curriculum guides of all descriptions. States now use subject area standards to determine curriculum.

Keep in mind that in middle level we view curriculum as more than just what is taught/learned in the classrooms. Don't lose sight of the broader view of curriculum as everything that is planned for students in our schools. But for the sake of the discussion that follows, we will deal with that part of the curriculum that is planned by classroom teachers for students. Listing the topics to come will help us organize our discussion. We will look at:

Curriculum standards

Subject-centered curriculum

Levels of curriculum connections

Service learning

Shared responsibility to teach reading

Curriculum Standards

Perhaps the most profound influence on what is taught/learned in schools is wielded by standards set by subject area organizations and states. Very simply, *standards* define what students should know and be able to do. "Standards are a balanced, coherent articulation of expectations for student learning" (Carr & Harris, 2001, p. 19). *Turning Points 2000* (Jackson & Davis, 2000) is very clear about recommendations for standards:

> Standards = What students should know + What students should be able to do

> Teach a curriculum grounded in rigorous, public academic standards for what students should know and be able to do, relevant to the concerns of adolescents and based on how students learn best. Considerations of both excellence and equity should guide every decision regarding what will be taught. Curriculum should be based on content standards and organized around concepts and principles (p. 23).

STANDARD 3

Knowledge 4: Middle level teacher candidates are knowledgeable about local, state, and national middle level curriculum standards and of ways to assess the student knowledge reflected in those standards.

Performance 2: Middle level teacher candidates use current knowledge and standards from multiple subject areas in planning, integrating, and implementing curriculum.

It's rare to pick up an education journal dated 1998 or later and not find numerous references to standards. Standards are here to stay. Standards documents will not be effective if we fail to make them living documents, subject to our best thinking, over time. While they won't (and shouldn't) be stagnant, the concept of standards will endure. *Turning Points 2000* provides criteria for excellent standards in Figure 7.1.

● State and National Standards

In 1989, the National Council of Teachers of Mathematics introduced us to standards for teaching and learning math in prekindergarten through grade 12. In the 1990s, national organizations for language arts, science, and social studies followed suit. Other classes taught at the middle level have also formulated standards. These subject area organizations have used groups of experts to determine essential knowledge and skills in the disciplines that students should master. Familiarity with these standards is essential for middle grades teachers as we specialize in one or two subject areas.

All 50 states now have standards documents that are followed by school districts. Most state documents are very similar to the standards of the national organizations. Most states have developed their own assessment criteria aligned with these standards. I can't overemphasize the impact of state assessment standards. You will no

---

FIGURE 7.1 Criteria for identifying excellent standards

Academic standards should be

   . . . concerned with the essential ideas.

   . . . useful and clear.

   . . . rigorous, accurate, and sound.

   . . . brief.

   . . . feasible, taken together.

   . . . accessible.

   . . . developmental.

   . . . selected and modified or supplemented by consensus.

   . . . adaptable and flexible.

Source: From *Turning Points 2000* by A. W. Jackson and G. A. Davis, 2000, New York: Teachers College Press.

doubt be handed copies of the standards for your teaching area(s) and grade level(s) and urged by your administrators and mentors and teammates to make the standards the guide and dominant "playbook" in your classroom. Your state standards will be the basis of your curriculum—perhaps the standards will actually BE your curriculum.

Currently there are efforts underway to establish national curriculum standards. This initiative, labeled as the **Common Core State Standards Initiative**, is the result, at least in part, of the recognition that some state standards are more rigorous than others. Uneven state standards make it difficult to judge the quality of teaching and learning. Two organizations are in the forefront, the **National Governors Association** (NGA) and the **Council of Chief State School Officers** (CCSSO). It will be a complicated task to find common ground and agree on standards for the entire country, especially because education is basically a states right. Still, subject area experts are working to establish national standards that will likely be part of your teaching career.

● Standards in the Classroom

Wormeli (2001) states without hesitation that we need standards in the classroom. Among his reasons are that standards

- Help us consistently move every child ahead
- Spell out what our communities consider essential and enduring knowledge
- Provide a guide rope that we can return to if we swim too far away during our investigations
- Give us a plan to follow as we create intellectually rigorous and developmentally responsive experiences (p. 65)

With rationale like these and others we move forward, embracing what has come to be called the standards movement. Standards should be viewed as empowering. They give us structure and consistency, without dictating instruction. All of the instructional strategies in Chapter 8 can be used to teach standards. Standards are not restrictive and don't necessarily dictate sequence. In most cases, we are free to take a set of standards for our subject(s) and grade(s) and move them around to match our classroom and team goals. They can be introduced in one unit, emphasized in another, practiced in another, and assessed and reinforced as often as desired. Within the structure of curriculum standards, we can create learning experiences that are developmentally responsive for middle grades students. "Every teacher deserves clear, manageable, grade-by-grade sets of standards and learning benchmarks that make sense and allow a reasonable measure of autonomy. Anything less is frustrating, inhumane, and counterproductive" (Schmoker & Marzano, 1999, p. 21).

Creating a standards-based classroom in the middle grades should be a collaborative effort, contributed to by teammates, administrators, central office personnel, curriculum leaders, and so on.

A reality check must be included at this point. Standards are often overwhelming. They may provide not only the skeletal structure of a body of knowledge, but also the detailed fleshing out of a discipline. Rather than fit and efficient, we often seem to have an obese body of prescribed knowledge that simply won't fit in a 180-day school year. Our best judgment tells us that something must be trimmed in order to spend ample time on more foundational aspects. Perhaps the best way to put our curriculum standards on a diet is thoughtful and ongoing discussions with colleagues about what to emphasize and what to minimize.

Subject-Centered Curriculum

As we discussed in Chapter 6, most middle school teams structure their days around subject areas—some very distinct, others blended to various degrees. While standards are typically organized by disciplines, this in no way prevents the blending of subjects. Both discipline-based curriculum and curriculum based on connections among disciplines are not only possible, but desirable. Concepts "can 'function' both within disciplines and across them" (Jackson & Davis, 2000, p. 48).

Each core subject area has its own national organization. These organizations are made up of teachers, administrators, subject experts, and others with keen interest in the discipline represented. The organizations have governance structures, position statements, multiple conferences, publications, resource guides, and websites. They have also taken on the responsibility of formulating standards. Middle school teachers derive numerous benefits from membership in these organizations. I urge you to go online and explore the organizations that represent the subject(s) you want to teach.

English Language Arts

Major Organization: National Council of Teachers of English (NCTE)

Website: *www.ncte.org*

Student membership: $20/year; regular membership: $40/year

Journals for middle grades: *Language Arts* (for elementary and middle level) *Voices from the Middle* (middle level)

Special feature: Middle Web (browse middle grades news, download curriculum guides, examine student work, take visual tours of high-performing schools).

Standards

The English language arts standards were written in 1996 through a joint effort of NCTE and the International Reading Association (IRA). The standards are designed to be suggestive, not exhaustive. There are 12 content standards that are interrelated and should be considered as a whole. Among other things, the standards address

- Range of materials students should read
- Importance of students' knowledge of language use, variation, and conventions
- Reading strategies
- Knowledge needed to use language in writing, speaking, and making visual representations
- Connections between reading and writing

- Research and inquiry
- Technology-driven modes of research and data synthesis (from *www.ncte.org* 2009)

Position Statements

NCTE has designated specific position statements for middle grades addressing selection of materials, gender-balanced curriculum, and incentives for excellence, tracking, writing, reading, censorship, assessment, storytelling, drama, class size, and culturally/linguistically diverse students.

Mathematics

Major Organization: National Council of Teachers of Mathematics (NCTM)

Website: *www.nctm.org*

Student membership: $39 (includes one journal); regular membership: $78 (includes one journal)

Journal for middle grades: *Teaching Mathematics in the Middle School*

Special feature: Illumination website with interactive multimedia investigations

Standards

The standards proposed by NCTM are based on members' core beliefs about students, teaching, learning, and mathematics. Recognizing that decisions made about content of school mathematics have important consequences for both students and society, the document *Principles and Standards for School Mathematics* was published in 2000 to provide guidance. One of its six principles is the Curriculum Principle that states, "A curriculum is more than a collection of activities: it must be coherent, focused on important mathematics, and well articulated across the grades" (NCTM, 2000, p. 14). Following this principle, NCTM developed ten basic standards categories. Five of the standards are process-oriented: problem solving, reasoning and proof, communication, connections, and representation. Five of the standards are content-based: number and operations, algebra, geometry, measurement, and data analysis and probability.

Position Statements

NCTM provides an extensive list of position statements on content topics and grade level issues. They propose that all teachers of math at the middle level have extensive preparation in content to create an atmosphere of confidence where the process standards of NCTM are emphasized—problem solving, reasoning and proof, connections, communication, and representation. We are urged to work with other teachers and to be sensitive to students and parents from diverse racial and cultural backgrounds.

Science

Major Organization: National Science Teachers Association (NSTA)

Website: *www.nsta.org*

Student membership: $32 (includes one journal); regular membership: $74 (includes one journal)

Journal for middle grades: *Science Scope*

Special feature: The Middle School Science Classroom—a Web link of articles, resources, teacher interactive section, discussion board

Standards

The National Science Education Standards outline what students need to know and be able to do in order to be scientifically literate. They promote excellence and equity for all students in science. The standards state that science should be an active process for students. In other words, science is something students do, not just read about, with inquiry central to science learning.

Position Statements

NSTA offers statements on a broad range of topics. The statement pertaining to middle grades addresses five major areas—needs of young adolescents, model programs, model teachers, necessary resources, and professional interactions (from *www.nsta.org*, 2009).

Social Studies

Major Organization: National Council for the Social Studies (NCSS)

Website: *www.ncss.org*

Student membership: $33 (includes one journal); regular membership: $59 (includes one journal)

Journal for middle grades: *Middle Level Learning*

Standards

The standards developed in 1994 for social studies encompass ten strands: culture; time, continuity, and change; people, places, and environment; individual development and identity; individuals, groups, and institutions; power, authority, and governance; production, distribution, and consumption; science, technology, and society; global connections; civic ideals and practices.

The integrative nature of social studies is a big factor in middle grades education. Most of the themes used in interdisciplinary instruction and integrative approaches are derived from social studies. No longer a subject where memorizing dates and names is paramount, social studies in the middle grades can and should be an exciting and worthwhile learning adventure. NCSS tells us that the primary purpose of social studies is to help students make informed decisions with the public good in mind as they actively support a democratic society with a culturally diverse population.

Position Statements

The position statements of NCSS address ability grouping, citizen education, commercialism, democratization of schools, multicultural and global education, and testing, all of which can be accessed online (from *www.ncss.org*, 2009).

● Related Arts

We established in Chapter 6 that most middle schools consider English language arts, math, science, and social studies to be the core subjects. A variety of other courses are typically offered, which I have chosen to call "related arts." These courses are important to middle level education.

Related arts courses may include art, physical education, health, vocal music, instrumental music, technology, home/consumer arts, industrial arts, foreign language, and more. While middle grades teachers and schools openly acknowledge the value of related arts to student development and learning, there often appears to be a rift, real or perceived, between core and related arts teachers. We should be careful using a term such as *core* when it is used opposite the word *noncore* to refer to related arts, or classifying courses as academic and nonacademic. This kind of terminology can be inflammatory. Scheduling restricts many related arts teachers from fully participating in team meetings and functions and makes contributing to interdisciplinary teaching and units difficult.

How can we attempt to remedy this rift? Doda and George (1999) give us some ideas.

1. Related arts teachers can be given advisory groups or co-advise with a core area teacher.
2. Related arts teachers can be placed on teams or assigned to teams on a rotating basis.
3. Related arts teachers can form their own teams and share common planning.
4. Related arts courses can contribute content for ongoing and specific assessment.
5. Administrators should make sure related arts issues and concerns are included in faculty meeting agendas.
6. School personnel such as administrators and counselors can take related arts concerns to team meetings.
7. Considerations should be made for related arts classes when teams decide to take students out of school for part of the day or when they attend core team meetings.
8. The schedule should allow for equal amounts of planning time for all teachers.
9. Related arts subjects should be included in interdisciplinary and integrative curriculum planning.

What follows are very brief discussions of some of the related arts areas.

myeducationlab

Go to the Assignments and Activities section of **Topic #4: Motivation** in the MyEducationLab for your course and complete the activity entitled "Motivational Strategies."

Arts Education   This broad category includes related arts courses typically available in middle school. Major arts-related organizations joined to create standards in 1994 that apply to what the Consortium of National Arts Educators Association consider the four categories of arts disciplines: visual arts, music, theater, and dance. The Music Educators

National Conference (MENC) developed goals for arts education that focus on understanding, appreciating, and being able to communicate within and through the arts.

Most middle schools offer visual arts classes, often allowing students to discover and demonstrate talent that hasn't yet become evident in other areas. Students with artistic talent should be encouraged to use and expand their talent in other courses.

Vocal and instrumental music courses are available in most middle schools, and most likely to be attended by choice, rather than as required fare. In elementary school, students are exposed to vocal music on a regular basis attributing to students choosing chorus as an option in middle grades. Students who take private music lessons may form the backbone of instrumental music in middle school. Music programs in some middle schools serve primarily to give students awareness of the art form, while in others musical groups present entertainment on occasion and participate in competitions. The preface statement for the music standards for grades 5–8 tells us that the middle grades are critical to how music will be perceived and used in adulthood.

Health and Physical Education Most middle schools require students to be part of physical education classes each year. Health education is approached in a variety of ways, varying by state and by district. Elements of health education are sometimes incorporated in science, but most frequently they are part of physical education. Some middle schools even contract with outside organizations to provide health education.

Young adolescents often amaze us with their dual nature. One minute they appear to be shy and unassuming, and the next they respond with wonderful talent and enthusiasm when given opportunities to excel in the arts or other areas beyond the core curriculum.

In 1995, the Joint Committee for National School Health Education Standards developed guidelines for school health standards. The topics include health promotion, disease prevention, healthy behaviors, influence of media on young adolescent health, goal setting, and decision-making.

Experts in the field of health education have identified 10 content areas as necessary for a comprehensive school health education and recommend a developmentally appropriate program based on community needs, with at least 50 hours per year of instruction in health-related areas. The 10 content areas are community health, consumer health, environmental health, personal health and fitness, family life education, nutrition and healthy eating, disease prevention and control, safety and injury prevention, prevention of substance use and abuse, and growth and development.

The content areas addressing personal health, fitness, nutrition, and healthy eating are vital in today's middle schools. Childhood obesity is at an all-time high and steadily increasing, with life-threatening consequences.

Technology Education The broader phrase associated with technology is "information literacy." We all know that there is absolutely too much information in any discipline for any of us to "know it all." Not only is there a wealth of information, the information is constantly changing.

Our libraries are now media centers. Regardless of the subject, we are all responsible for introducing students to resource generators and requiring that they use them. Many middle schools offer specific courses that are basically technology-centered. Courses in keyboarding are prevalent, as are courses that relate to software programs and how to use them. The International Society for Technology in Education (ISTE) guides us regarding technology skills appropriate in middle level education.

Industrial, Home Arts, and Consumer Education When I was in middle school (junior high), courses in this general category were simply called "shop" and "home ec." With advancements in technology and added sophistication, we have changed both names and content. Middle schools now offer courses with titles like "Family and Consumer Science," "Trade and Industrial Arts," and "Technology and Design." The classes are coed, with girls and boys learning similar information and skills. By virtue of their content, the classes are interactive and hands-on in nature, ideal attributes of courses for young adolescents.

Foreign Language Typically there are two levels of foreign language instruction in middle school. Foreign language classes with curriculum equivalent to what students encounter in courses for which they receive high school credit are usually offered to eighth graders who show promise and/or interest in languages.

Many middle schools have language classes that expose students to the culture of one or more countries, with minimal exposure to the associated language. Courses of this nature are often short in duration, possibly 6 weeks, allowing a student to become familiar with a number of cultures and languages. For instance, a

7th grader may have 6 weeks of Spanish culture and 6 weeks of French culture interspersed with other brief related arts courses.

The American Council on the Teaching of Foreign Languages (ACTFL) developed a vision statement that includes the philosophy that all Americans should be proficient in at least one language and culture in addition to English.

▶ See How They Grow

Maria • 7th Grade

As we know from Chapter 3, Maria grew increasingly restless being cooped up in the apartment she shares with her mother each afternoon and most weekends. When she was younger, TV and toys occupied her time. Now that she's in 7th grade, she frequently leaves the apartment and stays away for longer periods of time. She goes down the block to a corner grocery store and sits outside with neighborhood kids, not a bad thing in and of itself, but the potential for harm is present. On several occasions she has accepted rides with high school teens and knows her mother would not approve. She has tried beer and now will have one any time it's available. She has smoked cigarettes, but doesn't particularly care for them. She has been offered marijuana, but so far has turned it down. Many in the older crowd she now seeks dropped out of school and speak mostly Spanish.

Maria's mother knows she sneaks out occasionally, and they argue about it. Mom would like to have another job so she could be home more when Maria isn't in school, but she has had no luck finding other work. Maria's teacher, Ms. Esparza, is also concerned about her.

In Chapter 1 we recognized that the purpose of middle level education involves both academic and affective domains. The middle grades receive criticism both in philosophy and practice if less than optimal progress of middle level students on standardized assessments such as the National Assessment of Educational Progress (NAEP) and the Trends in International Mathematics and Science Study (TIMSS) is announced. In our efforts to strengthen this level of schooling, our focus must continually rest on what we teach and how we teach it—in both the four core subjects and the related arts. Strong programs require teachers who are competent and confident in the disciplines.

STANDARD 4

Performance 1: Middle level teacher candidates use their depth and breadth of content knowledge in ways that maximize student learning.

Connecting Curriculum

Most of us who have taught middle grades have realized the benefits of connecting curricular areas to whatever extent is feasible and appropriate. The terms *connecting* and *integrating/integration* are often used interchangeably in defining the process of looking for bridges or commonalities among historically distinct subject area curriculum strands. However, the writings of James Beane and others have redefined an integrated curriculum to encompass a much more sophisticated and comprehensive approach to connecting curriculum strands referred to as *integrative* curriculum. In the interest of clarity, when we discuss the various approaches to connecting curriculum, I'll refer to the four most widespread methods described briefly in Figure 7.2.

Regardless of definitions, procedures, and components, helping our students see and study connections within, between, and among subject areas can bring content alive, increase understanding, and more closely link "school learnin'" to real life. As teachers it is our responsibility to determine approaches to curriculum that work best for our students.

FIGURE 7.2   Connecting the curriculum

Simple ⟶ Comprehensive

Complementary Content and Skills	Multidisciplinary	Interdisciplinary	Integrative
• may alter timing	• alters timing	• alters timing	• alters timing
• uses content mapping	• uses content mapping	• uses content mapping	• uses content mapping
• subjects separate	• subjects separate	• subject boundaries blurred	• subjects interwoven
• teacher driven	• teacher driven	• teacher driven	• student and teacher driven
	• content-based	• content-based	• themes derived by student-teacher interaction and are based on student concerns and societal issues

STANDARD 3

Knowledge 2: Middle level teacher candidates understand the interdisciplinary nature of knowledge and how to make connections among subject areas when planning curriculum.

Disposition 5: Middle level teacher candidates are committed to implementing an interdisciplinary curriculum that accommodates and supports the learning of all young adolescents.

Three benefits derived from making connections among curricular areas that enjoy widespread acceptance, according to Weilbacher (2001), include

1. Teacher/student and student/student relationships are formed and fostered in positive ways.
2. Learning is made more relevant.
3. Connections are made not only among disciplines, but also within the community and students' own experiences.

What you're about to read represents both a compilation of what others have said about curricular connections and how I have come to understand and practice the broad concept.

STANDARD 4

Knowledge 2: Middle level teacher candidates know how to use content knowledge to make interdisciplinary connections.

● Complementary Content and Skills

Curriculum mapping, a process developed and promoted by educators such as Heidi Hayes Jacobs (2004), is an effective way for teachers to plan a year of instruction. The primary elements to consider include

- Process and skills
- Essential concepts and topics
- Assessment products and performances

Individual teachers arrange these elements on a calendar in sequences so the elements build on one another. A team of teachers then shares their calendars. Carefully, they view the curriculum of their fellow teachers. They look for gaps and repetitions in individual calendars and complementary fits among subject areas. When complementary content and skills are spotted, teachers negotiate timing so that a cohesive plan emerges that makes sense for student learning.

Through curriculum mapping, it is possible for teams of middle school teachers to recognize content topics and skills emphases that naturally fit together. For example, the science teacher may plan to use pendulum swings the second week in October as part of a 6-week study of physics. This would be an ideal time for the students to study circles, radii, and arcs in math. The language arts teacher may plan to study the elements of short stories, including Edgar Allan Poe's "The Pit and the Pendulum." The three teachers don't change their lesson plans. They alter the timing of topics. Pendulums do not constitute a theme, merely a focal point around which multiple content areas and skills fit.

The *complementary content and skills* approach requires little extra effort on the part of teachers. A curriculum map makes tweaking timing a relatively simple thing to do. The multidisciplinary approach also uses curriculum mapping, but in a more complex way.

Multidisciplinary Approach

In a multidisciplinary approach, teachers share their curriculum maps with the intent of choosing a theme around which complementary content and skills may revolve, a theme that unifies topics and concepts in two or more subject areas. Teams will typically determine a theme and then decide what each subject area can contribute and when and for how long the theme will guide and unite their disciplines.

myeducationlab

To hear Eric Langhost, the 2008 Missouri Teacher of the Year, tell how he makes history come alive through sharing stories of real people and real events, go to the Teacher Talk section of **Topic #7: Strategies for Teaching** in the MyEducationLab for your course.

Along with curriculum mapping, a process called *webbing* is valuable. In a thematic web used in multidisciplinary instruction (see Figure 7.3), the theme is in the middle and the subject areas form the web. In *multidisciplinary instruction*, the subject areas remain distinct, and, through the theme, students see connections. They see that content learning in one area applies to another area.

Multidisciplinary, or theme, teaching will only serve its purpose of enriching the curriculum through connections if those connections are not artificial. Just as connections should be meaningful, so should the choice of themes. The theme becomes even more important when we move to the interdisciplinary approach.

STANDARD 3

NMSA

Performance 4: Middle level teacher candidates develop and teach an integrated curriculum.

Interdisciplinary Approach

An *interdisciplinary approach* is a more involved strategy for connecting curriculum than a multidisciplinary approach. Themes tend to be more conceptual in nature rather than content-based. For example, multidisciplinary teaching may revolve around "seasons," while an interdisciplinary approach might have "change" as the theme. A theme of seasons is more limited with fewer avenues to explore than a theme of change.

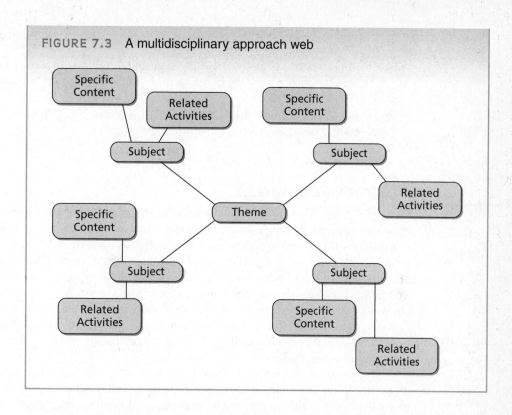

FIGURE 7.3   A multidisciplinary approach web

FIGURE 7.4   Conceptual themes

- Activism
- Beginnings
- Celebrating Differences
- Change
- Conflict Resolution
- Conservation
- Freedom
- Heroes
- Independence

- Innovations
- Interdependency
- Journeys
- Justice
- Prejudice
- Self-awareness
- Societal Dilemmas
- Symbolism
- Wellness

When teachers work together to explore a concept such as change by connecting multiple subjects, subject area boundaries are often blurred. Figure 7.4 lists some themes that are more concept-based as opposed to content-based.

Both curriculum mapping and theme webbing are excellent tools for planning interdisciplinary instruction. In Chapter 10 we explore the development of interdisciplinary units.

STANDARD 3

Disposition 4: Middle level teacher candidates realize the importance of connecting curriculum and assessment to the needs, interests, and experiences of all young adolescents.

Performance 3: Middle level teacher candidates incorporate the ideas, interests, and experiences of all young adolescents in curriculum.

Integrative Curriculum

Of all the terms used to describe connecting the curriculum, *integrative* elicits the most controversy. Not only do practitioners and researchers use it to mean different degrees of connections, but the concept itself is controversial and is the most complex of all the published versions of how the curriculum might be connected.

An *integrative curriculum* is intended to be the whole, planned curriculum of the middle school. A major distinguishing factor of this curriculum is that the themes chosen for study should result from the intersection of problem-based student concerns and large social issues. Students and teachers determine themes jointly and plan the direction of study together. A broad range of skills are necessary in integrative curriculum, including those in Figure 7.5.

An integrative curriculum should include both core and related arts subject areas blended in the study of meaningful themes. It should be conducive to heterogeneous grouping and accommodate individual differences. Teachers are facilitators who are also learners right along with students.

FIGURE 7.5   Skills for integrative curriculum

1. Reflective thinking, both critical and creative, about the meanings and consequences of ideas and behaviors.

2. Identifying and judging the morality in problem situations; that is, critical ethics.

3. Problem solving, including problem finding and analysis.

4. Identifying and clarifying personal beliefs and standards upon which decisions and behaviors are based; that is, valuing.

5. Describing and evaluating personal aspirations, interests, and other characteristics; that is, self-concepting and self-esteeming.

6. Acting upon problem situations both individually and collectively; that is, social action skills.

7. Searching for completeness and meaning in such areas as cultural diversity.

Source: National Middle School Association, 4151 Executive Parkway, Suite 300, Westerville, OH 43081, 1-800-528-NMSA, www.nmsa.org

Paul George (1996) questioned claims that integrative curriculum is superior to subject-centered curriculum. He maintained that all curriculum designs rest with well-prepared, committed teachers. With strong subject foundations and connections among disciplines established to any degree considered appropriate, curriculum in middle grades will foster learning and motivate interest and achievement.

STANDARD 3

Performance 1: Middle level teacher candidates successfully implement the curriculum for which they are responsible in ways that help all young adolescents learn.

Service Learning

"More and more schools across the country, recognizing the important role service plays in developing responsible, caring, active citizens, are including service-learning activities as a required part of the school curriculum. Their decision to include service learning is fully supported by research . . ." (Kaye, 2006, p. 34).

We often think of *service learning* as a nice addition to what we do in middle school, if time permits. That's a very different approach compared to making service learning an embedded part of a school's curriculum. These are two ends of the spectrum with most middle schools somewhere in between.

Service learning and volunteerism are not the same. Volunteerism has benefits to the volunteer and the person/group receiving the help. Service learning takes the service connected to volunteerism and adds the dimension of learning. "Although it is related to both community service and volunteerism . . . , service learning is unique in that it links community service and volunteerism with academic learning" (Fertman, White, & White, 1996, p. 3). The authors of *Service Learning in the Middle School: Building a Culture of Service* continue by saying that service learning is not an add-on to programs that exist, but rather "a methodology that infuses service into the school's curriculum" (p. 3).

Middle schools generally incorporate occasional service projects. Early adolescence is the ideal age for service experiences. When *Turning Points* (1989) called for connecting schools to the community, service opportunities certainly filled the bill then, and they continue to do so now.

> Service learning = Preparation + Service + Reflection + Celebration

There are four major elements of service learning: preparation, service, reflection, and celebration. Each element is vital, and none should be omitted.

STANDARD 1

Performance 7: Middle level teacher candidates engage young adolescents in activities related to their interpersonal, community, and societal responsibilities.

Dundon (2000) advises that teachers listen to students before beginning a service learning project. She suggests that we ask students what they care about rather than arranging projects ourselves. The payoff can be profound. Once the students have spoken concerning their priorities, the preparation part of the cycle can begin.

Kaye (2006, p.35) tells us that service-learning projects, accompanied by reflection and celebration, may lead to students who

- Apply academic, social, and personal skills to improve the community
- Make decisions with real results
- Grow as individuals, gain respect for peers, and increase civic participation
- Experience success no matter what their ability level
- Gain a deeper understanding of themselves, their community, and society
- Develop as leaders who take initiative, solve problems, work as a team, and demonstrate their abilities while and through helping others

When students see their actions positively affect others, they change. This is what happens "when learning and service connect" (Kaye, 2006, p.34).

Who wouldn't want young adolescents to experience this kind of growth? If you have opportunities to facilitate the service-learning model with your students, please do so. If your school doesn't already provide opportunities, creating the opportunities for service that leads to learning is a worthwhile mission.

We Are All Teachers of Reading

We often hear that children learn to read by third grade and then read to learn from then on. If only that were true. Two misconceptions exist. One is the expectation that students who enter middle school are proficient readers, particularly readers for literary experiences, including short stories and simple novels. The second is that students who have mastered reading for literary experiences will naturally read for information and for learning how to do something without direct instruction and guided practice. The solution to the first misconception may be best accomplished through reading specialists. In the absence of funding (or the fact that reading instruction is not a priority), it is up to all of us to teach the basics of decoding and comprehension. Many of us are not prepared to do this. Staff development is essential to accomplish the task.

STANDARD 4

Knowledge 4: Middle level teacher candidates understand how to integrate state-of-the-art technologies and literacy skills into their teaching fields.

Disposition 4: Middle level teacher candidates value the integration of state-of-the-art technologies and literacy skills in all teaching fields.

Performance 5: Middle level teacher candidates integrate state-of-the-art technologies and literacy skills into teaching content to all young adolescents.

The second misconception implies that all types of reading are the same. We must address this misconception if our students are to be successful. They must be able to read with comprehension, regardless of the subject area. Reading a math book requires rereading. Once through is rarely sufficient. Students may need to read a paragraph, consider examples, and then reread. Reading a science text often involves calling up prior knowledge to provide context. Social studies material is often laden with names of people and places that are difficult to decipher. We must help students understand how to get beyond pronunciation to substance, to envision an event and get the big picture of a sequence. When we use opportunities provided in the content we teach to reinforce reading skills, then reading has purpose and relevancy. We could tweak the reading adage to say "We read in middle grades to learn content and as we learn content our reading skills improve." After all, is there a content area that doesn't rely heavily on reading proficiency?

> Teaching reading = "Before reading" strategies + "During reading" strategies + "After reading"strategies

Strategies for Encouraging Reading

Regardless of the subject(s) you teach, there are steps you can take to increase both the reading skills and enjoyment of your students.

1. Know your students' reading habits. Do they read only because it's assigned? Do they read novels? Magazines? Comic books (graphic novels)? Newspapers? Internet websites? Text messages? When is reading meaningful to them?

2. Provide a variety of reading opportunities—individual, small group, whole group, for pleasure, to learn specific information, to learn how to do something, and so on.

3. Explicitly teach students how to read for a variety of purposes and in appropriate ways. We have to teach them to read poetry, a math book, information in journals or online for a report, a piece of historical fiction, the newspaper, and so on.

4. Establish a classroom library, no matter what subject(s) you teach. As a math teacher, I have favorite authors like Greg Tang who write wonderfully entertaining books that teach math skills. But I don't stop with books that deal with math. I buy books at book fairs, library sales, garage sales, 75% off tables at large bookstores, and flea markets . . . anywhere young adolescent-appropriate books can be found. Don't forget to include magazines like *Time for Kids, National Geographic, Wildlife, Sports Illustrated for Kids*, etc.

   Hartley (2008) tells us that she arranges for each of her students to select a book or two when the book fair comes to her school. These books are added to the classroom library. In this way she knows she will have books that appeal to her students. Students will more happily read books that interest them. Just ask Jacob, the student in the photograph on the first page of this chapter!

5. Consistently incorporate Sustained Silent Reading (SSR) or a Drop Everything And Read (DEAR) into the school day. A well-stocked classroom library will provide plenty of choices so that students may self-select what they read.

● Writing

A discussion of reading would not be complete without mention of writing. Reading is, of course, a prerequisite for writing. But more than a prerequisite, the two are inextricably linked. Good readers have most of the skills necessary for good writing, but instruction is necessary for students to successfully engage in the different genres and purposes of writing. Both reading and writing are necessary to succeed in our increasingly literacy-based society. Whether for pleasure, for information, or for knowing how to do something, reading and writing are essential skills. As middle grades teachers, we are all teachers of reading and writing.

myeducationlab

Go to the Assignments and Activities section of **Topic #4: Motivation** in the MyEducationLab for your course and complete the activities entitled "Motivation in Writing" and "Students' Sharing with Excitement."

▶ Teachers Speak

● Keith Richardson

I can't express strongly enough the benefits of a robust reading program. My classroom library is a vital part of teaching language arts, as is daily reading for pleasure. I see my responsibilities as a middle school teacher to do the following:

1. Teach kids to read with fluency and comprehension.
2. Teach kids to write with proper mechanics, to address particular audiences, and to express their thoughts clearly and concisely.
3. Encourage a love of, and appreciation for, language expression in all its many genres.

I have these responsibilities posted near my desk. Each day I challenge myself to engage students in their own learning to bring them closer and closer to these three goals. . . . It's work I love.

Reflections on Curriculum for Middle Level Education

Curriculum is more than textbooks, district guides, and lists of facts, and even more than standards. Curriculum involves all the aspects of students' interactions with teachers, with each other, with specific discipline-based knowledge, with connections among concepts, and with their worlds and beyond. Young adolescents are with us for only a few brief years. During that time they grow and change and become. Our daunting responsibility is to frame a curriculum that will bring out all their potential and catapult them forward with knowledge, skills, awareness, a sense of responsibility—all those positive and healthy attributes called for in *This We Believe*. You may hear the phrase "curriculum wars" referring to what some seem to perceive as conflicting viewpoints of curriculum—academic and affective. There is absolutely no need for conflict here. Developmental responsiveness does not adversely affect high academic expectations and vice versa. They work in concert and complement one another.

Teachers with strong content knowledge coupled with understanding of young adolescent development are prepared for discipline-based and connected curriculum designs. Balanced curriculum includes core and related arts subjects, service learning, support of affective growth—a wholistic approach to middle grades. In all these areas, our curriculum is to be "relevant, challenging, integrative, and exploratory" (National Middle School Association, 2010, p. 7).

GROUP ACTIVITIES

1. In groups, acquire your state standards for each of the disciplines for grades 5, 6, 7, and 8. All states will have math and language arts, most will have science and social studies, and many will have standards for related arts disciplines. Add these standards to your class files. You will use them in future activities.

2. Add to your school files by finding out what related arts courses are offered at each school. Are any of them required? Are any offered only at certain grade levels? Do any require auditions or other qualifications?

3. In groups of three to five, choose a theme from Figure 7.4. Draw a web similar to Figure 7.3. Write your chosen theme in the middle and fill in the core four subjects plus at least two related arts areas. Now spend 15 minutes brainstorming concepts that could be explored in the core and related arts areas to support the theme. You should have no problem filling a page. Conceptual themes invite so many interesting topics. Be prepared as a group to share an overview of the results of your brainstorming with other groups.

INDIVIDUAL ACTIVITIES

1. Consider the subject area(s) you want to teach. Was anything discussed in this chapter pertaining to that subject new information to you? If so, what?

2. Choose a subject area organization website to visit. Prepare a brief report of what's included to share with classmates.

3. Think of one related arts course that particularly stands out in your memory. Write at least five attributes of this course to share with your class.

PERSONAL JOURNAL

1. What was your favorite subject in middle school? In retrospect, was it your favorite because of the subject/curriculum or did other factors weigh more heavily? (teacher, instructional approach, time of day, cute boy/girl sitting in front of you, etc.)

2. Why have you chosen the particular subject area(s) you want to teach? What influences led to your decision?

Professional Practice

(It will be helpful to reread the profile of Carmen Esparza in Chapter 4 and the descriptions of Maria in Chapters 2 and 3.)

● Carmen Esparza

Ms. Esparza's career as a bilingual teacher is ever-evolving. The rapidly increasing interest in teaching English language learners provides new articles on the topic in many journals. She diligently seeks them out, reads what educators have to say, and adjusts her strategies. But at the end of the day it all boils down to one goal—English fluency. Ms. Esparza understands and appreciates the need to keep other cultures alive in her class and to validate home languages. But it doesn't change the fact that her students must learn to communicate in English, read it with accuracy and comprehension, and express themselves in written Standard English.

Ms. Esparza is particularly concerned about Maria, now a 7th grader. She has had her in class for almost two years and has watched her change from a shy, compliant 6th grader to a withdrawn, almost defiant, 7th grader. Her English skills showed improvement in 6th grade, but her lack of effort is showing in 7th grade.

1. Bilingual education has critics. Some people don't see its value. Among them are teachers. What can Ms. Esparza do to influence the perceptions of those who disparage what she does?
   a. be as informed as possible about studies addressing bilingual education and, when opportunities arise, reasonably express what she learns to others
   b. make the bilingual program more visible in the building through projects and posters
   c. ask her principal to talk with teachers about the need for support
   d. keep to herself and let teachers watch the progress

2. Which of the following should Ms. Esparza not do as she tries to positively influence Maria?
   a. ask a professionally successful Latina woman to meet with Maria and other girls to talk about issues she faced and what contributes to her success
   b. remind Maria daily of the value of speaking and writing fluently in English
   c. continue to speak in both Spanish and English in whole-group sessions, but change to mostly English when speaking with Maria
   d. involve Maria in afterschool activities

Constructed Response

As a non-bilingual teacher, how could you support Ms. Esparza's efforts to legitimize and promote bilingual education at Martin Luther King Middle School?

INTERNET RESOURCES

Education World

www.educationworld.com

This large site includes links to national subject area standards as well as state-by-state subject area standards information.

National Subject Area Organizations:

American Council on the Teaching of Foreign Languages (ACTFL)

http://actfl.org

Association for Supervision and Curriculum Development (ASCD)

www.ascd.org

International Society for Technology in Education (ISTE)

www.iste.org

Music Educators National Conference (MENC)

www.menc.org

National Art Education Association (NAEA)

www.naea-reston.org

American Alliance for Health, Physical Education, Recreation, and Dance

www.aahperd.org

National Council for the Social Studies (NCSS)

www.ncss.org

National Council of Teachers of English (NCTE)

www.ncte.org

National Council of Teachers of Mathematics (NCTM)

www.nctm.org

National Middle School Association (NMSA)

www.nmsa.org

National Science Teachers Association (NSTA)

www.nsta.org

ABCD Books

www.abcdbooks.org

This site connects literature and service learning through book selections, workbooks designed to make explicit links between what students read and service-learning projects, curriculum ideas, and professional development opportunities.

National Service Learning Partnership

www.service-learningpartnership.org

Founded in 2001, the Partnership is a national network of members dedicated to advancing service-learning as a core part of every young person's education, concentrating on strengthening the impact of service-learning on young people's learning and development, especially their academic and civic preparation. The Partnership supports members sharing resources, organizing change, and sponsoring innovation.

Youth Service America

www.ysa.org

Youth Service America concentrates on improving communities by increasing the number and the diversity of young people, ages 5–25, serving in substantive roles. They focus on mobilizing, supporting, and sustaining service activities.

8 Middle Level Instruction

Instruction is all about communication among teachers and students. We must first thoroughly understand the curriculum ourselves and then find ways to enhance the understanding and skill development of students with regard to the content and concepts we teach. This is the purpose of instruction. The more extensive our repertoire of strategies, the more effective we will be as teachers. Here focus teacher Jesse White is interacting with students at Lincoln Middle School.

instructional practices in the middle school should focus on what we know about the learning needs of young adolescents coupled with what we know about how learning occurs.

Knowles and Brown, 2007, p. 152

CHAPTER PREVIEW

Big Ideas of Instruction
- Brain-Based Learning
- Student-Focused Instruction
- Backward Design
- Differentiation of Instruction
- Thinking Skills
- Inquiry-Based Learning
- Cooperative Learning
- Technology in the Classroom

Instructional Strategies
- The Importance of Choice
- Nine Categories of Instruction
- Recommended Strategies

Reflections on Instruction

INTRODUCTION

The emergence of standards-based learning and assessment is focusing the attention of teaching on outcomes, not the process itself. We can "teach our hearts out" in the middle level classroom, but if students are not learning, then our efforts have little or no meaning. We haven't always viewed instruction this way. Some still don't. It's time to determine the success of instruction based on measures of student learning, not on teacher performance. There are instructional strategies that are middle-level appropriate and proven effective. If incorporated into a teacher's instructional repertoire, these strategies can result in greater student learning.

myeducationlab

To hear John Kline, the 2008 New Jersey Teacher of the Year, express his passion for his subject and how he encourages students to discover the fires of their own passions, go to the Teacher Talk section of **Topic #4: Motivation** in the MyEducationLab for your course.

STANDARD 5

Disposition 6: Middle level teacher candidates realize the importance of basing instruction on assessment results.

We focused on curriculum in the last chapter. Measuring student learning is addressed in Chapter 9. Once again keep in mind that separating curriculum, instruction, and assessment is artificial, but expedient, in a textbook. My hope is that as you study Chapters 7, 8, and 9, your appreciation of the interdependence of these three fundamental components of teaching will grow.

We begin this chapter by considering the big ideas of instruction, the underlying concepts of how we teach. Following our discussion of the big ideas of instruction are brief descriptions of middle level-appropriate strategies grounded in the big ideas. First, read these recommendations upon which to base instruction from *Turning Points 2000* (Jackson & Davis, 2000).

- Meet students where they are, since people learn best by connecting new information to old.
- Center classrooms on the students, not the teachers, since people also learn best when they exercise some control over their learning.
- Provide rich learning environments, since intelligence is fluid, not fixed, and will increase, given access to a diversity of materials, opinions, and options.
- Organize content around concepts, since the brain searches for meaningful patterns, connecting parts to wholes.
- Engage students in challenging work grounded in higher-order thinking, since people learn best when they have to stretch to succeed.
- Connect what happens in the classroom to the students, either directly or by helping them discover links to the world beyond the classroom, since people learn best when what they are learning has relevance to themselves or their society. (pp. 83–84)

As you read this chapter, remember our discussions of middle level organization, young adolescent development, student diversity, and elements of curriculum design.

STANDARD 5 MIDDLE LEVEL INSTRUCTION AND ASSESSMENT

NMSA   Middle level teacher candidates understand and use the major concepts, principles, theories, and research related to effective instruction and assessment, and they employ a variety of strategies for a developmentally appropriate climate to meet the varying abilities and learning styles of all young adolescents.

Knowledge 1: Middle level teacher candidates understand the principles of instruction and the research base that supports them.

Big Ideas of Instruction

In this section we will explore eight big ideas of instruction. These are foundational principles rather than individual strategies. It's important that we understand the premises that support the ways we teach.

Brain-Based Learning

Big Idea of Instruction ▶

Research on how our brains work is a dynamic area of science. Eric Jensen (2005), noted researcher and author concerning brain functioning, tells us that the field of brain-based learning is new and should not be considered a program or a package that will solve education's problems. It is, rather, a way of understanding how the brain works and how teachers may incorporate this valuable information into the classroom to increase student learning.

Renate and Geoffrey Caine (1994) are major contributors to the field of brain research and its implications for teaching and learning. They developed twelve principles based on facts about how the human brain functions. These principles include

- Each brain is unique.
- The brain processes what it hears, sees, and senses at the same time.
- Learning involves the whole person.
- Learning occurs in focused and peripheral ways.
- Learning is both conscious and unconscious.
- We understand and remember best when facts and skills are embedded in experiences.
- Challenge enhances learning; threat inhibits it.

Understanding how the brain works when it comes to learning can help us better utilize our time with students in the classroom. The potential benefits of using these principles are in direct proportion to our willingness to apply them to instruction and enrich the experiences of the learner.

Brain-based research tells us that enrichment has two critical ingredients—the learning must be challenging and interactive feedback must be present. Challenge may come through problem solving and critical thinking opportunities, relevant projects, and complex activities. Be aware that too much challenge may lead students to give up, while too little challenge will lead to boredom. Determining the right amount of challenge calls for us to know our students well, and then to individualize levels of challenge to maximize enrichment. Interactive feedback is the second ingredient of enrichment. Feedback should be specific and immediate. As we

Enrichment = Challenging learning + Interactive feedback

proceed through this chapter, keep challenge and feedback in mind. These two elements should be infused in every facet of our classroom instruction.

Student-Focused Instruction

Big Idea of Instruction ▶

Shifting our focus to learning as a means of measuring instructional effectiveness naturally calls for us to view instruction from a student perspective. To do so changes how we view our responsibilities. Student-focused instruction calls for us to create opportunities that empower students to be self-directed learners. "Learning is more likely to happen when students like what they are doing—when they are involved, active, and learning from and with other students" (Murphy, 2009, p. 24). Student-focused instruction requires us to be facilitators of learning, not merely dispensers of information and skill trainers. Filling our instructional toolboxes with the strategies discussed later in this chapter, and many more, allows us to tailor what happens in the classroom to meet the needs of our students. A balanced classroom will include student-directed activities, as well as more traditional strategies like lecture, notetaking, worksheets (no, this is not a four-letter word), and whole-class instruction. Regardless of the strategy, we must keep our focus on students. Some of the characteristics of student-focused instruction include

- Active student engagement
- Variety of strategies
- Student choice
- Student inquiry
- Student responsibility
- Built-in, ongoing assessment of learning

One of the most powerful student-focused instructional tools is the outdoors. Outdoor education is a subset of experiential learning, according to Herb Broda, author of *Schoolyard-Enhanced Learning*. He encourages us to view the schoolyard as an extension of the classroom. "Perhaps by taking kids outside at school, we might be able to occasionally spark that sense of wonder and feeling of 'Wow!'" (Broda, 2007, p. 151).

STANDARD 1

Performance 5: Middle level teacher candidates use developmentally responsive instructional strategies.

STANDARD 2

Performance 4: Middle level teacher candidates implement developmentally responsive practices and components that reflect the philosophical foundations of middle level education.

Outdoor education is student-focused. Using the schoolyard as an extension of the classroom is good for kids. Here focus student Gabe explores concepts with classmates.

● Backward Design

Big Idea of
Instruction ▶

The philosophy and practice of backward design brings curriculum, instruction, and assessment together. The link among the three has traditionally focused on the order in which the words were just stated—we decide what to teach, we develop ways to teach it, and then we determine if the learning occurs. Backward design changes this order. When Wiggins and McTighe (1998) published their book *Understanding by Design*, the seminal work that promotes backward design, the majority of teachers thought, "Hey, this makes sense. I want to know more."

Wiggins and McTighe (1998) tell us to brace ourselves for the fact that they ask us to think differently about "time-honored habits and points of view about curriculum, assessment, and instruction" (p. 6). Many teachers begin planning for instruction with textbooks, activities, and unit/lesson plans they've used before. Backward design calls for us to reverse our thinking and first consider our desired results. Next we determine what evidence would assure us the results are accomplished. Once these two decisions are made, we plan the experiences and instruction that will achieve the results and provide evidence of success.

Stage One of backward design involves identifying desired results. There is more content within the national, state, and district standards than can reasonably be addressed, so we have to make choices about what to include. To help us make our decisions about priorities, we are encouraged to view content on three levels.

- Concepts and skills considered *enduring* — those big ideas that students retain even when they have forgotten facts and details.

- *Essential* knowledge and skills — those we want students to remember from lessons and units.

- Knowledge and skills that are worth being *familiar* with — the ones that may be peripheral to what is studied and are merely introduced in the current lesson or unit.

Three categories of knowledge and skills = Enduring understandings + Essential to mastery + Worthy of familiarity

A major teaching responsibility involves knowing our subjects deeply and broadly enough to distinguish where along the continuum from enduring understanding to familiarity specific knowledge and skills belong. Experience, reflection, and collaboration among colleagues serve as our best sources of effectively fulfilling this responsibility.

Stage Two of backward design calls for us to determine what evidence will tell us that students have achieved the desired results. A wide range of assessment methods, including informal checks for understanding, observation, quizzes/tests, and performance tasks/projects serve as evidence.

Stages of Backward Design = Identify desired results + Determine evidence of achievement + Plan instruction to achieve and demonstrate results

Stage Three of backward design involves planning learning experiences and instruction to give students opportunities to achieve desired results and to demonstrate those results with appropriate evidence.

● Differentiation of Instruction

Big Idea of Instruction

Differentiating instruction calls for us to meet our students where they are, to accept them as learners with differing strengths and weaknesses, and to do all that we can to help each and every student grow as much as possible. Since the mid-1990s the words "differentiating instruction" have caused us to examine classroom practices in a new light. The concept of differentiated instruction is linked to Carol Ann Tomlinson (1999) and her book *The Differentiated Classroom*. In this book and many subsequent books and articles, Tomlinson makes a commonsense case for the importance of differentiating instruction, describes the philosophy and ways to begin, and provides classroom scenarios (many in middle level) that give us vivid pictures of what a classroom looks like when the instruction is differentiated to meet the needs of students.

Elements to differentiate = Content + Process + Product

Tomlinson tells us that we can differentiate content, process, and product as illustrated in Figure 8.1. We can use students' readiness, interests, and learning profiles to guide our differentiation practices. **Content** is what a teacher wants students to learn. **Process** includes activities that require students to use skills to make sense of ideas and information. **Products** allow students to demonstrate what they have learned. Keep in mind that differentiating one aspect of instruction will affect the other aspects. Tomlinson emphasizes that there is no one right way or time to differentiate.

Elements on which to base differentiation = Readiness + Interest + Learning profile

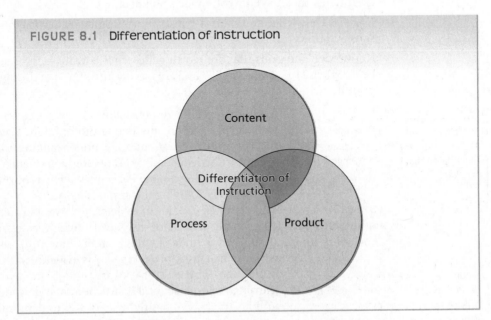

FIGURE 8.1   Differentiation of instruction

Source: Based on Tomlinson 1999.

Whole-class instruction is entirely appropriate in many instances. Tomlinson tells us, "Teachers may adapt one or more of the curricular elements (content, process, product) based on one or more of the student characteristics (readiness, interest, learning profile) at any point in a lesson or unit" (p. 11). She cautions us to "not try to differentiate everything for everyone every day" (p. 14). Tomlinson advises us to start small with a differentiated task that takes a limited block of time.

In order to begin to differentiate according to readiness, interests, and learning profiles requires us to know our students well. At the heart of middle level education is the premise that doing schooling right requires us to have knowledge of, and closeness to, our students. Wormeli (2001) tells us that knowing our students well is like "taking their temperature," not just once in August, but often as they grow and change (p. 87). Tomlinson (1999) says that in a differentiated classroom the teachers are diagnosticians. In this way instruction and assessment are inseparably linked. Some additional characteristics of a differentiated classroom include

Young Adolescent Diversity

- Student differences are considered.
- Diagnostic assessment is used to determine student needs.
- Multiple Intelligences Theory is utilized.
- Student grouping strategies are varied.
- Student interests, readiness, and learning profiles are considered.
- Student choice is exercised.

Thinking Skills

Big Idea of Instruction

Using thinking skills is a cognitive act that may simply involve awareness of surroundings or may be as complex as making judgments that lead to actions. Bloom's taxonomy (1956) presents the classic six levels of thinking: knowledge, comprehension, application, analysis, synthesis, and evaluation. In 2001, Anderson and Krathwohl provided an update to Bloom's taxonomy using the terminology in Table 8.1.

Each level may be accessed through the use of active verbs and questions. I strongly urge you to explore the levels fully, to read books and articles about them, and to internalize them. Regardless of the content area, we can provide thinking opportunities at all six levels. Teach them to your students. Then occasionally ask: "Which level of Bloom's taxonomy are we using here?" The flower in Figure 8.2 is a fun way to keep the levels visible in your classroom.

Bloom's taxonomy = Remember + Understand + Apply + Analyze + Evaluate + Create

STANDARD 5

Knowledge 3: Middle level teacher candidates know that teaching higher order thinking skills is an integral part of instruction and assessment.

TABLE 8.1 Bloom's taxonomy

Categories	Key Verbs		Question Stems
Remember (Knowledge)	recognize	retrieve	When did _____?
	identify	list	Who was _____?
	recall	define	Where is _____?
	memorize	duplicate	Why did _____?
			Can you list four _____?
Understand (Comprehension)	interpret	classify	How would you compare _____ to _____?
	summarize	compare	What is the main idea of _____?
	infer	explain	What is meant by _____?
	illustrate		
Apply	implement	dramatize	How would you use _____ to _____?
	use	illustrate	What approach would you use to _____?
	operate	solve	Can you _____ by _____?
Analyze	organize	categorize	What evidence can you find to conclude that _____?
	integrate	differentiate	What does _____ have to do with _____?
	focus	examine	
		test	
Evaluate	check	monitor	How would you change _____ to form _____?
	critique	defend	Can you propose a different way to _____?
	judge	support	How would you design _____ to _____?
Create (Synthesis)	generate	construct	What is your opinion of _____?
	plan	produce	How valuable is _____ for _____?
	design	develop	Why would you recommend _____?

Teaching students thinking skills can be accomplished through focused instruction outside a specific content area. Modeling is vital. We can model, for instance, the difference between reading and recalling the steps required to successfully learn to juggle two balls and actually doing it. We can read the steps out loud, close the book and recite them (*remember*), paraphrase the steps (*understand*), and then hold

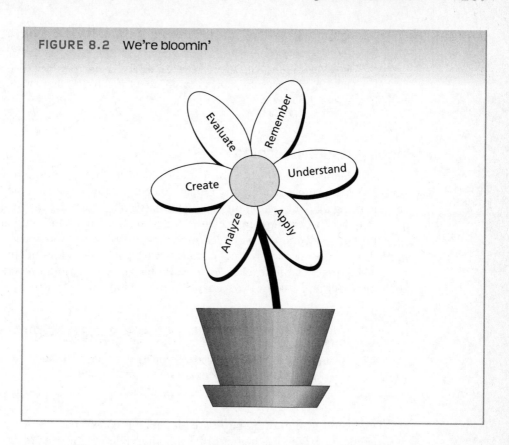

FIGURE 8.2   We're bloomin'

two balls and ineptly toss them into the air, bungling the process. We then explain to our students that remembering and understanding are quite different from applying. We would then ask students to *analyze* what went wrong when we attempted to *apply* what we knew and then to *create* a plan for learning to actually juggle. Finally, we would ask the students to predict the success of our attempts, or perhaps the value of learning to juggle (*evaluation*).

While it is possible to teach specific thinking skills in isolation, teaching thinking skills within the context of the curriculum should be ongoing. To extend a skill presented in isolation, such as categorization (*analysis*), a math teacher might give a small group of students a bucket of attribute blocks and ask them to develop categories in which the blocks might be divided and lists of blocks that fit each. A language arts teacher might ask students to read an essay, write a summary (*understand*), organize the main points (*apply* and *analyze*), compose an essay on the same topic (*create*), and then examine both essays critically to defend the value of each (*evaluate*). A science teacher might ask students to name the parts of an insect (*remember*), ask students to illustrate the parts (*understand*), dissect an insect into basic parts (*apply* and *analyze*), and build a model out of clay (*create*).

STANDARD 5

Performance 2: Middle level teacher candidates create learning experiences that encourage exploration and problem solving so all young adolescents can be actively engaged in learning.

Inquiry-Based Learning

Big Idea of Instruction

Inquiry-based learning is just what it sounds like—learning from questions and investigations. The process of inquiry is open-ended, beginning with a topic or scenario and involving a brief exploration or in-depth research. There are many levels of inquiry. A quick check in a reference book or a telephone call or an informal interview constitutes inquiry. Inquiry-based learning may involve a well-planned project with multiple levels. It is not passive, not characterized by middle grades students in straight rows taking notes as the teacher lectures. Inquiry-based learning is good for young adolescents because it cultivates students' responsibility for their own learning.

STANDARD 5

Knowledge 5: Middle level teacher candidates understand ways to teach the basic concepts and skills of inquiry and communication.

One manifestation of inquiry-based learning is constructivism. A teacher facilitating students as they use higher order thinking skills to construct their own learning, amounts to constructivism. Constructivism is good for young adolescents because most prefer active learning, they are generally very social creatures, and they have the capacity to be quite creative. Constructivism takes emphasis off teaching and places it squarely on learning and the learner. "An inquiry learning approach . . . takes advantage of students' own experiences to develop problems that will engage students in active learning" (Lemlech, 2004, p. 56). Constructivist strategies are time-consuming. While using them in every lesson is appealing, there simply isn't enough time in a school day, or school year. Constructivist strategies are most appropriate for complex learning such as analyzing events, proving theories, and scientific experimentation.

Cooperative Learning

Big Idea of Instruction

There's cooperative learning . . . and then there's cooperative learning. The two words can be a catch-all for any instance of students working together . . . or they can represent an instructional strategy with defined guidelines and requirements. Let's examine both viewpoints.

On any given day, in any middle school, you will probably hear teachers referring to cooperative learning or cooperative groups or simply group work. While

myeducationlab

To watch Traci Peters' lesson at Cario Middle School, as she demonstrates a structure that includes multiple basic lesson components, go to the Video Examples section of **Topic #7: Strategies for Teaching** in the MyEducationLab for your course and view the video entitled "Traci Peters' Lesson."

proponents of stricter definitions may wince, my opinion is that any time middle level kids work together, they experience both cooperation and learning. This has to be good for them.

Many school districts conduct professional development sessions based on the Johnson and Johnson (1999) method which proposes that cooperative learning must incorporate five basic elements in order to realize all the potential of students working together. These elements are

1. *Positive Interdependence*

   This element requires students to depend on one another in order to achieve the desired results.

2. *Face-to-Face Interaction*

   Students in cooperative groups have to work together to explain, discuss, complete assignments, problem solve, etc.

3. *Individual Accountability*

   Students are required to be accountable for individual tasks that contribute to the group goals.

4. *Interpersonal Skills*

   Students are encouraged to learn to collaborate with each other in socially acceptable ways.

5. *Group Processing*

   Students think and talk about how their group functioned as they accomplished their tasks through the use of the first four elements.

Cooperative Learning = Positive Interdependence + Face-to-Face Interaction + Individual Accountability + Interpersonal Skills + Group Processing

When these five elements are planned for in a lesson or project, students will experience a host of benefits. The presence of these elements, according to many researchers and teachers, sets "true" cooperative learning apart from more loosely constructed group work.

Both heterogeneous and homogeneous groups may be formed with regard to achievement levels, interest and experience levels, or other factors related to student differences. There are times when teachers designate groups and purposefully put particular students together. Then there are other times when students are grouped using random strategies or when students are allowed to choose their own groups.

The length of time groups remain intact will vary. Changing the size and composition of your groups depends on the activity or task. If you assign a group project, the groups of students will remain constant for the duration of the assignment. Some teachers have great success with forming heterogeneous cooperative groups that stay together for a quarter, or longer. The philosophy behind this is that students in stable

---

FIGURE 8.3   Getting started and maintaining cooperative learning

1. Read about and experience cooperative learning in university classes and staff development opportunities.

2. Determine to implement cooperative learning in your own classroom.

3. Give several simple tasks to students in random groups that will show them the benefits of working together. Make sure success is built into the tasks.

4. Define a task for cooperative groups in your classroom.

5. Make decisions about grouping students, roles for the task, materials needed, time guidelines, and desired results of cooperative work.

6. Plan for positive interdependence, face-to-face interactions, individual accountability, interpersonal skills, and group processing.

7. Talk with your students about the process of cooperative learning. Include your expectations, guidelines for interactions, and how work will be assessed.

8. Assign roles to students in groups.

9. Observe closely as groups work together. Take notes on what you see.

10. Involve students in debriefing the cooperative learning experience.

11. Plan your next venture into cooperative learning!

---

groups, with appropriate guidance, develop trusting and nurturing relationships, along with social skills and commitment.

The participants in cooperative groups are often assigned specific roles to help the groups function effectively and efficiently. The roles may include a facilitator to keep things moving, a recorder to take notes, a timer to keep members on schedule, a gatherer of materials, an encourager to ensure everyone provides input, and an artist to illustrate for the group.

Young Adolescent Diversity

There are multiple benefits of cooperative learning including development of racial and gender tolerance, promotion of friendships, increased understanding of children with disabilities, and greater abilities to problem-solve. With benefits like these, the practice of cooperative learning is a must in middle level education. The steps in Figure 8.3 will help you begin and maintain cooperative learning in your classroom.

● Technology in the Classroom

Big Idea of Instruction ▶

Turning Points 2000 refers to technology as an instructional resource that requires our vigilance (Jackson & Davis, 2000). There are so many instructional tools available. We make our choices according to lesson objectives, availability, our expertise in using the tools, and the appropriateness of the tool to the particular situation. Our challenge is to mesh curriculum, our students and their needs, and instructional tools to foster effective learning opportunities. The use of calculators, videos, audiotapes, and other tools considered "lower tech" in the 21st century is common. Most classrooms have computers, and middle schools have computer labs. SMARTBoards, streaming video, podcasts, and handheld computers are available.

Technology innovations such as the SMARTBoard can enhance learning.

Students are often more enthusiastic if a project involves working with technology. Access to information provided by the World Wide Web has the potential to enhance how we approach research in all content areas. The interactive nature of websites allows for simulations where students manipulate variables and receive immediate feedback. The possibilities are tremendous.

Now that we have established a foundation for instructional practices, let's examine some instructional strategies that are appropriate for young adolescents in middle level settings.

▶ Teachers Speak

● Jermaine Joyner

Using technology is so much a part of who I am and what I do. I teach kids about it all day long. I have my own website and blog. My phone is my means of voice communication, text messaging, surfing the Internet, reading books, etc. It's my alarm clock and my camera. I often joke that I'm married to it and don't need a traditional wife. But then I fully understand that I'm exaggerating. If I forget, my girlfriend gladly reminds me. My point is that I depend on technology and enjoy it as well. I view technology as a vital teaching tool and I have a hard time understanding teachers who don't take advantage of at least a few of the tools available. Fortunately, I have a principal who calms me down when I get agitated and frustrated by some colleagues' lack of interest and motivation to incorporate tools I know would benefit student learning. Calm or not, I'm on a mission to bring the wonderful digital world into every teacher's repertoire of strategies.

STANDARD 3

Knowledge 5: Middle level teacher candidates are fluent in the integration of technology in curriculum planning.

STANDARD 4

Disposition 4: Middle level teacher candidates value the integration of state-of-the-art technologies and literacy skills in all teaching fields.

Performance 5: Middle level teacher candidates integrate state-of-the-art technologies and literacy skills into teaching content to all young adolescents.

Instructional Strategies

Our instructional toolboxes should be overflowing with strategies in order to effectively address the learning needs of each student. To be developmentally responsive means that we accommodate the needs of students in our classrooms who are, by virtue of being young adolescents, developmentally unequal.

STANDARD 5

Knowledge 1: Middle level teacher candidates understand the principles of instruction and the research base that supports them.

Disposition 1: Middle level teacher candidates value the need for a repertoire of teaching/learning strategies that are appropriate for teaching all young adolescents.

Performance 1: Middle level teacher candidates use a variety of teaching/learning strategies and resources that motivate young adolescents to learn.

STANDARD 6

Performance 3: Middle level teacher candidates connect instruction to the diverse community experiences of all young adolescents.

● The Importance of Choice

Putman (2009) says of students that "choice must be used as a 'hook' to catch their interest and motivate them. Research has revealed that students need a feeling of control . . . and, once motivated, they demonstrate greater effort and persistence . . ." (p. 55). Having a full toolbox of instructional strategies allows us to carefully choose the ones that are appropriate for our students, as well as for the content, skill, and/or standard to be addressed. This toolbox also allows us to give students choices.

While hammers, saws, screwdrivers, and vise grips have differing uses for a carpenter, they are all valuable in the building process. The effective carpenter knows the capabilities of each tool, can decide which tool is most appropriate, and recognizes when to use each in the various stages of construction. This analogy applies to the classroom as well. Instructional strategies are tools. Teachers must ". . . rely on their knowledge of the students, their subject matter, and their situation to identify the most appropriate instructional strategies" (Marzano, Pickering, & Pollock, 2001, p. 9).

STANDARD 1

Knowledge 3: Middle level teacher candidates know a variety of teaching/learning strategies that take into consideration and capitalize upon the developmental characteristics of all young adolescents.

Choice is motivational; it is developmentally responsive and will pay off in increased learning. Let's look now at nine research-based categories of instruction.

Nine Categories of Instruction

In a meta-analysis of many studies of instruction, Marzano, Pickering, and Pollock (2001) found nine categories shown in Figure 8.4 that correlate positively and

---

FIGURE 8.4   Categories of instructional strategies that affect student achievement

Identifying similarities and differences—involves identification of important characteristics and then comparing, classifying, creating metaphors and analogies

Summarizing and note-taking—powerful study skills for identifying and understanding the most important aspects of what students are learning

Reinforcing effort and providing recognition—techniques that address students' attitudes, beliefs, and motivation concerning the connection of effort and success

Homework and practice—provide opportunities for students to refine and extend knowledge

Nonlinguistic representations—graphic representations and physical models that elaborate on knowledge

Cooperative learning—flexible and powerful tool for grouping students to promote collaboration

Setting objectives and providing feedback—process of establishing a direction for learning and then providing an explanation of what students are doing that is correct and what they are doing that is incorrect

Generating and testing hypotheses—process of understanding a principle, making a conjecture, and applying the knowledge to see if it holds true

Cues, questions, and advance organizers—techniques that activate prior knowledge and/or set the stage for and bridge the way to, new knowledge

---

Source: From *Classroom Instruction That Works* by R. J. Marzano, D. J. Pickering, and J. E. Pollock, 2001, Alexandria, VA: Association for Supervision and Curriculum Development.

most often with student learning. Some of the categories are stand-alone strategies, but others may encompass multiple individual strategies. The categories are all shown to be highly effective and, although they are listed in descending order of effectiveness, each comes highly recommended as a tool for classroom instruction. As we examine individual recommended strategies in the next section, refer back to Figure 8.4 to see how each strategy might fit into one or more of the nine categories.

Recommended Strategies

The big ideas of instruction provide the theoretical bases for the great variety of instructional strategies available to middle level teachers. Each is rich in possibilities. What follows are brief descriptions of instructional strategies that both fit in one, or more than one, of the nine categories of instruction and are vehicles for implementing the big ideas of instruction.

Lecture   Overuse and misuse of the lecture format, along with some of our own memories of fighting to stay awake through the Prussian Wars or the contributions of automation to the Industrial Revolution, have left many of us with a bad taste. However, with certain guidelines, the lecture, or mini-lecture, is a valuable teaching strategy to introduce a lesson, describe a problem, and/or provide information in concise ways.

A mini-lecture is simply a brief lecture. Keeping the mini-lecture to 10 minutes or so will allow it to be used effectively and as often as appropriate.

When planning a mini-lecture, identify the main points. Consider an attention-grabbing opener (advance organizer) that will set the stage for the content to come. Then decide on examples to include that will illustrate the main points. Finally, develop a summary of the content that refers back to the advance organizer and main points.

Lecture = Attention-grabbing opener + Illustrative examples + Summary

Demonstration   A demonstration is a way of showing students something that would be difficult to convey through words alone. Whether showing steps in solving a math problem or describing the symbols for editing and their applications, or conducting a science experiment, demonstrations can be very effective instructional tools applicable in every subject area. When coupled with a mini-lecture, a demonstration complements auditory learning with visual stimulation.

Demonstration = Showing + Telling

Teacher Think-Aloud   Modeling thinking processes through think-alouds shows our students how they might go about solving problems, approaching a task, or processing new information. "Think-alouds make invisible mental processes visible . . ." (Wilhelm, 2001, p. 26).

Here's an example of a think-aloud: Margo purchased a CD on sale that had an original price of $15.00. All the CDs on the rack were 20% off. The sales tax was 8%. How much change did Margo receive from a $20 bill?

Think-aloud = Organized thought + Verbalization

Focus teacher Sadie Fox routinely demonstrates science concepts and requires students to share demonstrations as well.

Think-Aloud

"Ummmm . . . Let's see what I know. The CD is on sale so she's not going to pay $15.00. Does she pay 20%? No, that's the discount. So I have to find 20% of $15.00. That's 3. I should subtract it because the CD is on sale. Okay, that's $12.00. Now I need to add the tax. I have to multiply again (write .08 × 12 on board and multiply). I subtracted the $3.00 but now I have to add the $.96 (write on board 12.00 + .96). That means she paid $12.96 for the CD. She used a $20 bill so I have to subtract $12.96 from $20 (do this on board). So she got $7.04 back in change."

Think-alouds can demonstrate to students how to bring personal background and prior knowledge into reading. Try reading an article or passage in a short story and then stop to verbalize an experience you had that relates to the text. In this way you are showing your students how to internalize what they read.

Aside from academics, try using the think-aloud strategy when you hear students arguing or you become aware of a friendship rift or when students have decisions to make. Think aloud about how you might deal with the situation. For young adolescents this is so much more effective than "preaching" or talking "at them."

Classroom questioning = Convergent + Divergent

Questioning   Effective questioning takes thought and planning. We can prompt our students to think on all six levels of Bloom's taxonomy on any topic in any subject by asking relevant questions.

Questions may be convergent and tend to have one best answer. These questions lead to exercising Bloom's remembering and understanding levels. Divergent questions are those that are open-ended and often have many possible responses. When we are looking for application in thinking, our questions should allow for a number

FIGURE 8.5   Questioning techniques

1. Plan key questions that are clear and specific to provide lesson structure and direction. Ask spontaneous questions based on student responses.

2. Adapt questions to student ability level. This enhances understanding and reduces anxiety. Phrase questions in natural, simple language.

3. Ask questions at a variety of levels. Keep Bloom's taxonomy in mind.

4. Respond to students in ways that encourage them to clarify initial answers and support their points of view and opinions.

5. Give students time to think before requiring an answer. Wait-time after asking a question should be five seconds or more to both increase the frequency of student responses and to encourage higher level thinking.

6. Encourage a wide range of student participation. Call on nonvolunteers, being careful to consider difficulty levels of questions.

7. Encourage student questioning. Prompt students to phrase questions that stimulate higher cognitive levels of thought.   .

of correct responses. Analysis is often personal and based on prior knowledge, so answers will vary. Creating can be engaging because we are asking our students to come up with something new based on what they know. The responses to questions aimed at evaluative thinking can take many directions. Figure 8.5 contains very practical guidelines for using questioning as a thoughtfully planned instructional strategy.

One of the best ways we can help our students learn a concept deeply is to guide them in framing good questions. After a reading assignment or an activity, rather than requiring students to write a summary or an outline, have them write questions. Without guidance you will likely get a lot of "When did . . . ?" "Who was . . . ?" "What happened when . . . ?" — all remembering, with maybe a smattering of understanding. To make the strategy effective, use question prompts like the ones in Table 8.1. As a homework assignment you might ask students to read a particular text and develop three questions using these prompts. The next day, form groups and have students exchange and answer each other's questions.

Class Discussions   Class discussions occur every day in almost every class in every middle school. It is the nature of most young adolescents to like to talk and voice opinions. Most want to be heard and have great things to contribute. Focus the discussion to keep it on track and ensure that everyone participates. Keep in mind that a discussion is a conversation, not just a question and answer session. Ideally student voices are heard more frequently than the teacher's.

Class discussion = Focus + Broad participation

Brainstorming   The goal of brainstorming is to produce as many responses as possible. All contributions are allowed without judgment (of course, within guidelines

FIGURE 8.6   K-W-L chart

Constitution of the U.S.		
K What We Know	**W What We Want to Know**	**L What We Learned**
• Written in 1700s • Tells how to run our country • Displayed in Washington • Fancy penmanship • Signed by a bunch of men • Has amendments	• Who actually wrote it? • Can it be changed? • What are some things that we hear about that are "unconstitutional"? • What do we do about things that aren't covered in the constitution?	This column is for students to record answers to their questions and other things of interest learned in their study. Have a way of adding lots of paper for a long list.

of good taste). We want students to think in divergent ways as they contribute. The results of brainstorming can be recorded in many ways using the chalk/whiteboard, chart paper, or SMARTBoard.

Brainstorming is also the first stage of a very popular and useful instructional tool, the K-W-L chart. Figure 8.6 shows a K-W-L chart and an example of how it might be used. The **K stands for what we KNOW**. Brainstorming fills that column. From the brainstorming will come questions, perhaps about things listed in the K column. The **W stands for what we WANT to know**, so the W column will be filled with questions. The **L stands for what we LEARNED**. The K-W-L chart should be displayed for the duration of the study of a topic so we can continually add to the columns.

> K-W-L = What we know + What we want to know + What we learned

Another important use of brainstorming is to begin the writing process. To write an essay, students can brainstorm all the things they might possibly want to include. They group them, and the groups become logical paragraphs. The paragraphs are then sequenced, and an introduction is written followed by the body paragraphs and then a conclusion.

When a class decision is needed, perhaps choosing a field trip location or a topic to be studied in more depth, brainstorming is a valuable tool to allow everyone to participate. Once students have experienced the process, it can be student-led rather than teacher-led. Brainstorming is an effective way to create ownership of decisions.

Notetaking   Taking notes is part of our everyday lives. We make lists for groceries and things to do, notes to help us follow directions to a location, instructions for how to order something we see on television, etc. Of course, this isn't the same thing as taking notes on a lecture or a reading assignment, but the reasons for notetaking are similar. Notetaking, whether practical or academic, helps us remember and saves us time.

> Notetaking = Listening + Deciding what's important + Writing

Ernst (1996) calls notetaking "listening with your pencil" (p. 71). Notetaking requires both listening skills and critical thinking skills as we decide what is important to remember, organize information to write, and determine if it's enough or if further clarification is needed. This is a lot to ask of a 10- to 14-year-old. We must model the process.

We can give students a framework for notes and have them fill in details either as they listen to a lecture, participate in a discussion, read text, or watch a video. For these guided notes you may want to simply write statements with key words and phrases omitted. Allow time for students to read through the guided notes before the lecture, discussion, or video so they will be reading or listening for specific information. This strategy focuses attention and also provides a study guide.

In an inclusive classroom you will likely have students for whom notetaking will be difficult because of some condition that impairs their ability to be successful with the skill. Try providing carbon paper for several students who are willing to share their notetaking abilities with students who need assistance.

Drill and Practice   Clarifying and consolidating material already learned and then repeating the information or skill is what the drill and practice strategy is all about. The process helps with long-term retention and aids in developing speed and accuracy (Burden & Byrd, 2007).

> Drill and practice = Clarifying + Consolidating + Repeating

When you use drill and practice, always make sure the material is familiar enough so students won't have to stop to look something up or ask questions. Students should be able to work independently and always have a way of knowing quickly how well they did. Using computer software to practice skills and recall information is both efficient and effective. Use drill and practice in moderation, but don't fail to employ it when there are obvious benefits.

Graphic Organizers   Graphic organizers are very powerful instructional tools that help us think critically as we visualize knowledge and comprehend relationships in organized ways. They enhance teaching and learning in any subject area to sequence events, prioritize actions, categorize information, compare and contrast ideas and objects, show part/whole relationships, illustrate connectivity, show cause and effect . . . you name it, and a graphic organizer can enhance it.

> Graphic organizers = Thinking critically + Visualizing knowledge + Comprehending relationships

Following a brainstorming session students can take all the random, scattered information and make sense of it using a graphic organizer. A simple web design (Figure 8.7) works well for this purpose where supporting ideas radiate from a central topic or theme like spokes on a wheel. Talking students through the creation of such a web is the best way for them to understand the process.

After reading a story or novel, an effective way to review the events is to use a sequencing organizer (Figure 8.8). You can do this as a whole class a few times, then assign the task to small groups of students who can post their graphic organizers for others to view.

You'll find that many students will start to really catch on to the significance of concepts such as *recognizing similarities and differences* when they understand the use of Venn diagrams. Do you remember from the beginning of this section that this is the top ranked category of instructional strategies in terms of student learning? Figure 8.9 shows a simple Venn diagram, one of the most useful graphic organizers.

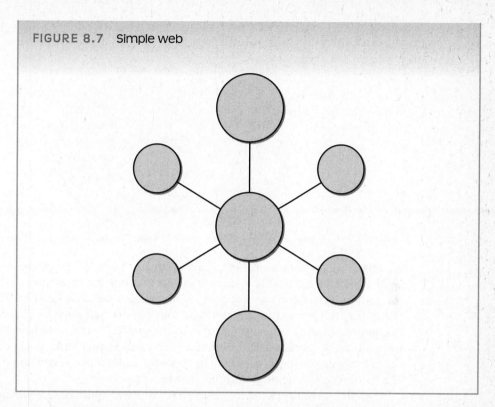

FIGURE 8.7 Simple web

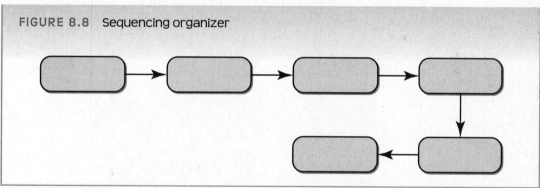

FIGURE 8.8 Sequencing organizer

Enhancing Vocabulary The more words students *own*, the higher their comprehension levels will be and the easier learning and conceptualizing will become. A word can be ". . . an instrument of learning, a vehicle for information, and a changer of history. . . . If we accept the importance of words, then a broad and comprehensive vocabulary has power . . ." (Powell, 2000, p. 14).

Enhancing vocabulary = Creating a word-rich environment + Giving opportunities to use words

Creating a word-rich environment will immerse our students in vocabulary. When a new word surfaces in class

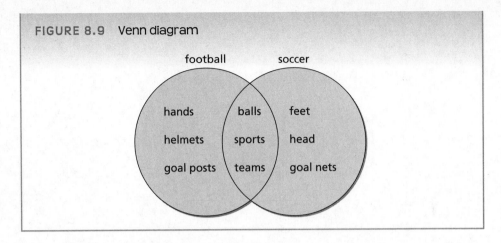

FIGURE 8.9   Venn diagram

readings, videos, discussions, etc., have a student write the word on an index card along with a definition that is appropriate for the context. Then have the student put the card in a classroom pocket chart with a pocket for each letter in the alphabet. In this way we create our own classroom dictionaries that are full of relevant words. Encourage students to use the words in the pocket chart in their writing. As the words increase, occasionally pull out all the cards in one letter pocket and review the words with students. Ask them to recall the context of the creation of each card. The words can also be used in games and exercises.

Graphic organizers can be very effective in vocabulary study. Knowing that visual stimulation promotes learning, graphically portraying words makes sense. Figure 8.10 shows two visually pleasing ways for students to study new words.

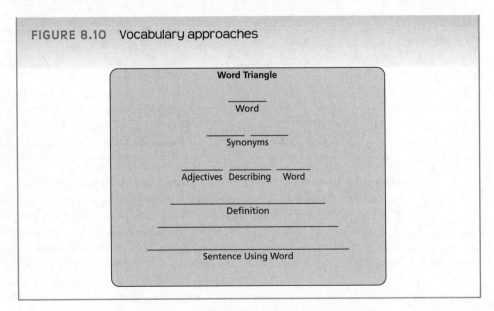

FIGURE 8.10   Vocabulary approaches

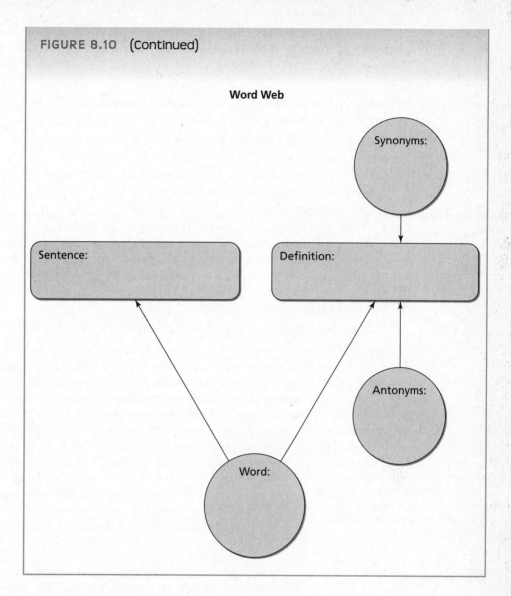

FIGURE 8.10 (Continued)

Word Web

Sharing Vocabulary   Every subject has a unique vocabulary. There are lots of ways to bring these unique vocabularies alive for our students. We no longer need to perpetuate the drudgery of writing an assigned word, indicating part of speech, then writing a dictionary definition along with a sentence that may or may not illustrate meaning, followed by the task of reading this structure over and over to memorize it. Far more interesting and productive strategies are available to us.

One of the richest benefits of the team structure in middle school is the possibility of sharing the vocabulary used in all our subjects all day long. Team vocabulary sharing can be accomplished in a very simple way. Here are the steps.

1. Devise a rotation system that designates one team teacher to be in charge of vocabulary each week.

2. On Thursday, pass a clipboard with a page similar to Figure 8.11 on it among team teachers.

3. Each team teacher writes a brief description of the next week's content/plans and five or six key vocabulary words. Include related arts teachers who teach students on your team.

4. By Friday the designated teacher should have the clipboard. This teacher makes a wall chart of the words for each team classroom and perhaps the gym, cafeteria, art room, etc. Colored paper from the big rolls available in most schools works well. A wide marker will make the words easily visible. Use the same color paper and marker for all classrooms for any given week.

5. Teachers post vocabulary lists in the same places in each classroom every week.

The lists are visual reminders of the words that will be key to understanding the concepts and skills emphasized during the week. All teachers should attempt to use every word on the list within the context of their classes. While *photosynthesis* rarely comes up in language arts, the word can still be examined because of its compound nature. The art teacher may use the word *symmetry* to describe a painting rather than just mentioning the balance of elements, while the math teacher works with the concept of symmetry. As you use a word, walk over to the list and point to it. Our students are then hearing the word in different contexts and seeing the word on the list. Great reinforcement! Sharing vocabulary lets our students know we talk and plan together. Students learn vocabulary in deeper, more contextualized ways. All this is accomplished through a painless process that takes very little time.

> Shared vocabulary = Deciding on key words + Sharing words among teachers + Using words in a variety of contexts

myeducationlab

To watch Deirdre McGrew's lesson at Cario Middle School, as she demonstrates how games and role-play can be useful teaching tools, go to the Video Examples section of **Topic #7: Strategies for Teaching** in the MyEducationLab for your course and view the video entitled "Deirdre McGrew's Lesson."

Role-Play   When students act out or dramatize a situation or idea in a class setting we call it role-play. To be useful as an instructional strategy, role-play requires structure that includes a clear purpose and role descriptions. Expectations and incentives are needed both for those actively participating, as well those students not actively filling the roles but who need to pay attention. It is vital to debrief a role-play session to make sure students get the point(s). Once the students are accustomed to role-playing, we can be more spontaneous about initiating it.

FIGURE 8.11   Shared vocabulary

Team _____

Week of _____

Subject:	Key vocabulary
Overview of plan:	
Subject:	Key vocabulary
Overview of plan:	
Subject:	Key vocabulary
Overview of plan:	
Subject:	Key vocabulary
Overview of plan:	

Role play = Structuring scenario +
Setting expectations +
Imagining/pretending + Debriefing

Role-play helps students gain empathy for others, test solutions to dilemmas, and more deeply understand an event or situation. Other benefits include increased verbal and nonverbal learning, encouragement of divergent thinking, enhanced mental stimulation, and expansion of communication skills.

Projects   I have watched with great joy as young adolescents suddenly "come alive" in the midst of a project experience that is full of choices. Students who seldom show any semblance of interest in school work often blossom when given the opportunity to choose a topic, a strategy, and/or a work product. Projects allow students to show initiative, take responsibility, be physically involved, make decisions, and create. In other words, students "bloom." Speaking of projects her students undertook, Hughes says, "They conducted interviews, read articles, watched documentaries, listened to music, and learned how to become researchers—knowledge seekers. They were engaged with relevant curriculum, and they grew to understand how to be responsible for their own learning . . . they seemed happy to be learning" (Hughes, 2009, p. 43).

The possibilities for projects are practically unlimited. They can be much "messier" than other strategies. They often involve field trips that give students real-world experiences. We must set expectations, ask questions that help students define their projects, assist them in sequencing tasks and organizing procedures (graphic organizers are ideal), remind them of problem-solving strategies for the big and small dilemmas that are inevitable, provide encouragement to stay on task, and celebrate with them as their work culminates into a product. In other words, we facilitate the acquisition and practice of life skills. Worthy effort!

> Projects = Setting expectations + Defining topics + Organizing procedures + Problem solving + Encouraging + Celebrating

Think-Pair-Share   Think-Pair-Share is a versatile and useful tool that can be employed almost any time, in almost any setting, and for any purpose. Here are the simple steps.

1. Ask a thought-provoking question or give a prompt.
2. Instruct students to think for 30 seconds or so.
3. Have students turn to a neighbor and briefly discuss their thoughts.
4. Ask for volunteers to share with the class what they have discussed.

Field trips provide ideal opportunities to share authentic, memorable experiences with young adolescents.

Think-Pair-Share = Prompting/
questioning + Individual thought +
Sharing thoughts with neighbor/
whole class

I often have students write brief notes about their think-ing before talking with a partner to lend some accountability to the process. You might want to establish a Think-Pair-Share journal where students date their thoughts and add their part-ner's opinions/answers to their own.

A variation of Think-Pair-Share, sometimes called Pyramid Think-Pair-Share, involves having pairs of students share with other pairs. In this way, a student goes from individual opinions/answers, to hearing from another student and building on ideas or possibly being persuaded to change an opinion, and then on to benefiting from two additional students' thought processes. This could be followed by whole-group sharing.

Jigsaw = Base groups + Assigned
topics + Expert groups + Students
teaching students

Jigsaw There is great power in students teaching students, and Jigsaw is an excellent technique that requires them to do so. Here are the basic steps involved in using the Jigsaw model.

1. Choose a reading that can be logically divided into sections.

2. Divide your students into groups the same size as the number of sections in the reading. For instance, if a chapter has four sections, your students should form "base" groups of four students each.

3. Within each group, have students number off one to four. Ask all the ones to get together, all the twos, all the threes, and all the fours. These groups become "expert" groups.

4. Assign each expert group a section of the reading to discuss. Their task is to formulate a plan to teach the material to members of their individual base groups. Encourage groups to develop graphics, written summaries, or other unique ways to make the material meaningful.

5. Reconvene base groups to teach each other the material they have mastered in their expert groups.

Figure 8.12 graphically shows how the model works. Students like the idea of being experts and teachers. Naturally, your watchful facilitation will play a critical role in the success of this valuable instructional strategy.

Learning Centers Broadly speaking, learning centers are designated places in a classroom, or possibly movable displays/activities, that provide students opportuni-ties to pursue interests and/or learn content and skills using a variety of modalities and in differing time frames. Learning centers are enjoying a resurgence of popular-ity due, in part, to a renewed emphasis on differentiating instruction (George & Alexander, 2003). With the advent of longer class periods made possible through block scheduling, learning centers are gaining popularity in middle and high schools (Callahan, Clark, & Kellough, 2002). Requiring time and thoughtful effort to set up

FIGURE 8.12   Jigsaw

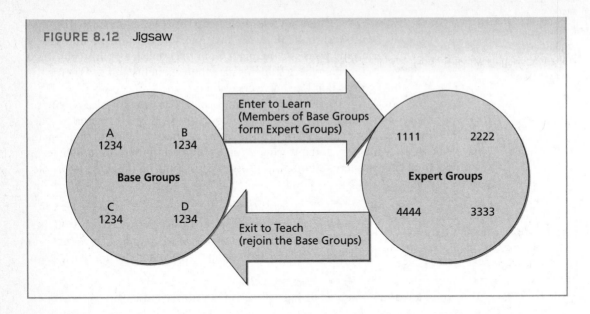

Learning centers = Planning + Durable materials + Procedures and expectations + Time to learn and enjoy

and maintain, learning centers provide enrichment and reinforce skills in ways that address different interests and ability levels.

Reflections on Instruction

To be effective, instructional practices must pass numerous tests—developmentally responsive, research-based, content/skill appropriate, time efficient, standards supporting, and so on. It takes time to build a repertoire of strategies and experience to make decisions about the what, how, and when of approaches.

We should choose our instructional strategies based on student needs, the concepts to be taught/learned, and the classroom situation at hand. Consistently using only one or two strategies is not developmentally responsive. Through variety we address multiple intelligences, learning styles and modalities, and all the areas of diversity discussed in Chapters 2 and 3.

GROUP ACTIVITIES

1. In small groups (3 or 4), agree on a broad topic that would be taught in middle school. Brainstorm aspects of the topic *content, process* of learning, and *product* that might be differentiated. Then think of ways to determine student *readiness, interests,* and *learning profiles* concerning the topic chosen. Organize your best collective thoughts for the six italicized areas, and be prepared to share with your whole class.

2. In pairs, make an appointment to talk with a middle school teacher. Ask about how he approaches heterogeneous classes. How often and in what ways does he differentiate instruction? Add your findings to your school files.

3. So far in this class you've had numerous cooperative learning experiences. As a class, discuss the experiences that seemed more successful than others. Can you determine the factors that may have affected the relative success of the experiences? List the factors, and then classify them into the five categories as defined by Johnson and Johnson.

4. There are sixteen instructional strategies in this chapter. In pairs, choose one strategy and write three questions about it using the question stems provided in this chapter. Use the questions to teach another pair more about your chosen strategy.

5. Think-pair-share time. Individually think of how using procedures to share vocabulary within your team is developmentally responsive. Write your thoughts on a note card. Now pair with someone in your class, and share what you have written. As a pair, connect with another pair, and share responses. As a whole class, debrief the process.

6. In conjunction with your instructor, decide on sections of Chapter 9 that appear conducive to using the Jigsaw model. Determine base and expert groups. Use this model to teach each other about various aspects of assessment.

INDIVIDUAL ACTIVITIES

1. Choose a topic within a subject you plan to teach. Write a narrative explaining how you might address each of the categories in Bloom's taxonomy in Table 8.1.

2. Think of a process or skill that would be included in a subject you plan to teach that lends itself to a teacher think-aloud. Plan what you would say to help students understand the process or skill and be prepared to think-aloud for your classmates.

3. During one of your university classes, pay attention to the dynamics of a typical class discussion. Pay close attention to process, as well as keeping up with the content. Take notes on what you observe. Write a critique of the experience and include ways the professor might have improved the discussion time.

4. By this point in your life you have no doubt developed notetaking techniques that you find effective for your learning style. Write a brief description of your technique to share with the class.

PERSONAL JOURNAL

1. Do you recall cooperative learning experiences in your middle grades years? Write about your participation in, and reactions to, the experiences.

2. Did you ever have that "lost" feeling in a middle grades class? What subject and what topic?

Now that you know more about differentiation, explain how your teacher could have done more to meet your needs.

3. How comfortable are you with classroom technology? Explain.

4. What motivated you as a student? Can you remember teachers, projects, or other circumstances that prompted you to achieve? Explain.

5. Were you an eager participant in class discussion? Why or why not?

6. Can you recall any time as a student when having a choice in your academic work made

a task more meaningful for you? When would choices have made an experience more productive?

7. What instructional strategies dominated your middle grades experience? High school? University?

Professional Practice

(It would be helpful to reread the description of Mr. White in Chapter 4, as well as the description of Zach in Chapter 3.)

● **Jesse White**

Recently Jesse White attended an inservice workshop designed to create awareness of how teacher-focused and student-focused methods of instruction differ. He has attended other workshops during his six years of teaching where he has learned about cooperative learning and the importance of differentiating instruction.

Mr. White decided to plan and implement a cooperative learning project that would take about four weeks to complete. Because the project will require significant monitoring and he wants to "work out the bugs" before implementing it with all 107 students he teaches, he decides to pilot the project in his first period class. He forms heterogeneous groups of five students each. He gives them an overview of the project and reminds them of the basics of their recent class study of media influences and the importance of an informed citizenry. Students are given the individual task of watching television news and reading newspapers for a week with the purpose of choosing one local, one national, or one international issue on which they would like their group project to be based. They are to be ready to defend their choices using notes that Mr. White will collect. The groups will decide on an issue and together write a statement justifying

their decision. They will create a poster. One side will include newspaper articles, summaries of television news reports, and personal commentaries that explain the issue. The other side will be used to follow up on other related events and/or solutions as they unfold over a period of two weeks.

Zach ● **seventh grade**

1. We first met Zach as a 6th grader in Chapter 3. While he is now on Ritalin for his diagnosed ADHD and appears to be better able to concentrate, he still lacks the motivation to work up to his potential. Mr. White recognizes this. Zach has warmed up to Mr. White, and this is a good first step. Every once in a while he shines in social studies. How might this project be most positive for Zach's usual lack of motivation?

   a. Zach will have an opportunity to use his creative streak to successfully design a good poster, something that he will likely enjoy.

   b. In the role of facilitator, Zach could prove to other kids that he can be a leader.

   c. From what Mr. White has heard from his teammates, Zach's interest level is more acute early in the day, so being a student in first period is a real plus.

   d. Zach may develop an interest in a current events topic.

2. Zach rarely participates in class. He is quiet most of the time. Mr. White knows Zach's

interest in academics will continue to decline if he isn't somehow "hooked" on learning. Which one of the following would be the least beneficial aspect of this project for Zach?

a. He may find an issue that sparks his interest.

b. He may feel a sense of belonging as a result of being part of a small learning group.

c. He will be expected to do some individual work.

d. Because there is an element of choice involved, he may find the project inviting.

3. As part of the information presented to Mr. White on student-focused instruction, he learned that using primary sources of data is desirable. Which one of these responses illustrates this concept?

a. As an authority in the class, Mr. White should give an overview of local, national, and international issues.

b. The posters will result from the work of the students in each group.

c. Students can ask the adults in their homes for opinions about the issues.

d. The project requires students to get information directly from newspaper articles.

Constructed Response

What aspects of teaming could Mr. White use to enhance this project? What characteristics of effective teams might help facilitate a project like the one described?

INTERNET RESOURCES

NCREL Instruction

www.ncrel.org/sdrs/areas/in0cont.htm

This part of the North Central Regional Educational Laboratories site is specifically geared to assist teachers by providing a synthesis of the research on issues of instruction along with practical classroom strategies.

Teachers Network

http://teachnet.org

This site, with a motto "By Teachers, For Teachers," is filled with ideas for the classroom including lesson plans, resources, professional development opportunities, and grant writing information.

Middle Web Writing/Reading Workshop Project

http://middleweb.com

This large site has a link for Writing/Reading Workshop Project to assist with literacy instruction.

Technology in Education Resource Center

www.rtec.org/

This valuable site provides links to numerous practical resources for schools and teachers regarding the use of technology in education to improve student achievement.

9 Assessment for Middle Level Learners

Young adolescents can show what they know and are able to do so in a myriad of ways, from traditional paper and pencil tests to projects and performances. They may illustrate, report, build, demonstrate, and so on. These students are building a habitat to meet particular specifications. Their teacher will use the project as a performance assessment.

Curriculum, assessment, and instruction are intertwined, each inevitably affecting the other two. Any effort to change curriculum and assessment without changing instruction, or to change instruction without considering curriculum and assessment, will fail.

Jackson & Davis, 2000, p. 26

CHAPTER PREVIEW

Assessment Overview
- Diagnostic Assessment
- Formative Assessment
- Summative Assessment

Classroom Assessment
- Seven Forms of Classroom Assessment
- Matching Instruction and Assessment
- Portfolio Assessment

Evaluating and Grading
- Rubrics
- Purposes of Grades
- Establishing Scoring Criteria
- Grading for Success

Standardized Assessment
- Comparing Standardized and Classroom Assessment
- Benefits of Standardized Assessment
- Preparing for Standardized Assessment

Reflections on Assessment in Middle School

INTRODUCTION

In Chapter 7 we looked at the many faces of curriculum, from discipline-specific to integrative, and various options that seek to combine aspects of both of these ends of the curriculum spectrum. In Chapter 8 we explored some big ideas of instruction, as well as a variety of instructional strategies. In this chapter's opening quote, the authors of *Turning Points 2000* tell us that it is absolutely necessary to match the flexibility and variety of curriculum and instruction that we employ in middle level classrooms with a wide and developmentally responsive spectrum of assessment methods.

STANDARD 1

Performance 6: Middle level teacher candidates use multiple assessments that are developmentally appropriate for young adolescent learners.

STANDARD 3

Knowledge 7: Middle level teacher candidates understand multiple assessment strategies that effectively measure student mastery of the curriculum.

STANDARD 5

Disposition 5: Middle level teacher candidates value the importance of ongoing and varied assessment strategies.

When we think of assessment, we generally classify it in two basic ways—classroom assessment and standardized assessment. For our purposes, *classroom assessment* is any form that occurs as a direct part of classroom teaching and learning. *Standardized assessment* may be in the form of commercially produced tests administered by local, state, or national mandate, or tests designed by individual states based on curriculum standards. Most states have devised their own standardized tests based on standards as discussed in Chapter 7 and mandated by No Child Left Behind. As you probably realize, classroom assessment provides richer and broader options than standardized assessment and will be the focus of the majority of this chapter.

Before delving into either classroom or standardized assessment, we need to consider some of the purposes of assessment.

Two classifications of assessment = Classroom + Standardized

Assessment Overview

In my first years of teaching, I considered assessment to be tests and quizzes given only for the purpose of assigning grades. As a student, I anticipated getting grades, and as a teacher I dreaded giving them. My hope is that you will begin your career with a more informed sense of assessment.

The most impactful purpose of assessment is the information it provides as we make instructional decisions that improve how we design the teaching and learning environment. Plainly stated, if the kids don't "get it," we find another way to provide learning opportunities. If they do "get it," we are free to move on, move up the Bloom's taxonomy hierarchy, and offer enrichment. In addition to using assessment to improve instruction, assessment allows us to monitor student progress, with a view toward promoting student growth. Another purpose is to evaluate student achievement (i.e., grading) in order to recognize accomplishment (or the lack of it). A fourth purpose involves the collection of data to substantiate

TABLE 9.1   Four purposes of assessment and their results

Purpose	Result
Making instructional decisions	Improve instruction
Monitoring students' progress	Promote growth
Evaluating students' achievement	Recognize accomplishment
Evaluating programs	Modify program

Source: NCTM, 1995.

making program decisions (NCTM, 1995). Deciding to modify, discontinue, or adopt new programs should be based on assessment results, generally gathered over time or from larger samples than one classroom. Table 9.1 lists the purposes and results of assessments.

STANDARD 3

Performance 8: Middle level teacher candidates use multiple assessment strategies that effectively measure student mastery of the curriculum.

STANDARD 5

Knowledge 9: Middle level teacher candidates understand the multiple roles of assessment in the instructional process (e.g., monitoring learning, evaluating student progress, and modifying teaching strategies).

Disposition 8: Middle level teacher candidates are committed to using assessment to identify student strengths and enhance student growth rather than deny student access to learning.

Assessment can and should serve multiple purposes. With this realization comes the responsibility to assess purposefully, in a variety of ways, and with an eye toward using the results to promote increased learning.

Three categories of assessment = Diagnostic + Formative + Summative

Regardless of the assessment used, there are three broad categories to consider—diagnostic, formative, and summative.

● Diagnostic Assessment

How can we plan curriculum and instruction if we don't have information about what our students know and don't know, what they can and can't do? Content area standards give us broad expectations by subject, topic, and grade level.

Within each standard is the "stuff" of teaching and learning. Classroom time is too precious to use on content and skills that students have already mastered. Conversely, jumping right into standards and realizing days later that students lack the prior knowledge necessary to relate meaningfully to new content, or lack the skills necessary to progress to new skill levels, also wastes valuable instruction time. The solution is *diagnostic assessment,* sometimes called pretesting. This form of assessment is an important teaching and learning tool that is often neglected.

STANDARD 5

Disposition 6: Middle level teacher candidates realize the importance of basing instruction on assessment results.

Diagnostic assessment may indicate deficiency or mastery of whole groups of students, or it may help us in planning for differentiation if we discover wide variations in prior knowledge or achievement levels. Diagnostic assessment makes us more informed about our students and better able to develop a classroom perspective more closely matched to reality. This information is power when it comes to effectively planning for teaching and learning.

Formative Assessment

The purpose of *formative assessment* is to monitor learning during instruction and take advantage of multiple opportunities to give feedback. Formative assessment methods vary according to content/skills and instructional strategies and may be as informal as teacher observation. The results of formative assessment should guide our instructional decisions and help us find out where our students are on the path toward mastery. "Formative assessments happen before and while students work on assignments. A significant element of effective classroom assessment is formative—the kind of ongoing, regular feedback about student work that leads to adjustment and revision by both the teacher and the students" (Andrade, Buff, Terry, Erano, & Paolino, 2009, p. 4).

The feedback provided by formative assessment helps students know where they are in relation to learning goals, as well as what they need to do to continue to improve. Feedback needs to be as timely as possible to allow us to take advantage of "teachable moments." Giving specific corrective feedback not only guides future efforts, but also tells our students loudly and clearly that what they do and learn is important to us, and therefore **they** are important to us. What we know about young adolescent development tells us that providing feedback promotes positive cognitive and emotional development.

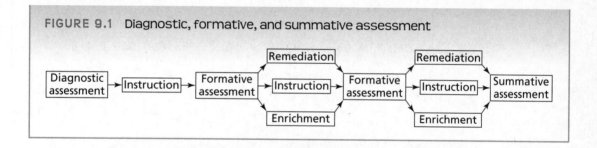

FIGURE 9.1 Diagnostic, formative, and summative assessment

STANDARD 3

Disposition 4: Middle level teacher candidates realize the importance of connecting curriculum and assessment to the needs, interests, and experiences of all young adolescents.

Summative Assessment

Summative assessment typically occurs at the end of a unit of study and is designed to make judgments about the quality of a process or product. It is more formal than diagnostic or formative assessment and is used as a major factor in determining student grades. Summative assessment should allow students to demonstrate what they can do with what they know. To be effective, summative assessments should not be limited to paper-and-pencil exams.

Because formative assessment occurs all along the journey toward mastery, it guides our instruction. Figure 9.1 shows the interactions among instruction, diagnostic assessment, formative assessment, and summative assessment. Notice that formative assessment provides multiple opportunities to alter instruction. Take a few minutes to follow the paths that exist between and among these four important aspects of teaching and classroom assessment.

Classroom Assessment

myeducationlab

To hear Chandra Emerson, the 2008 Kentucky Teacher of the Year, emphasize the role of enthusiasm in the creation and maintenance of a positive classroom, go to the Teacher Talk section of **Topic #3: Classroom Management** in the MyEducationLab for your course.

Classroom assessment can take multiple forms, from informal to formal. Any time we gather information about student achievement and behavior, we are assessing. Before we talk about various forms of classroom assessment, it is important to make the point that no assessment is truly objective. Some teachers refer to multiple choice and true/false tests as objective. You will often hear standardized tests that don't include essay items referred to as objective. Yes, there's generally one right answer, so grading may even be accomplished using a machine. But think about this . . . someone had to write the questions, and thereby make judgment calls about what's important enough to test.

STANDARD 3

Knowledge 4: Middle level teacher candidates are knowledgeable about local, state, and national middle level curriculum standards and of ways to assess the student knowledge reflected in those standards.

Knowledge 11: Middle level teacher candidates understand the key concepts within the critical knowledge base and know how to design assessments that target them.

STANDARD 4

Knowledge 3: Middle level teacher candidates are knowledgeable about teaching and assessment strategies that are especially effective in their teaching fields.

Performance 2: Middle level teacher candidates use effective content specific teaching and assessment strategies.

STANDARD 5

Disposition 5: Middle level teacher candidates value the importance of on-going and varied assessment strategies.

▶ Teachers Speak

● Deirdre McGrew

I've never been very comfortable with the whole idea of testing. As a student, I always felt like I knew more than any particular test might indicate. But tests are considered necessary in education, and, in my opinion, they are necessary evils. That being said, let me tell you what I've learned about assessment that makes it palatable to me.

An assessment is a snapshot of what a student knows and can do at a given time under particular circumstances. One snapshot is not an album. It takes lots of snapshots to get a real view of learning. The kids in our CARE program would still be in 5th grade if their capabilities were measured only by a once-a-year standardized test score. They know more than the state tests show. I take notes on what I observe them doing and what they tell me in interviews. I watch them work in small groups and listen as they teach each other. They complete lots of their work on the classroom computers, and the software tracks progress. When I view assessment as a collection of these measurements plus more, it makes sense to me. I'm exploring portfolio assessment for my students' collections. That may be a great way for them to follow their own progress.

● Seven Forms of Classroom Assessment

Marzano (2000) tells us that there are seven basic forms of classroom assessment. They are briefly stated in Figure 9.2. We will discuss each one—some in more detail than others. As we explore the seven forms, think about how each one might serve the function of being diagnostic, formative, and/or summative.

Forced-Choice Items   The first form of assessment is very traditional and is the most common type of both classroom assessment and standardized assessment. Students simply choose a correct response from the choices provided. Examples of forced-choice assessments include matching, true/false, multiple-choice, and fill-in-the-blank. Although fill-in-the-blank typically doesn't provide answer choices, only one response is generally considered to be correct.

Of these forced-choice assessments, multiple-choice is the most difficult to write. The hardest aspect of writing multiple-choice items is coming up with viable detractors. The incorrect detractors should be plausible enough to be considered, but inaccurate enough to be considered wrong by students who know the content. It is possible to write multiple-choice items that require higher-order thinking, but it's a very time-consuming proposition. True/false items are also difficult to write so that they are not strictly knowledge based or so blatantly true or false that they do not require careful consideration.

Essays   Essay questions require students to write responses in narrative form, to answer questions in complete sentences and in an organized fashion. In that respect, essay questions can assess knowledge (remembering), comprehension (understanding), application, analysis, synthesis (creating), and evaluation, as well as communication skills.

Short Written Responses   These are mini-essays requiring brief answers/explanations. An example of a short written response item in math would be: "Briefly compare a triangular prism and a triangular pyramid by telling about their

---

FIGURE 9.2   Seven forms of classroom assessment

1. Forced-choice Items
2. Essay
3. Short Written Responses
4. Oral Reports
5. Teacher Observation
6. Student Self-assessment
7. Performance Tasks

Source: From *Transforming Classroom Grading* (p. 87), by R. J. Marzano, 2000, Alexandria, VA: Association for Supervision and Curriculum Development.

bases, faces, edges, and vertices." In language arts a short written response item might be: "Briefly describe the bicycle stolen in *Pee-Wee's Great Adventure.*" These items don't require synthesis or evaluation. The math item asks for knowledge and comprehession-level aspects of the two polyhedra. The language arts item merely requires recall, but has some variability possible since an exact number of bicycle attributes are not specified as they would be in a forced-choice item.

Oral Reports   Oral reports are similar to essays in that they require organizing multiple facts/concepts to express information. Students must not only be able to write their essays coherently (even if they do not have to be turned in), but they also are required to deliver them orally, using visual tools as appropriate. It is possible then to assess not only levels of Bloom's taxonomy, but also organizational skills and oral communication ability.

Teacher Observation   Marzano (2000) tells us that teacher observation is "one of the most straight-forward ways to collect classroom assessment data" (p. 99). Observations are useful when assessing process-oriented skills such as reading fluency, spatial abilities as demonstrated through hands-on tools like tangram puzzles, dexterity skills used in the manipulation of science experiment materials, and so forth. While different students may have the same knowledge about how to do something, their process skills of efficiency and accuracy may vary.

Teacher observation may be the only way to assess nonachievement factors such as attitude, effort, behavior, time on task, and so on. Having definite aspects to observe, and then creating a system for recording those observations, are vital to lend consistency and a measure of objectivity (though admittedly small) when using teacher observation as a classroom assessment. Think about this—it's impossible *not* to observe in our classrooms. It will happen continually. The danger in using teacher observation in overt ways as a form of assessment is that the "squeaky wheel gets the grease." By this I mean that certain young adolescents may draw more attention than others, either positively or negatively. If we don't occasionally make teacher observation very purposeful, we are likely to miss key growth-enhancing or remediation opportunities.

One variation of teacher observation is the teacher-student informal interview. These sessions are time-consuming, but quite valuable when the right questions are asked and students are comfortable expressing themselves. Teacher-student interviews may be a luxury when you are on a five-person team and have more than 100 students. Finding the time needed could be one result of a block schedule and careful team planning.

Student Self-Assessment   "Although the most underused form of classroom assessment, student self-assessment has the most flexibility and power as a combined assessment and learning tool" (Marzano, 2000, p. 102). Understanding the developmental aspects of young adolescents, this makes sense. Self-assessment is definitely a skill that requires guidance to be both an assessment and a learning tool. Simply saying "Tell me how you think you did," or "Did you do a good job?" will not elicit thoughtful responses from most middle grades students. They need specific

Student teacher Sarah Gardner and her cooperating teacher, Ms. Cunningham, are discussing with students their progress on a research project they are working on together.

aspects to assess, an array of understood descriptors from which to choose, and a re-porting process that assures them respect and confidentiality.

Teacher think-alouds can be valuable for teaching students to self-assess. Through teacher self-assessment we can demonstrate to students how to think about progress, accomplishment, quality factors, and indicators of understanding.

Teachers who use student self-assessment extensively report that students tend to assess their own work quite realistically, with honesty and candor. Their remarks and criticisms are often more severe than those of the teachers. Having students self-assess following corrective measures builds independence and proactive behavior (Marzano, 2000).

A question to consider is whether student self-assessment, if recorded in some viable way, should have some bearing on a teacher's assessment or if it should be its own category added to many forms of assessment used within a unit of study. The answer to this question depends on circumstances such as how the self-assessments are gathered, how much guidance students have had in doing the self-assessment, and the stated purpose of the self-assessment.

Performance Assessment *Alternative* and *authentic* are words often used inter-changeably with performance assessment. *Alternative assessment* generally refers to any assessment that is not primarily a forced-choice, essay, or short written response.

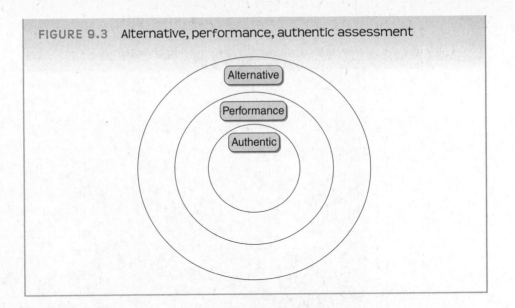

FIGURE 9.3   Alternative, performance, authentic assessment

STANDARD 5

Knowledge 3: Middle level teacher candidates know that teaching higher order thinking skills is an integral part of instruction and assessment.

Authentic assessment tends to be real-life in nature. *Performance assessment,* usually refers to tasks that require students to apply knowledge. **Performance** tends to be an umbrella term in that it includes both real-life and contrived aspects of assessment. The Venn diagram in Figure 9.3 illustrates that both authentic and performance assessments are alternative in nature, that authentic assessment is performance-based, and that performance assessment is broader than authentic assessment.

Performance assessment methods are generally considered to be those outside the realm of traditional assessment. O'Connor (2002) broadly describes performance tasks as demonstrations of knowledge and skills. Table 9.2 gives us Schurr's (1999) viewpoint of some of the characteristics of what she considers traditional and authentic assessment.

Jackson and Davis (2000) tell us that authentic tasks that we have established as performance tasks help students

1. Concentrate on complex tasks

2. Demonstrate what they can do

3. Make connections between themselves and the world

4. Reflect on their own understanding

5. Apply and transfer knowledge and skills in different contexts (p. 56)

This is an impressive list. It emphasizes the value of developing performance oppor- tunities for our students. Read about focus student Gabe's experience with perfor- mance assessment in **See How They Grow**.

TABLE 9.2   Characteristics of traditional and authentic assessment

Characteristics of Traditional Assessment	Characteristics of Authentic Assessment
1. Sequence of simple, distinct tasks	1. General, complex task involving interrelated sub-tasks
2. Recall of limited amounts of knowledge, despite ever-increasing scope of knowledge	2. Internalization and application of knowledge and thinking processes generalizable to all sorts of knowledge
3. Quick and easy to score objectively, even if there is little validity	3. Scoring requires complex and more subjective considerations
4. Tests breadth of knowledge better (e.g., by numerous questions)	4. Tests depth of knowledge better
5. Easy to compare scores	5. Scores tend to be too contextual to compare easily
6. Easy to standardize for all students regardless of differences	6. Adapts more to strengths, needs, and choices of unique students
7. Encourages low-level thinking to arrive quickly at one right answer	7. Encourages critical and creative thinking, taking time to arrive at the best of many possible answers
8. Requires only reactive response, usually by student in isolation	8. Involves students very actively and cooperatively in productive process

Source: From *Authentic Assessment: Using Product, Performance, and Portfolio Measures from A to Z* (p. 4), by S. Schurr, 1999, Westerville, OH: National Middle School Association. Adapted with permission from National Middle School Association.

▶ See How They Grow

Gabe • 8th Grade

Gabe is enjoying 8th grade much more than 6th or 7th, in part because his family no longer leaves the area for three months each year. Dad got a job working construction, with a back-up job in landscaping. The family now lives in a small house near Valley View Middle School. Gabe can walk to school.

Another reason for Gabe's renewed interest in school is his fascination with robotics. In Ms. Fox's science class he learned the basics and she en- couraged him to stay after school with the kids who are in the robotics club. He was hesitant because they already knew so much more than he, but soon discovered that his longtime love of transformers was good preparation for being part of the club.

For several years he searched the Goodwill store for transformers while his mom bought the family clothes. Occasionally she would buy one for him. Ms. Fox is very enthusiastic and asked if he would bring his collection to a club meeting. She brought the DVDs of both the transformer movies and loaned them to him.

No, this isn't what we think of as a traditional way to hook a student on school, but genuine attention from a teacher, coupled with a captivating topic, is probably the best way to keep reluctant learners coming back. Ms. Fox can use Gabe's knowledge as expressed through club activities as a performance-based indicator.

STANDARD 5

Knowledge 4: Middle level teacher candidates know how to select and develop formal, informal, and performance assessments based on their relative advantages and limitations.

● Matching Instruction and Assessment

We've looked at seven forms of classroom assessment, each fulfilling a need and serving a purpose depending on the content/skill and the methods of instruction. With the large variety of assessments available, it is possible to match assessment methods to instructional methods. For instance, if a unit in social studies involves students studying the Bill of Rights and then discovering events in history to which they apply, assessing the unit by using fill-in-the-blank items that call for verbatim recitation of the amendments would be inappropriate. A performance that requires students to write or analyze a scenario and then apply the amendments would be an assessment that matches the instruction. There will, however, be occasions when true/false and multiple-choice assessments are appropriate, particularly when the learning goal is retention of knowledge and comprehension of concepts.

STANDARD 5

Knowledge 2: Middle level teacher candidates know a wide variety of teaching, learning, and assessment strategies, and when to implement them.

● Portfolio Assessment

A *portfolio* is a collection of student work that may be selected to showcase best quality, show progress over time, or both. Portfolios are flexible vehicles for organizing and viewing all kinds of assessment tools, from traditional paper-and-pencil tests to performances that include teacher feedback and student self-assessments.

A comprehensive portfolio should emphasize both process and product and should serve as a short evolutionary record of progress toward learning goals.

STANDARD 5

Performance 8: Middle level teacher candidates implement a variety of developmentally responsive assessment measures (e.g., portfolios, authentic assessments, student self-evaluation).

As collections of work, portfolios allow individual differences to be seen as assets. Because students are given opportunities to make choices within guidelines as to what to include, they stand a good chance of being able to express their own multiple intelligences. For instance, they may have the opportunity to include artwork, video productions, photographs of sporting events, items from nature, Internet searches and results, annotated lists of books they've read, timelines, graphic organizers, poems . . . the list is endless. If a portfolio is to show what a student knows and can do in a discipline or multiple disciplines, then student choice leads to student self-expression. As with project learning discussed in Chapter 8, light bulbs go on in some young adolescents' heads when they see learning as a whole, rather than isolated assignments, and when they make decisions to shape a product they can proudly display.

In Shelbourne, Vermont, the middle school Alpha Team implemented the use of student portfolios as the cornerstone of their assessment program for their multiage team that loops 6th, 7th, and 8th graders. The reasons stated by two of the teachers, Carol Smith and Cynthia Myers (2001), include

- Teachers should provide varied opportunities for students to make sense of their learning.
- Students need time to reflect on their work.
- Students need to make connections between and among tasks and note improvement along the way.

They report that students learn to recognize quality and improve their decision-making skills as they look at other students' portfolios, as well as their own, over time. Their organizational skills improve, as do their self-assessment skills. According to the Alpha Team, the portfolio provides "concrete evidence of learning and represents the perfect format for students to discuss progress with their teachers and parents" (p. 11).

Many books and articles have been written about portfolios, detailing their development and benefits. Teams that use portfolios can share advice and the lessons learned in implementing them. Whole middle schools that use portfolios reap the benefits of having students view them as a "way of life" and excellent evidence of the depth and breadth of their learning and maturing progress.

Evaluating and Grading

We began this chapter with a discussion of performances and behaviors that tell us if our students are meeting specified learning goals. We examined broad categories of classroom assessment and discovered there are many ways to diagnose prior knowledge and skills, to monitor progress along the way through formative assessment, and to determine if goals are reached through summative assessment. We looked at single assignments as well as collections of performances in portfolio format.

Now we will address the issue of distinguishing degrees of understanding and clarifying the criteria for judging performance. Let's agree on some definitions of terms before addressing the details of determining degrees of quality and understanding.

evaluation—the process of judging levels of quality of student work/ performance/understanding

score—the number given to student work to indicate evaluation

weight—the value given to specific student work relative to other assignments

grade—the number or letter representing scores of evaluation received over time and reported to students and adults

For decades, some educators have questioned the wisdom of assigning grades to students. They have argued that grades are meaningless, do not represent understanding and the application potential of knowledge, are harmful to student self-esteem, impede progress if either too low or too high—the list goes on and each flaw has a degree of validity. But for Americans, grading and receiving grades is ingrained in our schools. Recently researchers have taken up the challenge of looking at grades in new ways. With the advent of standards and acceptance of differentiating instruction and multiple intelligences, we may see meaningful change in grading practices in the future.

STANDARD 5

Performance 9: Middle level teacher candidates maintain useful records and create an effective plan for evaluation of student work and achievement.

Rubrics

To assess in ways that speak to "how good is good enough," we turn to rubrics, both as valuable instructional tools and as means of assessment. A *rubric* is a scoring guide that provides the criteria for assessing the quality of a piece of work and includes a gradation for each criterion, generally from excellent to poor, with quality often indicated by numbers. You have probably experienced rubrics as scoring tools and have discovered their benefits in education courses. Figure 9.4

FIGURE 9.4 Generic rubric

Criteria	4	3	2	1	0
Choice of topic	Interesting and current	Interesting but not current	Generic and uninteresting	Not at all relevant	Not enough information for judgment
Depth of research	Evident and compelling	Evident but not compelling	Some research	Little evidence	Not enough information for judgment
Organization of ideas	Clear, easy to follow	Can be followed	Little organization evident	Ideas cannot be followed	Not enough information for judgment
Quality of information	Correct and detailed	Correct but without detail	Incomplete, some incorrect	Mostly incorrect or missing	Not enough information for judgment
Use of conventions	Correct usage of grammar and punctuation	Some errors but not distracting	Errors that interfere with content	Too many errors to be coherent	Not enough information for judgment

shows a generic rubric that could be adapted for specific topics in most any subject area. Figure 9.5 provides sample descriptors when numbers are used to judge work quality.

Some schools use rubrics frequently. Chances are that these schools had a few rubric zealots who attended a workshop or a session at a conference where rubrics were explained and the development process was clarified. Once teachers experience their benefits, they are willing to take the time to develop rubrics to assess the performances of their students.

When you share a rubric with your students, it becomes an excellent instructional tool. If detailed enough, a rubric lets students know the expectations for an assignment. Rubrics paint a clear picture, much better than simple directions. If you have examples of products, share them with students and discuss what each criteria looks like. Be sure to save products so you'll have some to show the next time you make similar assignments.

Rubrics serve as valuable communication tools between teacher and student, teacher and parent, and student and parent. The clear expectations and level of feedback communicate thoughtful, purposeful assignments with rubrics providing the basis of conversation about teaching and learning. Figure 9.6 summarizes some of the benefits of using rubrics.

FIGURE 9.5   Number scale for rubrics

4—Students understand the important information accurately and with detail.

3—Students understand the important information, but the details are fuzzy or nonexistent.

2—Students have a basic understanding of the information mixed with some misconceptions and/or gaps.

1—Students have so many misconceptions that the basic information is not understood.

0—Students provide insufficient indicators on which to judge their understanding.

FIGURE 9.6   Reasons to use instructional rubrics

Instructional rubrics . . .

- are easy to use and to explain
- make teachers' expectations very clear
- provide students with more informative feedback about their strengths and areas in need of improvement than traditional forms of assessment do
- support learning
- support the development of skills
- support the development of understanding
- support good thinking

Source: From "Using Rubrics to Promote Thinking and Learning," by H. G. Andrade, 2000, *Educational Leadership,* 57(5), pp. 14–16.

STANDARD 5

Performance 10: Middle level teacher candidates communicate assessment information knowledgeably and responsibly to students, families, educators, community members, and other appropriate audiences.

Purposes of Grades

Grades provide information. A grade assigned to a student serves multiple purposes depending on who views it.

As viewed by students. An obvious purpose of grades is to inform students about their achievement. With ongoing formative assessment, summative grades should not surprise students. What they do is lend seriousness to the whole assessment process. The surprise is often perceived by the adults who receive grade reports without adequate communication about sources of grades and student progress.

Low letter grades without accompanying details and descriptions of deficits have never been shown to be motivators. The threat of even lower grades if study habits aren't changed will probably prove to have negative effects. However, descriptive narratives, even if they contain negative comments, can be motivational if approached as opportunities for improvement (Burden & Byrd, 2010). Receiving a high grade, especially if it shows progress, can be motivating with or without an explanation. As with so many aspects of middle grades education, perspective and teacher attitude determine in large measure the receptiveness and dispositions of students toward grades.

● *As viewed by parents.* Grades are expected features of school. Attempts at the middle level to convey progress, or lack of it, with narratives alone (replacing letter grades) have generally been met with disapproval and been considered unacceptable by families. Grades are traditional, and even though parents may realize they are subjective measures, they usually still want to know if Johnny's work is of A, B, C, D, or F quality. Praise and punishment may both be doled out based on the grades received by students.

● *As viewed by teachers.* If grades and the process of grading do not guide instructional planning, then we are missing a major function of assessment and evaluation. We have already discussed the value of diagnostic assessment in decision-making. The same premise applies to grades. We look at the academic achievement of our students, or lack of it. We determine content depth, remediation, instructional strategies, sequencing, pacing, and so on. At the same time, individual student grades give us guidance for grouping/regrouping and differentiating instruction.

When considering placement in what are considered advanced courses in middle schools, such as Algebra I and foreign language, grades provide a guidance function. They also provide information used in determining summer school or afterschool options often used for remediation.

● *As viewed by administrators.* Administrators at school and district levels use grades as indicators of academic success of groups of students—classes, grade levels, and whole schools. Individual student grades influence promotion and retention and help determine placement of students in homogeneous or heterogeneous groups.

Your school and your team will have established grading procedures in terms of scales and reporting. Be sure you understand these procedures and what leeway you may have in determining student grades. Some schools will require a minimum number of grades per quarter or semester. Many principals will ask to see your record keeping system, and parents expect clearly defined criteria. As a team, you will want the message that grades send to students and adults to have a measure of consistency and absolute fairness.

● Establishing Scoring Criteria

Regardless of the assignment or assessment, scoring needs to be based on pre-established criteria. For forced-choice assessments, students need to know how many points each item is worth and then how those points translate to scores and figure

TABLE 9.3   Varying grade scales

A	B	C	D	F
90–100%	80–89%	70–79%	60–69%	<60%
93–100%	85–92%	78–84%	70–77%	<70%
95–100%	85–94%	75–84%	65–74%	<65%
95–100%	88–94%	81–87%	75–80%	<75%

into overall grades. For projects, students need scoring guides. Rubrics may be used to provide number scores when points are assigned to each descriptor of quality.

Clear and precise scoring criteria set targets for our students. With assignments that receive scores, and assessments that are evaluated, knowing what is expected in terms of standards to be met and the credit to be given adds clarity and definitive goals.

Having defined criteria helps us deal with the basic question of what grades mean. What, after all, is an A? How about a C? There are general notions, but consistency from state to state, school to school, and even classroom to classroom does not exist. As we look at the different percentages commonly associated with letter grades in Table 9.3, keep in mind that even with percentages established for a district, the assignments and assessments that are evaluated and scored to come up with the percentages are subjective.

What to Include   Even though academic achievement is the implied focus of grades, we know that other factors are often included. In some schools and on some teams, it is understood that dispositions such as effort, participation, attitude, and other behaviors receive weight in a grade. A noted researcher and author on the topic of grading, Ken O'Connor (2002), cautions us against including dispositions in academic scores to develop letter grades. He tells us that unless a nonacademic outcome or behavior process is part of a stated learning goal, it should not be part of a content area grade. "Hard work (effort), frequent responses to teacher questions, intense involvement in class activities, and a positive . . . demeanor are all highly valued attributes. However, they should not be included directly in grades" (p. 99). The attributes mentioned are difficult to define and even more difficult to measure.

Along with reporting academic grades, it is entirely appropriate to give feedback on dispositions and behavior. A commonly used rating sale for nonacademic outcomes includes descriptors such as superior, excellent, above average, average, satisfactory, and so on. An alternative to these scales, which sometimes lack specificity, are checklists of specific behaviors such as uses time wisely, organizes work well, works effectively with others, or completes assignments on time.

Weighting Grades   Some assignments and assessments are more valuable than others because they demonstrate learning more accurately and require more knowledge and skills to complete. For this reason, we don't want a homework assignment to be scored on a 0–100 point scale and a major writing project to also be scored 0–100. There are a number of ways to remedy this dilemma. You may want to designate the compiled or averaged scores of major assignments and assessments as a larger percentage of the overall grade. You might reserve 0–100 points for the bigger assignments and assessments and relegate fewer points (0–5) for daily work. This is what weighting is all about—an admittedly subjective process.

When using a rubric, you could have five criteria with a 0–4 scale for each. This would give a score range of 0 to 20. If the rubric applied to a major assessment, you would want to multiply the achieved score by a factor that would show its relative importance. For instance, if the assignment needs to be worth 100 points, simply multiply a score by 5.

An Alternative to Mean Average   When an idea required more than passive consideration, my mother would say, "Put your thinking cap on." Here's a concept so simple, yet so radical, that it may require your thinking cap. For me it resulted in a response of "Wow! What a revelation!" My experience leads me to believe that the overwhelming majority of teachers use the mean average to compute grades. Recall that the mean is the total of scores divided by the number of values. The mean is a measure of central tendency, and so is the median. The median is the middle value when the scores are placed in numerical order.

When using the mean, all scores or possible scores are added, even the zeros. The mean "emphasizes quantity over quality and completing all work rather than doing some superbly and missing some" (O'Connor, 2002, p. 143). Few students realize what one zero will do to an average. If a student has four scores, three of which are 100% and one of which is zero, the mean average is 75%. According to Table 9.3 that means a C, a D, or even an F. Do any of those three letters accurately indicate the student's achievement? Perhaps the median (100, 100, 100, 0) of 100 is not completely accurate either, especially if the zero resulted from a lack of understanding or skill. But chances are a zero indicates a behavior (nonacademic) outcome, and perhaps should not even be included in calculating a content-area letter grade.

Using the median as a measure of central tendency rather than the mean takes into consideration that we all stumble occasionally and have days when we are not at our best. If this philosophy applies at any age, it should apply in early adolescence. We expect variability. Being developmentally responsive calls for us to reward achievement and growth over time while diminishing the effects of social and emotional changes and traumas.

Take time to examine Table 9.4, which illustrates issues with the mean from *How to Grade for Learning*. Note that the mean for each of the four students is 63%. Now look at the medians. Consider the 10 scores for each student. Which students appear to have a solid grasp of the knowledge and skills? Should they all receive Ds and Fs? Their point totals are the same, but their degrees of understanding are certainly different.

Consider the value of using a combination of the mean and median. Discuss this issue with your teammates.

TABLE 9.4   Issues with the mean

Assessments in Order	Karen	Alex	Jennifer	Stephen
Assessment #1	0	63	0	0
Assessment #2	0	63	10	0
Assessment #3	0	63	10	62
Assessment #4	90	63	10	62
Assessment #5	90	63	100	63
Assessment #6	90	63	100	63
Assessment #7	90	63	100	90
Assessment #8	90	63	100	90
Assessment #9	90	63	100	100
Assessment #10	90	63	100	100
Total	630	630	630	630
Mean	63%	63%	63%	63%
Median	90%	63%	100%	63%

Source: From *How to Grade for Learning* (p. 142), by K. O'Connor, 2002, Arlington Heights, IL: Skylight Professional Development. Copyright 2002 by Pearson Education, Inc. Reprinted with permission.

Reporting Grades   Progress reports and report cards are standard fare in most middle schools. They should be considered the bare minimum in terms of efforts to communicate grades to students and parents/guardians. The traditional system calls for grade reporting every 4 to 5 weeks. Ideally your team will have a system to communicate progress, or the lack of it, more frequently in cases where outstanding progress is being made or a sudden or chronic lack of progress is noted.

Report cards vary in the amount and types of information included. This is often outside your control. You and your team will want to supplement communication in ways that keep parents informed and invite their participation.

● Grading for Success

Tomlinson (2001) tells us "grading grows from a philosophy of teaching and learning. It reflects what a teacher believes about learning" (p. 12). She outlines five guidelines for grading.

1. Grade so that students' degrees of success "reflect the degree of their own growth" (p. 14).
2. Assign appropriate work and "grade the student's work on the basis of clearly delineated criteria for quality of work on that task" (p. 14).

3. As a part of grading, "give students consistent, meaningful feedback that clarifies for them—and for me—present successes and next learning steps" (p. 14).

4. Look for growth patterns over time when assigning grades.

5. Show individual growth as well as relative standing among classmates.

To sum up Tomlinson's grading philosophy she writes, "Can grading be a part of efforts to help all students succeed? Absolutely, when it grows from a philosophy of teaching for maximum individual growth" (p. 15).

Standardized Assessment

myeducationlab

Go to the Assignments and Activities section of **Topic #1: Schools and Teaching Today** in the MyEducationLab for your course and complete the activities entitled "Using Test Results to Impact Student Learning."

Standardized tests are a fact of life in public education. With No Child Left Behind, the demand for accountability in our schools has never been higher. We hear it from parents, legislators, and citizen groups. Standards of learning established by subject area organizations and state departments of education provide goals. How to measure progress toward those goals, which include understanding and performance, is a dilemma. While calls for accountability lead to standardized testing, the process itself and the results are often viewed critically.

Validity and reliability are two concepts important for all assessment, but of particular importance for standardized assessment. Validity refers to the degree to which an assessment measures what it is supposed to measure. For classroom assessment, validity is within our control. For standardized testing based on imposed standards, validity can be verified through comparisons of standards and test items. However, most teachers do not have access to state items, so establishing validity is usually a state issue. Reliability refers to the consistency with which an assessment measures what it is meant to measure. Reliability can be complicated to establish, requiring field testing of sample populations. With classroom assessment, teacher judgment makes up for whatever an assessment lacks in terms of reliability.

Vital components of standardized assessment = Validity + Reliability

Comparing Standardized and Classroom Assessment

As classroom teachers we can follow the adage of "Teach what you test and test what you teach." If classroom assessment is interwoven with curriculum and instruction, and standards are incorporated, then the package of learning and testing can be neatly and cohesively bundled. Classroom assessment in its many forms derives content and skills to be tested from the learning opportunities of the classroom.

State standardized assessments derive content and skills to be tested from state standards documents. While we don't write the items, we have the standards they supposedly measure.

Most standardized tests derive content and skills from many sources including national subject area organizations and textbooks. They are written to match grade level expectations, but often contain items and/or complete sections that are unfamiliar to our students. We can use published preparation materials, but in doing so we may find that we actually end up presenting isolated facts out of context.

With classroom assessments, we are free to determine the value of items in the overall scheme of our planned assessment and measure student success against our learning goals. We then assign a score to the assessment and a weight to indicate its importance relative to other assessments. Assessing student success in meeting stated learning goals and expectations is referred to as *criterion-referenced assessment*. Student scores reflect what they know and the degree to which they know it. With *norm-referenced* assessments, students are rated relative to other students within a segment or population. Norm-referenced tests are expressed in percentiles. On a classroom assessment, usually criterion-referenced, an "85%" means that 85% of the knowledge and skills assessed were correct. On a standardized assessment, usually norm-referenced, an "85%" means that 85 of every 100 students tested lower than the student with 85% and 15 of 100 students tested higher. This simply compares student performance and provides little information about the level or mastery of learning goals. If most of the students actually did very poorly on the assessment, then a norm score of 85% would represent questionable success. If most of the students did exceptionally well on the assessment, then a norm score of 85% would represent outstanding success. Based on student success relative to learning goals, state standardized test results typically place students in one of four groups labeled "below basic," "basic," "proficient," and "advanced." This information is reported in ways that facilitate individuals being compared with other students within the same class, school, district, or state. In the same way, schools and districts are compared with others within a state.

Benefits of Standardized Assessment

Standardized assessment is not going away in the foreseeable future. The capacity, debatable as it is, to provide comparisons and gauge annual progress makes standardized assessment a fixture in public education. I have often referred to it as a "rite of spring," since most standardized assessments are administered March through May in traditional school calendars. Given their undeniable presence, our best stance is to be proactive. To be both proactive and positive, we must consider the possible benefits of standardized assessment. Figure 9.7 lists a sampling of those benefits.

Preparing for Standardized Assessment

There is a prevailing fear that preparing for standardized assessments will lead to almost exclusive drill and practice, or as some call it, drill and kill, instruction. Obviously, that would be very inappropriate, particularly for middle level students. Most researchers who study test preparation practices and their results tell us that we should avoid the temptation to drill isolated information not just because we know it's not developmentally responsive, but because it doesn't work. Classrooms that concentrate on the "big ideas," active student involvement, and a comprehensive

---

FIGURE 9.7   Benefits of standardized tests

Standardized tests . . .

- provide data on how well students, and consequently teachers, schools, districts, and states, are performing.
- if directly tied to standards, promote a common instructional focus.
- show patterns of strengths and weaknesses to guide decision-making.
- when results indicate mastery and/or improvement, build public trust.
- provide a mode of comparison, although approximate, for schools, districts, and states.
- may prompt us to ask probing and important questions concerning instructional practice as we analyze results.

---

curriculum are likely to see their students excel on standardized assessment. Here are some practices to consider.

1. *Be positive concerning the necessity of standardized tests.*   If we convey (even if we don't say out loud) the message, "We've got to put up with those stupid standardized tests in April," our students will sense our negativity and their preparation, and subsequently their scores, will suffer. If we approach standardized tests with an attitude of, "This is a great opportunity to show what we know and can do!" I guarantee you happier, more productive students along with the real possibility of higher scores.

2. *Focus on student reading ability,*   regardless of the subject area tested. Remember that we are all teachers of reading. Help students improve their reading skills within the context of your subject area and continually assist them with vocabulary acquisition.

3. *Know your state curriculum standards intimately,*   including the ones written for previous and subsequent grade levels, and incorporate them into your lesson plans.

4. *Obtain and use previous standardized test results for your students.*   Look for strengths, weaknesses, and both individual and team trends. Use these results diagnostically for instructional planning.

5. *Provide an abundance of authentic opportunities*   that call for not only knowledge and comprehension, but also application, analysis, synthesis, and evaluation.

6. *Emphasize problem-solving*   in all content areas. Math does not have a monopoly when it comes to problem-solving opportunities. After all, history is just one problem after another, with attempted resolutions along the way.

7. *Teach the skills of editing*   and then give lots of opportunity for practice. Help students recognize errors and areas for improvement in their own and others' writing.

8. *Provide frequent opportunities for students to interpret and create representations*   like tables, graphs, and maps. As with problem-solving, this is not the exclusive

purview of math. Some estimates tell us that 25% of the standardized test items in social studies and science involve charts, tables, graphs, and maps.

9. *Use a variety of assessment methods* to help develop student flexibility. We know it is beneficial to assess the same content and skills in many ways.

10. *Locate and use appropriate test preparation and test-specific materials* from publishers and as provided by state departments of education. Using material that is written in the same format as the test to be administered is advisable. After all, we don't want the test to measure format familiarity more than content knowledge and skills.

Preparation for standardized testing should not be thought of as separate from daily instruction. Using a variety of instructional practices to present a broad and comprehensive curriculum will be the best possible preparation.

Reflections on Assessment in Middle School

Curriculum, instruction, and assessment are interwoven. We have looked at each separately and examined components and issues. What we teach, how we teach it, and then how we gather evidence of learning must be developmentally appropriate and responsive, as well as interdependent. Diagnostic assessment informs our decisions concerning curriculum and instruction; formative assessment tells us if we need to move toward enrichment or remediation; and summative assessment provides information for grading and signals the timing for moving on to new curriculum.

Assessment can be accomplished through a rich variety of means, whether diagnostic, formative, or summative. Assessment allows us to evaluate student achievement and recognize accomplishment; make informed instructional decisions and improve instruction; monitor student progress and promote growth; and evaluate and modify programs.

Classroom assessment establishes hallmarks of understanding. To distinguish degrees of understanding and skill development, we use classroom assessment. Using rubrics allows us to set criteria of quality in advance of assignments, use narratives and descriptions to give feedback, and be specific and open in what otherwise can be a very subjective and vague process.

Performance assessment involves any task in which students are required to demonstrate understanding and skills. Paper-and-pencil tests that require more than recitation of facts, complex tasks requiring extensive planning, and every level in between may be considered performance assessment.

Standardized assessment is a stable feature of public education. It's not going away. Standardized assessment has limitations, but it also has benefits. Taking a proactive stance involves including strong instructional practices that strengthen learning and lead to improved standardized test scores.

Accountability is essential for all of us involved in teaching and learning. Assessment allows our students to show what they know and what they are able to do. The results of assessment serve as accountability measures for us. Schools and districts are responsible for providing support for teaching and learning. Assessment results hold them accountable to us and to our students. The important role of classroom and standardized assessment cannot be overstated. "Continuous, authentic, and appropriate assessment measures provide evidence about each student's learning progress. Such information helps students, teachers, and family members select immediate learning goals and plan further education" (National Middle School Association, 2010, p. 24).

GROUP ACTIVITIES

1. In pairs, interview a middle school teacher to discuss assessment. Take a list of the seven basic forms of assessment covered in this chapter and ask the teacher to comment on if and when she uses each. Write a summary of this information to be shared with the class. Include summaries in your school file.

2. In subject area groups, choose a standard and develop an overview of a performance that would assess a hallmark of understanding. Be prepared to share your overview and assessment with the class.

3. In subject area groups, write lists of items that might be included in a student portfolio for a particular topic of study.

4. Respond to these and other questions/prompts appropriate for your area/state.

- Does your state mandate a nationally produced standardized test? If so, find information on the administration of the test (timing, grade levels, frequency, use of results, etc.).

- What information is available concerning your state's standardized assessment? (grade levels, developers, website for preparation, uses of results, etc.)

- Locate state and district test results. Put in a form to share with the class.

- Locate state test results for the middle schools in your school file. Put in a form to share with the class.

Add information gathered to your class files.

INDIVIDUAL ACTIVITIES

1. What type of assessment can you remember from your middle school years? High school? College? Which type did you find easiest? Most difficult? Most meaningful?

2. Write a paragraph that compares and contrasts alternative, performance, and authentic assessment.

3. Do you think a missing homework assignment should receive a grade of zero? Why or why not? What might you do to lessen the impact of an "off week" for a student?

4. Discuss the pros and cons of using the median rather than the mean to determine grades.

5. How are the concepts of performance assessment especially appropriate for middle grades?

6. Write a letter you might send home to parents to explain the value of rubrics. Assume they are unfamiliar with the concept and you plan to use a rubric to assess a student project.

PERSONAL JOURNAL

1. How do you typically react to assessment? Do your grades generally mirror your self-assessment of knowledge/skill level?

2. Do you remember taking standardized tests? Achievement type? SAT or ACT? Praxis? Write about your anxiety levels for these tests.

Professional Practice

(It would be helpful to reread the descriptions of Joey Huber in Chapter 4 and Emily in Chapter 3.)

● **Joey Huber**

Joey is in his last week of fulltime student teaching. He can't believe it's almost over. Things have gotten a little tense at Madison because it's almost time for the state standardized tests. The principal at Madison is making a very big deal out of it, sending letters home asking parents to go over fact sheets and practice materials with kids. He's also planning a big test pep rally. The teachers have told Joey that at least an hour a day must be spent doing practice tests and then going over the material with the kids who, by the way, are less than enthusiastic about the whole thing. They're used to the testing, but that doesn't make them like it any more. They know that if they don't score in the basic category or above, they could be held back in 6th grade. Joey volunteered to conduct daily help sessions after school now that middle school baseball season has ended.

1. All of the following would be good things to do to prepare for the help sessions except
   a. find items in the same format as the tests and explain to the kids how to approach them
   b. make charts that show how the 6th grade students performed on the tests last year to give this year's kids something to aim for
   c. develop exercises that require students to take apart problem-solving scenarios to figure out steps to a solution
   d. find sample reading passages and accompanying questions for kids to use as practice

Emily ● 7th grade

2. Emily and her friends are particularly anxious about the tests. They get nervous every year, but the thought of not going to 8th grade is terrifying to them. Which of the following would be the most appropriate for Joey to say to them?
   a. Don't worry about it. You'll do fine.
   b. We have a week to go and I'll work with you to study for the tests.
   c. You've learned so much this year. Remember this as we review.
   d. These tests don't matter that much anyway.

3. Which order of assessments and instruction is correct?
   a. diagnostic, instruction, formative, instruction, summative
   b. diagnostic, formative, instruction, diagnostic, instruction, summative
   c. formative, instruction, diagnostic, instruction, summative
   d. formative, diagnostic, instruction, summative

Constructed Response

Why is the assessment rubric considered an important innovation? What are the major benefits of rubrics for both teachers and students?

INTERNET RESOURCES

Assessment Training Institute

www.assessmentinst.com

While this site primarily promotes a particular for-profit assessment training program, there are articles and information available on the site that make it useful for all teachers.

Education World

http://educationworld.com

Middle Web

www.middleweb.com

NCREL Pathways to Assessment

www.ncrel.org/sdrs/areas/as0cont.htm

This part of the North Central Regional Educational Laboratory website features articles on assessment that contain links to detailed explanations of key words and phrases relevant to understanding assessment.

Rubrics4Teachers

www.rubrics4teachers.com/

This site consists of information about rubrics, rubrics organized by grade level, sample rubrics for most subject areas and the main topics within each, and links to rubric-maker sites.

10 Planning for Teaching and Learning

Traci Peters and her teammates routinely plan together. They look for connections among the content areas and then adjust their individual plans to reflect those connections. Teams that plan together understand how much more meaningful content is for young adolescents when it is relevant to other things they are learning.

Although planning is a critical skill for a teacher, a well-developed plan will not guarantee the success of a lesson or unit or even the overall effectiveness of a course. But lack of a well-developed plan will almost certainly result in poor teaching. Like a good map, a good plan helps you reach your destination with more confidence and with fewer wrong turns.

Callahan, Clark, and Kellough, 2002, p. 61

CHAPTER PREVIEW

The Importance of Planning

Organizational Skills
- Study Skills
- Time Management
- School Supplies

Goals and Objectives
- Goals
- Objectives

Resources for Teaching
- Selection of Resources
- Textbooks

Collaborative Planning
- Same Subject Planning
- Planning with Students

Levels of Planning
- Long-Range Planning
- Single Subject Units
- Interdisciplinary Units
- Daily Lesson Planning

Reflections on Planning

INTRODUCTION

In this chapter we put it all together—curriculum, instruction, and assessment, tempered by what we know about our students' developmental characteristics and differences. This is a tall order, but it's the craft of teaching. Planning the days, the weeks, the semesters, and year is the task that will determine the level of success we, and our students, achieve in making the teaching and learning connection. It is serious business with tremendous consequences. Overwhelmed? Possibly—well, probably. But take heart. Like any other active endeavor that requires hard work and energy, planning for teaching and learning builds cognitive muscles that may seem overworked or incapable in the beginning but become stronger and more suited for the challenge as we gain momentum in the process. This isn't to say that it's ever easy, but with experience we become more comfortable with the planning process. Its importance should never be diminished regardless of how many years of experience we have.

The Importance of Planning

To understand how important planning is, simply consider some of the elements involved: content; sequence; strategies; who does what, when, where, and in what order; resources, materials; standards; learner needs; technology; homework; classroom climate; student assessment . . . the list could go on and on. The elements of planning involved on a daily, weekly, semester, and yearly basis must all be organized and coordinated. Decisions must be made that involve student needs and interests, curriculum requirements, and lesson delivery. Effective, comprehensive planning requires thoughtful and wise decision-making.

myeducationlab

To hear Melanie Teemant, the 2007 Nevada Teacher of the Year, express that teaching is a calling and that in the classroom we touch the future, go to the Teacher Talk section of **Topic #16: Professional Responsibilities** in the MyEducationLab for your course.

Planning for teaching and learning serves many purposes. Burden and Byrd (2010) tell us that among other things, planning can help us do the following:

- Give a sense of direction and, through this, a feeling of confidence and security. Planning can help you stay on course and reduce your anxiety about instruction.
- Organize, sequence, and increase familiarity with course content.
- Prepare to interact with students during instruction. This may include preparing a list of important questions or guidelines for a cooperative group activity.
- Incorporate techniques to motivate students to learn in each lesson.
- Take into account individual differences and the diversity of students when selecting objectives, content, strategies, materials, and products.
- Arrange for appropriate requirements and evaluation of student performance.
- Become reflective decision-makers about curriculum and instruction.

And you thought a plan was whatever you could squeeze into a 2-inch by 2-inch box on a page with many other boxes to remind you which pages to cover in a textbook! Let's take an in-depth look at this extremely important function of a classroom teacher.

In this chapter we discuss four distinct levels of planning—long-range, single subject units, interdisciplinary units, and daily lessons. Before doing so we need to look at some topics that will be integral factors in the planning process.

STANDARD 5

Disposition 3: Middle level teacher candidates believe that instructional planning is important and must be developmentally responsive.

STANDARD 1

Performance 3: Middle level teacher candidates create positive, productive learning environments where developmental differences are respected and supported, and individual potential is encouraged.

Performance 10: Middle level teacher candidates respond positively to the diversity found in young adolescents and use that diversity in planning and implementing curriculum and instruction.

STANDARD 7

Disposition 6: Middle level teacher candidates are committed to refining classroom and school practices that address the needs of all young adolescents based on research, successful practice, and experience.

Organizational Skills

Just as we are all teachers of reading, we are all teachers of the organizational skills required for success. Organizational skills involve forming habits. Our students are going to form habits with or without our guidance. Helping them be "creatures of habit" in positive ways that promote learning and success is one of our greatest services to middle school students. Planning for organizational skill acquisition involving productive habits will enhance students' chances of success in future academic situations and will also serve them later in life.

Organizational skills = Forming productive habits

The acquisiton of organizational skills is not an innate or inevitable process. D. Robert Sylwester, an expert on brain-based learning, explains that between the ages of 10 and 14 the brain's frontal lobe, which is associated with problem-solving, critical thinking, and organizational skills, develops. He used the term **hovering** to describe how he believes we should walk students through this maturation process (Dyck, 2002). The implication here is that we need to plan to include direct instruction, consistent practice, and monitoring when it comes to study and organizational skills. He concludes that

> This means we must put detailed structure into place, share successful organizational strategies and tools, and use varied methods of explaining new concepts to students. Then we need to repeat all these steps until the process of learning and retaining information becomes second nature to them (p 19).

● Study Skills

We have already discussed the necessity of directly teaching students how to read the material in specific subject areas—that reading a math text requires different emphases than reading a short story. Looking up vocabulary in a glossary and thinking about words in context, reading captions under pictures, understanding information in tables and graphs, knowing how to use a map legend, recognizing the importance of key names and time frames, taking time to dissect a formula and its applications, and reading a story carefully to determine characters, plot, setting, and voice—all of these skills require us to "hover" and guide. This should be part of our planning.

STANDARD 4

Disposition 3: Middle level teacher candidates are committed to using content specific teaching and assessment strategies.

Summarizing and notetaking are vitally important instructional strategies that correlate with student learning. As with reading in content areas, they must be explicitly taught and monitored. Outlining is a related skill that will prove invaluable.

The skills needed to study for a test often elude middle grades students. Some think simply sitting in class should be enough, even when they are unsuccessful over and over again. Others rely on last-minute cramming with possible short-term, but little long-term, success. Others don't have a clue. If we teach what we test, and test what we teach, then assessment in the form of quizzes and tests should not be a mystery. We need to help our students learn how to show what they know and can do.

Even with our emphasis on the big concepts and in-depth understanding, we ask our students to memorize numerous things in order to problem-solve, accurately complete a time line, perform an experiment, and so on. Most of us have tricks that work for our learning styles. Share them with your students. Try new ones yourself and then think aloud about them for your students as you model how they work. Figure 10.1 is a brief list of memorization techniques.

● Time Management

As adults we know how important time management is, not only to our productivity, but also to our comfort and enjoyment of both work and leisure. Middle grades students are moving from the dependency of childhood toward independence when their own personal decision-making concerning time will affect what they accomplish or fail to accomplish.

While in the classroom, with effective planning on our part, students work within a structure on various tasks. However, simply having the structure does not guarantee that young adolescents will use their classroom time productively. They may go from sitting alone in a desk with a book open during silent reading time, to

> **FIGURE 10.1** Techniques for memorization
>
> 1. Visualize the information. Create a picture in your mind that portrays what you want to remember.
> 2. Divide the information you want to memorize into small chunks. In dividing the information, do so as logically as possible. The act of categorizing will make retention even easier.
> 3. Recite out loud the information you need to remember. Listen to your own voice. When trying to recall, it is easier when you can remember what your voice sounded like as you recited.
> 4. Make flash cards. No, they're not just for math facts. You can use them for words/definitions, events/people and dates, sequencing, random bits of information, etc.
> 5. Create acronyms for lists or groups. Did you know that radar stands for "radio detection and ranging?" It's an acronym that is so accepted that it has become a word in itself. To create an acronym, simply arrange the first letters of each item you want to memorize into a real or made-up word.
> 6. Write what you want to memorize in varying ink colors. The color will help you visualize the information you want to recall.

sitting in a circle during group discussion time, and back to a desk for journal writing, and still accomplish absolutely nothing. To an outside observer they appear to have cooperated with the teacher and followed directions. Well, physically yes, cognitively no. Our emphasis must be on using class time wisely to engage students mentally. Interesting lessons requiring individual and group accountability will help engage and elicit participation from the reticent, sometimes mentally lazy, occasionally daydreaming kids who inevitably inhabit our middle level classrooms.

When given work/study time in school and homework to do at home, our students need to understand that assignments take time and that the amount of time varies from student to student. If, for instance, we ask Noah to show the solution steps and find the answers to three math items, read the social studies text section on reconstruction, fill in a lab sheet with science experiment data from class, and write a paragraph summarizing the setting of *The Cay*—all this while preparing for a band presentation at Tuesday's PTA meeting—we need to provide time management guidelines that realistically portray his Monday afternoon and evening. He needs to understand approximately how much time he'll have to devote to academics and how much time he'll have for other activities like sports, video games, dinner, home chores, and, perhaps most importantly to him, hanging out.

Many middle schools require students to use assignment pads. Some even provide these valuable organizational tools and insist that they be maintained in consistent ways. I agree with this practice. My calendar (adult assignment pad) is invaluable. It is my ultimate time management tool. Of course, having an assignment pad doesn't guarantee accomplishment, but when adequately filled in, and then consistently checked upon arrival home by a parent, a student stands a greater chance of managing time and completing work. Assignment pads also serve as reminders of what materials need to be taken both to class and home.

> Success using an assignment pad = Adequately filled in + Consistently checked at home

● School Supplies

Providing a team-coordinated list of required school supplies is essential. For instance, if your teacher team prefers mechanical pencils and black ink, then specifically state that these are necessary. If three classes require pocket and brad folders, then they should be on the list. Binders for subject areas and spiral notebooks for journaling, protractors and rulers for math, colored pencils for social studies—whatever is needed must be listed explicitly.

Some teachers provide an extra service for students by having a dry-erase board outside their classroom doors to list what is required for the day. For instance, vocabulary notebook, poetry anthology, and highlighters may be needed Wednesday, but not literature books with the opposite being true for Friday. Staples such as paper, pencils, and assignment pads are a given.

Depending on your particular situation, you may want to keep extra supplies in a drawer to be loaned to students who infrequently arrive without what they need. For students who perpetually forget or intentionally fail to have needed supplies, team action may be required to emphasize the importance of having necessary items.

Goals and Objectives

myeducationlab

Go to the Assignments and Activities section of **Topic #5: Instructional Planning** in the MyEducationLab for your course and complete the activity entitled "Matching Goals and Objectives to Standards."

To effectively plan instruction, we have to know where we're going and what the desired outcomes look like. In writing goals and objectives, we are practicing backward design as we state the desired learning. Backward design asks us to strengthen our goals and objectives by envisioning the final product or performance as we design paths to get our students where we want them to go.

● Goals

Goals are general statements of intent. They are broad and do not specify steps toward reaching them. An educational goal may be written at the national, state, district, or school level to provide a direction for learning. Goal-setting is an essential aspect of teaching that guides our instructional planning.

In writing goals there are three broad concepts to consider—needs of the learner, the subject matter, and needs of society (Gunter, Estes, & Schwab, 2003). With what we know about young adolescents, including all three of these components makes sense. Here are some examples of classroom goals.

- Students will understand how math is used in everyday life.
- Students will grasp the importance of conservation with regard to natural resources.
- Students will appreciate the musical contributions of major composers.
- Students will understand the influence of William Faulkner on the image of the South.

Objectives

"A learning objective is a statement of the measurable learning that is intended to take place as a result of instruction" (Gunter, Estes, & Schwab, 2003, p. 22). I like this definition for three reasons. First of all, the term **learning objectives** encompasses other terms you may hear like performance objectives, cognitive objectives, affective objectives, content objectives, and other modifications of the basic word *objectives*. We realize that regardless of what we want our students to know or do, and the source from which the knowing and doing emanate, the result we're going for is learning. The second thing I like about the definition is the emphasis on objectives as measurable. While goals may state ideals, objectives use verbs to define specific learning and provide ways to determine if the learning occurs. The third reason is that the objective is accomplished as the result of instruction. For an objective to be meaningful, it must guide instruction and be the reason for doing what we do in the classroom.

Using active verbs to describe the learning we want to occur makes it possible to select instructional strategies to bring about the learning and to design assessments to verify the learning. Most learning objectives begin with the statement "Students will" Keeping a chart containing verbs associated with Bloom's taxonomy, similar to Table 8.1 in Chapter 8, on your desk as you write objectives is a good way to check for inclusion of each of the six categories of learning while varying verb usage. Here are some examples of objectives and the category of Bloom they address.

- Students will recall the order of the major wars involving the United States. (remember/knowledge)
- Students will match the authors to the titles of the books listed on the Great American Authors chart. (remember/knowledge)
- Students will classify each polyhedron as a pyramid or a prism. (understand/comprehension)
- Students will summarize a paragraph, preserving the main idea. (understand/comprehension)

- Students will construct an equilateral triangle given their knowledge of angles and a compass. (application)
- Students will interview a community member on the topic of increasing voter participation given the recent study of communication techniques and the political process. (application)
- Students will compare and contrast the Dust Bowl era to the current drought situation. (analysis)
- Students will verify the relative accuracy of information from a variety of graphs. (analysis)
- Students will design an electrical circuit. (creation/synthesis)
- Students will compose a short story with all the prescribed elements. (creation/synthesis)
- Students will support one candidate for governor using recent newspaper reports. (evaluation)
- Students will defend their position on gun control. (evaluation)

Learning objectives are often included in state/standards, textbooks, and other instructional materials. If they express what you want your students to know and be able to do, then use them—if not verbatim, then as starting points. You will probably not have to write objectives from scratch, but you will be the decision-maker regarding both the depth of content and the order in which the desired learning will take place.

Writing your learning objectives in a particular place on the board each day gives students a sense of organization and purpose. Refer to the objective at the beginning of a class period and then draw student attention to it again toward the end of the class and ask for opinions on whether or not the objective was reached. If so, ask how we know. If not, ask what needs to happen to bring about the learning. Young adolescents are capable of this kind of critical thought. Let's give them opportunities to practice.

Resources for Teaching

There is an amazing array of resources for classroom teachers. Visit a teacher resource store and you'll find books, games, videos, CD-ROMs, manipulatives, and so on, for all subject areas and grade levels. In addition to what's available in the public domain, there are many teaching resources available through national organizations. The National Middle School Association (NMSA) and the Association for Supervision and Curriculum Development (ASCD) publish materials for teachers to use to increase their effectiveness in the classroom. Subject area organizations, such as the National Council of Teachers of Mathematics (NCTM), publish resources for teacher development as well as material that may be used in the classroom, as discussed in Chapter 7.

State departments of education and school districts provide resources for teachers and students. There are curriculum guides, benchmarks and standards documents, sample lesson plans on special websites, practice materials for standardized tests, and other resources deemed important by those who have oversight responsibilities.

● Selection of Resources

With all the print and electronic resources produced continually, the dilemma of what to use and when to use it requires commonsense decision-making. We can't use it all. We wouldn't want to use it all.

The resources published by companies not affiliated with school or national organizations should be chosen with care, with our choices guided by the curriculum content we teach and grade/developmental appropriateness.

Some districts and schools give teachers set amounts of money to spend each year on classroom resources. This is a luxury, and we need to be good stewards of these funds. Principals have resource budgets that allow them to take teacher requests and buy resources as far as their budgeted dollars will allow. Most teachers have more resources at their disposal than they will ever use over the course of a school year. Because of this, new teachers should never feel handicapped by lack of "stuff." Don't be afraid to ask.

There are many things to consider when choosing resources, including

- relationship of resources to course objectives and curriculum standards
- educational value in terms of curricular and instructional goals
- absence of bias concerning gender, race, religion, etc.
- relative worthiness of the time necessary to implement or use the resource
- motivational attributes from a student perspective
- accuracy and timeliness of content

Just because a workbook or lesson or manipulative is attractive and potentially fun to use does not qualify it as appropriate for our classrooms. If it does not have the potential to increase student learning, then it is wasting precious minutes.

STANDARD 5

NMSA

Knowledge 7: Middle level teacher candidates understand how to motivate all young adolescents and facilitate their learning through the use of a wide variety of developmentally responsive materials and resources (e.g., technological resources, manipulative materials).

Textbooks

When we talk about adopting a textbook series at the state, district, or school level, we are talking about more than a solitary book. Publishers have responded to the call for accountability and ever-burgeoning technology by providing amazing tools for teachers. Along with the basic textbook and teachers' edition, you may receive consumable workbooks (each student gets his own each year), CD-ROMs full of supplemental materials, booklets for student and parental interactive practice, special workbooks designed specifically for state standards test preparation, interactive software, supplemental literature books, packets of maps, boxes of math and science manipulatives, videos, black-line masters to reproduce, overhead transparencies, and powerpoint presentations. . . . Can we use all of these resources over the course of a semester or a year? Absolutely not. The choice of a text series will probably not be yours, but how and when you use the book and assorted "goodies" that come with it will probably be within your control.

Let's consider what a textbook (and its ancillary components) is not. It is not the curriculum, it is not the shaper of all instruction, it is not necessarily the sequencer of content, and it is not the only source of information in your subject area. However, a well-chosen text that aligns closely with national and state subject area/grade level standards can form a basis for our instructional planning.

There are things we can do in the beginning of the school year to make students more comfortable with the basic textbook. For instance, we can prepare a text scavenger hunt that requires students to look at the title page, table of contents, illustrations, organization of chapters, purpose of boldface print, index, appendix, glossary, and more. Middle grades students respond positively to creative activities of this kind. The time invested will pay dividends all year long.

Collaborative Planning

myeducationlab

Go to the Assignments and Activities section of **Topic #5: Instructional Planning** in the MyEducationLab for your course and complete the activity entitled "Understanding Differences in Planning."

While the ultimate responsibility for planning what occurs in your classroom is yours, some of the planning on any of the levels may be done collaboratively. In Chapter 6 we discussed that one of the major benefits of teaming is the possibility of planning with other teachers. Planning objectives and activities in your content area with a teammate whose

STANDARD 5

Disposition 4: Middle level teacher candidates value opportunities to plan instruction collaboratively with teammates and other colleagues.

Performance 3: Middle level teacher candidates plan effective instruction individually and with colleagues.

curriculum complements yours is not only a joy, but also a boon to student learning. Teachers on a team should compare their long-range plans to find connections. This is discussed in the next section. Now let's look at same subject planning and planning with students.

Same Subject Planning

If your school is large enough to have more than one team per grade level, you will have one or more colleagues who teach the same subject at the same grade level. This is a great benefit. Chances are you have the same curriculum guide, standards, textbook, and basic materials. The adage "two heads (or three or four) are better than one" applies here. We each approach content and instruction in our own way. When we put more than one approach on the table and collaborate in planning, the result will be richer and potentially better for our students.

Occasionally planning with same subject teachers on different grade levels is very helpful. This is *vertical articulation*—vertical because it crosses grade levels and articulation because of the communication factor. It is extremely helpful to understand the standards and instructional methodology your students experienced before they came to you, as well as the expectations that await them when they leave your classroom. Regardless of the size of your school, vertical articulation is valuable for looking at student experiences over time to see the big picture and enhance continuity among grade levels.

Planning with Students

Like every other aspect of education, there are degrees of implementation of teacher and student *collaborative planning*. Many middle grades classrooms encourage student input in the planning process. The concept of curriculum integration involves "a student-centered approach in which students are invited to join with their teachers to plan learning experiences that address both student concerns and major social issues" (Vars, 2001, p. 8). Student involvement in planning helps create a student-centered classroom regardless of the degree of curriculum integration. Erlandson and McVittie (2001) reported in the *Middle School Journal* "Collaborating with our students in planning . . . which included experiential, hands-on activities they had a voice in designating or selecting, would demonstrate our commitment to ensuring that the curriculum is both personally relevant and meaningful to our students" (p. 35).

Teachers are ultimately responsible for the curriculum and instruction in their classrooms. Involving students in the planning process does not diminish that responsibility. Determining when and how to bring students into the process may be based on many factors, including a teacher's comfort level with the required standards and the planning process in general.

Students like Janie who have favorite authors and/or strong interests appreciate opportunities to be part of planning for learning. Read about how Janie is changing in **See How They Grow**.

▶ **See How They Grow**

Janie ● 7th Grade

Of all our focus students, I'd say Janie changed the most between 6th and 7th grade. You have to look closely to know the girl in each picture is actually the same young adolescent. As you recall from Chapter 3, Janie became concerned about her weight right before entering Cario Middle School. Concern for physical development aligned with social development and a metamorphosis of sorts took place.

Janie's parents weren't thrilled with the transformation. When the first purple streak appeared in her hair, along with the black fingernails, they were horrified. Mom said she should have known when Janie's taste in literature went from Judy Blume to Jodi Picoult. Mom and dad called a parent-teacher conference to try to find out why their daughter had turned "goth." When Traci Peters and her teammates sat down with Janie's parents, they listened to their concerns and then began to reassure them. Had Janie gotten in trouble in any setting? No. Had Janie's grades fallen in 7th grade? No. Had she become withdrawn or rebellious? No. Of course the teachers noticed the change, but so far it was in outward appearance only. Teachers and parents agreed to stay in close touch and communicate any signs of problems immediately.

Levels of Planning

Too often when we think of planning we concentrate primarily on daily lesson plans. There are other levels that are significant to student learning that warrant careful consideration, and provide the context for daily planning. Figure 10.2 illustrates levels of planning and some of the factors that guide decision-making at each level. Long-range planning serves as a framework for unit planning. Unit planning provides a framework for both weekly and daily planning. By beginning with long-range planning, we are planning from whole to part.

● Long-Range Planning

Long-range plans are comprehensive guides for facilitating learning involving student profiles, content and sequencing, classroom management philosophy, instructional strategies, and overall organizational factors. Writing a long-range plan requires that we think ahead and consider the big picture.

> Long-range planning = Thinking ahead + Considering the big picture

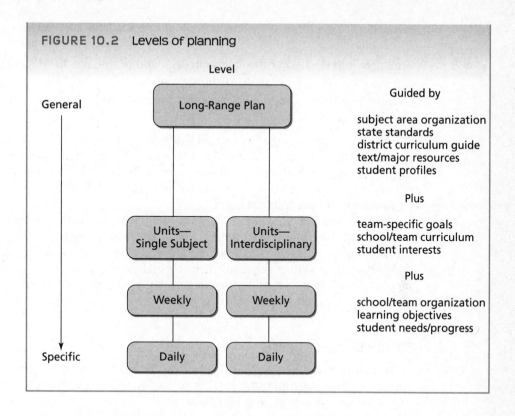

FIGURE 10.2   Levels of planning

Your district/school will probably require that you write a long-range plan for the school year. They may provide detailed guidelines for the plan and check to make sure certain elements are included. Even if you are not required to write a long-range plan, I strongly urge you to do so. Here are some key elements to include.

Student information: Develop a student profile by reading permanent files, looking at test scores, talking to teachers who have taught them, driving through the neighborhoods where your students live, considering socioeconomic factors such as free/reduced lunch status, and gauging student interests through some sort of survey in the first few days of school.

Content information: Identify the body of knowledge and skills that compose your course content.

Sequence: Determine the sequence of the content you will teach. Develop a time line.

Materials: List the instructional resources you will need to organize or order.

Assessment: Determine major forms of assessment for evaluating student progress.

Units of study: Determine large "chunks" of content that may be considered units of study.

Records: Select or design a system of record keeping for student progress and achievement.

Management: Develop rules, consequences, and procedures for classroom management, as well as noninstructional routines.

Communication: Determine ways to communicate with students, colleagues, parents, and the community.

Writing a long-range plan that includes all of these elements may seem like a daunting task, particularly if you don't have a mentor or teammates to emulate. Even if you do not produce a formal document to be reviewed, the process of thinking through the key elements and making notes concerning your plans will provide a structure for life in your classroom.

Developing and adjusting a long-range plan is part of being a reflective practitioner. Just as navigators rely on maps and charts to determine the track they want to follow from starting point to destination, teachers rely on plans and their decision-making abilities to effectively and efficiently orchestrate learning. Long-range plans should be thought of as working documents that are flexible enough to be altered to accommodate varied rates of learning or to respond to unforeseen events.

● Single Subject Units

As you create your long-range plan, you will be sequencing major chunks of content and skills in your subject area. These chunks may be organized into manageable units of study through *single subject planning*.

Most of the content and skills included in middle grades curriculum will fall neatly into units around themes. State standards and district curriculum guides are typically organized in ways that are "unit friendly" so that creating single subject units need not be forced or artificial. A unit can provide context for learning by revolving around, and being based on, a big idea. Let's look at some basic steps that lead to the creation of a unit. There are no set rules. The premise is simple—connect learning and build on prior knowledge concerning a unifying big idea. Here are some basic steps.

1. *Select a suitable theme.* The theme may be obvious, such as westward settlement, the writings of Mark Twain, photosynthesis, or measurement, or it may be necessary to combine or divide topics as they occur in your long-range plan.

2. *Determine goals and specific objectives for the unit.* These may be spelled out for you in your state standards documents or district curriculum guides. As you examine goals and objectives, you will likely see ways to incorporate standards that may not have been readily apparent. For instance, in a unit on measurement there will be many opportunities for students to practice their knowledge and skills regarding working with fractional and decimal numbers. In a unit on photosynthesis there will be opportunities to discuss the earth's relationship to the sun and other concepts of astronomy.

3. *With your goals and objectives in mind, determine assessments that will gauge learning.* Keep in mind the broad array of assessments discussed in Chapter 9.

4. *Develop preassessments to determine prior knowledge.* This may be as simple as a K-W-L session (see Chapter 8) on the unit theme or as traditional as a paper-and-pencil diagnostic test.

5. *Involve students in unit planning.* Tell them the overall goals and give them a sense of where you are heading. Allow them to brainstorm projects and activities that relate to the theme. Incorporate as many of their ideas as possible.

6. *Develop an outline of the breadth of the unit and an approximate time line.* If you use a textbook as a primary source, determine how much of the text will be included. Be conscious of the school calendar so that your timing makes sense and refer to your long-range plans to make sure your plans will allow for the other units you will teach during the year.

7. *Sequence learning objectives and make daily plans.* (More on daily planning in the next sections.)

8. *Gather resources and arrange for special events that will enhance the unit.* If books need to be reserved and videos ordered, see the media specialist. If guest speakers are desired, call them well in advance. If you want to use facilities other than your classroom, make the arrangements.

All of these steps may be taken independently or in collaboration with other teachers who teach the same subject in the same grade level. Make sure your team knows about your unit plans. Discuss curriculum regularly so that each of you is aware of what's being taught and learned by teammates and students. The whole process of sharing long-range plans leads naturally into discussions of units of study.

If you are fortunate enough to have teachers on your team who plan like Traci Peters, you will both see the benefits and learn a great deal. Read about Traci's philosophy of planning in **Teachers Speak**.

Next we consider planning that connects subjects and concepts in interdisciplinary ways.

● Interdisciplinary Units

As stated in Chapter 7, any time connections are made among concepts, within or among subject areas, our students benefit, whether the connections are labeled complementary, multidisciplinary, interdisciplinary, or integrative. The term *interdisciplinary* expresses the cooperative nature of well-planned units that can energize teachers and students and create meaningful learning opportunities for all involved. As you might imagine, there are numerous approaches for developing interdisciplinary units, and even more numerous possibilities for implementing them. I hope your interest will lead you to seek out, read, and use books and articles on the topic. What you are about to read is only the proverbial tip of the interdisciplinary unit (IDU) iceberg.

myeducationlab

Go to the Assignments and Activities section of **Topic #15: Collaborating with Colleagues and Families** in the MyEducation-Lab for your course and complete the activity entitled "Learning and Improving Together."

▶ Teachers Speak

● Traci Peters

I've lived with the adjective "obsessive" for my whole teaching career. To me it simply makes sense to plan, and then plan some more. When other teachers see my organization scheme and never see me in a panic in the workroom when the copier jams, it's because I know exactly what I want to do in my classes at least a week in advance. My classroom materials are organized. My groups of four desks each have a number that corresponds to the numbers on the classroom sets of calculators, scissors, rulers, protractors, etc. I teach my students how to retrieve materials and how to properly return them to their storage place. I walk into Cario each morning knowing my room is ready, my day's state objectives are on the white board, the "What did I miss?" classwork/homework board is complete, and everything I need for the lessons is in place.

I've been asked if this kind of planning carries over into my personal life. My answer is "It used to!" You see, I have a two-year-old son now and school is about the only place in my life that has any semblance of order! My husband and I enjoy life together so much, and our baby boy has just added to that pleasure. We hope to have several more children. As a math teacher I think about ratio and proportion and wonder, as my personal life gets messier, how can I possibly get any neater at school?

Let's explore the basic steps necessary for the creation of an *interdisciplinary unit*. Each step is important, but the order of accomplishing the steps can vary. Some teams might have units already written or previously implemented that may only need to be tweaked to make them more effective and engaging. A unit requires interest and communication among the teachers involved, along with ample time together to plan.

As we discuss the steps to create an interdisciplinary unit, refer to Figure 10.3, an interdisciplinary unit my team at Prairie Middle School in Colorado implemented with 8th graders. It will help you understand how the steps fit together.

1. *Choose a theme.* The choice of a theme is crucial. By comparing long-range plans it is possible for teams to choose a theme that accommodates the standards of each subject area. Typically we think of themes as either content based or concept based. A content theme is something tangible or specific, such as airplanes, Native Americans, Middle Ages, or the environment. There is nothing wrong with a content theme as long as related concepts become the focus of lessons and activities. According to Tomlinson (2001), "Concepts are the building blocks of meaning" (p. 24). A concept related to airplanes is flight. Flight is a richer theme than airplanes. In an IDU with a theme of airplanes we can certainly talk about flight. If the IDU theme is

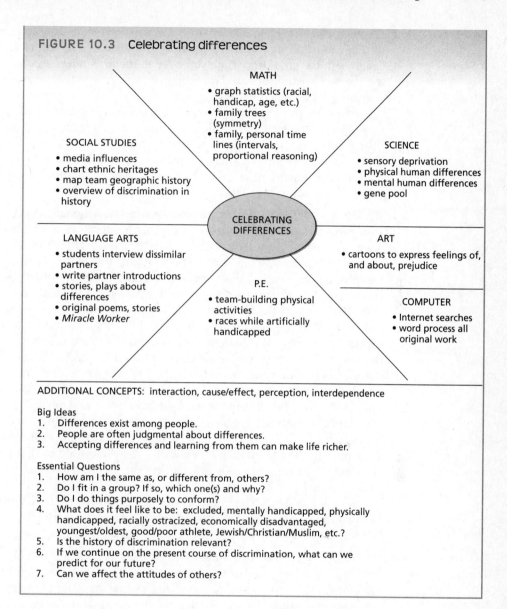

FIGURE 10.3   Celebrating differences

MATH
- graph statistics (racial, handicap, age, etc.)
- family trees (symmetry)
- family, personal time lines (intervals, proportional reasoning)

SOCIAL STUDIES
- media influences
- chart ethnic heritages
- map team geographic history
- overview of discrimination in history

SCIENCE
- sensory deprivation
- physical human differences
- mental human differences
- gene pool

CELEBRATING DIFFERENCES

LANGUAGE ARTS
- students interview dissimilar partners
- write partner introductions
- stories, plays about differences
- original poems, stories
- *Miracle Worker*

ART
- cartoons to express feelings of, and about, prejudice

P.E.
- team-building physical activities
- races while artificially handicapped

COMPUTER
- Internet searches
- word process all original work

ADDITIONAL CONCEPTS: interaction, cause/effect, perception, interdependence

Big Ideas
1. Differences exist among people.
2. People are often judgmental about differences.
3. Accepting differences and learning from them can make life richer.

Essential Questions
1. How am I the same as, or different from, others?
2. Do I fit in a group? If so, which one(s) and why?
3. Do I do things purposely to conform?
4. What does it feel like to be: excluded, mentally handicapped, physically handicapped, racially ostracized, economically disadvantaged, youngest/oldest, good/poor athlete, Jewish/Christian/Muslim, etc.?
5. Is the history of discrimination relevant?
6. If we continue on the present course of discrimination, what can we predict for our future?
7. Can we affect the attitudes of others?

flight, however, we can deal with airplanes and much more. An IDU with a theme of Native Americans can deal with culture, heritage, and gentrification. An IDU with a theme of heritage can certainly deal with Native Americans plus much more. Creating an IDU with a concept theme increases the possibilities of subject area standards being included in authentic and meaningful ways. Examples of concepts include change, conflict, interdependence, patterns, and power.

2. *Develop essential questions and big ideas.* Essential questions guide students through a unit. They frame the essence of what your class can realistically examine in the amount of time you have to spend. Subject area teachers should closely examine standards documents to ensure that relevant standards are included within the unit.

   The answers to essential questions, which may be many and varied, contribute to the big ideas of the unit. Think of the big ideas of a unit as the principles every student should take away from the unit. These are widely accepted ideas within our shared culture. Figure 10.3 includes additional concepts accompanying the theme of Celebrating Differences along with essential questions, big ideas, and a basic subject web.

3. *Web the theme.* Using a simple graphic organizer, the theme/subject web, team members and related arts teachers should spend considerable time brainstorming ways to use standards, activities, research, readings, etc., to address the theme. This can be a very invigorating exercise for teachers as we consider our own subject area(s) as well as a wider view of all possible connections. As a math teacher, I may have a vague recollection of a song that relates to a particular theme. I hum a line or two and the music teacher recognizes the tune and proceeds to fill in the lyrics that directly relate to the theme. I have experienced brainstorming sessions like this and have found them to not only be productive, but great fun! It's a teacher/team activity that reveals teacher interests and talents that may otherwise lay dormant.

   Now include students in this successful and enjoyable webbing experience. Hold on—they'll surprise you with their ideas and energy. Pick a time frame, perhaps advisory or a common time taken from a block of team time, for each team teacher to conduct a brainstorming session with a group of students. Put the theme in the middle of a web. Tell students that you want their help in planning a study of whatever the theme is and ask them for ideas. Because you have already had the benefit of thinking with others about the theme, you'll be able to prompt with suggestions if there is a lull. Remember that inviting and implementing student-generated curriculum infuses developmental responsiveness into our classrooms.

4. *Plan beginning, culminating, and schedule-changing events.* Let the brainstorming session(s) "gel" for a day or so and then plan the major events of the unit. Walking into class on a Monday morning and saying, "For the next few weeks we're going to study flight as it relates to living things. Please get out your textbooks and turn to page 146 and begin reading about Orville and Wilbur Wright" effectively takes a great theme like flight and turns it into instant drudgery. Try this scenario instead:

   > Gather your team into a large dark room. Play a recording of bees buzzing, then bird wings flapping, then geese honking, then helicopter blades whirling, and then jets soaring. On a large screen show footage of a rocket launch and then the historic "One small step for man, one giant leap for mankind" sequence. Then turn up the lights and announce that for three weeks we will

study flight in many forms and human's quest to soar. Now **that's** the way to begin a unit!

It takes planning—from an attention-garnering beginning through schedule-changing events to a meaningful and unforgettable culmination. Guest speakers, field trips, research projects, community involvement, permission forms, bus transportation, parent participation, supply gathering, and more all take time to arrange. Where imagination takes you, and practical/realistic constraints allow you to go, plan ahead and enjoy the process.

5. *Write daily plans.* In the next section of this chapter we'll discuss writing daily lesson plans. For the sake of this discussion of units, I'll simply say that this step will make or break the cohesiveness of any unit. A meaningful and well-written unit depends on the everyday classroom experiences to draw together the connections related to the theme within and among the subject areas. For instance, the study of aerodynamics, the examination of statistics of passenger airline service, analysis of the significance of President Kennedy's inaugural promise of a man on the moon within a decade, and the study of literature about man's quest to fly all require careful planning and coordination within the unit time frame.

As teachers begin planning what, when, and how to teach aspects of a unit, they need to talk frequently and share tentative plans. There will be overlaps and obvious connections on which to capitalize. Some topics and activities may be jointly approached because subject area boundaries are blurred. Combining classes, co-teaching, supporting activities, lengthening/shortening class time—so many educationally sound variations are possible within an interdisciplinary unit.

6. *Plan assessments.* In step two, the essential questions and big ideas are planned, fulfilling the concept of backward design. We know what we want to accomplish in the unit. Once teachers have talked through the parameters of the unit (what, when, how), it's time to view the unit as a whole. In this step we create ways of determining what students know and are able to do as a result of the unit.

This is not a time for "assessment as usual." Units present wonderful opportunities for combining subject standards in projects and group activities. Students could develop portfolios of their unit work, present a simulation of an event that demonstrates understanding, conduct a research project individually or in groups that incorporates big ideas and new vocabulary, and perform in many other authentic ways.

You might want to approach the students and ask, "How will I know what you have learned?" They will undoubtedly surprise you with unusual assessment ideas. For instance, when asked this question in connection with a unit based on the theme of flight, one 12-year-old suggested that he make a set of wings for our principal using what he would learn about flight. The principal would then jump off the second-story roof. If he could fly, then learning had taken place. If not, oh well. We all had a good laugh (and, fortunately, so did the principal as the story was told during a faculty meeting). The suggestion broke the ice and students brainstormed other ways that actually became part of the unit assessment plan. All of the student suggestions were experiential in nature.

7. *View unit as a whole.* Several weeks before implementation, teams need to reexamine the big picture of the unit and focus on support issues. Here are some examples of questions to address:

  - Are all the planned activities meaningful with opportunities for higher-order thinking?
  - Have all arrangements been made? Facilities reserved, permission forms written, phone calls made, materials ordered, transportation confirmed?
  - Have we been realistic in our planning, or overly ambitious?
  - Are the media specialist and others aware of our plans and prepared for the increase in activity resulting from the unit?
  - Has everyone who would be affected by schedule changes been informed?
  - Have responsibilities been equitably delegated?

As with most anything we undertake in middle grades education, flexibility should rule. We pay attention to our students' needs and follow their lead when possible. When planning a unit, always have mechanisms for monitoring and adjusting. As with any planning and implementation, if something isn't working, change it and move forward.

8. *Enjoy the unit.*

9. *Evaluate the unit.* Allow everyone involved to give feedback. Team teachers and related arts teachers all need to give detailed feedback in a meeting and/or in writing. Debriefing is vital to future success. Figure 10.4 provides sample questions to consider.

Provide comment/suggestion forms for guest speakers, administrators, personnel at field trip locations, even parents. If you call a parent and say, "We'd like your feedback on the unit we just finished" and the parent replies "What unit?" there's a good chance that the impact on your students was not what you had hoped. Along with unit-related questions, give parents and community participants an opportunity to comment on their interactions with students. In the middle grades, we understand our responsibility to teach the whole child, including attitudes and behaviors.

Asking students to evaluate a unit, or anything else for that matter, requires that our adult egos be intact. Most students will respond to our surveys thoughtfully and with candor, but be aware that there are boyfriend/girlfriend breakups, "I can't say anything positive" attitudes, and "Hey, it will be fun to write nasty stuff" mindsets that may enter the picture. So hold on to your hat when you try a student evaluation similar to Figure 10.5.

FIGURE 10.4   Unit evaluation for teachers

Unit _____ Team _____ Date _____

1. Did the plans address the big ideas?
2. Did the plans address essential questions?
3. Were all subject area standards adequately addressed?
4. Did all students have the opportunity to succeed?
5. Were all students challenged in some way?
6. Were higher-order thinking skills promoted?
7. Were all levels of Bloom's taxonomy addressed?
8. Was the pace of the unit satisfactory?
9. Are there other resources that may have enhanced the unit?
10. Were the student assessments appropriate?
11. Was there a balance of independent work and group work?
12. Have we asked the students to evaluate the unit?
13. Have we involved the appropriate people in debriefing the unit?
14. Was there school-wide or community involvement/interest in the unit?
15. Was the unit successful enough to justify the time and effort it took to plan and implement?

---

10. *Make a detailed log of the unit.* It's very important to keep a comprehensive summary of the planning, implementation, and feedback for each unit. I suggest a three-ring binder to organize plans, lessons, notes, resources, phone numbers, websites, evaluations, pictures—all the artifacts you can gather. While you may think the unit will remain fresh in your memory, there are details and reminders that will slip your consciousness by the time you want to implement the unit again. A review/critique session and a comprehensive log actually serve to make the next implementation less work. Why reinvent the wheel each time?

● Daily Lesson Planning

The quality of day-to-day classroom experiences depends in large measure on the quality of teacher-designed lesson plans. You have probably been exposed to several philosophies of, and formats for, lesson planning. There is no one right way to plan a lesson. The variability of our students and our subject areas determine appropriate approaches.

> Quality of planning = Quality of classroom experiences

FIGURE 10.5 Unit evaluation for students

Name _____ Unit _____ Date _____

1. Three of the most important or interesting things I learned:
_____
_____
_____

2. One question I still have is:
_____
_____

3. The thing(s) I liked best about this unit:
_____
_____
_____

4. The thing(s) I liked least about this unit:
_____
_____
_____

5. If my teachers do this unit again, I would recommend that they:
_____
_____

6. Here are some unit themes I would enjoy:
_____
_____

7. Comments and suggestions:

Very few teachers can "wing it" successfully, at least not for long. Certainly experience helps, but the process of writing a lesson plan in an organized way is beneficial to 30-year veterans as well as first-year teachers. The mere act of putting in writing what we envision for our time with students will lead to more ideas, changes that will enhance, material/resource reminders, and structuring that will alert us to gaps. You have probably seen lesson plan books in resource stores or in classrooms during field experiences. Could all the information needed to successfully teach a lesson possibly fit in a 2-inch by 2-inch square? Absolutely not! What plan books do is provide overviews,

myeducationlab

To hear Traci Peters, 7th grade math teacher at Cario Middle School, explain the importance of and procedures for daily lesson planning, go to the Video Examples section of **Topic #5: Instructional Planning** in the MyEducationLab for your course and view the video entitled "Traci Peters' Interview about Planning."

STANDARD 3

Knowledge 1: Middle level teacher candidates understand that middle level curriculum should be relevant, challenging, integrative, and exploratory.

Disposition 4: Middle level teacher candidates realize the importance of connecting curriculum and assessment to the needs, interests, and experiences of all young adolescents.

Disposition 5: Middle level teacher candidates are committed to implementing an integrated curriculum that accommodates and supports the learning of all young adolescents.

Performance 2: Middle level teacher candidates use current knowledge and standards from multiple subject areas in planning, integrating, and implementing curriculum.

Performance 3: Middle level teacher candidates incorporate the ideas, interests, and experiences of all young adolescents in curriculum.

Performance 4: Middle level teacher candidates develop and teach an integrated curriculum.

Performance 6: Middle level teacher candidates provide all young adolescents with multiple opportunities to learn in integrated ways.

STANDARD 4

Knowledge 2: Middle level teacher candidates know how to use content knowledge to make interdisciplinary connections.

Disposition 2: Middle level teacher candidates are committed to the importance of integrating content.

Performance 4: Middle level teacher candidates teach in ways that help all young adolescents understand the integrated nature of knowledge.

usually a week at a time. They serve a valuable purpose in that they give us a bird's-eye view of our weeks. They help organize and sequence days and structure whole weeks. Many administrators require teachers to submit copies of a week's worth of plans on Friday or Monday. This accountability check is necessary, unfortunately, as an impetus for some teachers to structure their content and delivery practices. Teachers who thoughtfully plan with or without periodic accountability checks shouldn't mind administrative oversight. The weekly plan book is actually a great way to map out 5 days at a time within a single subject or interdisciplinary unit. For instance, if you know from unit planning that you will spend 4 weeks on Egypt and Egyptian history in sixth grade social studies, dividing the unit into four major chunks will help organize and give direction to your unit.

Keeping a three-ring binder of daily plans is a positive habit you will value more and more with time. When you have thorough, written plans, it is simple to transfer the main points to a weekly planner. The binder provides a complete picture of classroom activities that will aid in future planning.

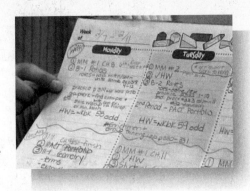

Teacher planning books provide the structure for an overview of daily and weekly plans.

Components of Lessons   Regardless of the lesson planning format you choose, there are basic components to consider when structuring a class period. However, not every component will be present in every class period. Many times your basic plan will extend into a second, or even a third, day. The components of a lesson have been described by many authors and delineated in school and school district guidelines. One of the most well-known experts on lesson planning is the late Madeline Hunter. The components advocated by Hunter (1984) are basic and valuable in most any lesson planning.

1. *Anticipatory Set.* This is the beginning of the lesson that helps learners focus on what's ahead. Focus can be established in many ways. You might want to try . . .
   - reading a current events article
   - telling a relevant brief story or joke
   - placing an object in the room to garner attention
   - projecting a picture on the ceiling
   - demonstrating something interesting
   - asking a provocative question

   Just as the beginning of a unit is important to its success, the beginning of a lesson makes the difference between our students anticipating what's ahead or simply following along when and where they are led.

2. *Objective Clarification.* Thoughtful planning will include a clear view of the lesson's objective(s), often established through state content standards. Just as rubrics let students know expectations for products, objectives tell students what they are expected to learn and be able to do as a result of the lessons. A clear objective communicated to students, along with an attention-getting anticipatory set, will "kick start" a lesson.

3. *Presentation of New Knowledge and Skills.* This step is wide open in terms of instructional strategies. All of the strategies discussed in Chapter 8 may be used in this step of lesson planning. The decisions we make about the appropriateness of strategies based on the content, and student interests and needs, must be made during the planning process, as well as decisions about individual and/or group work.

4. *Guided Practice with Feedback.* Practice can take many forms, depending on the content, skills, and classroom circumstances. If what has been taught/learned can be practiced in a traditional paper-and-pencil way, then it is entirely appropriate. If, however, practice involves a more authentic approach, then students may attempt to replicate a demonstration, perform a skill, respond to questioning, and so forth. Guided practice typically occurs during class and is brief enough to allow time for feedback. Teachers may choose to post answers or results and ask students to determine their own success. Students working in pairs or small groups may check each other's work as feedback. Teachers may "spot check" or simply ask students if there are problems or questions. Whatever the method, it's important to gauge student understanding of reasonable chunks of content and skills before moving on to independent practice or new knowledge and skills.

 Further student inquiry or reteaching may be necessary. The results of the guided practice will tell us. This part of the planning step cannot be bypassed. As you give feedback or receive information about student understanding, you will need to make decisions about continuing whatever strategies you used in step 3 or changing gears to other instructional strategies. Flexibility is a must throughout the planning process, and nowhere more than in the Guided Practice with Feedback phase. Experience helps, but we are all occasionally surprised by the levels of understanding, as well as the pace of understanding, whether rapid or halting.

5. *Assignment of Independent Practice.* While guided practice generally takes place in class, independent practice usually amounts to homework. A discussion of homework comes later. Holding students accountable for completing independent practice is important and worthy of careful consideration. Not everything students do requires a grade, but students need their work acknowledged, and, when not complete, they need a consequence. Finding a balance where independent practice is valuable to student learning and valued by them as a means to greater understanding and proficiency is one of our planning challenges.

6. *Closure.* A lesson should not end because the bell rings. Flexibility dictates that we not insist on completing all we have planned in a class period just because we wrote it as a class period "package." Closure may come about as planned in the form of summarizing the lesson, asking students to do a brief reflection exercise, or discussing how the lesson relates to what's ahead. Then again, you may glance at the clock and discover you have four minutes left and your lesson is still in the Guided Practice with Feedback phase. Regardless of the phase, you need to focus the students' attention on a closure that helps them see what has been accomplished during the class period and a brief comment about what's to come.

Formats for Lesson Planning   The basic components of a lesson can be formatted in many ways. Figure 10.6 shows a commonly used planning form that includes aspects of standards and student variability. Forms such as this one work well because they remind us to include important components. I often need much more space than a single sheet of paper provides. Some lessons need to be "scripted" to a greater extent than others. For instance, if my lesson involves the examination of characters

FIGURE 10.6 Sample lesson plan format

Teacher _____ Class _____ Date _____

Standards to be addressed:

Lesson objective(s):

Opening:

Procedures:

Whole group—

Small group—

Individual—

Plan for differentiation—

Guided practice:

Feedback:

Independent practice:

Assessment:

Closure:

Materials and resources:

in a short story, I know that appropriate questions to direct student thinking need to be planned and organized. I would want to write the questions I plan to use to elicit thoughtful responses. On the lesson form I may write "Lead class discussion of characters by asking questions." Then I would attach a sheet of the questions.

Middle grades students are wonderfully creative and imaginative. If part of the planned lesson brings out these traits and learning is taking place that perhaps wasn't part of what you anticipated, allow yourself enough flexibility to go with the momentum. On the other hand, if a concept or skill you assumed to be either already mastered or easily grasped turns out to be surprisingly difficult or time-consuming, be ready to slow down, change strategies, reteach, or simply allow time for processing. Madeline Hunter is perhaps most famous for the phrase "monitor and adjust." Effective teachers are sensitive to levels and pace of student understanding and are willing and able to direct classroom activities to accommodate needs.

Varying Class Lengths   Chapter 6 helped us understand that class lengths vary greatly in middle schools. Some may be as brief as 45 minutes and others as long as 100 minutes. Teams that use the flexible blocks may occasionally have classes that are 2 to 3 hours long. The strategies discussed in Chapter 8 may be more or less appropriate depending on the length of the class period. The value of knowing about, and having experienced, a wide variety of strategies is that we can pick and choose what will be best, given the circumstances of the day.

As you plan for a class, keep in mind that there are few activities or assignments that will engage young adolescents for more than 20 minutes or so at a time. A lab experiment, an active group project, or an invigorating class discussion may be exceptions, but planning for variety is the best policy. A brief class period may require only two distinct changes of pace, while a longer block of time may require five or six different activities/strategies to motivate and engage students.

Planning for a longer block of time is not as simple as putting two short plans together back to back. The need to check for understanding will be different, the pacing of activities will vary, assessments may change in both nature and scope, and independent practice will certainly be different from the simple combination of two separate assignments. As discussed in Chapter 6, longer blocks of time with our students have many benefits, and the thorough nature of the planning process that is needed to effectively use the gift of more time is worth the effort.

Practical Advice   Here are some tips to consider when planning lessons.

1. Overplan rather than underplan to avoid wasting valuable class time. It's much easier to eliminate plan elements than it is to improvise in meaningful ways.

2. Check for levels of Bloom's taxonomy, use of multiple intelligences theory, differentiation to meet student needs—all the aspects that help ensure effective instruction.

3. Regardless of where you are in your plan, allow time for closure that wraps up the lesson.

4. Never leave school without a written plan for the following day.

5. Gather materials and arrange for resources at least a day ahead. The copier seems to know when we wait until the last minute and breaks down to teach us to plan ahead!

6. Be flexible. This is possible when we know the content, practice a variety of instructional strategies, and plan thoughtfully. Interruptions happen. They are inevitable. Altering our plans may be necessary for academic reasons as well as any number of other occurrences totally outside our control.

7. Spend time reflecting on lessons. Consider what worked well, what could have been better, and how to alter/adapt plans to be used in the future. Remember, there's always tomorrow. We can fill in gaps and make adjustments in the following day's plans if we take the time to reflect on our lessons.

8. Keep notes about the things you might change or add as resources for future planning.

Homework   For every ardent supporter of homework you may find a naysayer. Harris Cooper (2001), a noted expert on the topic, tells us that the homework controversy is not new and will likely never be resolved. His research shows that every 15 years or so there's an outcry alternately for more or less homework. The call for increased homework coincided with the launch of *Sputnik* in the 1950s, while in the late 1960s homework was viewed as undue pressure on students. Following the publication of *A Nation at Risk* in 1983, homework gained favor. In the late 1990s concern grew over stressed-out students and overworked parents.

Opinions aside, Cooper conducted a meta-analysis of the relationship of homework to academic achievement. He found that for elementary students assigning homework has little, if any, effect on achievement. For high school students, the benefits of being assigned and completing homework are substantial. For middle school students, the benefits are more evident than for elementary students, but no more than half as effective as for high school students. Cooper says that for young adolescents, improvement in achievement appears to continue through about an hour or so of homework and with more than an hour, achievement does not improve.

There are many variables when it comes to why students complete, or do not complete, homework. Home circumstances play a role. Some students have quiet study areas and adults who check assignment pads and encourage students to do their homework. Then there are the rest of the students. While many believe that education is the "great equalizer," homework definitely is not. We can provide equal working conditions in our classrooms, but the home is basically outside our realm of control. A principal I know recently posed a question to a large gathering of teachers. He asked, "At what point do students stop doing homework?" Most teachers answered with grade level guesses. The principal then said, "No, it's when their parents no longer understand the material." Thought provoking, isn't it?

Homework—to assign or not, how much, what kind, what percentage of the grade it will be worth—should be a matter of team concern. One of the beauties of middle grades teaming is the possibility of coordinating the whole school experience for our students. The answers to the questions about homework should be guided by the needs and characteristics of our students.

If homework is assigned, then students should be held accountable for turning it in and given some sort of credit. To assign it and never require that it be completed is unfair to students and to the process. If it's important enough for students to use their out-of-school time to complete, then it's important enough to warrant checking, at least for completion or attempted completion. I view homework (and tests, papers, any assignment) as so important that I feel a strong obligation to provide as rapid feedback to students as possible. At the college level, I aim for returning student work with comments by the next class period and view the "midnight oil" it sometimes requires as well worth it. My students are demonstratively appreciative of the extra effort. Middle school students need immediate (or close to it) feedback to enhance their knowledge and skill building. Homework can be used to build responsibility in our students as it reinforces learning. We can model responsibility with our respect and acknowledgment of their efforts.

Not every student will turn in homework on time. As in every other area, there is a great deal of variability. One way to attempt to instill personal responsibility in students is to not only require work, even if late, to be completed, but to also require documentation as to why the work was not completed on time. A form similar to Figure 10.7 may work for your classroom, and perhaps for your whole team.

FIGURE 10.7   Student responsibility form

Name _____ Class _____

Today's date _____ Date assignment was due _____

Assignment _____

I did not turn in this assignment on time because

(check all that apply)

_____ I was absent on _____ .

_____ I forgot to do it.

_____ I did not understand how to do it.

_____ I had extra home duties including _____ .

_____ I did not take the right materials home.

_____ I did not have the assignment written down.

_____ I did it, but left it at home.

_____ I did it, but could not find it when it was time to turn it in.

Here is what I plan to do to make sure my assignments are completed and turned in on time.

_____

_____

_____

_____ (signature)

When assigning homework, here are some ideas to consider.

- Arrange with your team/school to provide an afterschool setting for students who want to stay to complete assignments.
- Check homework every time it is assigned to provide feedback, but only record grades for homework periodically.
- Give assignments in advance if appropriate, especially if they will be due following a holiday or on a Monday.
- Make homework only a small percentage of the total grade.
- Allow students to take "open homework" quizzes and tests occasionally as an extra motivation to complete assignments.

We need to think about **designing** homework, as well as **assigning** homework. Instead of asking students to answer questions about a section, we might ask them to write questions about what they read using question stems associated with Bloom's taxonomy. Or maybe we could ask students to talk to three others about a current events issue and take notes on their responses. When math practice is needed, 10 problems will often do as much good as 40.

Cooper (2001) proposes the "ten minute rule" which says the optimum time homework should require is 10 minutes per grade level. So, sixth graders should have 60 minutes maximum (total for all subjects), seventh graders 70 minutes, and eighth graders 80 minutes. Making homework reasonable, as interesting as possible, and doable without parental assistance will encourage students to complete it.

Reflections on Planning

In the introduction to this chapter I stated that with experience we become more comfortable with the planning process. Exactly what will experience do for us in this process? Now that you have a glimpse at what's involved in long-range, unit, and daily planning, consider some benefits experience will bring.

- Your understanding of the content you teach will be deeper and broader allowing for more within-discipline and among-discipline connections to be made naturally as you plan.
- You will have a larger toolbox of instructional strategies to use in your planning.
- You will become more confident in your knowledge of student development leading to the ability to be more responsive to the needs of young adolescents.
- Your peripheral vision in the classroom will grow wider to allow for more effective observation of students.
- You will know more about available materials and resources to use in lesson planning.
- Your lesson planning will become more sophisticated as you understand how to use student prior knowledge to build on the potential of your class.

Most of us find ourselves in charge of a middle grades classroom and 70 to 120 students with only part of a semester of student teaching under our belts. All the benefits of experience lie out ahead of us as we mature in the teaching profession.

Planning is a series of decisions, each building on other decisions. Thorough, thoughtful, written plans determine to a large extent the learning that happens in your classroom.

GROUP ACTIVITIES

1. In pairs, interview a teacher in one of the local schools in your school files. Ask the teachers for information concerning:

   homework policy

   long-range planning

   frequency of interdisciplinary units

   lesson planning formats

   If possible, obtain copies of long-range plans, formats for planning, and IDU plans to share with the class.

2. In groups of three or four, brainstorm ways to involve students in the planning process.

3. Form groups composed of different subject area concentrations. Agree on an interdisciplinary theme and create a web of possible topics/ideas similar to Figure 10.3. Include relevant concepts. Be prepared to explain your web to the whole class.

INDIVIDUAL ACTIVITIES

1. Briefly describe the memory enhancing devices that work for you. Be prepared to share with the class.

2. Choose a subject area and find at least three websites that provide subject-specific resources that are user friendly and free.

3. Did you experience an interdisciplinary unit when you were in middle school? If so, briefly describe its impact. If more than one, list the themes you can remember. If not, describe other ways you may have experienced subject connection.

PERSONAL JOURNAL

1. Write about your memories of homework in the middle grades. Did you have a place at home conducive to completing academic work? Were your parents or siblings encouraging and helpful? Were you conscientious about completing independent practice assignments?

2. Do you have the organizational and time management skills to regularly develop thoughtful, written lesson plans? List reasons for an affirmative answer. Think of habits to create or break that may help you develop necessary skills if you feel this is a weak area for you.

Professional Practice

(It would be helpful to reread the descriptions of Jesse White in Chapter 4 and Zach in Chapter 3.)

● **Jesse White**

In Chapter 4 we saw that Lincoln Middle School has challenges that they share with many urban middle schools. The socioeconomic status of most of the students is low or poverty level and many live in crowded government projects in neighborhoods that have an element of danger. They likely have few role models of academic and professional success. While this is not an excuse for low levels of achievement and behavior difficulties, the reality is that in many cases, this is life in and around urban middle schools. The district administrators have chosen to not grant magnet status to Lincoln as they did to Jefferson Middle School. Instead, they have decided to do something considered pretty radical and controversial. Next year Lincoln Middle School will be two schools in one, and each will be single-gender.

Mr. White observed a suburban school in the district try single-gender math and science classes with supposedly excellent results. The kids, along with some parents, fought it vehemently when the plan was announced. But after two years, praise for the innovation is almost universal. The teachers are happy, the kids are happy, and the parents are happy. Standardized test scores in math and science have improved and behavior office referrals have decreased.

1. Some Lincoln teachers object to the change to single-gender. Mr. White is respected among his colleagues. What would be best for him to focus on in discussions with the hesitant teachers?
   a. The district has made a decision and to fight it is futile.
   b. There are books on the learning differences between boys and girls that they can read during summer break.
   c. There is a district school where some objected to the change in the beginning that appears to be very successful and happy with the initiative.
   d. Things can't get a whole lot worse at Lincoln in terms of overall achievement and behavior, so single-gender is worth a shot.

2. To prepare for next year when he will have all boys in his classes, Mr. White should
   a. Read books by authors such as Gurian and Sax.
   b. Arrange to visit with teachers at the school that is successfully implementing single-gender education, at least on a limited scale.
   c. Look for websites that address learning differences and think about strategies to tweak in some way to best suit boys.
   d. All of the above

3. The teams at Lincoln will change as teachers express their preferences for either girls or boys. Which of the following would probably work best in terms of team formation once decisions are made about who will teach boys and who will teach girls?
   a. Allow the faculty to form their own teacher teams.
   b. Ask the faculty to privately submit who they would like to team with, as well as who they absolutely would not want to team with. Then the principal could negotiate team formation.
   c. To be fair, teacher names by subject area could be placed in a bowl. Then math, language arts, science, and social studies names could be drawn and each group of four becomes a team.
   d. The principal, who knows about teacher styles from a broad perspective and has information only the school "overseer" would have, should put teachers together for this first year of single-gender classes.

Zach ● eighth grade

4. Zach seems to not care one way or the other about the single-gender decision. Which of the following is probably not a benefit for boys in the single-gender school scenario?

a. The boys in a single-gender class may feel more at liberty to talk about things the way they would when Mom isn't around, allowing for more freedom of expression, i.e., gross topics that seem to fascinate boys in puberty.

b. When only boys are in a middle school classroom, there may be less "posturing" to impress the girls and more attention given to learning.

c. Because boys tend to learn through kinesthetic activity more than girls, teachers can actually build in more active learning opportunities.

d. Assignments can be geared more toward typical boy interests, with other choices of course, since not all boys prefer trucks and frog guts.

Constructed Response

From what you have read, possibly experienced, and think at this point, compare and contrast coeducational and single-gender school settings with regard to academic learning, behavior, and socialization. Do this by completing a chart similar to this one.

Criteria	Coeducational setting	Single-gender setting
Academic learning		
Behavior		
Socialization		

INTERNET RESOURCES

AskERIC Lesson Plan Collection
http://ericir.syr.edu/Virtual/Lessons

This site is part of the Educational Resources Information Center (ERIC), a service funded by the U.S. Department of Education. It provides more than 2,000 unique teacher-written lesson plans organized by subject area and grade level.

Education World
www.educationworld.com

This large site is loaded with practical information and strategies to assist teachers with lesson planning. There's a section titled "Tips for New Teachers," as well as information on the use of technology in classroom instruction.

Teachers Network
http://teachnet.org

11

Maintaining a Positive, Productive Learning Environment

A positive and productive learning environment is one in which students thrive. They experience physical, emotional, and academic safety within a structure that gives them confidence and a sense of belonging. Creating and maintaining this environment promotes optimal learning and growth for young adolescents. Here we see focus student Emily working cooperatively with her peers.

Creating and maintaining a positive and productive learning environment is complex and compelling—complex because there are multiple variables to consider, and compelling because without a positive and productive learning environment, teaching has little effect.

Powell, 2009, p. 204

CHAPTER PREVIEW

Creating a Positive and Productive Learning Environment

- Membership
- Cultural Considerations
- Connecting with Students
- Self-discipline

Physical, Emotional, and Academic Safety

- Physical Safety
- Emotional Safety
- Academic Safety

Prevention of Classroom Problems

- Prevention through Good Instruction
- Routines
- Rules and Consequences

Intervention When Classroom Problems Occur

- Unobtrusive Intervention
- Implementing Consequences
- Peer Mediation

Within Our Control

- Understanding Our Role
- Getting Off to a Good Start
- Easier to Love Than to Like

Reflections on Maintaining a Positive, Productive Learning Environment

INTRODUCTION

We often hear that there are few absolutes in life, and I suppose that's true. But there is one certainty when it comes to teaching that is irrefutable—without effectively managing the classroom environment, learning will be adversely affected and you will not enjoy your job. Years of experience teaching in the classroom, observing new and veteran teachers, and serving as both a cooperating teacher in the field and as a college supervisor of student teachers have all confirmed this absolute for me.

Creating a positive climate, ensuring that curriculum and instruction are engaging, and applying discipline measures when appropriate all contribute to maintaining a positive and productive learning environment. In a type of orchestrated oversight, we see that literally everything we do and everything that occurs in the classroom enhances or detracts from both student learning and our personal satisfaction with the profession of teaching. Keep in mind that nowhere is developmental appropriateness more critical than when we consider the learning environment.

STANDARD 5

Performance 7: Middle level teacher candidates employ fair, effective, developmentally responsive classroom management techniques.

People who wince at the thought of teaching middle school don't do so because we study ancient civilizations in sixth grade or learn about the Pythagorean theorem in seventh grade or read *The Outsiders* in eighth grade. They wince at the thought of being the lone adult in a room full of young adolescents. Memories of themselves and classmates, perhaps visions of their own 10- to 15-year-olds, and the general portrayal of middle grades kids as disturbed links between sweet childhood and maturing adolescence all contribute to the maligning of this wonderful age group. Sure, some of it is justified. There's no denying the element of challenge in middle level classrooms, but there's also no denying that teaching middle grades kids is an extraordinary adventure. Young adolescents want parameters. They want their teachers to manage the environment so they can safely learn and grow.

Chris Stevenson (1992, p. 219) recommends guidelines we may use to create and maintain a positive learning environment. He tells us that considering these four components will accomplish the order needed for learning while helping middle grades students use their energies to work toward autonomy that allows them to make choices about how to behave. Here is a brief description of the four components.

1. *"Interpersonal climate"* Teachers are approachable as they promote good relationships with students. Where there is mutual respect, students are cooperative in the teaching-learning process.

2. *"Worth and dignity assured"* Students are encouraged to believe in themselves and to develop positive self-esteem. No one in the classroom is allowed to belittle, tease, embarrass, or humiliate another.

3. *"Approximating democracy"* Whenever possible, students are allowed to have a say in choices affecting individuals, classes, and teams. An open forum for discussion and solution seeking fills the student need for self-determination. This process in middle school contributes to more enlightened citizenship as adults.

4. *"Redemption is always close, not closed"* Remembering that human growth and development occur in spurts, and are highly individual, leads teachers to

Positive learning environment =
Creating an interpersonal climate +
Ensuring worth and dignity +
Approximating democracy + Making
redemption available

address undesirable behaviors and offer fresh beginnings. It is vital to separate the offense from the student identity. Some students make many mistakes and require teacher maturity to forgive and move on.

Knowing what we do about middle grades student characteristics and development, Stevenson's four provisos make sense. Embedding these components both in our classroom environments and within our team procedures is advisable.

In this chapter, we explore the creation and maintenance of a positive and productive learning environment as well as the perpetuation of academic, emotional/social, and physical safety. We discuss both prevention of problems and the when and how of intervention when prevention just isn't enough. Then we explore what our students expect of us and how we should respond to their expectations.

Creating a Positive and Productive Learning Environment

In Chapter 4 we discussed what it means for a classroom to be a community of learners. If it has been several weeks, or even months, since you read that section, it would be helpful to reread it now. Both *Turning Points* (Carnegie, 1989) and *This We Believe* (NMSA, 2010) exhort us to pay special attention to the creation and maintenance of a learning environment that has the earmarks of a caring community. In this section we look at the value of students having a sense of membership; we explore the importance of cultural considerations, and ways to form positive teacher-student relationships. Then we examine the ultimate goal of a positive learning environment—student self-discipline.

STANDARD 5

Performance 6: Middle level teacher candidates establish equitable, caring, and productive learning environments for all young adolescents.

Membership

A positive and productive learning environment is characterized by a sense of community where each person (student and teacher) feels connected to both the group and the subject matter. In middle school the whole notion of teaming, with its lengthy list of benefits, is based on the value of membership. In a school where each teacher plans for and implements strategies that lead to classrooms as caring communities, the teams, the grade levels, and the entire school become productive learning environments.

Productive learning environment =
Connection to group + Connection
to subject

Feeling comfortable with a group of friends is important to healthy social development.

Young Adolescent Diversity

An environment where acceptance and membership are the norm is especially important for at-risk students whose backgrounds of failure in school, indifference at home, and little support from communities outside the school all threaten their success. Just as membership in a learning community affects academic success, academic success brings a sense of membership. Conversely, students who fail academically seldom feel accepted in a learning environment and often seek membership in antisocial settings.

Cultural Considerations

The role of culture in determining strategies for managing the classroom environment cannot be overstated. Rothstein-Fisch and Trumbull (2008) tell us, "Our premise is that cultural values and beliefs are at the core of all classroom organization and management decisions. In parallel fashion, cultural values and beliefs are at the center of students' responses to teachers' strategies and of students' own attempts to engage in and influence interactions in the classroom" (p. xiii). One of the main points made in their book *Managing Diverse Classrooms* is that the majority of schools emphasize the individualistic values of the dominant European American culture. An individualistic approach to school and learning emphasizes the individual and the quest to become independent through growth and development. Much of the world is based on a collectivistic culture with emphasis on individual development while staying very close to family, whose well-being is foremost.

An example of an individualistic classroom practice is almost exclusively asking students to work alone on assignments and projects. A collectivistic approach encourages sharing of notes and ideas and the solving of problems as a group effort. A management expectation of "Raise your hand when you wish to speak," although likely included in many middle level classroom rule sets, is individualistic and will be difficult for students whose cultures are collectivistic in nature.

The implications of managing the learning environment with consideration for the cultures of your students are important, and pretty daunting. I encourage you to read books like *Managing Diverse Classrooms* and consider the message. In general terms, the authors recommend that the organization and management of our classrooms reflect the understanding that

- Students are active learners whose development takes place within particular social and cultural contexts and is influenced by those contexts.
- Home socialization practices influence how students interact and solve problems.
- Good classroom organization and management tap existing skills and dispositions while building new capacities.
- As they mature, students can take increasing responsibility for regulating their own learning and ensuring harmony in the classroom (p. xv).

Connecting with Students

To maintain a positive and productive learning environment where all feel like accepted members, we need to continually find ways to identify with our students. "Taking time to connect with our students, to win them over, is the first step in classroom management" (Cummings, 2000, p. 14). Just as young adolescents display a wide array of qualities, our approaches to connecting with them—to "winning them over"—will vary. Here are some suggestions.

- Before school starts, write a personal postcard welcoming the students who will enter your class. Yes, it's time-consuming and the cards and postage will cost (ask your principal to finance it), but the short- and long-term benefits are invaluable. I did this as a middle school teacher and continue the practice at the university level. I consider it a "must." (Parents love it, too!)
- Greet your students at the door the first day, and every day, of class.
- Learn student names very quickly, using whatever mnemonic device (memory aid) that works for you. Use names often in and out of the classroom. Even if you see 120 students on a team, you should know every name by the end of the second week of classes. It can be done.
- Use "getting to know you" surveys. Kids, like all of us, enjoy talking and writing about themselves. Give them an opportunity to do so and then use the information throughout the year to connect more personally with them. A simple survey is shown in Figure 11.1.
- Let students know that you understand their need to connect with each other. Experience shows us that if we don't provide socializing opportunities for young adolescents, they will use our instructional time to talk to each other. A policy of no talking in the halls or the cafeteria is deadly. Not only is it unenforceable, it's developmentally wrong. I am comfortable allowing socializing time in my classroom. Five minutes of free talking time helps ensure attention during the rest of the class period.

FIGURE 11.1   Introducing myself

Name _____

1. I was born in _____.
2. I have lived here for _____ (years, months, weeks).
3. There are _____ people living in my house.
4. My pets are _____, a _____; _____, a _____; and _____, a _____.
5. My favorite subject is _____.
6. My least favorite subject is _____.
7. The best thing I did this summer was _____.
8. After school I most like to _____.
9. On weekends I like to _____.
10. My favorite music group is _____.
11. My favorite movie is _____.
12. The best book I ever read is _____.
13. My favorite food is _____.
14. If I could travel anywhere, I'd most like to go to _____ because _____.
15. The people who know me best would use these three words to describe me:
    _____ , _____ , _____ .

Source: From *Wayside Teaching: Connecting with Students to Support Learning,* by S. D. Powell, 2010, Thousand Oaks, CA: Corwin Press.

Self-Discipline

Helping middle grades students develop self-discipline is one of our highest callings. Young adolescents are in the midst of the transition from dependence to independence. Most have been accustomed to being told what to do, how to do it, and when to do it in elementary school. In middle school it should be to a lesser degree. We want our students to develop self-discipline as members of a community that exists in a positive and productive learning environment.

Teaching students how to monitor their own behavior is an important task. We need to remind them to be aware of their actions and attitudes and to adjust them when needed. Self-monitoring is the ultimate form of classroom management. Burden and Byrd (2010) suggest that we teach self-monitoring as a means of achieving self-discipline by prompting students to ask themselves questions when they are tempted to violate a rule or feel like they are about to lose self-control. The questions might include, "Is this worth the trouble it will cause me?" and "Is this what I want to happen?" As with other traits we want our students to acquire, teaching through the modeling of self-discipline techniques is very meaningful.

Physical, Emotional, and Academic Safety

A positive and productive learning environment will include physical, emotional, and academic safety. In recent years we have become increasingly aware of the need for physical safety. From the shocking events at Columbine High School in 1999 to the daily reality of violence toward and among school age children and youth, our heightened focus on physical safety is justified. As important as physical safety is, it is imperative for educators to recognize the need for emotional and academic safety as well. "We must create a learning space in which children—their bodies, hearts, and minds—are pro-

---
Safety in school = Physical + Emotional + Academic
---

tected" (Belair & Freeman, 2000, p. 3). This protection includes minimizing and, when possible, eliminating threatening events that may be physical, emotional, or academic in nature.

Physical Safety

Physical safety requires the elimination of threatening and/or real scenarios including

- Fear of pushing, shoving, tripping in the hall
- Fear of having personal items stolen
- Worries about plans to escalate a disagreement after school
- Verbal threats about impending violence
- Fear of being caught up in a fight
- Fear of weapons being used in school (Cummings, 2000, p. 121)

In an interview printed in *Middle School Journal* (Erb, 2000), Gerald Bourgeois, a respected educator for more than four decades, talks in detail about school safety. Bourgeois says we must examine what is happening both in school and out of school. The cause of violence in schools is usually not what he terms "school stuff" (p. 5). The roots of the violence may be family-oriented and related to child abuse, domestic abuse, alcohol/drug abuse, viewing of violence in the media, availability of weapons, and other family or social problems happening outside of school. For this reason he tells us that school safety should be addressed from many perspectives. He suggests a community audit to recognize problems. Concurrently, a school audit should include situations like vandalism, harassment, and bullying. Both audits can identify needs and match resources to address them.

Bourgeois recommends thorough consideration of school security both in daylight and at night, assessing access to the grounds, dark/hidden places, windows, lighting, door closures, and safety hazards. This assessment should lead to security precautions and changes. Next he recommends the writing of a building-specific contingency plan that goes beyond district safety policies and answers such questions as what do we do if

- An intruder enters the building
- A bomb threat occurs
- A suicide is attempted or occurs
- A natural disaster threatens or occurs
- A shooting is imminent or occurs
- A gasoline tanker overturns in front of the school
- A fire occurs or is nearby, releasing toxic fumes (p. 7)

In addition, Bourgeois urges principals to establish procedures for teachers in the event of fights, sudden health problems, a classroom intruder, students with weapons, and so on.

Many middle schools employ resource officers who serve to prevent safety crises and maintain order. These officers are most useful when they do more than respond to rule infractions and act as police officers. Some coach sports, develop personal relationships with students, act as positive role models, and lend support when needed. Resource officers are typically members of the local police force assigned to school safety.

Schools may employ student concern specialists. These valuable individuals can serve as a second pair of eyes for a principal, concentrating on the physical well-being of the students. They can prevent acts of violence, intercept threats to student safety, and handle discipline problems. An effective student concern specialist listens carefully and watches constantly, interacting and intervening when appropriate. When physical safety is present, students will be more emotionally secure.

Many middle level schools employ resource officers who often do much more than prevent or address violence. They may become part of the learning environment, befriending kids who trust them as adult role models.

Emotional Safety

We have spent considerable time discussing the emotional development of young adolescents and how the sensitivity and vulnerability of their emotions should be acknowledged and addressed in middle school. Educators who understand and care about middle grades students know the impact of an environment that provides *emotional safety*. Young adolescents need to be able to count on the school environment to provide a stable atmosphere where expressed emotions receive consistently caring responses. Their homes and communities may not provide emotional safety.

Some critics of the middle school emphasis on affective issues and growth are quick to say that we should concentrate on academics and not on what they may call the "touchy-feely" aspects of early adolescence to chance. In *What Every Middle School Teacher Should Know*, Knowles and Brown (2007) report on a number of research studies that have linked a caring environment (emotional safety) to cognitive growth. They make a case for positive student-teacher interpersonal relationships as vehicles for the improvement of the quality of learning.

Emotional safety entails minimizing stress for students. Knowles and Brown (2007) tell us that many situations initiated by teachers may cause needless stress for young adolescents. They include

- Frequently yelling at one student or an entire class
- Applying punishment inappropriately
- Threatening students
- Making fun of students
- Establishing unrealistic academic demands or expectations
- Requiring students to open their lockers, get the appropriate books and notebooks, and get to their next class on time—all in less than 4 minutes
- Pushing students to learn abstract principles that are beyond their cognitive capabilities
- Assigning extensive homework that requires at least an hour or more of work each evening for each subject
- Embarrassing students in front of their most significant audience—their peers (pp. 92–93)

Knowles and Brown (2007) also say that we may disrupt the emotional stability needed for optimal student learning in subtle, and often unwitting, ways by

- Refusing to lend a pencil, protractor, or paper to students
- Caring more about completing the textbook than meeting each student's needs
- Treating each student the same regardless of differences in learning abilities or learning styles
- Preventing students from interacting socially during class time
- Assessing student learning in only one way

- Designing lessons that are primarily teacher directed without hands-on opportunities for student learning
- Refusing to be flexible in curriculum design, instructional processes, or scheduling
- Using quizzes to "catch" students who may not understand material
- Ignoring young adolescents' stages of cognitive, social, and emotional growth (p. 93)

We see that making our classrooms less than emotionally safe can be quite inadvertent. It's pretty scary to know how much power a word, a look, a policy never intended to do harm, a withholding of support, and so on, may have in the life of a young adolescent. We must be very aware of our influence.

Bluestein (2001) tells us there are practices that characterize a school with an emotionally safe climate. Among these practices are

- Recognizing positive behavior
- Meeting students' needs for attention in positive ways
- Being aware of changes in student behavior
- Maintaining a sense of how students are doing
- Recognizing when students are in crisis
- Being willing to listen
- Respecting student confidentiality
- Being aware of how students treat each other
- Responding immediately to bullying and harassment

Perhaps one of the most proactive things we can do to promote emotional safety is to listen to our students without condemning or even offering solutions. If they know we care about them, respect their absolutely natural fluctuations in mood, and are willing to allow them to grow, make mistakes, and begin again (and again!), they will tend to perceive emotional safety in our classrooms. Remember that emotional development and cognitive development are linked. So if students perceive emotional safety, they are likely to sense academic safety as well.

Academic Safety

Academic safety is a concept rarely discussed, and yet it is addressed regularly by teachers intent on creating a positive and productive learning environment. What exactly does academic safety mean? It means, in the words of *Turning Points* (1989), "Ensuring success for all students: All young adolescents should have the opportunity to succeed in every aspect of the middle grade program, regardless of previous achievement or the pace at which they learn" (p. 49). Success begets success. The corollary, unfortunately, is also true—lack of success begets lack of success.

"No adult would be foolish enough to participate in a losing effort for 180 days a year for thirteen consecutive years; yet we expect struggling students to return to school year after year despite their inability to succeed" (Knowles & Brown, 2007,

p. 106). When we succeed, we are willing to exert effort and take risks to attempt new and more challenging feats. Unfortunately, academic risk-taking is buried in many students before they even reach middle school. For some it is a casualty of middle school. Our task as teachers is to minimize feelings of inadequacy by ensuring that every student succeeds at something.

One way to ensure some measure of success for each student is to internalize and act on our understanding of adolescent development by operationalizing the concept of differentiation as discussed in Chapters 7 through 9. Using what we know about multiple intelligences theory, learning styles and modalities, varying motivational levels, and maintenance of high expectations, we create a learning environment that at once validates cognitive progress and raises the bar to preserve momentum.

STANDARD 1

Disposition 3: Middle level teacher candidates hold high, realistic expectations for the learning and behavior of all young adolescents.

The negative effect peers can have on the academic success of members of their social groups always surprises and dismays me when I witness it. In middle school awards assemblies, I have heard kids jeer as one of their own is called to the front to be recognized for an accomplishment. As adults we understand that underlying the jeers is a tender jealousy that hasn't matured enough to recognize it for what it is, much less lead to a comment of "Good job, my friend." The student being jeered could not care less about the psychological origins of "Geek," "Teacher's pet," "Smarty pants," or other taunts I have heard but am reluctant to put in print. This same kind of thing happens daily in many middle grades settings.

The opposite kind of embarrassment is even more prevalent. Our students are afraid of failing in front of their peers. After feeling stupid in the eyes of their classmates, many will simply clam up and not participate. To them, no notice is better than negative notice. A sudden headache or need to go to the bathroom may occasionally work to get them out of the academic spotlight of perhaps reading aloud, going to the board to work a problem, or answering questions about an assignment. When headaches and bathroom breaks are exhausted, many turn to misbehavior as a refuge from the academic arena. We need to recognize these avoidance tactics as we find ways to move each student toward some measure of success.

Once again we call on Knowles and Brown (2007) to focus us on concrete ways to promote academic safety. They ask us to consider how we would entice young adolescents to return to our classrooms day after day if school was not mandatory. A sobering thought to ponder, isn't it? Here are some comments on what academic safety means for kids.

- No one laughs at them when they attempt to ask or answer a question.
- Teachers establish realistic academic expectations and outcomes for each student.
- Students' efforts are recognized, as well as the products of those efforts.

- Teachers eliminate competitive situations that create inequity among students.
- Teachers develop cooperative grouping strategies that encourage students to collaborate in their learning and share their knowledge and expertise with one another.
- Teachers play the role of facilitator to encourage student independence.
- Teachers choose alternative instructional strategies to meet each student's learning style.
- Teachers recognize and appreciate talents other than academic skills.

STANDARD 5

Disposition 2: Middle level teacher candidates value the need for providing and maintaining environments that maximize student learning.

Physical, emotional, and academic safety are imperative for a positive and productive learning environment. When all three are attended to, our classrooms are healthier places for our students. However, even when physical, emotional, and academic safety measures are in place, student discipline issues will arise. Now let's look at ways to prevent problems in the classroom in order to maintain a positive and productive learning environment where students are physically, emotionally, and academically safe.

STANDARD 1

Performance 8: Middle level teacher candidates create and maintain support-ive learning environments that promote the healthy development of all young adolescents.

Prevention of Classroom Problems

The old saying goes, "An ounce of prevention is worth a pound of cure." The more proactively we address classroom management, the less reactive we will have to be. Everything we do in our classrooms might be characterized as either preventing the bad by promoting the good, or reacting to the bad and attempting to turn it into the good. I'd much rather spend time on the former than the latter.

Curwin, Mendler, and Mendler (2008) tell us there are three broad categories of students in a typical classroom and suggest the "70–20–10 principle" that goes like this:

- Seventy percent of students rarely break rules. They are reasonably motivated to learn and accept the parameters of the classroom. They have experienced enough success to expect to be successful in the future. For them, rules and consequences are realistically unnecessary.

- Twenty percent of students break rules regularly. They can be completely on or completely off, depending on numerous factors. Their achievement range is vast and unpredictable. They need rules and consequences with a good measure of structure to keep them from disturbing the whole class.

- Ten percent of students are chronic rule breakers and tend to be out of control much of the time. They typically have experienced failure over and over, either academically or behaviorally (or both), and see no hope of success.

"The trick of a good discipline plan is to control the 20 percent without alienating or overly regulating the 70 percent and without backing the 10 percent into a corner" (p. 33). Given the 70–20–10 principle we might expect a middle school class of 30 to have 21 or so students who pose no discipline problems, 5 or 6 who are behaviorally volatile, and maybe 3 who consistently challenge both our patience and resourcefulness.

> Typical classroom behavior = 70% rarely break rules + 20% regularly break rules + 10% often out of control

Jacob Kounin (1970) found when studying classroom management that teachers differ little in how they handle problems once they arise. The differences were dramatic, however, when observing what successful classroom managers do to prevent classroom problems. Kounin concluded that the skills demonstrated by successful classroom managers could be categorized in three areas—their "withitness," their ability to overlap activities, and their management of movement. As you observe classrooms or reflect on scenarios, think about what you would do in Kounin's three categories to be a proactive successful classroom manager.

Now let's look at ways to prevent classroom problems, including good instruction, productive routines, valid rules and consequences, and the instituting of uniforms for students.

STANDARD 5

Knowledge 8: Middle level teacher candidates know effective, developmentally responsive classroom management techniques.

Prevention through Good Instruction

Planning for instruction, implementing developmentally appropriate practices, and maintaining vigilant and responsive peripheral vision in the classroom are key elements of effective management that result in learning and enjoyment for students and teachers. Instructional planning and classroom management are inseparable. Students are less likely to misbehave when the work is interesting and challenging, when there are routines, when resources are sufficient, and when they know their teachers will grade their work and give feedback. These are all aspects of good instruction.

Planning for instruction as discussed in Chapter 10 and using a variety of appropriate strategies such as those in Chapters 8 and 9 with a challenging and integrative curriculum as discussed in Chapter 7 will go a long way toward preventing classroom management problems. On the flip side, teachers who do not plan well may be distracted by unrelated matters, not have a clear notion of where the lesson is going, and communicate disorder to their students.

Motivating students through good instruction is the best preventive medicine. Doing so requires our full attention.

Motivated students cause fewer discipline problems. Enthusiastic teachers who present their material in stimulating, meaningful ways and treat students with respect and dignity almost always have fewer behavior problems than those who do not. When students are actively learning content that they can personally relate to, they usually have neither the time nor the energy to create discipline problems. Conversely, when students feel that they are passive receptacles for irrelevant knowledge, they become bored, turned off, and find satisfaction in acting out (Curwin, Mendler, & Mendler, 2008, p. 168).

● Routines

Students occasionally get thirsty, need to use the bathroom, forget supplies, are tardy or absent, need to see a counselor, or experience emotional crises. Each individual occurrence of this nature may have only a minor impact on the classroom. Collectively, these interruptions can significantly detract from the learning environment. Team and classroom routines are essential in minimizing the impact of relatively minor interruptions. *Routines* are rules organized around a particular time, concept, or place that help guide students and teachers to accomplish tasks in the quickest and most efficient manner possible. Speaking of the benefits of well-established routines, Borich (2003) says "they allow the teacher more time to teach and learners more time to become engaged in the learning process" (p. 105).

Established routines are not meant to be restrictive. Rather, they free us to concentrate on curriculum, instruction, and assessment more fully with fewer distractions. We may want to establish routines to address taking/reporting attendance, changing seating arrangements, turning in late work, distributing and gathering materials, beginning and dismissing class, seeing the nurse, and going to lockers. Anticipating times, concepts, and places that may be better addressed through routines, as opposed to repeating instructions over and over, will waste less time and help our classrooms run more smoothly.

Before establishing classroom routines it is important to consider the full range of school policies that might relate to the areas to be addressed. For instance, the guidance counselor will likely have a procedure for students to follow who feel the need for counseling; the office will have mandatory ways for reporting attendance, although the method of taking attendance is usually up to individual teachers; there will be a general policy for time allowed to make up work following an absence; and students will likely need some sort of identification when in the hallways. Many routines can be established as a team. If all of a student's teachers do something in the same way, the likelihood of the student following the routine is heightened.

Perhaps the most useful of all routines is one that allows us to get the attention of a group of students—the 30 or so in our classrooms, or the 100 or more in the cafeteria or on the field. The routine I have used for years is the hand-raising technique. Here's how it works. When you raise your hand, students raise theirs. During cooperative group work when many students are not facing you and most are actively engaged and not keeping their eyes on you, the few who may see your raised hand will raise theirs and other students will see them and follow suit. The key here is that when hands are raised, mouths are closed. When all hands are raised, all mouths are closed. You lower your hand and students do the same. Then you can speak, but the students can't. This technique works for 20 and for 200 if it is practiced from day one of school. It's most effective if whole teams consistently use it.

> Getting attention of group = All raise hands + Student mouths close

One routine that builds responsibility in students and saves needless repetition for teachers is the use of a "What did I miss?" notebook. This is a binder with a page designated for each school day. At the end of each day the teacher writes a description of what happened in class. You may have only one preparation per day as part of an interdisciplinary team, or two or three different preparations if you cross disciplines or teach on a two-person team. Regardless, keeping an updated "What did I miss?" notebook in your classroom is worth the time and effort.

A large calendar with important dates clearly indicated will help students stay organized. Insisting that students check the "What did I miss?" book and the calendar before asking about events/assignments is a routine that will save precious instructional time.

Designating baskets for each class period is a good idea. Students know they can turn in assignments or leave notes for you, and that they can pick up worksheets/handouts they may have missed from folders that are kept in their class basket.

Organizing materials/resources in a specific area and having a system for designated students to gather what's needed for themselves and others is an antichaos routine. Maybe one person per cooperative group is the material gatherer or the first person on each row in a more traditional classroom arrangement. Habits of picking up and putting away materials must be taught and practiced.

Classroom interruptions are inevitable. Late students, announcements, teachers and support staff at your door—the list could go on and on. Wise administrators do their best to protect instructional time, but schools, their occupants, and the public are unpredictable and you can count on being interrupted on a regular basis. Teaching your students how to react to interruptions is a valuable lesson. For instance, when the public address (PA) system comes on, teach your students to instantly be silent. This doesn't mean the announcement is in any way more important than what's happening in class, but listening and dealing with the request or information quickly will get you back on track sooner. When someone appears at your door, teach your students to freeze if you're in a whole group activity, or to lower their voices if they are doing group work to free you to respond to the visitor.

Time spent actually teaching and practicing routines in the beginning of the school year will pay dividends throughout the year. Our students are going to form habits with or without us. How much better it is for all of us if the habits they form coincide with the efficient management of our classrooms. Don't overlook or minimize the role of well-established routines as part of your classroom management plan.

Wouldn't it be great if good instruction and productive routines actually prevented all classroom problems? Unfortunately, rules and consequences are usually necessary to maintain a positive and productive learning environment. The combination of engaging instruction, effective routines, and appropriate rules and consequences will go a long way toward prevention of classroom discipline problems.

Rules and Consequences

Rules define what is and what is not acceptable in the classroom. *Consequences* define what will happen when rules are broken. In addition to providing the structure for acceptable behavior, rules communicate expectations and help maintain a positive and productive learning environment.

Some rules are dictated by school and/or district policies. Some middle schools have a prescriptive plan of very specific rules that directly affect your classroom. If so, the plan may have a sequence of consequences that all teachers are to follow for specific infractions. I have seen whole school plans successfully administered, but I've also witnessed problems when school discipline policies conflict with what teams of teachers feel is best for their students. As a new teacher, you may sense that your hands are tied, and indeed they may be. Remember, however, that policies, agreeable or not, do not dictate your relationships with students.

As with routines, it's a good idea for teams to develop rules and consequences together when possible. The team is a unit that should function smoothly in logical and consistent ways. It is my experience that teachers rarely agree on all the routines and rules needed for middle grades students. Part of being a good team member is understanding the value of compromise and being willing to enforce some rules that may seem relatively minor to you, but are viewed by teammates to be of greater importance. We all have our "pet" procedures, likes, and dislikes when it comes to students and classroom management. Keep a sense of perspective in this area. For instance, if there is no school policy concerning gum chewing but your teammates are opposed, allowing students to chew gum in your classroom, even if you think it's fine, would undermine the other teachers. The gum would not always be spit out as they left your class, and students might unjustly label other teachers as "mean" for enforcing the "no gum" rule in their classes. If you think it's less than a big deal for shirts not to be tucked in but your teammates feel the rule is important, it's not going to hurt you to notice and ask students to comply. I have found that abiding by team rules vigilantly is best for everyone, even when I am not personally convinced of their worth.

Guidelines for Establishing Rules   Borich (2003) contends there is no one single best set of rules for classrooms. "Rules make a statement about the type of climate desired in a behavioral setting. They are a message system whereby the teacher's beliefs and philosophy about academic and conduct-related behavior are communicated to students" (p. 101). Burden and Byrd (2010) provide guidelines for establishing rules that are straightforward and comprehensive. Their guidelines include

1. Make classroom rules consistent with school rules.
2. Involve students in making the rules to the degree that you are comfortable and to the degree that the students' age level and sophistication permit.
3. Identify appropriate behaviors and translate them into positively stated classroom rules.
4. Focus on important behavior.
5. Keep the number of rules to a minimum (4–6).
6. Keep the wording of each rule simple and short.
7. Have rules address behaviors that can be observed.
8. Identify rewards for when students follow the rules and consequences for when they break the rules. (p. 237)

Taking a Positive Approach   It is important to state rules in positive terms. Our goal is to promote appropriate behavior and, in doing so, curb inappropriate behavior. We want rules to state what our students should do, not what they shouldn't do. For example, a positively written rule would state "Be in your seats when the bell rings" as opposed to "Don't be out of your seat when the bell rings." Small differences in wording can have a real impact on how students respond. Positively stated rules are clear to students and provide observable behaviors for teachers to praise. Negatively written rules focus on what's wrong and put our classrooms in punishment mode.

Examples of positive rules that involve powerful "I" statements include

- I will be the best student I can be.
- I will respect others and the environment.
- I will follow directions the first time they are given.

Using positive reinforcement simply means recognizing appropriate behavior, acknowledging it privately and/or publicly, and possibly rewarding it beyond acknowledgment. When rules are stated in positive terms, we can simply say "Thank you for being in your seat when the bell rang." The acknowledgment carries with it a reinforcement because students hear the rule repeated. For the 70% of our students who rarely break rules, positive reinforcement is generally enough to ensure appropriate behavior. For the 20% whose behavior vacillates between rule compliance and rule defiance, positive reinforcement stands a good chance of upsetting the balance between compliance and defiance in favor of appropriate behavior. For the 10% of our students who are chronic rule breakers, positive reinforcement (typically awarded the other 90%) allows them to hear and see what happens when rules are followed. Although not a common cure, finding occasions to positively reinforce this needy 10% will likely have an effect. It can't hurt. All of us seek attention. Disapproval is attention and so is approval. We want our chronic misbehavers to experience the difference between positive attention and negative attention. Our goal is to make the positive attention more enjoyable than the negative so "attention getting" might be redirected by the student. Our chronic misbehavers have so much room for improvement that we should have many opportunities to catch them doing better. Our responses to these students have much to do with their escalation or de-escalation.

George and Alexander (2003) give us an example of a positive set of simple, straightforward rules.

1. Be prompt.
2. Be prepared.
3. Raise your hand when you wish to speak.
4. Follow directions.
5. Treat others with respect.

Teaching Responsibility   Teaching students to be responsible is much more complex than teaching them to obey (Curwin, Mendler, & Mendler, 2008). Although we may be tempted to simply say "Just do what I say" to our students, Pavlov's experiments with food, bells, and salivating dogs is hardly an appropriate model to use when considering rules and young adolescents. With our emphasis on developmental appropriateness and our quest to foster critical thinking, asking students to simply "obey or else" is incongruous. The work and time required to teach responsibility for actions is part of our jobs as teachers of young adolescents.

Teaching responsibility when it comes to compliance with rules should be approached like any subject. We can use a variety of strategies and Bloom's guidance to promote knowledge (rules posted), understanding (rules discussed), application (rules practiced), analysis (reasons for rules acknowledged), synthesis (rules applied in new situations), and evaluation (rules perceived as classroom governance). Stopping at the knowledge level or simply posting the rules and expecting compliance

Requiring young adolescents to develop and follow their own sets of responsibility rules makes classroom conduct and learning personal.

will be very disappointing. We know learning that leads to any kind of action requires more of the taxonomy than the first level.

Teaching responsibility entails the promotion of decision-making skills. Making decisions about rule compliance happens on a conscious level. Teaching students that they have choices and how to make the choices that will be best for them and everyone else involved is teaching responsibility.

For the first week of school it's a good idea to spend 5 minutes or so each day discussing, modeling, and having students role-play rules. We may ask them to write what compliance to a certain rule might "look like," or perhaps what the classroom would

> Reinforcing rules = Discussion + Modeling + Role-play

be like without a particular rule. For some classes, it may be helpful to do some rule-related activity each Monday. After long holidays it's very appropriate to emphasize rules again.

Developing Consequences   Curwin, Mendler, and Mendler (2008, p. 83) explain the main differences between consequences and punishments:

> Punishments are done to others. The goal is to achieve the proper amount of misery so that the behavior will not recur. . . . Consequences are what we do to ourselves. They are the results of our choices. . . . A consequence helps us learn to make better choices. It gets us to look inside and take responsibility so we can fix our mistake.

These authors continue with this wisdom and advice.

- A consequence may not be predetermined because it is the result or effect of something else.
- Students should not only have a say in our classroom rules, but also in the consequences that result from the breaking of the rules.
- It is best to have a menu of consequences from which teacher and student may select, rather than a lockstep list (i.e., 1. warning, 2. phone call home, 3. detention, 4. suspension) because each situation is different. A phone call home may do it for one student while, for basically the same offense, another may need detention. This is another reason to know our students well. We are wisely reminded that being fair doesn't always mean treating kids the same.
- Preserve student dignity if at all possible.
- Use consequences as teachable moments for modeling and encouraging responsibility.

Before leaving the topic of prevention of classroom problems, let's discuss a schoolwide initiative that has proven to be effective for some middle schools in helping create a positive and productive learning environment—school uniforms.

Uniforms   I am a believer in uniforms for middle grades students. After some initial resistance, most schools that adopted uniforms in the 1980s and 1990s have stayed with the practice of requiring students to wear one of several variations on a clothing theme. While the practice is started for different school-specific reasons, all relate to middle school philosophy and student well-being.

Some of the benefits often associated with the initiation and continuance of uniforms in middle school include

- The lessening of socioeconomic rifts among students
- Fashion becomes less important, with increased attention to learning
- Decreasing visible presence of gang identity and activity
- Decreased cost of school clothing
- Greater levels of identity within the school

One of the keys to successful development of a uniform policy is parental support. Parent-teacher committees generally select a variety of shirts/pants/skirts from an easily accessible vendor. Because instituting a mandatory uniform policy is risky, in the beginning at least, when it comes to student morale, having a uniform fashion show with student models and then allowing students to vote for colors and styles within the adult committee's parameters is a great idea. Given the choice, students would probably never initially say "yes" to uniforms. However, it is typical to hear comments such as "I don't have to decide what to wear" or "Everybody dresses alike, so we can think about other stuff" or "Now it's more fun to put on other clothes when I go places." If students are required to wear uniforms in elementary school, the requirement in middle school is a smoother transition. Many look forward to high school where uniform programs are not as widespread.

For uniform policies to "stick," they must be mandatory. Dress codes are a matter of school policy and can be difficult to enforce because of the generally subjective nature of the rules and the time/attention required of teachers to be vigilant when there are so many other instructionally important tasks to tend to. Uniform violations are easy to spot. To avoid any legal questions that would be time-consuming and costly to address, an

> Prevention of misbehavior = Engaging instruction + Routines + Rules and consequences

Uniforms have many benefits, including providing a sense of belonging either as a whole school or, in the case of focus teacher Jesse White's school, a grade level. Each grade level has its own distinct colors.

"opt out" policy for parents who feel strongly about their students not wearing uniforms is advisable. In my experience, this option is exercised very rarely.

Intervention When Classroom Problems Occur

We must use prevention as our first line of defense—effective instruction that engages learners, well-established routines, and appropriate rules and consequences. While the prevention of misbehavior is our goal, there are times when intervention is necessary. It may be unobtrusive or involve implementation of consequences that may require aggressive action on our part. Students can actually help other students with behavior improvement through peer mediation. Let's explore these methods of intervention.

Unobtrusive Intervention

Effective classroom management involves the ever-vigilant peripheral vision discussed earlier along with rational, calm decision-making. We have to determine when to do what, as well as when to do nothing. This may sound contradictory to consistently applying predetermined consequences to broken rules, but it isn't. I'm not implying that we should "do nothing" when clearly there is an infraction. However, classrooms are plagued most days not with major rule infractions, but by small disruptions that require a dose of plain old common sense to know when and how to intervene. Purkey and Strahan (2002) give us some questions to ask ourselves when deciding whether or not a situation is a matter of concern.

myeducationlab

To watch Traci Peters' room tour at Cario Middle School, as she shows us how classroom disruptions can be minimized through organized facilities and procedures, go to the Video Examples section of **Topic #3: Classroom Management** in the MyEducationLab for your course and view the video entitled "Traci Peters' Room Tour."

1. Will this situation resolve itself without intervention?
2. Can this situation be safely and wisely overlooked?
3. Does this situation involve a matter of ethics, legality, morality, or safety?
4. Is this the proper time to be concerned about this situation? (p. 102)

Small disruptions include a student asking another for a pencil during individual work time; a normally on-time, ready-to-work student slipping into class just as the bell stops ringing; and two students suddenly laughing loudly while gathering materials. To stop class momentum to address these small things would waste more time than they're worth. If you're conducting a class discussion of a reading passage and a student is just sitting with his book closed, publicly saying "Sean, open your book and sit up straight" will only alienate Sean and interrupt the thought processes of others. Casually walking toward Sean and opening his book, accompanied by a knowing look, may do the trick. This is an unobtrusive intervention.

Unobtrusive intervention serves in many ways as a form of prevention. It is intervention because students do something that requires a response. It is prevention because it will likely prevent escalation that would result in the need to implement consequences. Here are some unobtrusive things you might try doing to curb inattentiveness, annoying behavior, lack of participation, off-track distractions, and so on.

- Give "the look"—one your students recognize as disapproving.
- Move toward the student(s) in question.
- Pause and silently stare for a moment.
- Walk to the student's desk and put your hand on it.
- Use the student's name in an example.
- Ask the student to sum up what has been said or to repeat directions just given.

If necessary (and it often will be), you can be more assertive and still relatively unobtrusive by doing one of the following:

- Say "Sean, how should we be participating right now?"
- Ask the student to move to another part of the classroom.
- Ask the student to see you privately after class.

Cummings (2000) calls what has just been described "The Law of Least Intervention" (p. 137). When preventive measures are in place, simple unobtrusive intervention will keep most class periods running smoothly. Not using unobtrusive measures quickly and confidently will allow minor disruptions to escalate.

Implementing Consequences

When disruptions and rule violations interfere with your teaching and/or student learning, they require more than unobtrusive intervention. If appropriate, the consequence may be a reminder. When the misbehavior occurs again, a warning might be given. If it occurs one more time, the next step is taken. Some misbehaviors don't begin benignly. They may burst into being blatantly enough to require implementation of predetermined consequences. A behavior may require instant action to curb the behavior or to remove the student from a situation.

Rule violations actually provide opportunities for us to interact with students in ways that demonstrate maturity, restraint, concern for the overall good of the class, care for the misbehaver's well-being and growth, and wisdom. When we view instances of misbehavior as opportunities, we will address them in more positive ways.

Now let's look at some important factors affecting the implementation of consequences.

Parents   One of my favorite interventions, and one I included as often as possible as a classroom consequence, was parental contact. Some teachers report that there is an increasing number of situations when contacting a parent or guardian is less than effective. There are many students who, sadly, experience little support and/or guidance outside school. Unfortunately, these are often the very students who require the most intervention. They need and deserve our best efforts. There are many students, however, who respond with panic to the thought of a call home saying there is a behavior problem. For these kids, parental contact is an excellent motivator. For others, administrative intervention may be necessary.

Administrative Assistance   When consequences are dictated by you or your team, implementing them without the assistance of administrators is preferable. The more office referrals you write, the more diminished your power will be as a classroom manager. However, there are times when it is very appropriate to ask for administrative assistance. If a student reaches a consequence level that dictates an office referral, not giving one will send the message that you do not believe in the rule-consequence package that governs the classroom/team/school. There are violent misbehaviors that call for immediate administrative assistance. Verbal outrage, throwing objects in anger, instigating a fight, verbal abuse of teacher or another student, physical abuse (or the threat of), possession of contraband of any kind—these situations and others warrant calls for help. Read about one incident that involved focus student Darma in **See How They Grow.** Sometimes even students who are conscientious and well behaved are involved in potentially dangerous altercations.

▶ See How They Grow

Darma ● 8th grade

After over eight years of a clean behavior record, Darma has a blot. In Chapter 3 we read that Darma's last name, Suparman, won him a nickname among his friends of *Superman*. He liked it and grinned widely when his buddies would use the name. Well, that was before Darma found himself in a heterogeneous class with kids he had never shared a class with before. A couple of the boys heard one of Darma's friends call him *Superman* and they began to taunt, "Hey, *Superman*, what are your powers?" and "Ladies, ladies, did you know *Superman* is in our class?" Lots of laughter, stares, and sarcasm by both boys and girls was focused on Darma. He was so stunned by the negative attention that he verbally lashed out and said, "Yes, I'm Superman with a brain, unlike you illiterate retards." At that a couple of boys jumped up, knocked over their desks and started toward Darma who stood up and started swinging at them. The teacher, who had been standing in the hall, ran in and called the office on the intercom. Within a minute a male assistant principal ran in, but not before there was an all-out fight going on.

The Lake Park zero tolerance for fighting meant that Darma and two other boys were suspended for three days. This was not only humiliating for Darma at school, it was considered shameful at home. Darma's first name means "doer of good deeds," as he was reminded by his dad. So Darma suffered at school because he had to be out and could not make up his work, and at home because he knew he disappointed his parents. Yes, he'll get past this and go on to be a successful student, but he'll never forget it. He is determined to not let incidents like this get to him in the future.

While we hope these scenarios occur rarely, we know that in some settings they are frequent. Students who repeatedly cause major disruptions are sometimes referred to as being out of control.

Out of Control Students   Let's discuss approaches to students who repeatedly challenge your classroom management skills. We all have them. I can still name the students who, over the years, have presented me with more challenge than I could handle with prevention techniques or the occasional implementation of consequences. These are students who don't willingly become constructive members of our classrooms and who appear to enjoy disrupting the learning process. They often actually become legends in the school. Sixth grade teachers will have heard about them before they hit the middle school. If interventions have not had long-term positive effects, eighth grade teachers will have had years of warning.

The first step should be to seriously look at the student's history. Has she been referred for diagnostic testing? Are there home/family concerns? What interventions have been tried? Chances are the student has intellectual potential that isn't obvious from her grades. Helping her break out of the "I'm trouble" mode should be a group effort—the whole team plus the guidance counselor, school psychologist, administrators, and so forth. All may need to be involved to find in-school solutions.

There are students who need more help than we are equipped to give. Chronic misbehavior, after interventions have failed to modify it, is a sign that alternative placement may be needed. The regular classroom is not the place for all students. The education of the vast majority of students should not be jeopardized by students who need more than we can give. Districts that provide a variety of school settings for students with special needs and special interests are doing a real service for all students.

More Than One Student   No doubt there will be occasions when two or three students misbehave at the same time. When this happens you will be very glad you followed middle school philosophy that emphasizes the importance of understanding developmental processes and knowing your students well. Spending time analyzing the social dynamics of your classes pays off when faced with multiple behavior problems at once. If two or three students are involved, choose the one considered to be more of a leader. This could be the one who is most respected or considered funniest, or who, for whatever reason, wields the most influence. Concentrate on correcting or controlling this student's behavior. This may take care of the behavior of the others. If not, continue intervention down the "influence chain."

Dealing with misbehavior that appears to involve half or more of your class is cause for concern. The first step is to get their attention. Yelling is never the solution. If you use the hand-raising technique regularly, it will work in the majority of cases when there is more misbehavior than normal. Try turning off the lights. If you've never used this attention getter it may work. If you do it often it will not be effective in getting the students quiet enough to hear your directions. Standing silently in the front of the room with your arms folded may get their attention once you are noticed. On a few occasions when students were excessively agitated, I closed my classroom door loudly to get attention. It worked, but I would use it only as a last resort. Once you have students' attention, you can proceed. At this point you must address the causes of the disruption. A class meeting is called for, as well as appropriate consequences. You are responsible for figuring out, with the help of your students, how to make changes to prevent similar behavior problems in the future. Displaying calm reasonableness will help ensure resolution and prevent a repeat performance. Never hesitate to ask other teachers how they would handle situations.

Avoiding Power Struggles   When a teacher implements a consequence and the student refuses to comply, a power struggle is in the making. Power struggles, especially in a classroom, hallway, or cafeteria full of students, should be avoided. Quietly say to the student, "I feel a power struggle coming on and that's not the way I operate. Let's talk about this privately (or later or after class or . . .)." Some students have experienced "winning" a power struggle and have been viewed as tough by peers after succeeding in making the teacher angry, or exhausting the teacher to the point of getting out of the consequence. These are students who take pride in initiating verbal struggles.

It's good to find a way to acknowledge a student's feelings by paraphrasing what the student expresses. For instance, you might respond to "It wasn't my fault and I'm not serving detention for it," with "I understand you feel it's not your fault and that you don't believe you deserve a detention. So we have a problem. Let's talk about a solution after class." Use of the pronoun *we* indicates that maybe there's a solution that can be reached that is not all about punishing him.

Stopping a power struggle before it starts is important, and so is the procedure we use to follow up. If a rule has been broken, then a resolution must occur. Ideally it will be the prescribed consequence, if one exists. If the student attempts to engage in a power struggle publicly, we can't expect an easy private conversation, but it will give us the opportunity to actively listen, acknowledge feelings, show understanding, and say things like, "I sure don't like our relationship to be like this. Work with me here." Most young adolescents want to be heard. Listening and being willing to engage in conversation goes a long way toward not only peacefully resolving a current behavior problem, but also paving the way for future communication.

Many middle grades students find themselves on the verge of, or in the midst of, a power struggle before they realize what's happening. The whole situation may be defused by a sense of humor on our part. Often students are secretly hoping we will have a way to lighten up the mood and clear the air when they're not quite sure how to back off.

Will you always be able to calmly resolve potential power struggles? Unfortunately, no. There will be times when administrative assistance will be called for. Students will be suspended, in and/or out of school. Consequences will be imposed that none of us particularly like, or even think best for individual kids who have complicated personal circumstances. In these situations it is extremely important for the teacher to show public support for the administration, even if we privately want to take issue with the consequence imposed.

We are responsible for doing the best we can, even in uncomfortable and difficult situations. Our students depend on us to be adults and to remain in control and keep them from crossing the line and getting into deeper trouble that causes consequences to become more and more severe.

For teachers, a level head and a sense of humor can diffuse would-be power struggles. Giving kids a chance to back down gracefully will often avoid behaviors that may lead to negative consequences.

● Peer Mediation

As a supplement to teacher/administration classroom management procedures, some schools implement *peer mediation*. It may take many different forms, but basically peer mediation provides opportunities for students to problem-solve concerning their disputes in the presence, and with the help, of a student acting as a mediator. If successful, peer mediation can lead to students taking increased responsibility for their actions as they learn socially acceptable ways of solving conflicts. It can lead to greater self-control and an understanding of alternatives to aggression, which almost always results in emotional and/or physical harm.

A study reported by Robinson, Smith, and Daunic (2000) reveals five major areas of conflict often dealt with in peer mediation sessions.

1. Minor issues such as arguments over inconsequential topics or "having a bad day"
2. Personal attacks (e.g, picking on or insulting another student, spreading rumors)
3. Social skills deficits (e.g., failure to see another's viewpoint, inability to communicate, inability to control one's temper)
4. Typical teen issues (e.g., disputes with parents about staying out late or chores, boyfriend/girlfriend issues)
5. Status (e.g., attempting to boost one's reputation through self-aggrandizement or exaggeration) (p. 25)

To successfully help students settle disputes and acquire skills for handling future problems, a peer mediation program needs enthusiastic and dedicated teachers, counselors, and administrators to sustain the program's momentum. Resources include adult trainers who understand young adolescent development; curriculum that is developmentally appropriate and relevant to how kids process information; a plan that allows sessions to take place during the school day on an as-needed basis; a private, comfortable space to meet; and a system of deciding who will benefit and how they may access the program.

The only way a peer mediation program can hope to have an impact on the school environment is for it to be considered a valid alternative for conflict resolution by the kids themselves. This kind of validity does not come easily in middle grades. The program must be presented to the whole student body as an attractive plan that may provide a way not only to peacefully coexist, but also to avoid consequences imposed by adults. Peer mediation will not be used if it is perceived as a "nerdy" or "wimpy" thing to do. The choice of peer mediators is crucial. They should be representative in terms of grade level, peer group identification, socioeconomic status, special program involvement, race, and gender. Recruitment and training of the right students in the school population is vital.

The Robinson, et al. (2000) study revealed a benefit of peer mediation that should be noted. Their research shows that the mediators reported that the training involved helped prepare them to solve their own conflicts. So regardless of their efficacy with their peers' disputes, the mediator gains life skills because of the training. This implies that perhaps the whole school could benefit from peer mediator training. A valuable use of advisory time!

Now that we understand more about the prevention of inappropriate behavior, as well as what to do when disruptive and unproductive behavior occurs in our classrooms, let's examine some personal aspects of managing the learning environment. In the next section we consider our role in shaping the learning environment and how to get off to a good start in the classroom. We also examine how we can positively approach the young adolescents in our classrooms to help ensure a positive, productive place where learning and growth abound.

Within Our Control

myeducationlab

To hear Mike Geisen, the 2008 Oregon Teacher of the Year, tell us that he is both a scientist and an artist in the classroom as he develops relationships with students, go to the Teacher Talk section of **Topic #4: Motivation** in the MyEducationLab for your course.

We influence, but cannot always control, students, colleagues, parents, and resources. However, we can control the key variable in effectively managing the classroom learning environment—ourselves. The Haim Ginott (1993) quote in Chapter 4 bears repeating here. In fact, it bears repeating on a daily basis.

I've come to the frightening conclusion that I am the decisive element in the classroom. It's my personal approach that makes the climate. It's my mood that makes the weather. As a teacher I possess the tremendous power to make a child's life miserable or joyous. I can be a tool of torture or an instrument of inspiration. I can humiliate or humor, hurt or heal. In all situations, it is my response that decides whether a crisis will be escalated or de-escalated, a child humanized or dehumanized (p. 15).

Effective classroom management requires self-assured, competent adults to be effective. Whatever combination of strategies we choose, and in whatever set of circumstances we find ourselves, we are key to the management of the learning environment.

Here's a pledge we can make to our students, either explicitly or as a personal reminder of our responsibility as the teacher.

- I will not give up on you.
- I will not quit on you.
- I will not lose control with you.
- I will not yell at you.
- I will not be angry with you.
- I will always be here no matter what.
- Because I am a teacher and my job is to show you a better way, I will not take personally what you do or say when I do not like it (Curwin, Mendler, & Mendler, 2008, p. 133).

Understanding Our Role

"The challenge is to be with them without being like them . . ." (Stevenson, 1992, p. 25). Understanding our students—their development, interests, concerns, and habits—is vital. Our ongoing purpose is to be with our students as they grow. We have already grown, at least out of adolescence. We are not, and shouldn't attempt to be, like our students. Joining the student culture in an attempt to win their acceptance or popularity is a mistake. Read what Joey Huber has to say on this topic in **Teachers Speak**.

STANDARD 7

Knowledge 3: Middle level teacher candidates are knowledgeable about their responsibility for upholding high professional standards.

As a teacher, you are both the instructional leader and the classroom manager. Middle grades students don't need or want a teacher who at one moment is 13 and, in an instant, becomes the adult trying to control the classroom. The consistent message needs to be "I am the adult, you are the students. We will respect one another and learn from each other." To do otherwise is to send mixed messages. Joey learned this valuable lesson as a student teacher.

As adults we have a wide spectrum of personalities and life experiences. It's good to let students get to know us. Believe me, what we don't reveal, they'll make up! So be yourself—your adult self. An adult has emotions, hopes, problems, a sense of humor. Our students should see how thoughtful, mature people handle life. Remember, even if young adolescents appear to learn little else, they learn *us*.

▶ Teachers Speak

● **Joey Huber**

Reflecting on my student teaching experience feels surreal because it seems like just a week or so ago I was trying to figure out how I would survive, and now I'm trying to figure out how to say goodbye. I learned so much. When I first started observing and working in my student teaching classroom, I think I stepped over the line and became too much of a buddy figure to the students. This eventually caught up with me when it was my turn to instruct the students. They were not prepared to take me seriously as an authority figure. This, in turn, led to many incidents where students could not understand why I had to correct them. Students became frustrated, and it was tough to get them back on task. There was actually one point when a student said, "What's going on here, Mr. Huber? You used to be our friend and now you are one of *them!*" So, as you can see, the students were a bit confused and not willing to accept me as their teacher because of my desire to be their buddy. I understand that now. My transition from observer/classroom helper to teacher would have been much smoother if I had drawn that proverbial teacher–student line from the beginning. We could have still had fun, but the kids would have understood our relationship more clearly.

My student teaching experience will always be part of who I am in the classroom. The lessons I learned and the relationships I made will make me a wiser and more effective teacher.

● Getting Off to a Good Start

Students, as well as teachers, are often nervous about the first days and weeks of school. We can reassure our students and ourselves that the school year will bring positive experiences by doing some basic things such as

- Making the classroom organized and inviting
- Greeting students warmly and sincerely

Sharing extracurricular activities with kids is a great way to influence them, as well as have a good time forming meaningful relationships. During his student teaching experience, Joey Huber helped coach his school's baseball team to a 12-0 county championship.

- Establishing and explaining classroom routines
- Establishing and clarifying rules and consequences
- Conducting a survey of students' interests and concerns
- Creating ways for students to get to know us and each other
- Forming cooperative groups and conducting an activity in which students will experience success
- Clarifying the major learning goals for the class
- Explaining grading criteria

It takes lots of preparation to begin a school year in a proactive and engaging style. It's serious business. I strongly recommend that you read Harry and Rosemary Wong's book *The First Days of School*. It is filled with practical advice on starting and keeping the momentum of a positive learning environment.

Easier to Love Than to Like

I can honestly say that I have loved my students—all of them. I have cared deeply for them and always wanted the best for their lives. However, I have to tell you there have been individual students I have had difficulty liking. Teachers are human. We are capable of loving the unlovable. However, liking the unlikable is much harder.

How can we make the most of a situation where we feel the responsibility to address the needs of every student, even the one or two we like the least? The first step is to view the student as a "work in progress." Understanding both the developmental certainties and the possibilities of early adolescence will help us conjure up an attitude of excitement to see what a school year of maturing might do to make students more likable. Another tactic that helps is to purposefully spend time talking to the student you find hard to like about topics other than school. Finding a common interest will do wonders for a relationship. Try complimenting the student on a daily basis. Even the most unlikable middle grades student will have some trait that can be viewed as positive. Finally, realize that if you find it this difficult to like a student, there's a chance you may be the only adult who is even trying to do so. It is within our control to at least treat each and every student with kindness and respect, regardless of the level of our personal affinity, and to do our best to appreciate them.

Being prepared for each new day, having commonsense rules, possessing confidence that shows through in our relationships with colleagues and students—these actions are within our control. Managing the learning environment will become second nature to us when we recognize the personal power we possess to make a positive difference.

We will conclude this section about how much of the learning environment is within our control by considering some of the 12 processes that form the foundation of an effective discipline program according to Curwin, Mendler, and Mendler (2008) in *Discipline with Dignity*. Each process has been touched on in the chapter. There is value in this kind of summary, found in Figure 11.2, as we consider how we can make these guidelines realities in our classrooms.

FIGURE 11.2 Foundations of an effective discipline program

1. "Let students know what you need, and ask them what they need from you" (p. 21). The first part is easy, but be sure to include the second.

2. "Differentiate instruction based on each student's strengths" (p. 21). Assessing the academic levels of students and adjusting instruction to meet them where they are and take them forward are vital in providing both success and appropriate challenge. This will help prevent behavior problems.

3. "Listen to what students are thinking and feeling" (p. 21). Listening actively, identifying with student feelings, and conveying understanding and empathy can help prevent behavior problems.

4. "Use humor" (p. 22). Humor can set a friendly mood and diffuse small problems. Using a sense of humor in a middle school classroom, even if there are times when the kids don't get it, makes the atmosphere comfortable. Never, ever make students the butt of jokes or use sarcasm toward them.

5. "Vary your style of presentation" (p. 22). Disruptions often accompany inattentiveness and restlessness that result from using the same instructional approach over and over. Keep in mind that middle grades students need a change in activity every 15 minutes or so.

6. "Be responsible for yourself and allow kids to take responsibility for themselves" (p. 24). This is part of allowing, and even prompting, students to move from dependence to independence that requires them to be responsible for their actions.

7. "Realize that you will not reach every child, but act as if you can" (p. 24). When a student continually chooses misbehavior despite all our preventive measures and interventions, she needs more than we can give. This will happen occasionally. We need to ask for help, move on, and be at our best for all the other students we positively influence.

8. "Start fresh every day. What happened yesterday is finished. Today is a new day. Act accordingly" (p. 24).

Source: From *Discipline with Dignity* (pp. 21–24), by R. L. Curwin, A. N. Mendler, and B. D. Mendler, 2008, Alexandria, VA: Association for Supervision and Curriculum Development.

Reflections on Maintaining a Positive, Productive Learning Environment

Every concept and practice we have discussed in this chapter has as its ultimate goal the creation and maintenance of a classroom environment that supports learning. Managing the learning environment is a complex task. The part of the task that often receives the most attention is classroom management focusing on student behavior. We need to realize that student behavior is dependent on numerous variables, many of which are strongly influenced by our actions as teachers. Creating a positive and productive learning environment involves ensuring physical, emotional, and academic safety. Preventive measures include providing consistently engaging instruction; well-established and efficient routines; and appropriate and enforceable rules and consequences. When preventive measures are not sufficient, intervention becomes necessary. Deciding when and how to implement consequences, as well as wisely using resources such as parents, peer mediators, and other school personnel, are key to effective intervention.

As we have added to the description of effective classroom teachers discussed in Chapter 4, we see that many of the factors contributing to managing the learning environment are within our control. Knowing ourselves, addressing our personal maturity, and thoroughly planning our initial and ongoing encounters with our students will lead us to, as Haim Ginott admonishes, "create the climate" and "make the weather" in our classrooms with the students for whom we are responsible.

GROUP ACTIVITIES

1. In pairs, arrange to visit with a team of middle school teachers to find out how they
   - Begin the school year in welcoming ways
   - Establish and maintain routines
   - Develop rules and enforce consequences

   Add findings to your school files.

2. In groups of three or four, write a set of classroom rules you consider appropriate to post in a middle school classroom. Make a poster of the rules and be prepared to justify them.

3. As a class, brainstorm consequences for the rules posted in activity 2. Spend time discussing whether each item on the brainstormed list is a logical, related-to-the-rule consequence or if it more resembles punishment.

INDIVIDUAL ACTIVITIES

1. In addition to the suggestions given for connecting with students, describe another way you might "win them over."

2. Did you ever feel physically threatened in school? If so, describe the circumstances. If not, tell about the factors that helped you perceive safety in your middle school.

3. Why is sarcasm an inappropriate form of humor to use in middle grades classrooms? Will you have trouble controlling your use of it?

PERSONAL JOURNAL

1. Did you feel accepted as a member of a caring community in your middle school? If so, what did being accepted feel like? If not, what made you feel like you were not accepted?

2. Do you recall your emotional safety being jeopardized by something a teacher may have said or done? Write about the memory.

3. Do you anticipate having difficulty knowing where and when to draw the teacher–student line because you want to identify with your students? Will your desire to be liked by them sometimes cloud your judgment? If you had a teacher for whom this was a dilemma, write a description of the circumstances.

Professional Practice

*(It would be helpful to reread the description of Sadie Fox in Chapter 4 and her **Teachers Speak** feature in Chapter 6.)*

● **Sadie Fox**

Ms. Fox has never been a big "rule" person. When she was in school she rarely caused a problem or got in trouble. But when she thought a rule was unfair or unreasonable, she found a way around it or removed herself from the situation that required the rule. When she began teaching at Valley View, Ms. Fox was pretty smug about classroom management. She has a lot to offer kids and figured that's all it would take for them to behave in class. She decided to have a classroom without rule signs. All she wanted was for the kids to respect her and each other, and to behave and learn. It didn't quite work out that way.

Because she was hired about a week after classes started when another teacher suddenly resigned, school was in full swing when she met the team teachers, was shown her classroom, and was given her books and materials. Word got out that Ms. Fox didn't believe in rules and, kind of like Las Vegas, what happens in Ms. Fox's room stays in Ms. Fox's room. For a while it all seemed to work. The kids were delighted with the non-teacher-like attitude.

Ms. Fox's lessons were engaging and things were great for a few weeks.

1. The first sign of trouble for Ms. Fox was when five boys in her first period science class walked into second period social studies class with their uniform shirts untucked. It never occurred to Ms. Fox that this wasn't acceptable. After all, what's the big deal about a shirttail hanging out? When asked by the second period teacher, the boys said, "Oh, we forgot. Ms. Fox doesn't care." Because of this, the social studies teacher immediately found herself resenting Ms. Fox's apparent slackness. All of the following would have been appropriate ways of avoiding this scenario except
   a. Even though they were busy, the team teachers should have spent time with Ms. Fox to fill her in on team rules.
   b. Ms. Fox could have asked about team expectations.
   c. The principal should have shared the team rules with Ms. Fox.
   d. Ms. Fox should have noticed by the time of this incident that the boys always had their shirttails tucked in.

2. After the shirttail incident, the other three team teachers decided they needed to meet with Ms. Fox specifically about the team rules they had developed. When Ms. Fox heard them and was given a chart that listed them,

she was surprised at how petty she considered them, including "No gum," "Walk on the right side of the hall during passing period," "Only one restroom pass per day," and "Even if the proper materials are not brought to class, students may not go to their lockers during class." What is the best way for Ms. Fox to respond to the teachers?

a. Ask for the reasons behind the rules and determine to enforce them as a team player.

b. Tell the teachers that as long as there are no problems in her classroom, she prefers to not enforce the team rules.

c. Choose the rules she will follow and ignore the rest.

d. Ask to join a different team.

3. Routines serve many purposes. All of the following are benefits of routines in the middle level classroom except

a. Routines minimize the impact of relatively benign interruptions.

b. Routines give young adolescents more time to socialize.

c. Routines save instructional time.

d. Routines free teachers to concentrate on instruction.

Constructed Response

Explain unobtrusive interventions and why they are important. Give at least two examples.

INTERNET RESOURCES

Education World
http://educationworld.com

Middle Web Ideas for New Teachers
www.middleweb.com

This part of the Middle Web site features tips on management routines and procedures, as well as classroom discipline strategies.

Middle Web Middle School Diaries
www.middleweb.com

This part of the Middle Web site features first hand accounts from new and experienced teachers on a variety of topics that change regularly.

Northwest Regional Educational Laboratory
www.nwrel.org/national/

The U.S. Department of Education Office of Educational Research and Improvement supports this large site. It contains a link to the National Resource Center for Safe Schools that provides information to help schools create safe school environments.

The Really Big List of Classroom Management Resources
http://drwilliampmartin.tripod.com/classm.html

This site provides over 400 links to information about classroom management.

They Are All Our Children

12

Acknowledging that *they are all our children* requires everyone—educators, families, and members of the community—to work together to fulfill our responsibilities to nurture and empower young adolescents to recognize and make the most of opportunities for learning and growth.

$\mathcal{M}$aking these several school years momentous in ways that can lead kids to continue developing their minds, bodies, and souls in directions that are compatible with the educational values that our schools are charged with accomplishing is a formidable but critical mission. But it is also a possible one. Whether this mission is accomplished in any particular classroom or school, however, depends more on the teacher's vision and commitment than on any other factor.

Stevenson and Carr, 1993, p. 184

CHAPTER PREVIEW

21st Century Knowledge and Skills

No Child Left Behind

Family Involvement
- Involvement Decreases
- Getting to Know Families
- Familiarizing Families with Middle School
- Communication
- Opportunities for Involvement

Community Involvement
- Communities Matter
- A Success Story
- Afterschool Programs
- Business Partners
- What We Can Do

Transitions
- Entering Middle School
- Moving On
- Our Nine Students

Recognizing an Exemplary Middle School

Reflections on the Past and Future of Middle School

INTRODUCTION

This chapter is all about sharing—and ownership. Not until we consider all young adolescents our own will we understand our part in the shared responsibility for their growth. Only then will we understand and view each unique child as a significant individual around whom our efforts center. "Research shows that where there is shared responsibility for student learning, student achievement—for every sub-group—improves" (Conzemius & O'Neill, 2001, p. 3). Since we know that shared responsibility is the key, our mandate as teachers is not only to do our part as best we can, but also to draw others into the process, including families and the community.

STANDARD 6

Performance 2: Middle level teacher candidates act as advocates for all young adolescents in the school and in the larger community.

Schools where shared responsibility is a reality most often exhibit the following evidence of success:

- Rising standardized test scores
- Classroom-, school-, district-developed assessments that show steady improvement for every individual and every group of students
- Increasing rates of student, parent, teacher, and community satisfaction on a variety of indicators important to these constituents
- Improved efficiencies in the use of resources such as staff development dollars, curriculum choices, staff development decisions, and time
- Evidence of renewed energy for teaching, learning, and leading
- Students actively engaged and taking responsibility for their learning
- Deeper, more enduring connections among students, teachers, parents, administrators, and the community (Conzemius & O'Neill, 2001, p. 4)

Sharing responsibility with family and community is considered so vital by the National Middle School Association that one of the seven Performance-Based Standards for Initial Middle Level Teacher Preparation is devoted to the concept. Standard Six, titled Family and Community Involvement, states, "Middle level teacher candidates understand the major concepts, principles, theories, and research related to working collaboratively with family and community members, and they use that knowledge to maximize the learning of all young adolescents."

Throughout this chapter we examine the knowledge, dispositions, and performances that flesh out this standard. We explore the No Child Left Behind Act, family and community involvement, ways to help students transition into and out of middle school, and how to recognize an exemplary middle school. But before discussing these topics we need to consider the concept of 21st century knowledge and skills that will impact all of us.

21st Century Knowledge and Skills

Now that we are well into the 21st century, it is becoming more and more obvious that economic globalization and the full-blown arrival of the digital age requires that a more complex and challenging variety of knowledge and skills be taught in school.

FIGURE 12.1   Sample 21st century skills for students and teachers

21st century-ready students and teachers will be . . .

- Critical thinkers
- Problem solvers
- Effective communicators
- Positive collaborators
- Self-directed learners
- Media literate

- Globally aware
- Engaged in community
- Economically literate
- Ethically responsible
- Adaptable
- Personally productive

Businesses and state departments of education are abuzz in attempts to define exactly what knowledge and skills should be emphasized in the future.

How will young adolescents acquire the knowledge and skills necessary for today and tomorrow? Yes, as teachers we are responsible for much of the learning that takes place in middle level settings, but families and communities share this responsibility as well. Thus the title of this chapter, *They Are All Our Children.*

Lists abound of what should be included in any summary of 21st century knowledge and skills. They are eloquently stated and loudly applauded by both educational experts and government officials. To incorporate them in our K–12 schools requires awareness and determination. As state departments of education ask public schools and teacher preparation programs to retool to make sure students are prepared for a successful future, we all need to consider how to make this a reality.

The knowledge and skills considered necessary for success in the 21st century tend to revolve around themes such as global awareness, financial/economic literacy, information and technology literacy, civic literacy, and health and wellness. Within these themes are descriptors of student skills that must be in place for success. Most documents addressing 21st century knowledge and skills also describe teacher attributes that will help us lead our students into successful futures. In most documents, the skills for students and teachers are the same. Figure 12.1 includes sample skills for both students and teachers.

No Child Left Behind

The title of this chapter—*They Are All Our Children*—echoes the intent of the federal legislation passed in January 2002—the No Child Left Behind Act (NCLB). The objectives of the act are right in line with NMSA's beliefs that every child, regardless of circumstances, should receive a quality education (George, 2002).

While we will not argue with the impetus behind the legislation to provide quality education for all children, the challenges presented to middle schools by the mandates and deadlines of the act are daunting. The success of a school, according to NCLB, rests solely in student achievement as measured by standardized tests. The mandates of NCLB are accompanied by a time line for accomplishment. The act proposes financial support for schools that need it most to facilitate changes necessary for meeting the deadlines. This is a positive step, as long as the funds are a reality and the human and material resources are available.

NCLB calls for all students to score at proficient levels or above by 2014. States must present their definitions of proficiency in math, reading, and science and their assessments for measuring student achievement to the U.S. Department of Education for approval. Schools whose students are not making adequate yearly progress toward proficiency must provide options to parents, including transfers to other schools and Title I funding for tutoring. Provisions are made for replacing a school staff after 4 years of failure to make adequate progress and a state takeover of a school with 5 years of failure.

Particularly problematic for middle schools, again not in intent but in feasibility, is the provision for a "highly qualified" teacher in every classroom. NCLB defines "highly qualified" as having a degree in the content area taught or passing a Praxis content area exam. Being a content specialist is very important and we should all be working toward that goal. However, many middle school teachers have degrees in elementary education, and not enough universities offer middle level degrees requiring adequate coursework in a subject area.

NCLB emphasizes the importance of family/community involvement with schools. If schools attempt to meet the standards outlined in the legislation alone, the likelihood of success is doubtful. However, with family and community support the standards are more within reach.

This is a very cursory discussion of No Child Left Behind. As states struggle to fulfill the mandates and middle level educators attempt to reconcile the demands of the act with the balance of developmental responsiveness and academic rigor, no doubt there will be adjustments and compromises along the way.

We'll now turn our attention to families and communities as we attempt to involve them as our partners in educating young adolescents in excellent and equitable ways.

Family Involvement

As discussed in Chapter 3, the definition of family has changed and expanded. While most books and articles discuss parent involvement, I choose to use the word

Families = Traditional + Nontraditional

family to encompass biological parents, stepparents, grandparents, aunts/uncles, older siblings, and others who either live in the home or share guardianship of our students. So while the word *family* in this chapter is still synonymous with the word **parent** for the majority of our students, the implications should be stretched to more realistically encompass all our students and their individual circumstances. The principles are the same, even if the players are changing.

STANDARD 6

Knowledge 1: Middle level teacher candidates understand the variety of family structures.

No matter how we define family, involving those closest to our students in the life of the school, and specifically in their students' schoolwork and relationships at school, has a positive impact on learning. "Positive family dynamics have been deemed a vital ingredient in the academic success of middle level students. The benefits of parental involvement on student achievement and attitude toward school have been documented" (VanHoose & Legrand, 2000, p. 32).

STANDARD 6

Knowledge 9: Middle level teacher candidates understand the roles of family and community members in improving the education of all young adolescents.

Performance 1: Middle level teacher candidates establish respectful and productive relationships with family and community members that maximize student learning and well-being.

● Involvement Decreases

A discouraging fact of life in most middle schools is decreasing family involvement compared with elementary schools (Downs, 2001). Most middle schools experience sharp decreases in family involvement between grades 6 and 8. Let's face it. How often do you hear someone say, "Gee, I wish I were 13 again." Few of us have fond memories of our own self-image and we would probably not wish to be back in a junior high/middle school setting as students.

Jackson and Davis, the authors of *Turning Points 2000*, report that families "check out" as their children progress to and through middle school. They tell us that many families genuinely believe that their involvement should decrease to promote independence. Another reason for withdrawal of involvement stems from many young adolescents' negative view of their families being part of their school experiences, even their lives in general. Families and teachers can tell humorous, and not so humorous, stories of students ignoring family members who attempt involvement. After a couple of "funny" instances, families decide to back off and give their students the space they appear to want.

A very real reason many families decrease involvement is academic intimidation (L'Esperance & Gabbard, 2001). When schoolwork becomes too difficult for family members, they shy away from school. Perhaps they dropped out before high school graduation or were never successful academically. Immigrant families often experience intimidation due to language barriers. English language learners are increasing in numbers, and finding ways to involve their families is becoming a dilemma of growing magnitude. Along with language barriers, cultural differences can create misunderstandings and reluctance. Some immigrant families don't realize that direct contact with schools and teachers is desirable, and that asking questions and giving input with regard to teaching and learning are sure to improve the process. Understanding reticent families and approaching them in sensitive and appropriate ways about a variety of opportunities for their involvement will benefit all of us.

Young Adolescent Diversity

Getting to Know Families

A commitment to involving families means making efforts to get to know them. Inviting families to get involved needs to be guided not only by what schools have to offer them, but what they have to offer schools. Matching potential family contributions to school needs, and then being sensitive to what families expect of schools will make for positive and productive relationships.

STANDARD 6

Disposition 1: Middle level teacher candidates respect all young adolescents and their families.

There are many questions we can ask families in order to find out what they want and expect from us, as well as what they have to offer the home-school partnership. A questionnaire might be used in a before-school contact. This is an ideal initiative for teams. Each teacher takes responsibility for a homeroom or advisory group. The questionnaire can be sent with a letter of welcome. If possible, a stamped, self-addressed envelope is a good idea to increase the probability of a high rate of return. As an alternative, send the questionnaire home with students in a packet of materials to be signed and returned. A contest to see which homeroom or advisory group has the highest return rate may help get information back from a large percentage of students. Figure 12.2 shows a sample form to send home. If you communicate electronically with families, e-mail is an excellent option.

Familiarizing Families with Middle School

If families understand middle grades philosophy with its student-centered focus on developmental appropriateness, their concerns may be at least partially allayed. A study reported in 2001 found that "Parents reporting high familiarity with middle level practices were more likely to report positive attitudes and engagement at their child's school . . ." (Mulhall, Mertens, & Flowers, 2001, p. 60). The study also showed that middle level practices are a mystery to the majority of parents. Table 12.1 shows the results of a survey of 20,584 parents with students in 131 Arkansas, Louisiana, and Mississippi schools at various stages of middle school implementation. From the chart you can see that none of the practices reached the "very familiar" status with even one quarter of the parents. In fact, only cooperative learning made the "somewhat familiar" or "very familiar" status with half, and cooperative learning is a strategy used in elementary schools as well as middle schools.

We are aware of how important each of the six survey practices in Table 12.1 are to middle level philosophy. If families are unfamiliar with what we do all day with their children, then their concerns are understandable. As we will discuss later in the chapter, we are our own best public relations specialists. If familiarity with middle level practices equates to more positive attitudes and increased family participation, then public relations specialists we need to be!

FIGURE 12.2   Sample questions for getting to know families

1. Who lives in your household?
   Name _____ Age _____ Relationship to student _____

2. What do you think your student's greatest strengths are?

3. What is your goal for your student during this school year?

4. Are there certain concerns, home situations, or medical problems we should be aware of in order to work more effectively with your student?

5. What activities does your student enjoy?

6. What one subject area do you think your student will struggle most with this year?

7. What does your student do after school? Is someone home when he/she arrives? Does he/she have regular activities?

8. Would your student benefit from regular after school sessions designed to help with homework? Would transportation be needed to take him/her home?

9. One of our team goals is to expand opportunities for our students to explore many interests. What special interest do you have that you would share with us this year (e.g., occupation, hobby, talent, etc.)?

10. Because we believe that education is a home-school partnership, we ask that you participate in ways in which you are comfortable. Here are some possibilities.
    Please check ways you would like to be involved occasionally.

    bake for events _____   field trip chaperone _____

    collect project supplies _____   homeroom parent _____

    tutor after school _____   big brother/sister program _____

    organize fundraisers _____   field day volunteer _____

    assist in classroom _____   materials preparation _____

    "phone tree" leader _____   career day speaker _____

    How would you prefer we communicate with you?

    mail _____   address: _____

    e-mail _____   address: _____

    phone _____   number: _____ best times: _____

    notes sent with student_____   addressed to: _____

Communicating the value of interdisciplinary teaming, advisory, integrated lessons, heterogeneous grouping, exploratory, and cooperative learning is an ongoing process. These practices, after all, permeate what we do. It's important to show how the practices are interrelated and, to a great extent, interdependent.

TABLE 12.1   Parents' familiarity with middle level practices

Middle Level Practices	Familiarity with Middle Level Practices (% responding)			
	Not at all familiar	*A little familiar*	*Somewhat familiar*	*Very familiar*
Interdisciplinary teaming	42	17	20	20
Advisory programs	52	18	17	13
Integrated lessons	43	22	21	14
Heterogeneous grouping	41	20	21	18
Exploratory	29	24	27	20
Cooperative learning	24	24	28	24

Source: From "How Familiar Are Parents with Middle Level Practices?" by P. F. Mulhall, S. B. Mertens, and N. Flowers, 2001, *Middle School Journal, 33*(2): p. 58. Copyright 2001 by National Middle School Association. Reprinted with permission from National Middle School Association.

● Communication

Getting to know families and familiarizing them with middle school philosophy and practices happens through effective communication. Ongoing communication with families enlists them as partners as long as the communication includes listening as well as giving information by both families and teachers.

STANDARD 6

Knowledge 4: Middle level teacher candidates know how to communicate effectively with family and community members.

Disposition 7: Middle level teacher candidates realize and value the importance of communicating effectively with family and community members.

School and home communication = Face-to-face + Telephone + Written + Electronic

Some communication vehicles are schoolwide such as open house and report cards. Others are initiated by teams and individual teachers. Most communication between home and school is either face-to-face, by telephone, in writing, or accomplished electronically.

A very real barrier to school–home communication may be language. The English language learners in your classroom will likely live in homes where English is not spoken fluently, nor read with comprehension. In fact, many of your students who speak adequate English in your classroom may have families who speak little or no English at home. You need to know this. Many schools have translators available,

Even though focus student Darma speaks English fluently, his parents have difficulty at times with school communications.

Young Adolescent Diversity

perhaps even a teacher on staff. Talk with your principal and other teachers about how best to communicate with families if there are language barriers. Be very aware of this challenge, regardless of the means of communication you choose.

Face-to-Face   Most middle schools have an open house at the beginning of the school year that many call *back-to-school night*. Typically, a family is given their student's schedule that they follow through each of the periods, which are shortened to 10 to 15 minutes. This allows them to meet all of their student's teachers and get a feel for the paths the student walks each day. Back-to-school night provides a wonderful opportunity to make a positive first impression on families. Here are some guidelines for success.

- Make your room as neat and attractive as possible. Even though it's the beginning of the year, be sure you already have some student work displayed.
- Greet families at the door with a smile and firm handshake.
- Give families a handout that may include your background, a brief statement about the importance of your subject area, a list of needed materials/supplies, classroom management policies, grading policies, etc.
- Pass around a sign-in sheet asking for student name and family member name(s), as well as how they prefer to communicate.
- Prepare to speak for about 5 minutes and then welcome questions. It is preferable that this brief speech be planned. Experienced teachers can give you ideas about questions your students' families will typically ask.
- Offer a clipboard on which families can request individual conferences. Back-to-school night is not the time to discuss individual students.
- Thank families for attending and express the need and desire for their participation throughout the year.

Family–Teacher (Parent–Teacher) Conference   A critically important face-to-face communication opportunity that seldom receives more than a mention in preservice education is the *family–teacher (parent–teacher) conference*. Often the skills and tactics for these potentially stressful "little talks" are learned on the job through trial and error. Most schools have organized times when families are invited to sign up for 15- to 30-minute conference times with either individual teachers or teams of teachers. Some schools have half days or evenings when teachers are available to talk with families. These conferences may be for exchange of information with mostly positive, affirming dialogue, or they may entail the necessity of corrective plans dealing with academics or behavior. Some schools designate a day following report card distribution when families are invited to the school. Three to four opportunities may be scheduled for conferences of this nature each school year. Up-to-date student folders with sample work and any notes about the student should be readily available along with an accurate and complete list of assignments and grades.

myeducationlab

Go to the Assignments and Activities section of **Topic #15: Collaborating with Colleagues and Families** in the MyEducation-Lab for your course and complete the activity entitled "Preparing for the Conference."

Conferences that are initiated for specific reasons require another level of preparation. If you are conferencing as an individual teacher, you will want to have the same resources listed in the previous paragraph. You will also want to make some notes to organize the information you want to convey as well as the questions you want to ask. Some tentative action plan ideas are helpful. If you are conferencing as a team, each teacher needs to be ready, with one of you leading the conference. This person is responsible for stating the main purpose of the conference, keeping the discussion focused, and summarizing the agreed-upon strategies to be implemented. Another teacher needs to take notes during the conference and complete a form similar to the one in Figure 12.3. Make sure at least one teacher can open the conference on a positive note to help put the family more at ease. You can see how efficient a team conference can be. As an individual teacher conferencing with a family, the whole responsibility falls on you. You still must document the conference fully and file your conference form.

STANDARD 6

NMSA

Performance 7: Middle level teacher candidates demonstrate the ability to participate in parent conferences.

Family conferences may be initiated either by teachers or by families because of specific concerns. These may occur anytime during the year. I strongly recommend that teams of teachers meet with families. I have seen the positive dynamics, the cohesive solutions, and the growth of empathy that is possible when a group of adults share information and formulate proactive strategies to benefit an individual student. Here's a fairly common scenario.

Maurice's grades are slipping and it's only the sixth week of school. He has been referred to the office several times for behavior problems. He became very angry in

---

FIGURE 12.3   **Sample family conference form**

Student name _____ Date _____

Family attending   _____
                    _____

Teachers attending _____
                    _____

Others   _____
                    _____

Notes: (continue on back as needed)

Summary of concerns:

Plan of action:

Follow-up communication plan:

---

fourth block yesterday and loudly called an eighth grade girl a bitch during social studies. He was sent to the Behavior Improvement Room for the rest of the day and his mom was called. She agreed to meet with Maurice's team of teachers at 7:30 the next day. The team got together after school the day before the conference to talk about Maurice. They discovered, as almost always happens, that one or more teachers have not seen the dramatic grade drop, nor do they regularly see any misbehavior.

When the conference begins, the teachers who are having relatively more success with Maurice speak first and give the positive side. Then a designated teacher explains the problems the other teachers are observing as well as the office referrals and BIR incidents. Teachers express their desire for Maurice to succeed and ask his mom to talk about anything she has observed, to ask questions, to give insights, etc. The conversation then becomes one about planning ways to help Maurice find both academic and behavioral success.

The resulting value of the whole team and the family meeting together depends in large measure on the attitude and demeanor of the teachers. There is a very real chance that Maurice's mom could have been intimidated and overwhelmed by four or five teachers sitting in desks where they are very comfortable and confident. Friendliness and the offer of coffee or a soft drink go a long way toward making the conference one of honest, sincere communication. Bottom line is that we all have the same goal—Maurice's success. Say it often, and mean it.

Room arrangement is important for conferences. A circle of chairs works best. Using all student desks will prove embarrassing. Provide at least two sturdy, armless chairs so that all sizes of family members and teachers can be seated comfortably. Teachers should never sit behind a teacher desk with family members on the other side.

Another consideration is our choice of words. We are the experts in education, but most families are the experts on their students. We would not expect them to spout adolescent development theory, but rather to use straightforward language to convey their concerns and descriptions of circumstances. So should we. Education jargon should be eliminated as much as possible. For instance, saying "Jennifer sometimes doesn't respond to what pedagogical research tells us is most aligned to the content" is journal talk, not family talk. Instead, try, "Jennifer doesn't seem to understand what we're talking about in class. I need your help to find ways of teaching that will help her 'get it.'"

Always have at least two positive things to say about a student with whose family you are meeting. This allows you to employ what teachers sometimes call the "sandwich formula." You place negative slices between layers of positive comments at the beginning and end of the conference. The "sandwich" will be much more palatable than a steady diet of negative information!

"Sandwich" conference = Positive comments + Negative concerns + Positive comments

There is an ongoing debate about the value of a team policy that calls for students to, almost without exception, be present for conferences. I've been on teams where the majority insisted that students attend with their families, and I've been on teams with the opposite philosophy. I see the benefit of both positions and have concluded over the years that it's a good idea to make student attendance dependent on individual circumstances. It's true that we want students to learn and practice responsibility, and participating in a family conference allows all parties to hear the same things at the same time while actively involving the student in the specified improvement plan. However, there are times when families may have information to share with teachers that they prefer not to discuss in front of their students. There are also cultural considerations. Some families may

Young Adolescent Diversity

abide by the "seen but not heard" philosophy of childhood. I recommend that families be asked their preference and that teams abide by that preference. During the adult-only conference a time can be set for the group to meet with the student to convey specific concerns and/or praise or to talk about the improvement plan.

Student-Led Conferences   Growing in popularity for a wide array of reasons, *student-led conferences* have the potential to bring more families into the teaching-learning process. In *Classroom Connections*, an NMSA publication, student-led conferences are defined as events "in which parents and students sit down and talk about one of the most important aspects in their life—school. The student is not only the focal point of the conversation, they are the leader of the conference" (Berckemeyer, 2001, p. 1). Schools implementing this innovative way of informing families of student progress and goals report very favorable results. It is clear that the most vital elements of a student-led conference are the student and the family. The teacher's role is one of consultation and encouragement.

> Student-led conferences = Student responsibility + Student analysis of achievement + Student/parent communication

Here are some reasons for having student-led conferences.

- Student ownership of the quality of academic work
- Provision for student-family interactions based on student effort and accomplishment
- Focal point that is academic rather than behavioral
- Process of organizing portfolio that gives student a sense of "wholeness" and connectedness of work
- Student acquisition and practice of communication skills
- Student goal-setting for academic progress
- Greater family participation (families usually show up in larger numbers when their students are involved)

Students need guidance as they begin to prepare for student-led conferences. Students should be asked to outline, if not script, what they will say to their families. If time permits, they benefit from practicing with peers. It's a great idea to choose a student to work with privately on his presentation. Then role-play as the family member of the student to demonstrate what a conference might look and sound like. Few strategies teach more efficiently and effectively than modeling. This is also an ideal time for students to learn communication skills, as well as basic manners. Dressing appropriately, opening doors for families, and introducing families to teachers are appropriate life skills for conferences. Speaking clearly, asking for and answering questions, and communicating organized points are skills that can benefit students for a lifetime.

Families also need to be prepared for the student-led conference. Sending a letter home informing parents about what to expect in a student-led conference is advisable.

We know how important it is to evaluate new or different efforts from several perspectives. Figure 12.4 contains samples of evaluations that can be completed by families and students.

FIGURE 12.4 Student-led conference evaluations

Student Evaluation

1. What was the best thing about your family conference?

_____

_____

2. What would you change about the conference?

_____

_____

3. Were your family's reactions what you expected? Explain.

_____

_____

4. How will you prepare for the next conference?

_____

_____

Family Evaluation

Thank you for joining us today for your student-led conference. Please take a minute to give us some feedback about your experience by circling the response closest to your opinion.

1. The student-led conference was
   - very worthwhile
   - worthwhile
   - not worthwhile
2. The time we spent in conferencing was
   - too short
   - the right amount
   - too long
3. The amount and nature of what our student presented was
   - revealing and informative
   - adequate, but still leaves questions
   - inadequate
4. Access to team teachers before, during, and after our conference was
   - satisfactory
   - unsatisfactory

If you have comments you would like to share with us, please write them below or call us. Thank you for participating in this important event with us!

Telephone Communication   After a face-to-face conversation, the next most personal communication is a telephone call. That dreaded "call from the teacher" has given this form of communication a bad rap. However, calls can and should be made for positive reasons as well as for problem situations.

Reaching families by phone during the day can be difficult and the proliferation of message services makes our phone etiquette important. If you are suddenly faced with a recorded message, never just hang up. With caller ID, the family will know someone from school called. If you are calling with a student compliment, you may want to cheerfully deliver the positive message and say that if the family would like to hear more good things they can feel free to reach you during your planning period. Be sure you are readily available if the family member returns the call during the times you specify. If the subject is less than positive, always let them know that the student is fine, but that there is a matter you'd like to discuss at their convenience. Ask the family to call you the following day during your planning period or to leave a message in the office, giving a time and number where they can be reached later in the day. If the situation warrants a more immediate response or definitely requires a conference, your message should indicate the appropriate sense of urgency and let the family know you will keep trying to reach them in the evening if you or the office hasn't heard back by the end of the school day.

If you call a family and discover that the phone number has changed or the phone has been disconnected, let your administrators know immediately. They will follow up to get the most recent information.

Written Communication   Probably the most frequently used form of communication between school and family is the written word. Often it's one-way communication and, if we rely on students to deliver the message, it's likely to be "no-way" communication. Written communication is by far the easiest way to relay information. Because it seems easy, it often has a tendency to become sloppy. I can't overemphasize the need to proofread everything that is sent to families, or to the public in general. We are educators, and we are expected to be educated. Our communication should show it. Educational jargon and obscure vocabulary are neither necessary nor desirable. Plain, to the point, informative writing is called for—with no grammatical or spelling errors.

Written communication can take many forms: progress reports, report card comments, general school information typically sent in the beginning of the year, announcements of meetings/events, letters about school picture day, fund raising information—the list is long. Your team will send a welcome letter with multiple bits of information; you'll send your own letter about your subject area, expectations, grading, and behavior policies; and your team may opt to send home periodic newsletters featuring student activities, outlining projects, recognizing accomplishments, and announcing future events.

Sending individual notes that are less than positive home with students and expecting them to be promptly delivered is unrealistic. If you have problem-oriented subjects to convey, better use the telephone or the post office. On the other hand, positive and complimentary notes almost always end up under a refrigerator magnet. The yearlong benefits of occasional "happy notes" cannot be overstated. Family appreciation and support will likely be yours for just a few minutes of your time in recognizing a positive trait or action. All students have them. It may not be for outstanding academic progress, but all young adolescents have something to their credit that can be praised. Find that something and be proactive about developing family relationships.

Electronic Communication   In *Meet Me in the Middle,* Rick Wormeli (2001) discusses the use of online postings to communicate with families. He posts class/team announcements, assignments, and due dates. He reports that close to 100% of his students do their homework because everyone knows the expectations. Using free sites such as schoolnotes.com and blackboard.com to electronically communicate with home may prove very successful in some communities. In others, where families either do not have Internet access or don't have enough time or concern to use it, only a small percentage of your students may benefit.

E-mail is another option to investigate. For families who work in places with computer access and those who habitually check their e-mail, this is a time efficient, and usually "kid proof," way to communicate.

Why We Hesitate to Communicate   It's one thing to say school-home communication is important, or hear it said in a teacher workshop, and quite another to regularly practice communication in varied formats. Why? Let's take a minute to consider this.

New teachers often say that the thought of talking to families is terrifying. And why shouldn't it be? Many of the parents of middle grades students are old enough to be the parents of some new teachers. Talking with them with confidence and authority takes practice and time. Listening as experienced teachers communicate with families is a great way to pick up tips and phrases, and a sense of composure. However, actually talking with parents is the only way to acquire the skill. It gets easier with time, but the butterflies in the stomach will probably never stop fluttering entirely. It's one of those challenges of teaching that we had better not avoid, because avoidance will come back to haunt us sooner rather than later.

Time constraints often pose problems. There are only so many hours in a day and, yes, we do have lives—hopefully rich, full ones—outside the classroom. In terms of positive communication, set some goals. I found it very reasonable to make five "happy calls" a week along with sending at least five "happy notes" home. These are nonconfrontational, even fun, communications that take surprisingly little time, but often go undone solely for lack of resolve.

Letting problems fester because we are either too nervous or too short on time to communicate with families is detrimental to the student and the learning environment in our classrooms. Lack of academic progress needs to be addressed early in order to be remediated, or at least improved, with family help. Although families should keep a close watch on student progress, and many do try, weaker students rapidly become experts in communicating only good news about school while concealing the less positive aspects of their actual performance. Calling home the week before the end of a grading period is not using communication effectively. It's very frustrating for families to realize that it's almost too late to have any real effect. When behavioral problems are allowed to fester because of our reluctance to communicate, not only will the student's behavior problem escalate, but chances are other students will be affected and our efficacy will be diminished.

In some cases, families may be seen as part of the problem rather than partners in seeking solutions. This view may or may not always be justified. Jumping to the conclusion that families contribute to whatever the problem may be is dangerous. Every option of involving families in solution paths should be explored and utilized.

There are experienced teachers who, in some situations, have become jaded when it comes to encouraging family involvement. They live with a history of unsuccessful attempts to positively involve families in the education of young adolescents. A succession of ignored attempts, and even blatant refusals to work toward solutions, have colored their view of the value, or even the feasibility, of families being part of the process. They may be justified in their skepticism, but you may hold the key to reaching families by merit of tenacity, untried strategies, or the strength of your personality. While I generally hesitate to advise new teachers to pay little heed to experienced teachers, in this case my hope is that you will consistently communicate with families, even those with reputations of reticence, and extend multiple invitations for them to participate in their students' education.

● Opportunities for Involvement

So far we've explored face-to-face, telephone, written, and electronic avenues of communication that involve families in the school life of our students. The involvement already discussed centers on individual student progress. Beyond this focus is a whole world of possibilities for families to volunteer time and energy. Rarely do families of middle schoolers eagerly approach the school and ask to be part of the activities. It is usually up to us to initiate and organize opportunities. The form in Figure 12.2 asks families to volunteer for a number of service needs. If a family member checks an area, by all means find a way to invite him to participate in that area at some point during the year.

Families have a wealth of knowledge, experiences, talents, hobbies, and special skills that can be used to enrich the lives of the students on your team. You'll probably never know the extent of the possibilities until you ask. A simple form such as the one in Figure 12.5 may be used.

It's helpful to compile and organize responses as a team. There will be "natural fits" that can be easily incorporated into the planned curriculum. If the topic of driving an 18-wheeler doesn't leap out as a curricular bright spot, it may fit nicely into an afternoon "Buffet of Exploration" where students sign up to attend four 20-minute sessions according to their interests. Clogging, fly tying, kite building, a day in the life of a CPA, baseball card collecting—what an interesting assortment you're likely to find. I've found that families greatly appreciate an acknowledgment when they are open enough to say "Here's what I do and I'm willing to share it with the kids."

FIGURE 12.5   Family interests survey

Because we strongly believe that middle school is an ideal time for students to explore and discover their own interests and talents, we'd like to invite you to share yours with us. From time to time we organize opportunities for family members to tell about and/or demonstrate what they do professionally or how they enjoy their leisure/hobby time. Your special skills and training may fit perfectly into an area of study or be appropriate for a "Buffet of Exploration" involving many adults and their areas of expertise. Sound like fun? You bet! We'd love to hear from you.

Name _____

Student _____

I would like to share my interest in

_____

_____

You may contact me at (phone or e-mail)

_____

Thanks for your time. You are our partners in learning here at Lincoln Middle School!

A postcard, telephone call, or e-mail note will complete the communication loop and let you express your appreciation.

Here are some more volunteer opportunities to offer families. Those who are not comfortable in the spotlight of a career day or an afternoon of interest sharing may, if asked, be willing and often pleased to help out in other ways.

- Participating in school "spruce up" days including grounds work, cleanup, painting, fixing, etc.
- Translating to help language minority families communicate with teachers and school
- Participating in service learning ventures
- Sponsoring clubs and special events
- Performing clerical duties related to a special event
- Setting up and monitoring "phone tree" communication
- Assisting in the school office or library

Family volunteers should be treated with respect and courtesy. They should not have to wonder what to do or how to do it. Specific directions and time frames provide the structure to keep everyone in a comfort zone. Always acknowledge the value of volunteerism in whatever ways you can. A handshake with a sincere thank you is the minimum. A note, a call, or a listing of volunteers in a newsletter will help ensure repeaters.

Community Involvement

The word **community** to this point has been used to describe the goal for our classroom, team, grade level, and even our entire school. In Chapter 4 we discussed the creation of a community of learners, building on Sergiovanni's (1996) definition that says communities share ideas and ideals to the point of going "from a collection of 'I's to a collective 'we'" (p. 48). However, some clarification is necessary for this section. When I speak of community here, I simply mean people who live in the same geographical area, "a collection of 'I's."

STANDARD 6

Knowledge 5: Middle level teacher candidates understand that middle level schools are organizations within a larger community context.

Our schools function within communities of people of all ages who inevitably have different lifestyles. Finding ways to draw them into the teaching-learning cycle of our middle schools is a challenge worth pursuing. The community is involved with public education in one way, like it or not, and that is financial. The federal government funds about 6% of public education costs, while state and local taxes share close to equally, in most cases, the remaining 94%. With or without children of school age, and whether they approve or disapprove of school board decisions, are bothered by the noise of P.E. classes on the field, or comforted by the enthusiasm of youth, the public still funds the overwhelming portion of public education. Our schools run the gamut from sources of pride for the community to sources of embarrassment. Pride and embarrassment, and everything in between, stem from perceptions of what we do and the results of our efforts. Sometimes the perceptions are based on accurate information, but many times they are not. If a school is perceived negatively, getting the positive word out when things are going well is difficult, but doable.

Communities Matter

I have known many young adolescents over whom I wish only our school teams had influence. These are the kids who have to grow up way too early in an attempt to cope with the cards of life they have been dealt. They're the ones for whom we may say, "If I only had the money to run a great big happy home for dozens of kids, this one I could help." No matter how physically, emotionally, and academically safe we make our learning environment, when the school is locked up for the evening, our kids go out into the community and away from our protection and influence. Jackson and Davis (2000) put it this way:

> It doesn't take a rocket scientist to realize that the middle grades school experience is only one of a myriad of influences on the trajectory of an adolescent's development. What happens to young people within their families, neighborhoods, peer groups, religious institutions, out-of-school programs and a wide range of formal and informal relationships and settings can easily have as much or more impact on how young people "turn out" as the middle grades school (p. 209).

Young Adolescent Diversity

Some communities have qualities that enhance, or at least don't appear to hinder, our teaching-learning efforts. They offer physical comfort and relative safety, family participation, recreational and cultural options, and at least give lip service to the value of education. What generally distinguishes these communities from those in the previous paragraph? You guessed it—socioeconomic status. Statistics will bear this out, but just because it seems to be so doesn't mean it can't be changed. A growing number of communities are refusing to rest on excuses for failure and are committing to what the title of this chapter states—They Are All Our Children. The school, the children, and the community are, for better or worse, inextricably linked. We can't expect 10- to 15- year-olds to lead the way and, without passionate leadership, communities by themselves seldom bring about school (and thereby student) reform. The school is in a position to make a difference for 7 to 10 hours a day. In partnership, the community and the school can grow together in claiming all the children as their own.

A Success Story

The staff of Guilford Middle School in Greensboro, North Carolina, determined to involve students in low-income settings. A comprehensive program called "Expanding Horizons" was initiated. Families and others interested in the well-being of the students at Guilford Middle School formed a resident association. Community participants, with the support and guidance of the school staff, established the following goals:

1. Promote academic success and greater interest in school by students through afternoon assistance and tutoring.
2. Provide materials and programs to promote positive decision-making.
3. Provide opportunities for success that would contribute to personal growth, increased self-esteem, and a positive self-concept.
4. Provide positive role models in the program through local organizations and colleges.
5. Coordinate information between the middle school, community, and agencies involved in the outreach program.
6. Initiate fundraising activities to establish an ongoing media resource center in the community center to be used for tutoring, homework, and self-improvement.

7. Use community resources to foster the development of a safe and orderly environment for the resident families.

8. Increase cultural awareness among young people by facilitating attendance at activities in the larger community and beyond (p. 34).

Expanding Horizons has experienced success in reaching its comprehensive goals due in part to the willingness of educators to spend the time and energy needed to reach out to their community. At the same time, it took courage for families and community members to join and sustain the efforts (VanHoose & Legrand, 2000).

> Successful community involvement = Inform + Invite + Coordinate + Appreciate

This success story speaks of ownership and a realization that they are all our children. The community and school acknowledge a shared responsibility for all children, clearly demonstrating the value, and the necessity, of collaboration among schools, families, and communities.

● Afterschool Programs

"The mere fact of being without supervision seems to have malignant effects on young adolescents, and all too many children find themselves home alone after school every day" (Jackson & Davis, 2000, p. 213). In *Turning Points 2000,* a research project is reported to have found significant differences in levels of self-esteem, behavior problems, depression, and academic success of "latchkey" young adolescents compared with students who were with or around adults after school in a home setting or organized program. Afterschool programs not only enhance students socially and cognitively, but they also prevent unhealthy encounters and behaviors.

Some afterschool programs are exclusively established and staffed by school personnel. However, the majority are the result of coalitions among community groups and schools. Sponsors of these programs may include Boys and Girls Clubs, 4-H, YMCA, YWCA, churches, youth service organizations, chambers of commerce, and parent organizations. Effective programs aim to provide three components: positive relationships between adults and young adolescents, enriching activities, and a safe place to be. Often the most successful programs have found a way to link and balance recreational and academic content. "After-school programs should not primarily be 'more school, after school,' but rather an opportunity to learn for the sheer joy of learning" (Jackson & Davis, 2000, p. 215).

● Business Partners

Some schools have formed partnerships with local businesses. *Business partners* support the school in whatever fashion suits their expertise. For instance, a pizza restaurant may occasionally donate pizzas for some special student recognition or event. An industry may offer field trip tours to explain how a business operates. A dry cleaning business might clean school curtains or band uniforms. A catering business might contribute goodies to a back-to-school gathering. And of course cash donations are seldom refused! Besides tangible contributions, employees may volunteer their time to tutor or mentor individuals and/or be part of an afterschool program. Recognition is vitally important. The school should publicize the fact that a particular business has agreed to be a partner in education through newsletters and signs in and around the school. Teachers and staff should always welcome volunteers and be overtly appreciative of those willing to partner with us.

What We Can Do

To accomplish widespread community initiatives, the involvement of entire schools or school districts is required. However, there are ways that we, as individual teachers and teams, can promote positive perceptions and relationships within the community. Here are 10 categories to consider.

1. *Be informed.* Information is power. There's a lot to understand about public education. As the adults closest to the "action," we should not only know what's going on, but also be aware of the influences that determine the who, what, when, and where of education locally, statewide, and nationally.

2. *Be positive public relations agents.* To people who do not have students in school or are not at all involved in schooling, we **are** the school. We may provide the only portrayal of education some people see, aside from an occasional news story, and these are often negative. The overriding image of what we do in schools should be positively portrayed.

3. *Acknowledge problems, suggest solutions.* If we are informed, and if we determine to be positive public relations agents, we can and should acknowledge problems in a forum that allows for more than cursory discussion. It is also our responsibility to seek solutions and offer them publicly. If there are glaring achievement gaps at your school, you should admit to it and be able to facilitate discussions within the community about solution paths.

4. *Don't overemphasize the need for funding.* You probably have heard community members make a blanket statement similar to "Throwing money at schools won't fix anything." No, blindly throwing money won't do much for us. However, additional funding could make huge differences in upgraded facilities, salaries to attract the best and the brightest to our profession, ongoing professional development opportunities, fully funded afterschool programs available to all students, appropriate technology for all schools, and more. An adequately funded and well-managed budget **will** make a difference. When we propose greater funding, let's be able to back up the request with how it will make a difference.

5. *Use the media proactively.* The influence of television and newspapers is tremendous. Part of being informed involves watching news reports and reading articles about education. If you are infuriated by negative publicity to the exclusion of what's happening that's positive, do something about it. Call the media about positive events, and write intelligent letters to the editor while encouraging students to do the same.

6. *Spotlight students.* Search for ways to get student work in front of the community. From artwork in galleries to ideas on public issues, our students are so very capable of contributing to the community good.

7. *Invite the community in.* When the community feels welcome and has positive reasons to walk through the school doors, they are likely to feel a sense of identification and ownership.

8. *Actively participate in the community.* We can be positive ambassadors for our schools in the community by being actively involved in things that interest us, including civic, religious, service, and social groups. The wider our sphere of influence, the more opportunities we have to promote community awareness and involvement in our schools.

9. *Promote community service.* We have discussed the impact service learning has on our students. Let's not underestimate the impact of service learning on the community. Not only do the deeds involved make a difference, but the community perception of our students can be greatly enhanced when they know about or see firsthand the services our students perform.

10. *Know about community resources.* There are times when it is beneficial to extend our classrooms into the community to take advantage of the wealth of knowledge and facilities available. In addition, community resources provide family counseling, medical assistance, legal advocacy, and a tremendous number of services to assist students and their families. We may not know the extent of these services, but we should be able to point those who trust us in the right direction so that they can take advantage of community resources.

STANDARD 6

Knowledge 6: Middle level teacher candidates understand the relationships between schools and community organizations.

Knowledge 7: Middle level teacher candidates know about the resources available within communities that can support students, teachers, and schools.

Disposition 3: Middle level teacher candidates value the variety of resources available in communities.

Disposition 4: Middle level teacher candidates are committed to helping family members become aware of how and where to receive assistance when needed.

Disposition 8: Middle level teacher candidates accept the responsibility of working with family and community members to increase student welfare and learning.

Performance 4: Middle level teacher candidates identify and use community resources to foster student learning.

Performance 5: Middle level teacher candidates participate in activities designed to enhance educational experiences that transcend the school campus.

Transitions

When considering shared responsibility for all our children, we realize that the responsibility extends to the *transitions* of students who are about to enter middle school and those who are completing their middle school years. "The transitions from elementary to middle school and from middle to high school have the elements of many adolescents' worst social nightmares—not knowing anyone, being ignored by peers, getting lost, and confronting demanding classes and teachers" (Allen, 2001, p. 1). Understanding young adolescent development issues prompts us to want to do everything we can to make the "into and out of" middle school transitions as smooth and painless as possible.

Entering Middle School

The fear of the unknown can be daunting for 10- and 11-year-olds. They have been in an elementary setting for years and are typically comfortable with how things work. In fact, they are the "big kids." Now it's time to go to middle school—usually a larger, more adultlike facility; as many as seven teachers and classes a day; multiple books and supplies to be put in and taken out of lockers; much older and more mature eighth graders to both fear and avoid; new kids in classes from other elementary schools—so many unknowns.

Articulation between the upper grade elementary teachers, typically fifth grade, and the lower grade middle school teachers, typically sixth grade, is important. To ease the transition to middle school, a coalition of these key people makes sense. "Recognizing the need and choosing to make a difference in easing the transition is the first step. This conscious choice on the part of principals, teachers, counselors, and parents, coupled with commitment, precedes the formation of a plan" (Powell, 2000, p. 24).

Here are some strategies to help ease the transition into middle school.

1. Sixth grade teachers, counselors, and the middle school principal visit elementary schools to talk with fifth graders and answer their questions.

2. Sixth grade students visit elementary schools to talk about "kid stuff," including the things they may remember worrying about a year earlier. It's very encouraging to hear survival stories.

3. Make a video of the middle school to be shown to fifth graders. I have organized several of these, with students carrying the camera and narrating the tour. It's great fun for the kids who make the video and equally so for the ones who watch. The middle schooler's sense of humor shines through, putting the rising sixth graders more at ease.

4. Offer tours of the middle school for fifth graders to take as a group. They have the security of their buddies with them as they walk around the new environment, listen in on classes, meet teachers and students, and see where they will enjoy the next 3 years. Include a "walk through" of a typical

schedule and a demonstration of how to open and secure lockers. If possible, let the fifth graders try opening a locker, preferably with success. As silly as it may seem to us, there is an inordinate amount of fear linked to lockers, both how to use them appropriately and how to avoid being stuffed into one.

5. Send information to families and students about class scheduling, team assignments, books and supplies, school hours, transportation, and dates of special open houses only for rising sixth graders and families. This information might also be published in the local newspaper.

Figure 12.6 is a survey you may want to give the first week of 6th grade to gauge the fears of the middle school "newbies."

● Moving On

There is an abundance of research that points to 9th grade as the year of unprecedented absenteeism, high academic failure, and excessively high student dropout rates. Communities and high schools are recognizing the dire need to better care for our students as they move from middle school to high school. Some high schools have 9th grade academies where 9th graders are set apart from the rest of the high school. They have their own administrators and elements that help them create their own identity, like separate facilities for classes and lunch. Continuing middle school practices into 9th grade such as teaming to whatever degree possible is advisable. If 8th graders know they will be eased into high school, their fears can be at least partially allayed. Remember that transition is a process, not an event.

Figure 12.7 is a survey you may want to give during the last month of 8th grade to gauge the fears of young adolescents as they transition to high school.

● Our Nine Students

myeducationlab

To hear Susan Ryder, the 2007 Colorado Teacher of the Year, tell us how she encourages students to realize that they are the authors of their own stories, go to the Teacher Talk section of **Topic #4: Motivation** in the MyEducationLab for your course.

There is one overriding theme in this book that by now should be second nature in your thoughts about teaching. The message is that the diversity of background, ability, motivation, and life circumstances of our students must be considered in everything we do in and out of our classrooms. Middle school may be the last, best hope of incorporating enough differentiation to reach our students in ways that will bring out their potential and give them hope and confidence for the future.

Young Adolescent Diversity

We have met 9 young adolescents and followed them from 6th grade to 8th grade. Take a last look at our 9 students as they approach high school where the complexity of the program, the size of the institution, and the potential for "slipping through the cracks" may make a strong middle school foundation even more important.

FIGURE 12.6   What worries me about going to middle school

WHAT WORRIES ME ABOUT GOING TO MIDDLE SCHOOL

Name: _____

Put an X in the box that best describes your level of concern.	Not Worried at All	A Little Worried	Pretty Worried	Very Worried
Moving from class to class				
Getting lost				
Finding the bathroom				
Making new friends				
Work will be hard				
Changing in front of others in PE				
Locking and unlocking my locker				
Who to sit with in the cafeteria				
Learning new rules and routines				
School is bigger				
Older kids in the hallway				
Being made fun of				
Looking different from other kids				
Being bullied				

Other things that worry me about going to middle school:

Source: From *Wayside Teaching: Connecting With Students to Support Learning* (p. 151), by S. D. Powell, 2010, Thousand Oaks, CA: Corwin Press.

FIGURE 12.7 What worries me about going to high school

WHAT WORRIES ME ABOUT GOING TO HIGH SCHOOL

Name: _____

Put an X in the box that best describes your level of concern.	Not Worried at All	A Little Worried	Pretty Worried	Very Worried
Deciding which classes to take each year				
Getting lost				
Finding the bathroom				
Making new friends				
Work will be hard				
Knowing which clubs/ activities to join				
Playing on a sports team				
Who to sit with in the cafeteria				
Learning new rules and routines				
School is bigger				
Older kids in the hallway				
Knowing how to act like I'm not a freshman				
Looking different from other kids				
Being bullied				
Not having a driver's license				
Finding (or not) a boyfriend or girlfriend				
Pressure to do things that make me uncomfortable				

Other things that worry me about going to high school:

Source: From *Wayside Teaching: Connecting With Students to Support Learning* (pp. 152–153), by S. D. Powell, 2010, Thousand Oaks, CA: Corwin Press.

▶ Meet the Students

Zach ● 8th grade

Zach had his share of ups and downs in middle school, but seems to be doing all right as 8th grade ends. As you can see by comparing his 8th grade picture to his 6th grade one in Chapter 3, he has gravitated toward individualism a bit. Mom is not too pleased with his long hair, but, since he takes his Ritalin regularly and makes decent grades, she's happy. She has just signed the papers to buy a home in the suburbs for herself, Zach, and her parents. This will mean that Zach won't go to the urban high school next year. He's unhappy about leaving his friends, but will try to stay in touch with them. Zach doesn't make friends easily and will probably be uncomfortable for a while in his new school, but he has a good support system at home and an acceptable level of interest in doing well in school. He should be fine.

DeVante ● 8th grade

DeVante still lives in the same apartment with his granny, but he no longer hangs around after school and in the evening with the guys who are gang-related. Through Jefferson Middle School, Mr. Joyner and other teachers who saw his potential, and Kim's family, DeVante has become a high achieving student and is showing emerging leadership skills. He was granted admission to the district's technology high school. He's very excited and is looking forward to school next year. He's disappointed that Kim won't be joining him at Ravenwood Technology Academy, but understands that her interests are in broadcasting, and possibly drama. They promised each other that they will talk every day. DeVante could very possibly earn a college scholarship. He will need someone, possibly a guidance counselor, to help him channel his interests and skills to make the most of high school, and into a college that matches his ambitions.

Emily ● 8th grade

Emily entered 8th grade with a new sense of confidence. Her grades were good, she enjoyed a growing group of friends, and found that boys were noticing her. In 8th grade she actually started feeling popular as she was included in lots of activities. Her parents decided to find a private speech therapist for her, and she has made significant progress. One of her boyfriends told her he thinks her slight lisp is sexy. Her earlier embarrassment due to speech difficulties is mainly a memory now. Emily is excited about going to high school. She has friends and is anxious to meet more kids from other middle schools that feed into the one large high school in her district. She's even thinking about trying out for the 9th grade cheerleading squad. Emily has flourished since we first met her in 6th grade.

(Continued)

Kim • 8th grade

Kim has blossomed throughout middle school. She is comfortable in social settings, has made all A's and B's in her classes, and is anxious to move on to Washington High School for the Performing Arts. Her parents are very happy with Kim because she worked hard to make good grades even in subjects she doesn't particularly care for. Kim still wants to be a broadcaster, but has expanded her ambitions to possibly include drama. She's still crazy about DeVante and will miss him next year. Kim's challenge in high school will be to study enough to continue to achieve good grades, even if she doesn't particularly see the point of some of the required courses, so that she can get into a college of her choice. She's looking that far forward primarily because college is a nonnegotiable in her family.

Gabe • 8th grade

Gabe is ending his middle school experience in a much better place than when he began. His grades and standardized test scores allowed him to pass from 6th to 7th to 8th grade, but just barely. This last year in middle school was one of progress. His interest in robotics and Ms. Fox's encouragement kept him gladly showing up each day. His confidence improved and he ended the year with no grades lower than C. But even with this progress, Gabe is going to have some challenges in high school. The work will be harder and the teachers and students aren't teamed. One key to Gabe's success as he progresses through school will be a teacher who will show a special interest in him. He has the potential to be the first in his family to graduate from high school. There will probably be some discouraging moments when the work will be difficult for him and extra encouragement will be needed to get him through.

Janie • 8th grade

Janie changed so much between 6th and 7th grade that her parents worried about her. After meeting with her teachers, they felt better, but still kept her close to them and were watchful. Comparing Janie's 7th grade picture in Chapter 10 to her 8th grade picture tells the story of how she matured. Janie's circle of friends changed some in middle school, as it expanded beyond her immediate neighborhood. For a while she gravitated to kids and families her parents considered outside the mainstream, but by the fall of 8th grade the purple streak in her hair went away and hasn't returned. Now at the end of 8th grade she continues to read a lot and has started writing a novel. She's even anxious to take English courses in high school and learn about writing. She will enter high school with a 3.1 GPA and is determined to do well.

Andy • 8th grade

Andy isn't faring well as his middle school experience ends. In 6th grade he began bullying several smaller boys. By the end of 7th grade his reputation was known throughout Hamilton Middle School as someone to be avoided. In 8th grade he was suspended three times for verbal abuse of teachers and expelled once for fighting. After Andy spent a month out of school, his dad went to the school board and asked that he be reinstated and promised to keep a close watch on him. He finished 8th grade with all Cs, Ds, and an F, but passed the state standardized tests and was promoted to high school. Andy is often seen driving his dad's truck without a license, and the other kids say he drinks large quantities of beer each evening. He's only 14, and the smile in his 8th grade picture masks his undesirable behavior. Andy will need a very strong mentor teacher in high school who will call him on his behavior toward others, try to teach him about personal responsibility, and insist that he do his schoolwork. That's a lot to expect of a teacher, but this is likely Andy's only hope of successfully completing high school.

Darma • 8th grade

Darma determined to not let anything stand in the way of his success. His sudden loss of temper during the behavior incident in 8th grade shocked him, and he has given the whole situation a great deal of thought. Math and science continue to be his favorite subjects. He will enter high school with a perfect 4.0 GPA. He and his parents expect nothing less. Darma and his friends remain close and are excited about going to high school. Their local school offers a wide array of interesting electives, including engineering, astronomy, and a sequence of advanced math courses. The future is bright for Darma.

Maria • 8th grade

Maria's English is improving with Ms. Esparza's help. In fact, Ms. Esparza is the only teacher at MLK Middle School that Maria has warmed to, partially because of the language they share. As she leaves 8th grade with mostly Cs, Maria is still hanging out with older teenagers who have dropped out of school. She has become the girlfriend of an 18-year-old who works at odd jobs occasionally and lives with his older brother near Maria's apartment. Ms. Esparza is apprehensive about Maria going to high school. While there is a bilingual program there, the school is much larger, and she fears Maria will get lost in the crowd and drop out without anyone even noticing. Ms. Esparza plans to meet with the high school bilingual teachers, as she does every year, to talk with them about how to possibly shepherd some of her students who have little support outside school.

Recognizing an Exemplary Middle School

I wish I could say that recognizing an exemplary middle school is as easy as compiling a master list of characteristics from *This We Believe, Turning Points*, the comparison of junior high and middle school traits, and the many other sources available, and then checking off say, 75%, and *voila!*, you've found an exemplary school! That would certainly simplify our task as educators. However, defining a successful or "true" middle school is, like most things in life, a complex issue. There are few, if any, black and white areas. Most have abundant shades of gray with occasional contradictions thrown in. There are middle schools I would term exemplary that exhibit only some of the tenets that have been discussed. There are combinations of characteristics that "work" for different reasons in different settings.

There is no one best prescription for success. Yes, there are some basics without which it is more difficult to create and maintain a developmentally responsive middle grades school. For instance, teaming carries with it so many possibilities for success that it is considered by most educators to be an absolute for middle schools. Heterogeneous grouping is another structure that has been shown over and over to be best for all students—the motivated and the unmotivated, and the high-achievers as well as the low-achievers. Connecting elements of the curriculum using active learning strategies, and measuring knowledge and skills with authentic and varied assessments leads to a more cohesive bonding of teaching and learning. Decisions about what to do and when, where, and how to do it should be based on the needs, strengths, and diversity of our students and our community.

The concept of balance needs to be applied when we examine individual tenets of middle grades practice. Every one of them has the potential to lose effectiveness, and perhaps even be detrimental, if carried to extremes. These "extremes" may distort the intended positive qualities of a tenet or may prevent other tenets from fulfilling their promise. For instance, if we emphasize "flexible organizational structures" from *This We Believe* to an extreme and lose the basic concepts of consistency and routine (valuable elements in the education of young adolescents) we are not providing the best environment for our students. From the *Turning Points* (Carnegie Council on Adolescent Development, 1989) tenet "Empowering Teachers and Administrators" we read, "Creative control of young peoples' educational experiences should clearly be the responsibility of teaching teams" (p. 18). If we as teachers fail to include parents' and students' views in our decisions about educational experiences, then we risk losing valuable insights.

The key to creating balance in our middle schools is equipping ourselves with options and the judgment to know when and how to implement and adjust. This has everything to do with recognizing (and creating!) exemplary middle level settings. The better we know our students and the broader our grasp of practices that reflect middle level philosophy, the more likely it is that who we are and what we do will bring us closer to a school environment that works for young adolescents. We must use our knowledge, skills, creativity, and energy as teachers "If we want our children to be smart but not arrogant, flexible but not easily deterred from their hopes and dreams, compassionate toward others but not overly accommodating, self-confident but not too preoccupied with themselves, proud but not exclusive . . ." (San Antonio, 2006, p. 12).

Reflections on the Past and Future of Middle School

It has been more than 40 years since the words **middle school** were proposed as an alternative structure within which to educate young adolescent students. Middle schools grew out of both dissatisfaction with the junior high philosophy and a realization that the middle years, typically 10 to 15, are unique and require a developmentally responsive philosophy to effectively bridge the gap between childhood and full-blown adolescence/young adulthood. Recognition of the legitimacy of early adolescence as a life stage needing and deserving its own special educational experience has garnered the attention of more and more educators and researchers. What has evolved over more than four decades is a middle grades teaching and learning philosophy that is coherent in its unwavering dedication to developmental responsiveness and academic rigor. Perpetuation of these two basic tenets depends in large measure on you, the future generation of middle level leaders.

"If middle school leaders expect to soon cross the finish line now that the 21st century has dawned, maybe they have not set their goals as high as they should" (George & Alexander, 2003, p. 584). These are Paul George's final words in the new edition of *The Exemplary Middle School*. He reminds us that when we see our goals almost fulfilled it's time to raise the bar. Some middle schools have implemented all the tenets of *Turning Points* and embraced the philosophy of *This We Believe*. For these schools, and the teachers who are the backbone, heart, and head of the organization, the challenge is to continue serving young adolescents in developmentally responsive ways that promote even greater academic rigor fostered by developmentally appropriate practice. They should look toward modifying and/or adding tenets to our guiding documents as students, society, subject matter, and political realities evolve.

For many schools and teachers, George's "finish line" is so far away on the cluttered landscape of their circumstances that the danger lies in losing sight of the ideals needed to guide their efforts. If in your first years of teaching you find yourself in such a situation, perhaps your greatest gifts to the school and students will be your optimism and recent indoctrination into the possibilities of middle level education.

It's just as difficult for me to end this second edition of *Introduction to Middle School* as it was to end the original text. My head and heart are still in the contents. I love my career in education, and specifically middle level education. Teachers are my heroes. There is no finer profession. One of my mantras is "Teachers make all other professions possible." What a privilege and what a joy. I congratulate you on your choice to teach middle school. You will never be bored. You will always be challenged. And you will have fun along the way. Welcome to the adventure!

GROUP ACTIVITIES

1. Visit a school in your class file and ask the following questions:

   a. How is back-to-school night orchestrated in your school or by your team?

   b. Do you send an individual and/or team "welcome to school" letter? (Ask for a copy.)

   c. How do you/your team use community resources such as business partners, service organizations, mentors, etc.?

   d. How do you/your team conduct family conferences? Have you tried student-led conferences? (Be ready to explain how they work.)

2. Divide the 9 focus students among your class members. Each of you will write a paragraph describing what you might have done as one of the students' teachers to make his/her middle school experience more successful than indicated in the Professional Practice sections. Be prepared to share your ideas.

INDIVIDUAL ACTIVITIES

1. Write a brief narrative that you might use on back-to-school night to introduce yourself and your philosophy of teaching young adolescents.

2. While in the mall you run into a parent who is quite angry about a decision her student's teacher team made. The team is on your grade level. You are well aware of the situation and disagree with the decision that was made. Write a narrative of how you would handle the situation.

3. How has No Child Left Behind affected your plans to teach middle school? Does your coursework provide enough hours in a subject area to allow you the status of "highly qualified"?

PERSONAL JOURNAL

1. Do you remember when you entered middle school/junior high? Write about how you felt and your first impressions.

2. Was your family involved in your school while you were in middle school? If so, in what ways? If not, did you want them to be?

3. When it was time for you to go to high school, what were your main concerns? Was it a difficult or pleasant transition?

INTERNET RESOURCES

National Parent Teacher Association (PTA)
www.pta.org

This site supports the traditional school PTA and provides information for families and communities.

NCREL—Afterschool Programs
www.ncrel.org/after/beyond/linkage

This site offers information on how to establish and maintain quality afterschool programs.

Schools to Watch
www.schoolstowatch.org

This site provides a visual tour of four high-performing middle schools selected by the National Forum to Accelerate Middle Grades Education.

Turning Points
www.turningpts.org

Turning Points is a comprehensive education reform model that focuses on improving student learning. The organization assists member schools in strengthening the academic core of middle school while establishing a caring, supportive environment that values young adolescents. Information about schools at various stages in the reform process is available.

The Partnership for 21st Century Skills
www.21stcenturyskills.org

The mission of The Partnership for 21st Century Skills is to build collaborative partnerships among leaders in education, business, community, and government in order to assure that K–12 schools incorporate knowledge and skills necessary to develop 21st century children. These children will become effective citizens, workers, and leaders.

Glossary

ability grouping: assigning a student to classes based on academic ability and achievement

abstract thinking: adult-like thinking characterized by ability to generalize and visualize

academic safety: an environment that ensures opportunities for success for all students regardless of previous achievement or pace of learning

academic self-esteem: a personal perception of a student's level of ability and academic accomplishment

accountability: being held responsible for student progress and efficient/effective use of resources

ADD: attention deficit disorder; often characterized by an inability to focus for a sufficient length of time

ADHD: attention deficit hyperactivity disorder; ADD often accompanied by a lack of impulse control

advance organizer: a way of focusing attention on, and generating interest in, the beginning of a lesson; in Hunter, also referred to as anticipatory set

advisory: a special time regularly set aside for a small group of students to meet with a specific school staff member

affective learning: learning that is connected to, and/or dependent on, attitudes, feelings, interests, and values

alternative assessment: generally any assessment that is not a traditional pencil-and-paper test

ASCD: Association for Supervision and Curriculum Development

assessment: methods to gather evidence of student learning

at-risk factors: conditions/behaviors that endanger student success

auditory modality: learning through hearing

authentic assessment: assessment that involves, and occurs within, a meaningful and/or real-life context

back-to-school night: an event designed to introduce families to the middle school environment

backward design: planning for curriculum and instruction by first making decisions about the desired learning results and methods of assessment

bilingual education: education option for English language learners delivered in two languages

block schedule: any schedule that allows for more time to be spent in a given class than the traditional fifty minutes

brain-based learning: using what we know about how the brain functions to guide decisions concerning curriculum content and instructional strategies

bullying: aggression with intent to harm; use of power in a relationship to hurt or humiliate

business partners: businesses that agree to support schools in a variety of ways, depending on their expertise and/or interest levels

classroom assessment: any form of assessment that occurs as a direct part of classroom teaching and learning

classroom management: maintaining an ordered environment in which learning may be accomplished

collaboration: working together to accomplish a task or goal

collaborative planning: planning for instruction with other teachers, typically team members (interdisciplinary) or those who teach the same subject

Collegiate Middle Level Association: organization for college students interested in middle level teacher preparation; affiliate of the National Middle School Association

common planning time: time set aside during the instructional day when teams of teachers meet

community of learners: close, trusting school-based relationships that encourage both personal and intellectual growth

complementary content and skills: content and skills that relate to one another in ways that enhance meaning and relevance

concrete thinking: child-like thinking characterized by the organization of experiences and information around what's visible and familiar

conflict resolution: the settling of student disputes

consequences: define what will happen if rules are broken

constructivism: students using higher-order thinking skills to construct or discover their own learning

cooperative learning: students working together in small groups to accomplish a learning task or a learning objective

core curriculum: subject areas generally considered basic for middle school—language arts, math, science, and social studies

creative thinking: thinking "outside the box," using imagination and ingenuity

criterion-referenced assessment: assessing what students know and are able to do according to stated learning goals

critical thinking: higher-order thinking requiring purposeful objectivity and consistency

culture: specific shared values, beliefs, and attitudes that characterize a group of people

curriculum: planned aspects of what students experience in school; typically thought of as the "what" of teaching

curriculum map: calendar-based plans for the sequence of what is taught; a tool for recognizing repetitions and gaps, comparing plans within a team in order to find potential areas for integration

cyberbullying: bullying accomplished through technology

developmental appropriateness: actions and attitudes attuned to developmental needs and interests of students

diagnostic assessment: assessment that determines existence and level of mastery for purposes of planning curriculum and instruction

differentiation of instruction: providing differing learning opportunities in terms of content, process, and product based on students' levels of readiness, interests, and learning profiles

dispositional theory: characterizes multiple intelligences in terms of sensitivities, inclinations, and abilities

diversity: differences among students that may include, but are not limited to, gender, learning style, interest, family structure, race, culture, socioeconomics, and multiple intelligences

early adolescence: period of life typically considered ages 10–15

emotional safety: an environment that provides a stable atmosphere where expressed emotions receive consistently caring responses

English language learners: students who have little or no proficiency using the English language

ESL: English as a Second Language

ethnicity: sense of group identification, political and economic interests, and behavioral patterns

ETS: Educational Testing Service

evaluation: making judgments about the quality of work or products of work

exceptionalities: abilities and disabilities that set students apart from other students

exploratory class: course that encourages students to take a broad, overview-oriented look at a subject or interest area; typically six to nine weeks in length but may last an entire school year

family/parent–teacher conference: an opportunity for family members to meet with teacher(s) to discuss student progress in work/performance/understanding/behavior

flexible block: schedule that allows teachers to divide class time in a variety of ways as appropriate to best address specific academic plans

formative assessment: ways of monitoring learning and providing feedback to students and teachers on progress toward mastery

gifted and talented students: students who may excel in intellectual, creative, artistic, and/or leadership abilities

goals: broad statements of intent without specific steps to fulfillment and often lacking in means of measuring success

grade: number or letter representation; score of evaluation received over time and reported to students and adults

graphic organizers: visual representation of knowledge that emphasizes relationships

guidance counselor: professional who addresses students' affective needs and concerns that impact personal and academic growth

heterogeneous grouping: grouping of students without consideration of academic abilities or achievements

homogeneous grouping: see *ability grouping*

house: a word that designates a "school-within-a-school"

hovering: in Sylwester, a term describing a philosophy of closely monitoring young adolescents as they mature

IDEA: Individuals with Disabilities Education Act

IEP: Individualized Education Plan

inclusion: assignment of students with special needs to regular classrooms; sometimes referred to as *mainstreaming*

inquiry-based learning: learning by questioning and investigating

integrative curriculum: subject areas are interwoven around a conceptual theme chosen as a result of student needs and interests

interdisciplinary instruction: subject areas are related and blended, often blurring subject boundaries

interdisciplinary planning: planning for instruction with teachers of different subject areas, typically in a team setting

interdisciplinary teaming: see *teaming;* interdisciplinary because different subjects, or disciplines, are represented

interdisciplinary unit: a unit of study addressing a theme with individual subject areas contributing and sometimes blending, and with subject boundaries often blurring

IRA: International Reading Association

junior high: a precursor to middle school, with departmentalized organization much like a high school, typically encompassing grades seven through nine

kinesthetic modality: learning through movement

learning centers: designated places in a classroom with information and activities to promote independent or small group learning using a variety of modalities; sometimes called learning stations

learning disabled (LD): a designated special-needs category, manifested in many forms

learning style: how students perceive and internalize knowledge and skills

long-range plan: comprehensive guide for facilitating learning involving student profiles, content and sequencing, classroom management philosophy, instructional strategies, and overall organizational factors

looping: a team of teachers and students who stay together for more than one academic year

LRE: Least Restrictive Environment, an environment in which students with special needs function that incorporates the fewest possible restrictions; for many of these students, the LRE is the regular classroom setting

magnet school: public school that offers a different focus involving curriculum, instruction, or both

mainstreaming: policy of blending students with special needs with the general student population; sometimes referred to as *inclusion*

membership: in middle school, a sense of community where each person feels connected to both the group and the subject matter

metacognition: the process of thinking about one's own thinking

middle school: a school specifically structured to meet the developmental needs of young adolescents, typically 10- to 15-year-olds

MSBA: a fictitious degree that stands for Middle School By Accident

MSBD: a fictitious degree that stands for Middle School By Design

multiage grouping: students of two or more grade levels intentionally placed together as ability and/or interests dictate

multicultural education: purposeful process of incorporating opportunities for students to gain insights about cultural differences locally and globally with the goal of increased acceptance and appreciation

multidisciplinary instruction: instruction in which subjects remain distinct, but are linked together by a common theme

multiple intelligences: theory that expands the narrow notion of intelligence beyond the traditional view to include verbal-linguistic, logical-mathematical, visual-spatial, bodily-kinesthetic, musical, interpersonal, intrapersonal, naturalist, and existentialist; individuals may have varying combinations of the intelligences in a wide spectrum of degrees

NAEP: National Assessment of Educational Progress

NBPTS: National Board of Professional Teaching Standards

NCATE: National Council for the Accreditation of Teacher Educators

NCLB: No Child Left Behind federal legislation

NCSS: National Council for the Social Studies

NCTE: National Council of Teachers of English

NCTM: National Council of Teachers of Mathematics

NMSA: National Middle School Association

NSTA: National Science Teachers Association

nonlinguistic representations: graphic or physical models that elaborate on a basic concept

norm-referenced test: compares individual student performances relative to the overall performance of a group of students using percentile rankings

objectives: statements of measurable learning that results from instruction; more specific than goals

peer mediation: opportunity for students to problem-solve concerning their disputes in the presence, and with the help, of a student acting as mediator

performance assessment: involves tasks that require students to apply knowledge

physical safety: the elimination of threatening and/or real scenarios such as theft, verbal abuse, weapons, and unwanted horseplay

portfolio: collection of student work that may show progress over time or may be limited to the students' best quality products

Praxis: series of tests developed by the Educational Testing Service to assess the knowledge and skills of preservice and practicing teachers

privilege gap: gap between haves and have nots based on socioeconomic status

professional learning community: teams of educators working collaboratively toward common goals

puberty: biological transition between childhood and young adulthood

race: categorizes individuals based on certain outward physical characteristics

reflection: purposeful analysis of actions and/or experiences with the goal of altering and improving future actions and/or experiences

related arts: courses other than core (language arts, math, science, social studies); also known as exploratory or encore courses

reliability: refers to the consistency with which assessment measures what it is meant to measure

role-play: assuming another person's perspective and mimicking circumstances when given specific parameters

rubric: scoring guide that provides the criteria for assessing the quality of a performance or product and includes a gradation for each criterion, generally from poor to excellent, with quality often indicated by numbers

rules: define what is and what is not acceptable in the classroom

Schools-to-Watch: designated exemplary middle schools with criteria established by the National Forum to Accelerate Middle-Grades Reform

school-within-a-school: a segment of teachers and students of a large school population who function as a unit with regard to organization, use of space, and scheduling

score: number given to student work to indicate evaluation

service learning: students providing services to individuals and groups with volunteerism accompanied by academic learning

sexting: sending text messages about sex

single subject planning: planning lessons within one specific subject

socioeconomic integration: blending of students of differing social and economic backgrounds

socioeconomic status (SES): a measurement of economic conditions using several criteria including income, occupation, and education; most often thought of as a measure of wealth

standard: a benchmark against which progress is measured; what a student should know and be able to do

standardized assessment: assessment with content typically representing a broad base of knowledge and administered to many segments of a general population, usually either nationwide or statewide

Structured English Immersion (SEI): delivery of education to English language learners with English instruction involving the majority of the school time, with other subjects secondary

student-focused instruction: creating opportunities that empower students to be self-directed learners

student-led conference: event during which families and teachers focus on, and are led by, the student in discussions and displays of classroom accomplishments

student-oriented: developed explicitly for student benefits and dependent on high levels of student participation

students with special needs: students who require special services due to differences in physical and/or mental characteristics, and sensory and/or processing patterns

summative assessment: means of making judgments about the quality of a process or product; typically administered at the end of a unit of study and used as a basis for assigning grades

synergy: created by individual actions working together to result in greater good; the whole is greater than the sum of the parts

tactile modality: learning through touch

teacher think-aloud: teacher verbally models the thinking process involved in problem-solving, approaching a task, or processing new information

teaming: a specific group of teachers (usually two to five) representing different subject areas and responsible for collaboratively facilitating the academic and social growth of a designated group of students

team planning: see *interdisciplinary planning*

texting: written text messages sent through cell phones

thematic instruction: subjects are linked by a common theme

This We Believe: position statement of the National Middle School Association

TIMSS: Trends in International Mathematics and Science Study

tracking: placing and keeping students in specific ability groups (see *ability grouping*)

transescence: term for developmental life phase used interchangeably with young adolescence

transitions: moving from grade to grade for middle school, and the time when students leave elementary school and the passage into high school; in the classroom, the process of going from activity to activity

Turning Points: 1989 publication by the Carnegie Council on Adolescent Development that outlines middle level education philosophy

Turning Points 2000: written in 2000 by Jackson and Davis, it serves as an update of the 1989 *Turning Points* document, with strategies for implementation of middle level philosophy based in part on the experiences of schools that have attempted to implement the original *Turning Points* tenets

underachievement: occurs when ability exceeds accomplishment

undersocialization: absence of healthy socialization resulting in missed learning and developmental opportunities

validity: refers to the degree to which an assessment measures what it is designed to measure

vertical articulation: communication with teachers in other grade levels

visual modality: learning through sight

wayside teaching: extracurricular opportunities to teach for which there are no official lesson plans, such as encounters with students in the hallway or cafeteria, or at the bus stop

webbing: a graphic way of connecting subject areas to a common theme

weight: value given to specific student work relative to other assignments

whole language: learning to read and write within an authentic context as opposed to learning skills in isolation

"withitness": in Kounin, a teacher's ability to see everything in the classroom; the competent and confident management of classroom movement

young adolescents: generally considered 10- to 15-year-olds

References

Agirdag, O. (2009). All languages welcome here. *Educational Leadership, 66*(7), 20–25.

Alexander, W. M., & McEwin, C. K. (1989). *Schools in the middle: Status and progress.* Columbus, OH: National Middle School Association.

Allen, R. (2001). Passages to learning: Schools find ways to help students make transitions. *Education Update, 43*(9), 1–7.

Anderson, L. W., & Krathwohl, D. R. (Ed.). (2001). *A taxonomy for learning, teaching, and assessing.* New York: Longman.

Andrade, H. G. (2000). Using rubrics to promote thinking and learning. *Educational Leadership, 57*(5), 13–18.

Andrade, H. G., Buff, C., Terry, J., Erand, M., & Paulino, S. (2009). Assessment-driven improvements in middle school students' writing. *Middle School Journal, 40*(4), 4–12.

Anfara, V. A., & Waks, L. (2000). Resolving the tension between academic rigor and developmental appropriateness. *Middle School Journal, 32*(2), 46–51.

Arth, A. E., Lounsbury, J. H., McEwin, C. K., & Swaim, J. H. (1995). *Middle level teachers: Portraits of excellence.* Columbus, OH: National Middle School Association and National Association of Secondary School Principals.

Azzam, A. M. (2005). The funding gap. *Educational Leadership, 62*(5), 93.

Banks, J. A. (1991). *Teaching strategies for ethnic studies* (5th ed.). Boston, MA: Allyn & Bacon.

Banks, J. A. (Ed.). (2004). *The handbook of research on multicultural education.* San Francisco: Jossey-Bass.

Batalov, J., Fix, M., & Murray, J. (2007). *Measures of change: The demography and literacy of adolescent English learners.* New York: Migration Policy Institute, Carnegie Corporation.

Beane, J. A. (1993). *A middle school curriculum: From rhetoric to reality* (2nd ed.). Columbus, OH: National Middle School Association.

Belair, J. R., & Freeman, P. (2000). Protecting bodies, hearts, and minds in schools. *Middle School Journal, 31*(5), 3–4.

Berckemeyer, J. C. (2001). Student-led conferences. *Classroom Connections, 3*(3), p.1.

Bloom, B. S. (1956). *Taxonomy of educational objectives, handbook I: Cognitive domain.* New York, NY: Longmans, Green.

Bluestein, J. (2001). *Creating emotionally safe schools.* Deerfield Beach, FL: Health Communications, Inc.

Borich, G. D. (2003). *Observation skills for effective teaching.* Upper Saddle River, NJ: Merrill Prentice Hall.

Boynton, M., & Boynton, C. (2005). *The educator's guide to preventing and solving discipline problems.* Alexandria, VA: Association for Supervision and Curriculum Development.

Broda, H. W. (2007). *Schoolyard-enhanced learning: Using the outdoors as an instructional tool, K-8.* Portland, ME: Stenhouse Publishers.

Brown, T. E. (2007). A new approach to attention deficit disorder. *Educational Leadership, 64*(5), 22–27.

Brown University Child and Adolescent Behavior Letter. (2003, March). Keep your eye on bullying. *19*(3), 2.

Burden, P. R., & Byrd, D. M. (2010). *Methods for effective teaching: Meeting the needs of all students* (5th ed.). Boston, MA: Allyn & Bacon.

Caine, R. N., & Caine, G. (1994). *Making connections: Teaching and the human brain.* Menlo Park, CA: Addison-Wesley.

Callahan, J. F., Clark, L. H., & Kellough, R. D. (2002). *Teaching in the middle and secondary schools.* Upper Saddle River, NJ: Merrill Prentice Hall.

Caram, C. A. (2001). The best-kept secret in at-risk education. *Kappa Delta Pi Record, 37*(2), 70–73.

Carbo, C. A. (Ed.). (1995). Educating everybody's children. In *Educating everybody's children: Diverse teaching strategies for diverse learners* (pp. 1–7). Alexandria, VA: Association for Supervision and Curriculum Development.

Carnegie Council on Adolescent Development. (1989). *Turning points: Preparing American youth for the 21st century.* Washington, DC: Author.

Carnegie Council on Adolescent Development. (1996). *Great transitions: Preparing adolescents for a new century.* New York, NY: Carnegie Corporation of New York.

Carr, J. F., & Harris, D. E. (2001). *Succeeding with standards: Linking curriculum, assessment, and action planning*. Alexandria, VA: Association for Supervision and Curriculum Development.

Chesboro, J., Berko, R., Hopson, C., Cooper, P., & Hodges, H. (1995). Strategies for increasing achievement in oral communication. In *Educating everybody's children* (pp. 139–165). Alexandria, VA: Association for Supervision and Curriculum Development.

Coloroso, B. (2003). *The bully, the bullied, and the bystander*. New York: Harper Resource.

Conzemius, A., & O'Neill, J. (2001). *Building shared responsibility for student learning*. Alexandria, VA: Association for Supervision and Curriculum Development.

Cooper, H. (2001). Homework for all—in moderation. *Educational Leadership, 58*(7), 34–38.

Cummings, C. (2000). *Winning strategies for classroom management*. Alexandria, VA: Association for Supervision and Curriculum Development.

Curwin, R. L., Mendler, A. N., & Mendler, B. D. (2008). *Discipline with dignity* (3rd ed.). Alexandria, VA: Association for Supervision and Curriculum Development.

DeAngelis, T. (2004). Size-based discrimination may be hardest on children. *Monitor on Psychology, 35*(1), 62.

Dickinson, T. S. (Ed.). (2001). *Reinventing the middle school*. New York: Routledge Falmer.

Dobrin, A. (2001). Finding universal values in a time of relativism. *The Educational Forum, 65*(3), 273–278.

Doda, N. M., & George, P. S. (1999). Building the whole middle school community: Closing the gap between exploratory and core. *Middle School Journal, 30*(5), 32–39.

Downs, A. (2001). It's all in the family: Middle schools share the secrets of parent engagement. *Middle Ground, 4*(3), 10–15.

DuFour, R., DuFour, R., Eaker, R., & Karhanek, G. (2004). *Whatever it takes: How professional learning communities respond when kids don't learn*. Bloomington, IN: Solution Tree.

DuFour, R., Eaker, R., DuFour, R., & Many, T. (2006). *Learning by doing: A handbook for professional learning communities at work*. Bloomington, IN: Solution Tree.

Dundon, B. L. (2000). My voice: An advocacy approach to service learning. *Educational Leadership, 57*(4), 34–37.

Dyck, B. A. (2002). Hovering: Teaching the adolescent brain how to think. *Middle Ground, 5*(5), 18–22.

Dyck, B. A. (2006). Becoming a multicultural educator. *Middle Ground, 9*(4), 27.

Education Vital Signs. (2006). *As educators face a childhood obesity "epidemic," other indicators of well-being improve*. Retrieved March 30, 2006, from http://www.asbj.com/evs/06/studenthealth.html

Erb, T. O. (2000). Interview with Gerald Bourgeois: Voice of experience on school safety. *Middle School Journal, 31*(5), 5–11

Erb, T. O. (2006). Cyberbullying: A growing threat to young adolescent well-being. *Middle School Journal, 38*(2), 2.

Erb, T. O., & Stevenson, C. (1999). From faith to facts: *Turning Points* in action—What difference does teaming make? *Middle School Journal, 30*(3), 47–50.

Erlandson, C., and McVittie, J. (2001). Student voices on integrative curriculum. *Middle School Journal, 33*(2), 28–36.

Ernst, J. (1996). *Middle school study skills*. Huntington Beach, CA: Teacher Created Materials.

Estrada, V. L., Gomez, L., & Ruiz-Escalante, J. A. (2009). Let's make dual language the norm. *Educational Leadership, 66*(7), 54–58.

Fege, A. F. (2000). From fund raising to hell raising: New roles for parents. *Educational Leadership, 57*(7), 68–70.

Feistritzer, C. E. (2005). *Alternative teacher certification: An overview*. Retrieved May 25, 2005, from www.ncei.com.

Fenter, R. C. (2009). The power of looping and long-term relationships. *Middle Ground, 12*(3), 29.

Fertman, C. I., White, G. P., & White, L. J. (1996). *Service learning in the middle school: Building a culture of service*. Columbus, OH: National Middle School Association.

Frey, N., & Fisher, D. (2008). The under-appreciated role of humiliation in the middle school. *Middle School Journal, 39*(3), 4–12.

Fullan, M. G. (1993). Why teachers must become change agents. *Educational Leadership, 50*(6), 12–17.

Garcia, E. E., Jensen, B. T., & Scribner, K. P. (2009). The demographic imperative. *Educational Leadership, 66*(7), 8–13.

Gardner, H. (1999). *The disciplined mind: What all students should understand*. New York, NY: Simon and Schuster.

Gathercoal, P., & Crowell, R. (2000). Judicious discipline. *Kappa Delta Pi Record, 36*(4), 173–177.

George, P. (2002). *No child left behind: Implications for middle level leaders*. Westerville, OH: National Middle School Association.

George, P. S., & Alexander, W. M. (2003). *The exemplary middle school*. Belmont, CA: Wadsworth/Thomson Learning.

George, P. S., & Lounsbury, J. H. (2000). *Making big schools feel small: Multiage grouping, looping, and schools-within-a-school*. Westerville, OH: National Middle School Association.

Ginott, H. G. (1993). *Teacher and child*. New York: Collier Books, MacMillan Publishing Company.

Goldstein, L. (2003, April 16). Special education growth spurs cap plan in pending IDEA. *Education Week, 22*(31), 1–17.

Goleman, D. (1995). *Emotional intelligence*. New York, NY: Bantam Books.

Gunter, M. A., Estes, T. H., & Schwab, J. (2003). *Instruction: A models approach* (4th ed.). Boston, MA: Allyn and Bacon.

Haskins, R., Paxson, C., & Donahue, E. (2006). *Fighting obesity in the public school*. Policy Brief of The Future of Children. Retrieved April 6, 2006, from http://www.futureofchildren.princeton.edu/briefs/FOC%20policy%20brief%20spr%202006.pdf

Hughes, H. (2009). Multigenre research projects. *Middle School Journal, 40*(4), 34–43.

Hunter, M. (1984). Knowing, teaching, and supervising. In P. L. Hosford (Ed.), *Using what we know about teaching* (pp. 169–192). Alexandria, VA: Association for Supervision and Curriculum Development.

Infoplease. (2004). *Teen birthrates continue to decline*. Retrieved April 7, 2006, from http://www.infoplease.com/ipa/A0193727.html

Jackson, A. W., & Davis, G. A. (2000). *Turning points 2000: Educating adolescents in the 21st century*. New York: Carnegie Corporation of New York.

Jensen, E. (1998). *Teaching with the brain in mind*. Alexandria, VA: Association for Supervision and Curriculum Development.

Jensen, E. (2005). *Teaching with the brain in mind* (2nd ed.). Alexandria, VA: Association for Supervision and Curriculum Development.

Johnson, D. W., & Johnson, R. T. (1999). *Learning together and alone* (5th ed.). Englewood Cliffs, NJ: Prentice Hall.

Jorgenson, O. (2001). Supporting a diverse teaching corps. *Educational Leadership, 58*(8), 64–67.

Jung, C. (1923). *Psychological types. (H.G. Baynes, Trans.)* New York, NY: Harcourt, Brace & Co.

Kahlenburg, R. D. (2000). The new economic school desegregation. *Educational Leadership, 57*(7), 16–19.

Kass, D., Evans, P., & Shah, R. (2003). *Bullying prevention is crime prevention*. Washington, DC: Fight Crime: Invest in Kids.

Kaye, C. B. (2006). Service learning and literature: Creating a dynamic, engaging school culture. *Middle Ground, 10*(2), 34–36.

Kienholz, K. B. (2001). From Dewey to Beane: Innovation, democracy, and unity characterize middle level education. *Middle School Journal, 32*(3), 20–24.

Kindlon, D. J., & Thompson, M. (1999). *Raising Cain: Protecting the emotional life of boys*. New York: Ballantine Books.

King, K., & Gurian, M. (2006). Teaching to the minds of boys. *Educational Leadership, 64*(1), 56–61.

Knowles, T., & Brown, D. F. (2007). *What every middle school teacher should know* (2nd ed.). Westerville, OH: National Middle School Association.

Kommer, D. (2006). Considerations for gender-friendly classrooms. *Middle School Journal, 38*(2), 43–49.

Kounin, J. (1970). *Discipline and group management in classrooms*. New York: Holt, Rinehart, and Winston.

Lawton, E. (1993). *The effective middle level teacher*. Reston, VA: National Association of Secondary School Principals.

Lemlech, J. K. (2004). *Teaching in elementary and secondary classrooms*. Upper Saddle River, NJ: Merrill/Prentice Hall.

Lemonick, M. (2005, April 18). The bully blight. *Time*, 144–145.

L'Esperance, M. E., & Gabbard, D. (2001). Empowering all parents. *Middle Ground, 4*(3), 17–18.

Lipsitz, J. (1995). Prologue: Why we should care about caring. *Phi Delta Kappan, 76*(9), 665–666.

Lounsbury, J. H. (1991). *As I see it*. Columbus, OH: National Middle School Association.

Lounsbury, J. H. (1997). Forward. In J. L. Irvin (Ed.), *What current research says to the middle level practitioner* (p. xi). Columbus, OH: National Middle School Association.

Manning, M. L. (2000). A brief history of the middle school. *The Clearing House, 73*(4), 192–195.

Marzano, R. J. (2000). *Transforming classroom grading*. Alexandria, VA: Association for Supervision and Curriculum Development.

Marzano, R. J., Pickering, D. J., & Pollock, J. E. (2001). *Classroom instruction that works: Research-based strategies for increasing student achievement*. Alexandria, VA: Association for Supervision and Curriculum Development.

McCarthy, B. (1997). A tale of four learners: 4 MAT's learning styles. *Educational Leadership, 54*(6), 47–51.

McEwin, C. K., Dickinson, T. S., & Hamilton, H. (2000). National board certified teachers' views regarding specialized middle level teacher preparation. *The Clearing House, 73*(4), 211–213.

McEwin, C. K., Dickinson, T. S., & Jenkins, D. M. (2003). *America's middle schools in the new century.* Columbus, OH: National Middle School Association.

McHugh, J. (2005). Synching up with the kids. *Edutopia, 1*(7), 32–35.

Mee, C. S. (1997). *2,000 voices: Young adolescents' perceptions & curriculum implications.* Columbus, OH: National Middle School Association.

Mendez, L. M. R., Young, E. L., Mihalas, S. T., Cusumano, D. L., & Hoffmann, L. L. (2006). What teachers can do to reduce hidden stressors for girls in middle school. *Middle School Journal, 38*(2), 13–22.

Mulhall, P. F., Mertens, S. B., & Flowers, N. (2001). How familiar are parents with middle level practices? *Middle School Journal, 33*(2), 57–61.

Murphy, P. (2009). Using picture books to engage middle school students. *Middle School Journal, 40*(4), 20–24.

National Board of Professional Teaching Standards. Retrieved May 20, 2009, from www.nbpts.org.

National Center for Education Statistics. (2003). Common core of data surveys 2003. Retrieved May 15, 2005, from http://www.nces.ed.gov/programs/projections

National Center for Education Statistics. (2006). *Public elementary/secondary school universe survey, 2003–2004, and State non-fiscal survey of public elementary/secondary education, 2003–2004.* Retrieved January 7, 2008, from http://www.nces.ed.gov.

National Clearinghouse for English Language Acquisition. (2006). *The growing numbers of limited English proficient students: 1993/94–2003/04.* Washington, DC: Office of English Language Acquisition, U.S. Department of Education.

National Council of Teachers of Mathematics. (1995). *Assessment standards for school mathematics.* Reston, VA: Author.

National Forum to Accelerate Middle-Grades Reform. (2001). *National forum policy statement: Student assignment in the middle grades: Towards academic success for all students.* Newton, MA: Author.

National Middle School Association. (2010). *This we believe: Keys to educating young adolescents.* Westerville, OH: Author.

O'Connor, K. (2002). *How to grade for learning.* Arlington Heights, IL: Skylight Professional Development.

Palmer, P. J. (1998). *The courage to teach.* San Francisco, CA: Jossey-Bass.

Paxson, C., Donahue, E., Orleans, T., & Grisso, J. A. (2006). Introducing the issue. *The Future of Children, 16*(1), 3–15.

Perkins, D., Jay, E., & Tishman, S. (1993). Beyond abilities: A dispositional theory of thinking. *Merrill-Palmer Quarterly, 39*(1), 1–21.

Perkins-Gough, D. (2006). Do we really have a "boy crisis"? *Educational Leadership, 64*(1), 93–94.

Piccuci, A. C., Brownson, A., Kahlert, R., & Sobel, A. (2004). Middle school concept helps high-poverty schools become high-performing schools. *Middle School Journal, 36*(1), 4–11.

Pipher, M. (1994). *Reviving Ophelia: Saving the selves of adolescent girls.* New York: G.P. Putnam's Sons.

Pollock, S. L. (2006). Counselor roles in dealing with bullies and their LGBT victims. *Middle School Journal, 38*(2), 29–36.

Powell, S. D. (2000). Forming middle and high school partnerships: Easing the transition. *Voices from the Field, 2*(2), 24–28.

Powell, S. D. (2000a). *Super strategies for succeeding on the standardized tests: Reading/language arts.* New York: Scholastic Professional Books.

Powell, S. D. (2009). *Introduction to education: Choosing your teaching path.* Upper Saddle River, NJ: Merrill.

Powell, S. D. (2010). *Wayside teaching: Connecting with students to support learning.* Thousand Oaks, CA: Corwin.

Prensky, M. (2006). Listen to the natives. *Educational Leadership, 63*(4), 8–13.

Purkey, W. W., & Strahan, D. B. (2002). *Inviting positive classroom discipline.* Westerville, OH: National Middle School Association.

Putman, M. (2009). Running the race to improve self-efficacy. *Kappa Delta Pi Record, 45*(2), 53–57.

Rakow, S. (2007). *Teaching to the top: Understanding and meeting the needs of gifted middle schoolers.* Westerville, OH: National Middle School Association.

Rance-Roney, J. (2009). Best practices for adolescent ELLs. *Educational Leadership, 66*(7), 32–37.

Rasool, J. A., & Curtis, A. C. (2000). *Multicultural education in middle and secondary Classrooms: Meeting the challenge of diversity and change.* Belmont, CA: Wadsworth/Thomson Learning.

Renold, E. (2002, November). Presumed innocence: Heterosexual, heterosexist and homophobic harassment among primary girls and boys. *Childhood, 9,* 415–434.

Richardson, R. C., & Norman, K. I. (2000). Intrinsic goodness: Facilitating character development. *Kappa Delta Pi Record, 36*(4), 168–172.

Rimm, S. (1997). An underachieving epidemic. *Educational Leadership, 54*(7), 18–22.

Robinson, T. W., Smith, S. W., & Daunic, A. P. (2000). Middle school students' views on the social validity of peer mediation. *Middle School Journal, 31*(5), 23–29.

Rothstein-Fisch, C., & Trumbull, E. (2008). *Managing diverse classrooms.* Alexandria, VA: Association for Supervision and Curriculum Development.

Ruder, S. (2000). We teach all. *Educational Leadership, 58*(1), 49–51.

San Antonio, D. M. (2006). Broadening the world of early adolescence. *Educational Leadership, 63*(7), 8–13.

Sarason, S. (1993). *You are thinking of teaching.* San Francisco, CA: Jossey-Bass.

Scherer, M. (2009). In the neighborhood. *Educational Leadership, 66*(7), 7.

Scherer, M. (2001). Improving the quality of the teaching force: A conversation with David C. Berliner. *Educational Leadership, 58*(8), 6–10.

Schlozman, S. C., & Schlozman, V. R. (2000). Chaos in the classroom: Looking at ADHD. *Educational Leadership, 58*(3), 28–33.

Schmoker, M., & Marzano, R. J. (1999). Realizing the promise of standards-based education. *Educational Leadership, 56*(6), 17–21.

Science Daily. (2009, May 5). *Poverty is rooted in US education system, research finds.* Retrieved May 31, 2009, from www.sciencedaily.com/releases/2009/05/090505111652.htm

Schurr, S. (1999). *Authentic assessment from A to Z.* Westerville, OH: National Middle School Association.

Sergiovanni, T. J. (1996). *Leadership for the schoolhouse.* San Francisco, CA: Jossey-Bass.

Silver, H. F., Strong, R. W., & Perini, M. J. (2000). *So each may learn: Integrating learning styles and multiple intelligences.* Alexandria, VA: Association for Supervision and Curriculum Development.

Smith, C., & Myers, C. (2001). Students take center stage in classroom assessment. *Middle Ground, 5*(2), 10–16.

Sodexo Foundation. (2008). *Impact of school breakfast on children's health and learning.* Retrieved May 31, 2009, from www.SodexoFoundation.org

Springer, M. A. (2009). Seeing the future of middle level education requires a mirror rather than a crystal ball. *Middle School Journal, 40*(5), 23–26.

Stevenson, C. (1992). *Teaching ten to fourteen year olds.* White Plains, NY: Longman Publishing Group.

Stevenson, C., & Carr, J. F. (1993). *Integrated studies in the middle grades: "Dancing through walls."* New York: Teachers College Press.

Stop Bullying Now. (2004). Retrieved October 17, 2006, from http://stopbullyingnow.hrsa.gov/index.asp?area=effects.

Strahan, D. B. (1997). *Mindful learning: Teaching self-discipline and academic achievement.* Durham, NC: Carolina Academic Press.

Strahan, D. B., Smith, T. W., McElrath, M., & Toole, C. M. (2001). Profiles in caring: Teachers who create learning communities in their classrooms. *Middle School Journal, 33*(1), 41–47.

Taylor, A. T. (2000). Meeting the needs of lesbian and gay young adolescents. *The Clearing House,* March/April 2000, 221–224.

Teach for America. (2009). *What we do.* Retrieved May 27, 2009, from www.teachforAmerica.org/mission

Teemat, A., Bernhardt, E. B., Rodriquez-Munoz, M., & Aiello, M. (2000). A dialogue among teachers that benefits second language learners. *Middle School Journal, 32*(2), 30–38.

Tell, C. (2001). Who's in our classrooms: Teachers speak for themselves. *Educational Leadership, 58*(8), 18–23.

Tolan, M. (2001). The new kid on the block. *Middle Ground, 5*(1), 10–13.

Tomlinson, C. A. (2001). Grading for success. *Educational Leadership, 58*(6), 12–15.

Tomlinson, C. A. (1999). *The differentiated classroom: Responding to the needs of all learners.* Alexandria, VA: Association for Supervision and Curriculum Development.

Tomlinson, C. A., Moon, T. R., & Callahan, C. M. (1999). How well are we addressing academic diversity in the middle schools? *Middle School Journal, 29*(3), 3–11.

Turnbull, R., Turnbull, A., & Wehmeyer, M. (2007). *Exceptional lives: Special education in today's schools* (5th ed.). Upper Saddle River, NJ: Merrill/Prentice Hall.

Urban Schools: Executive Summary. (2000). *Urban schools: The challenge of location and poverty.* Retrieved May 14, 2006, from http://ncees.ed.gov/pubs/96184ex.html

U.S. Census Bureau. (2002). *Current population survey, 1960–2002 annual demographic supplements.*

Retrieved April 28, 2005, from www.census.gov/prod/2002pubs/p60–219.pdf

U.S. Census Bureau. (2006). *Public education finances 2004*. Washington, DC: Author.

U.S. Department of Justice. (2005). *Indicators of school crime and safety: 2005*. Washington, DC: Author.

U.S. General Accounting Office. (2002). *School finance: Per pupil spending differences between select inner-city and suburban schools varied by metropolitan area.* Washington, DC: Author.

VanHoose, J., & Legrand, P. (2000). It takes parents, the whole village, and school to raise the children. *Middle School Journal, 31*(3), 32–37.

Vars, G. F. (2001). Can curriculum integration survive in an era of high-stakes testing? *Middle School Journal, 33*(2), 7–16.

Wadsworth, D. (2001). Why new teachers choose to teach. *Educational Leadership, 58*(8), 24–28.

Wardle, F. (2000). Children of mixed race: No longer invisible. *Educational Leadership, 57*(4), 68–72.

Weilbacher, G. (2001). Is curriculum integration an endangered species? *Middle School Journal, 33*(2), 18–27.

White-Hood, M. (2006). Targeting the school bully. *Middle Ground, 9*(4), 30–32.

Wiggins, G. P., & McTighe, J. (1998). *Understanding by design*. Alexandria, VA: Association for Supervision and Curriculum Development.

Wilhelm, J. D. (2001). Think alouds boost reading comprehension. *Instructor, 111*(4), 26–28.

Williamson, R. D., & Johnston, J. H. (Eds.). (1998). *Able learners in the middle level school: Identifying talent and maximizing potential*. Reston, VA: National Association of Secondary School Principals.

Willis, J. K., & Johnson, A. N. (2001). Multiply with MI: Using multiple intelligences to master multiplication. *Teaching Children Mathematics, 7*(5), 260–269.

Wolfe, P. (2001). *Brain matters*. Alexandria, VA: Association for Supervision and Curriculum Development.

Wormeli, R. (2001). *Meet me in the middle: Becoming an accomplished middle-level teacher*. Portland, ME: Stenhouse Publications.

Name Index

Subject Index

RECEIVED

NOV 2 0 2012

BY: